The Many Faced Jewel

The Many Faced Jewel
volume one
Traditional Witchcraft
Frater Sabellicus

Topaz House Publications
Washington State, USA
2024

Copyright Topaz House Publications, 2024
http://www.topazbooks.pub
ISBN: 9780998821337

All rights reserved. No portion of this book may be reproduced without permission of the publisher, except for scholarly usage.

I'd like to think L., my first teacher, for all our "Tête-a-têtes", J. and K. for moral support, and the University of Washington Libraries, without which this book would not have been possible.

Contents

Introduction.........13
Chapter 1
Traditional Witchcraft History.........21
    The Inverse Tradition.........30
    Templars and Esoteric Islam.........32
    Shia and Sunni.........36
    Ismailis.........38
    Nusayri and Bektashi.........44
    Manicheans and Zoroastrians.........54
    Zoroastrianism..........61
    Joseph von Hammer-Purgstall and Baphomet.........66
Chapter 2
The Sabbat.........75
    Hyperborea..........79
    Sabbat and Sabbath.........85
    Baphomet.........88
Chapter 3
The Heavenly Temple.........93
    Paradise, Jesus, Neoplatonism, the Sabbat 93
    Paradise and the Heavenly Jerusalem.........95
    The Grail and the Temple..........99
    20th Century Extensions.........102
Chapter 4
Jesus and Lucifer.........111
    Lucifer and the Place of Jesus in the Craft. 111
    Jesus Himself.........114
Chapter 5
Madeline Montalban.........125
    Lucifer vs. Lumiel 125
    Tarot on Lucifer.........129
    Randall-Stevens and Atlantis.........131
Chapter 6
UFO Literature and the Craft 139

Chapter 7
Doctrine..........147
    Questions of Evil..........147
    The Reverse Masks and the Mystery religions. 152

Chapter 8
The Megalithic Civilization..........159
    The Draconic Tradition Relating to the Megaliths. 165

Chapter 9
The Cabiri..........171
    Druids and Cabiroi..........173
    Faber..........177
    The French Astrotheist and Phallicist Cabiri..........186
    Lenormant..........193
    Conclusion 196

Chapter 10
The Pickingill Papers..........201
    Gardner 202
    Edward Davies and Dudley Wright..........204
    Benjamin Walker and Others..........206

Chapter 11
Masonry and Massey..........211
    Pickingill and Conway: Knight of the Sabean Square..........211
    The Masonic Rite..........213
    The Rite Itself..........218
    Conway and the Welsh tradition..........225
    Other Correspondences..........229

Chapter 12
Gerald Massey 235
    Welsh Mythology through an Egyptian lens. 237
    Troy Town..........248
    Seven Taas..........251
    The Inner Significance of Massey's Three and Four..........257
    Gods of the Four Quarters..........264
    The Watcher Angels as "Taas"..........266
    Heptanomis..........268
    Ancient Egypt in the Azoetia..........270
    Ancient Egypt, Creation. 275

Chapter 13
AOS Witchcraft, Chaos Magic, Massey, Chumbley.........283
   The Focus of Life..........283
   Some Extensions.........288
   Wilhelm Reich and Self-Undoing.........297
   W.E. Butler.........302
   Chumbley in Relation to Massey and Spare.........305
   Aesthesis. 310
   Other uses of Aesthesis.........314
   Aetheric I and Autochthonic I.........315
   Memory and Recollection.........318
   Azoetia Notes.........319

Chapter 14
The Toadstone.........327
   Truth and the Lie. 328
   Three Centers.........331
   Alchemical Extensions.........334
   Meditation and the Toad Stone. 336
   The Church of the East.........340
   Corbin, Shi'ite Gnosis and the Stone. 341
   The Stone and the Grail.........343
   Masonic Internal Alchemy.........346
   Extension into Traditional Witchcraft 348

Chapter 15
Grimoire.........353
   Part 1, Cosmology and the Gods.........354
      The Three.........356
      The Three in the Circle, and on the Earth.........362
      The Four:.........366
      The Frame of the World.........370
      The Functioning of the World 373
      The Gods of the Circle and their Correspondences. 377
      Hu Gadarn, Goe-Magog, Hercules, Tubal-Cain.........378
      Bride, Habundia, Freya, Rahab, Massey Isis.........380
      Arianrhod, Hekate, Ononshu, Massey: Nephthys.........382
      Death, Mahaziel, Odin, Herne the Hunter.........383
      The Four as Found in Paul Huson's work.........387

Part2, Elaborations.........388
    Tools of the Circle:.........388
    Zodiac Arrangements and Time..........392
    Celebrations..........394
    Planets and the Compass..........395
    The Heavenly City and the Circle. 396
    Alternate Reading of the Four..........398
    The Hand and the Eye, Mouth and Phallus. 400
    The Hand as a Map of the Four, the Five. 409
    The Eight Paths. 413
    Sexual Permutations, the Quadriga. 418
    The Non-Sexual Working Quadriga. 419
Part 3, the Ritual..........421
    Circle Casting with the Three and Four..........421
    Casting the Circle..........424
    Ritual Format with the Three and Four 426
    Ingress Rite Frame..........430
    Using Consecration of All Things, Secrets of Helios..........431
  The Different Levels of Reality. 433
Appendix..........441
  Other Witchcraft: Aradia. 441
  Witchcraft and Fanny Hill 442
  Celtic Commentary. 450
Works Cited..........461

Introduction

Before going into the book, I should tell you some things about myself. I have been involved in the occult and magic for 30 years. Of those 30 years, I've been seriously practicing magic for 20 years. Of those 20 years, I've focused purely on Traditional Witchcraft for 10. In the previous part of those 20 years, I focused on a variety of different currents, including Thelema, particularly Typhonian Thelema, Chaos Magic, general Ceremonial magic, Neo-Paganism, Wicca, and Traditional Witchcraft itself. Ten years ago, I decided to devote myself to Traditional Witchcraft, and on top of devoting myself to its practice, I decided to take on a research project to find out what the roots of witchcraft actually were. This book is the result of that project. Around the same time, I performed a modified version of the Toad Bone rite, which has lead to over a decade of daily internal alchemical practice related to the traditional craft.

Now, it's important to define our terms: traditional witchcraft, in the sense in which I mean it, is characterized by two things. First, it deals with a religious reality which goes beyond cursing and blessing, although it includes these as well. Second, these are practices which existed before Gerald Gardner announced his revival of Wicca. Many people would object to calling Traditional Witchcraft a religious tradition, because of general opposition to institutional religion, but it revolves around a core mystical reality which is by its very nature religious. It's this overarching mystical and religious reality which is embodied by the traditions that make use of the witches' Sabbat, which set traditional witchcraft apart from other cunning traditions of blessing and cursing.

This book is split up into three parts, "Foundations", "The Nineteenth Century", and "Practice". The first part deals with the origin of the classical tradition of witchcraft associated with the witches' Sabbat itself. The second part deals with the 19th century forebears of 20th century traditional witchcraft, while the last part is my own grimoire which explains my basic worldview and contains practical rituals, within the context of the ingress rite and its cosmology.

I don't trace the origin of the witches' Sabbat back to a matriarchal society, or to a pure paganism. Instead, I believe that it came about as a synthesis of heretical Christianity associated with the Cathars, beliefs brought back by the Knight's Templar from the Middle East, and the survivals of Greco-Roman mystery cults. These are combined with local, non-Greco-Roman, paganisms from the Celtic and Germanic worlds.

The second part of the book, in looking at some of the forebears of 20th century Traditional Witchcraft, points out various strands of thought such as Welsh Neo-Druidry and the French Astrotheist and Phallicist traditions which I believe influenced pre-Gardnerian witchcraft. In this, I believe that these sources were used to supplement and to extend pre-existing witchcraft traditions. I don't believe that these currents of Traditional Witchcraft were manufactured from nothing, using these sources.

The Traditional Witchcraft of part three, "Practice", to which this part is background is that which is collectively described in the works of Robert Cochrane, Paul Huson, Andrew Chumbley, the pseudonymous Pickingill Letters, the works of Nigel Pennick, and the tradition of Charles Cardell's "Coven of Atho". To this can be added the Welsh cunning tradition described by David Conway, author of "Magic: an Occult Primer". Though these works may appear disparate, I believe that they all describe the same central reality, viewed from different perspectives. On top of this, I believe that knowledge of one of these traditions gives one insight into the others.

My method of working has been to use the books to contact the reality which they describe, let this reality teach me, and then look for historical precedents to what I've seen and been taught. In this way, we move from what has been called "Unverified Gnosis" to

"Verified Gnosis". In the end, the products of the historical research are brought once more into harmony with the traditions described in the books.

Some of the things in this book are highly documented, from a somewhat academic perspective. Other claims are things which either, by their very nature, are unprovable, such as supernatural assertions, or are things which even though theoretically provable, do not have the level of surviving evidence which would satisfy scholars. Let the reader beware, then, and see the truth.

With regards to the second part of the book, which looks at the background of these traditions in the 19th century, my intent has been to strip away the accretions which have come from the works of Margaret Murray, James Frazer, and Robert Graves. Though Margaret Murray's thought has been thoroughly criticized, and her influence detected, the same is not true of the other two. In particular, some traditional witchcraft writing has apparently substituted Robert Graves for Murray, discarding one mask but putting another in its place. This stems from Robert Cochrane's embrace of Graves. Cochrane, in doing this, was elaborating on his own tradition with contemporary writers who he felt were describing a similar reality. However, people have since paid more attention to the supplement and the extension than to the the original ideas that they were meant to clarify.

This is an unfortunate situation in many ways, the biggest being that unlike Murray, Graves was a person whose writing had more in common with the mythomaniacs of the 19th century than with modern anthropology or history. The history that he puts forward about the origins of different concepts was proven to be false over a hundred and fifty years ago, if not more, and by adopting this framework as being literally true, practitioners are similarly binding themselves to a past where historians believed things which we know are categorically not true.

Similarly, James Frazer's concepts about divine kings, and their being killed and rising again has had a somewhat negative effect on pagan thought. Among other things, the notion that Rufus, the son of William the Conquerer, was killed as a sacrificial king is completely unhistorical. While some pagan traditions have incorporated the idea of a dying and rising king into a comprehensive theological framework, such as the Cochrane tradition, other neo-pagan groups have just blindly subscribed to it while attaching to it no real higher meaning.

However, in doing this research, I discovered a very interesting thing: Frazer and Murray, and also Graves, were not original in their ideas. Once these three are removed, another layer of myth making, this from the 19th century, which all of these drew on, presents itself. I believe that this layer itself influenced traditional witchcraft before these later writers' works were incorporated into traditional witchcraft, and Wiccan, beliefs.

Frazer's mythology was in many ways a codification in English of ideas associated with the French Astrotheists and Phallicists, who had been propagating them since the end of the 18th century. These ideas had their own, extensive, influence on the esoteric world before Frazer published his "Golden Bough", particularly through the medium of high grade Freemasonry, such as the rites of Memphis-Mizraim. The particular connection between Memphis-Mizraim and these ideas will be examined in volume 2 of this work. As for Margaret Murray, though her idea of witchcraft originally describing a matriarchal society is unique to her, the idea that witchcraft was a continuation of paganism in another form is not. Among other places, it can be found in the "Teutonic Mythology" of the brothers' Grimm, obviously in a Germanic context. Beyond witchcraft, the idea that folk festivals in Britain and in other places, in general, were survivals of pagan rituals is a concept that goes back as far as the 17th century. At that time, the antiquarian John Aubrey wrote his "Remaines of Gentilisme and Judaisme", which argued that British customs could be related to Roman pagan practices as well as Jewish ones, this latter being linked to the Old Testament. This was only posthumously published almost two centuries after it was written, but it demonstrates that the idea was "In the air", as it were. Similarly, the idea that these practices were fundamentally related to fertility is also a very old concept, with this being a central argument of the French Astrotheists themselves.

Graves' mythomania is prefigured by the writings of Godfrey Higgins, Gerald Massey, and a number of lesser writers such as Thomas Inman and James Forlong. These writers, in turn, drew on

French Astrotheism, and in fact worked the idea of folk festivals as the survivals of pagan fertility religions into their thought, with Massey and Higgins explicitly saying this. Additionally, Massey applies the same analysis to accounts of the Witches' Sabbath. In trying to peel back one layer of accretion, I found many more layers, ones which are more central to these beliefs themselves.

As I said, I am not a member of the groups associated with the people I'm writing about. My knowledge has come from work with the spirits, and from historical research. I believe that it's much more honest to state, quite extensively, the influences on my thought in this, instead of trying to mystify people by inventing a supposed tradition when it's very obvious to anyone who is knowledgable about these things where the various bits come from. Also, stating these sources is a recognition of the fact that we live in a time when a good amount of information on traditional witchcraft has already been made public. If this is so, and people work with that information, why should we insist that writers, in order to be authentic, present themselves as pure initiates who have had no connection with any other part of the occult world, instead of recognizing that this work, though in many ways secondary, can be as valid as that which has come before it?

Part One
Foundations

Chapter 1
Traditional Witchcraft History

Before we get started, it's necessary to define some terms. What this book is about is Classical Witchcraft, which I define as the witchcraft practices that are most stereotypically associated with the subject, which are centered on accounts of the witches' Sabbat. Because of this, these practices are the "Classic" idea of what Witchcraft is in the West. The word "Classic", here, should not be meant to imply an association with witchcraft as portrayed in Greco-Roman writings, but is instead medieval. Though there's a great deal of overlap between this idea of "Classical Witchcraft" and that of the Sabbatic tradition, which also deals with the witches' Sabbath, because this book is not endorsed by the Cultus Sabbati it would be inappropriate to refer to it as "Sabbatic" in that sense. Therefore, another term is needed. Though several current traditional witchcraft groups descend from this tradition, I'm opting to refer to these practices as "Classical Witchcarft", instead of traditional witchcraft in general, in order to not imply that what I'm describing is universally believed in by these groups. Instead, what's described here is something much broader, which may or may not reflect the beliefs of these groups.

Here, the historical part of this book should be taken separately from the practical portion of the book. This portion, based on my own practice and studies, is in fact explicitly linked to various current traditional witchcraft traditions. However, this does not imply that these traditions approve of, or agree with, these interpretations.

Now, Traditional Witchcraft is pre-Gardnerian witchcraft, that is to say witchcraft that goes back to traditions that predate Gardner's publicization of Wicca in the mid 1950s. These traditions are diverse. Some of them involve basic ideas of healing and cursing, and can be considered closer to practical magic than to religious reality. Some of them involve mystery traditions which bring a person to communion with the heart of reality itself. Others involve both. Within the mystery related traditions are some that have deific aspects, ones which are either modifications of Christianity or dual faith observances. These include pagan deities that have been absorbed as Saints but still retain parts of their original character. These deific traditions, in part, form a bridge between the purely practical and the mystery traditions. Within the mystery traditions in turn, are several different strands. Within paganism, there are several different trends in and of themselves, including both Germanic, Celtic, and Greco-Roman faiths. It should be remembered that Britain, as well as a great deal of continental Europe, was incorporated into the Roman Empire for centuries, and that these traditions did not necessarily die off with the fall of that empire.

Some of these pagan traditions, in turn, hearken back without much other influence on their core structure, while others can be highly syncretic, having been affected on a basic level by not only Christianity in general but heretical Christianity. This is where the what I'm calling "Classical Witchcraft" comes in. What became known as the archetype of witchcraft in Europe was a synthesis of a number of different streams of thought, which we'll examine in turn. Unfortunately, one of the reasons that this synthesis became known as the classical picture of witchcraft is that it was inscribed in lurid form in the handbooks of the inquisitors and witch finders. This caused opponents of the craft to look for this form of the craft everywhere, and to manufacture confessions based on this model, given through torture by people who didn't actually practice it. Though this was the case, the misapplication of this model by the witch hunters does not mean that the basic model itself never existed as a practical reality.

Traditional Witchcraft in the sense I mean it has three major sources, and many more minor ones. These three major sources are Greco-Roman mystery religions, the Cathars, and the Templars. The Greco-Roman mystery religions involved draw on religious Neoplatonism and Platonism, Sun worship in the form of the worship of Apollo, and Roman Mithrism, with symbolism from the Dionysian mysteries also being present. To this can be added survivals from Celtic paganism, some Germanic paganism, and other

Christian heresies such as the Free Spirit. The type of traditional witchcraft that I'm referring to is the kind that is centered around the witches' Sabbath and exhibits the full spectrum of activities.

To start with, Jeffrey Burton Russell, author of "Witchcraft in the Middle Ages", and a very good scholar, links higher cases of witchcraft accusations to places with a previous Cathar presence. The book, in and of itself, is good to consult in order to sift some of the wheat from the chaff regarding witchcraft in Europe.

This kind of traditional witchcraft as such began in France with the Cathar movement as a break away tendency that came into being after their official suppression. What and who the Cathars were has unfortunately been unnecessarily shrouded in mystery for a long time, with the mistaken opinion being that no Cathar works survived. In fact, a number of Cathar works survived, including a very important one called "The Secret Supper", that was also subscribed to by the related Bogomil movement. "The Secret Supper", with other Cathar texts, is translated by Wakefield in his "Heresies of the High Middle Ages" and is also included in Willis and Barnstone's "Gnostic Bible". "Heresies of the High Middle Ages", in particular is highly recommended in that it reproduces and translates a substantial amount of Cathar related documents. Here are a few of the sources from "Heresies of the High Middle Ages" and what they contain.

"The Secret Supper"

This document, narrated by John the Evangelist, describes Satan as a co-creator of the world, as taking the basic unformed, watery world that the Good God had made and creating the world we know on it. Satan in this creates humanity as well, who are all fallen angels. There are interesting features here which don't jibe with later speculation. For instance, John the Baptist is specifically condemned, and Enoch is similarly condemned, and the Enochian literature specifically condemned as false. This is strange, in that the "Secret Supper" itself is arguably descended from this same Enochian material. The work is not inverse, in that the evil God is supposed to have both created the Garden of Eden and the serpent in the garden, and so to have been responsible for the fall, which is artificially contrived to hurt humanity. The treatise adopts the Book of Revelations and states that the corrupt world created by Satan will be burnt and purified and replaced with the New Heaven and the New Earth of Paradise.

"Vision of Isaiah"

This contains the positive vision of the fullness of Heaven, or Paradise, with Jesus at its center. It's derived from the Enochian Merkabah-Hekhalot literature, and fills in the blanks that are missing in "The Secret Supper"

"Book of the Two Principles"

This work contains large sections criticizing the God of the Old Testament for his hypocrisies, arguing that this God has to be a false god based on his contradictory behavior and statements.

"A 'Manichean' Treatise",

Fragments from a lost work by a Cathar, presents the idea of two worlds in explicit detail, the good creation being heaven and Paradise, the false world being the present one, ruled by evil.

Moneta of Cremona, "Summa Against the Cathars"

Very good information, accurate though from a hostile source.

"The Summa of Rainerus Sacconi"

Also good information, but more focused on secondary issues like divisions within the Cathar movement itself.

The Cathars believed that the real, original, world is a world of light, the Ideal realm of Neo-Platonism, and that angels living in this realm were tricked into descending into the material world by an evil god. This evil god lead a revolt against the good god, who existed in the Ideal realm. The angels of the Ideal realm were promised to be kings and rulers of the material world, but instead the evil god entrapped them, stole their memories, and condemned them to constant reincarnation within human form. The evil god also partially created the material world. These fallen angels, with no memory, became some of the first humans, and the evil god presented himself to them as their god, the true god, who forced them to obey him. This God is understood to have been the Judeo-Christian god of the Old Testament.

The angels of the realm of Ideals, seeing their brethren trapped, out of mercy sent down a series of messengers to remind them of their true home in the realm of Ideals, the world of light. These messengers culminated in Jesus Christ, who was the son of the true god, the good god, and who gave his life to both sanctify the partially evilly created material world and to set the captive angels free. Jesus opened the path, but the path has to be taken by the various angels who have fallen and are now incarnate within human form. The path of redemption includes repenting for rebelling against the good god and engaging in contemplative practices that culminate in returning to the pleroma, the Ideal world, in the mind, which will then lead into returning to the Ideal world after death. This is also the meaning behind the Holy Grail, understood as the sacred stone that fell from the brow of Lucifer into the world. The stone is the angelic soul of the fallen angels, which fell into earth through the rebellion of the angels against the good god.

The origin of the Cathars, and Cathar belief, is through the Bogomil movement of Bulgaria, north of the Byzantine Empire of the time. It was thought for a long time that there was a direct connection between Manichean thought and the Bogomils, but scholar Yuri Stoyanov in his excellent work "The Other God", casts doubt on this. Instead of a lineal descent from the Manicheans, what Stoyanov presents is a profusion of post-Manichean dualistic cults existing in the medieval Byzantine Empire around Constantinople, that coalesced into Bogomil belief. This belief was tolerated to a higher degree in the Bulgarian Empire, a new Christian state the bordered the Byzantine Empire, than it was in the Empire itself. From Bulgaria, the Bogomils sent emissaries to western Europe to spread the world, leading to the formation of the Cathars, who not only existed in southern France but in northern Italy as well.

The Cathars were violently suppressed by the Church, but they lived on underground. People have a misconception that the Cathars who disliked the body and saw it as part of the false world could not, or would not, engage in the transgressive actions attributed to witches. Because of this, it has been suggested that there was a separate group of "bad Cathars" who decided to break the rules. This is not the case. Instead, witchcraft was formed and influenced by the division of the Bible by the Cathars into a part by the false god and a part by the good god, the father of Jesus. This happened after the suppression of the movement itself, and so the following would not have been approved of by the Cathars in their classical form.

The Old Testament god, and the rules that he established, were seen as creations of the evil god, including various laws. The bible was thought to contain a falsified account of the world, where the good forces were portrayed as bad, and the bad forces were portrayed as good. The figures such as the serpent in the garden of Eden, who were supposed to have ruined mankind, were interpreted as emissaries of the good god who were trying to help mankind. Therefore, Lucifer, and the various figures present in the Book of Revelations, such as the Dragon, were interpreted as being the good god and his court in disguise. Jesus, in this is seen as being Lucifer, the same Lucifer who offered the apple to Adam and Even in the Garden.

This is the case even though Jesus himself makes quite an appearance in the Book of Revelations. Later on in our story of the Craft, other interpretations of the Book of Revelations will be introduced which, though conflicting with this, were thought to reflect the same underlying reality.

Here, though, in what could be called a Cathar reversion, the true form of God the Father was equated with the Dragon of the Book of Revelations, and Jesus was equated with Lucifer, making Jesus the son of the Dragon. The court of heaven, the Ideal realm, is the angelic court around Jesus/Lucifer. It's immensely important to realize that the Dragon and Lucifer in this are the good gods, and that this Lucifer never rebelled against God. Instead, the entity who presented himself as the true God to the trapped angels, was the being who revolted against God. He is Satan, though he presented, and presents, himself as the good god, as Jehovah. Likewise, the Church, as much as it serves base and material causes instead of the transcendent, serves Satan, not the true God.

Within the inverse tradition, the prohibition against eating the apple, and the fear that those who did so would be as gods, can be interpreted to mean that Adam and Eve would see the truth about their Satanic captors, and become equal to or superior to them. They would no longer be under their influence, and would be able to ascend back home to the pleroma, the First Sun, from which they fell as a result of their rebellion.

This inversion of parts of Christianity, reached out in the countryside of France and combined with various survivals of Greco-Roman mystery religions and Celtic religions which existed at the same time, this being the 11th and 12th centuries.

I would like to make it completely clear that though these craft traditions talk about the God of the Old Testament as the evil god, that anti-Semitism is not part of the craft. The Cathars existed in a world where the Biblical theory of history was the only theory of history out there, and the inversion of it was a way of making sense of spiritual reality within their cultural context. Their main enemy was not people who are Jewish, but the Church, who they saw as serving the Evil God. They saw the Old Testament god as exhibiting arbitrary human behavior and cruelty unfitting for a transcendent entity. It goes without saying that people who are Jewish disagree with this position, and don't find the actions and responses of the Old Testament god to be without reason.

During the Middle Ages, people lived within a Biblical worldview. Like many people today, they implicitly considered the history of the Jewish people within the Old Testament to be part of their history, with the patriarchs of the Old Testament being taken as a type of ancestor. This type of inversion, wherever it occurs, does not refer to an out group and its God, but to the group itself and its God.

Currently, there isn't enough data to determine if the Cathars in the south of France treated people who are Jewish differently than the Catholic Church of the time did. However, I'd like to point out that the interpretation of the God of the Old Testament being an evil god which demonizes Jews themselves is not the only interpretation possible. Though I don't have proof this is what people believed, it's possible to interpret the story of the evil god being the God of the Old Testament in a way that paints Jewish people as the victims of this god. The bad acts by the God of the Old Testament were frequently, but not always, directed at the Jewish people themselves. In this, the Jewish people would be mislead by this malevolent force presenting itself as a good force. Related to this, though, the prophets of Judaism who proclaimed the message of Jehovah would be seen as forces of evil. The early advocates of this position, like Marcion and his followers, were located in the Middle East itself, and likely drew their support from Jewish converts. In fact, if you think about it, why would a pagan in the Middle East who worships Shamash, the Babylonian sun god, or Osiris, be concerned about whether or not the god of the Jewish people was a good or bad?

The Greco-Roman Religions followed the path of ascending to the First Sun, which is the Divine Mind, which is the Ideal realm. This was syncretized with a Platonicized understanding of Christianity where the One was God the Father and the Divine Mind, the First Sun, was Jesus in his true form, Jesus the personality being the good god within the First Sun. Jesus, in turn, as Word, was also the Platonic Demiurge, the world creator, who was, in this, partially responsible for the creation of the Earth. The Demiurge, here, is also Jupiter, Zeus, but also Hephaestius, Vulcan, who became synthesized with the Biblical figure of Tubal-Cain as the first Smith, this being one of many borrowings from the Bible of otherwise minor characters to represent Greco-Roman gods.

In turn, the idea of the Inverse tradition was combined with this through the commonality of Lucifer as signifying brightness being linked to the sun god, to Apollo, as king of the Divine Mind, later understood as Baphomet. Here, we come full circle: Lucifer is a bright god, the sun is bright, the source of light, Jesus is the force of the Divine Mind, which in turn is the First Sun, therefore Lucifer, Apollo, and Jesus are all the same person. The craft as it evolved featured a continuation of sun worship through an inverse Cathar lens, combined with a Christianized Neo-Platonism. This is what is under the mask of inversion. We shall directly examine this Greco-Roman underlay of the craft in our chapter on the Sabbat itself, and on Baphomet.

The relation of the inverse tradition to the Greco-Roman cults, and to paganism, was that the pagan aspects of how Christianity saw evil allowed the inverse tradition to work with these cults and admit them into the Cathar version of Christianity.

Additionally, Jesus was seen as secretly being Lucifer. The snake in the garden of Eden was secretly Jesus in his form of Lucifer, giving liberation to humanity from the Evil One. Jesus' sacrifice and resurrection, which redeemed the earth, are seen as secretly being that of Lucifer, who redeemed humanity and the world. In this, Jesus was a real being, who was really sacrificed, and was also the incarnation of a cosmic figure who transfigured the evil in the earth that had been put there by the Evil One, breaking the power of this evil, though remnants of it still remain, with his secret identity being Lucifer. We shall return to this subject.

The tradition within witchcraft, in general, is that both the good God and the Evil One were responsible for the creation of the world, probably as a variation of the Cathar understanding of the good God as creating the world in its unformed state and the Evil One as finishing it. However, this is moderated some, in that the part of the world that still exists within purity and goodness, such as untouched wildernesses, is reflective of the good God while the dysfunctional, blighted, parts of the world are related to the Evil One. There's more to say on this subject in relation to Abel and Cain, and with the Cainite tradition, but this is a good basic summary. Jesus, as well, appears in some witch traditions as someone who redeemed and purified the earth itself, as well as allowing for the captives to be freed from the domination of the Evil One. Nevertheless, even in these beliefs the Evil One still has power and needs to be countered.

Human beings, within traditional witchcraft, are also thought to be divided between those who possess an angelic soul, who are reincarnated angels, and those who aren't, with not every human being the incarnation of a fallen angel. The mechanics of this incarnative process are somewhat diverse. In one legend, the serpent in the Garden, a representative of the good God, in the process of trying to free humanity from living in obedience to the false god, also laid with Eve and beget Cain, with the descendants of Cain being those in whom the disembodied fallen angels could reincarnate. The same sort of supernatural relations can apply to those whose legendary forebears are thought to be fairies or elemental nature spirits.

Here, the Pleroma of Jesus/Lucifer, the First Sun, the Divine Mind, was the original home of the angels who fell to earth, and returning to the Divine Mind, the Pleroma, after repenting for making war on God, which is making war on Jesus/Lucifer and the Dragon/the One, is the path to liberation for the fallen angels. The Pleroma, the Ideal world, the First Sun, the Divine Mind is the Sabbath of the Ages. It is the super-celestial Sabbat itself. Going to the Sabbat is going to the Divine Mind.

Bringing the Sabbath down to earth is just that, bringing the Divine Mind down to earth and recreating the feelings of purity and Paradise which exists within the Divine Mind. The Ideal realm of the Divine Mind is the uncorrupted pure land, which the fallen angels existed in before being enticed down into the material world. Regeneration leads to the resumption of a pure, pre-fall, state of purity, which, in turn, is not against different forms of sexual indulgence, which can be partaken of in purity by the regenerated, as part of the enjoyments of paradise.

Also, the combination of the invalidation of Old Testament rules and the opposition to procreation on the part of the Cathars, and some of their descendants, is most likely the source of the doctrine associated both with some of the Bogomils and Cathars and with witches: that sexual activity is permitted when it doesn't lead to procreation.

The Inverse Tradition

To continue with this variation on Cathar doctrine, the people who were regarded as the villains of the Bible were looked at as secret heroes. Cain is a hero, as is Ham, and Nimrod. This brings up the interpretation of the famous "Watchers" in the Bible. It's not clear to me if this evolved purely from the Cathars, from the combination of the Cathars and Templars, or from all of these and something else. People have severely mistaken this story. The Watchers who descended from heaven were emissaries of light from the Pleroma, from the Sabbat, from the Ideal realm, who were sent to help humanity. The things that they taught humanity were supposed to help free humanity from the domination of the evil false god. As such, the particular skills that are recorded in various apocryphal material as belonging to the particular fallen angels are very important, and the fallen angels can be considered "Patron Saints" of those skills, who can be prayed to for assistance in learning them. These skills can be interpreted as gifts given by the angels to help us in fighting the Evil One. The sexual relations of the fallen angels and the daughters of men, considered to be the children of Cain, creating giants and men of reknown, was a positive thing that helped to establish the angelic bloodlines within the world. These bloodlines are important because they provide the means by which the disembodied fallen angels, who sometimes present as fairies or nature spirits, can achieve incarnation, which, in turn, is necessary for repentance and for ultimate reascension to the Sabbat and freedom from the earth.

The Ante-Diluvian civilization of the Watchers, then, is interpreted to be a very good civilization, and not to be wicked. The flood, which destroyed parts of humanity, was thought to be a vengeful counter-action by the false god, who did not want the fallen angels to be freed from his domination. Later traditions identified the Ante-Diluvian civilization with some very real prehistoric traditions that weren't eliminated by a flood, but through a cultural crisis which we'll treat later.

Similarly, the building of the tower of Babel was/is looked at not as a bad thing but as a very good thing, as an attempt to counter the evil, false god, with Nimrod being a hero in this. Nimrod, in particular, is looked at not only as a human messenger of the Sabbat, but as an embodiment of Baphomet or Tubal-Cain himself, with the court of Nimrod at the tower of Babel, with the 72 languages of people around him, echoing the court of heaven at the Sabbat of the Ages. Similarly to the flood, the destruction of the tower of Babel and the dispersion of the languages and peoples was thought to be the work of the evil, false god trying once again to control the fallen angels whom he had convinced to rebel against the Sabbat and to descend to earth. Nimrod's knowledge, and that encoded in the tower of Babel, is, then, a continuation of Ante-Diluvian knowledge.

Related to this, the Pickingill Papers repeatedly assert a Cathar presence in East Anglia through which the craft was transmitted. They relate this specifically to the "French Craft". In this, weavers came over from the Low Countries who were Cathars/Witches, and settled in the area, bringing their beliefs with them. Characteristically, the Pickingill Papers in question give no detail about how Cathar belief is potentially related to traditional witchcraft, but instead just state that the connection exists.

Also, the Papers constantly refer to the "French Tradition" of witchcraft. This, I believe, relates to this Cathar based witchcraft, as opposed to the native witchcraft which existed in Great Britain before its appearance in the Middle Ages. What existed before this strand of witchcraft, associated with the most iconic and classic depiction of witchcraft, arrived in the British Isles, was probably something along the lines of what certain people today think witchcraft is: a synthesis of remaining pagan beliefs with cunning practices of blessing, healing, and cursing that probably had Christian influences incorporated into them.

Templars and Esoteric Islam

This brings us to the Templars, and their relationship to traditional witchcraft. The Templars brought back the wisdom of gnostic sects from the east and combined it with the wisdom of the Cathars, who had similar points of view. That this was possible is now able to be adequately documented. The Templars, in engaging in the Crusades and overthrowing the Seljuk Turkish dynasty, made allies of the different sects in the Middle East that were considered to be heretical and non-Islamic. These sects were gnostic, and had an affinity with Christianity in their beliefs, to the point where some of them, such as the Nusayri, were actually classified as Christian groups by later Colonial powers. The Crusdaers allied with the Nusayri, with some of the Druze, and, I believe, had contact with the Sabians of Harran, as well as with the Ismailis. The Nusayri live in modern day Syria, and were part of the Crusader state of Antioch, while the city of Harran was adjacent to the County of Edessa, which was a Crusader state established in modern day Syria and Iraq.

The Sabians of Harran are often invoked as a source of paganism, and the story of the residents presenting the works of Hermes Trismigestus as their holy book to avoid persecution by Muslims is well known, but few works directly testifying to their beliefs have been widely available. This has changed with the publication of the translation of the Encyclopedia of the Ikhawn al-Safa, the Brethren of Purity, an Ismaili mystical and philosophical group that was centered in modern day Iraq. There, in the volume that deals with "Magic", they provide an account of the beliefs and deities of the Sabians.

Though many people know that the Sabians of Harran presented Hermes Trismegistus as their prophet, less known is the context in which this appeared. Specifically, they said that their prophet was Seth, the son of Adam, who was the first Prophet. Seth was understood in the Islamic world to be the same as Hermes Trismegistus, for obscure reasons. Among other things he was said to have both created the famous pillars inscribed with knowledge which survived the flood, and in other traditions to have built one of the pyramids. Muslim writers, including the Ikhwan al-Safa, believed that Seth was their prophet, and this had the consequence of the Sabians being regarded as having knowledge stemming from the first prophet. This primacy of knowledge was not as important in Islam as it would be in Christian esotericism, in that Muhammad was regarded as giving the complete and clear revelation, with the knowledge of the earlier prophets being more and more corrupted the further back you went.

Going by the Ikhwan al-Safa, the main deity of the Sabians was Abraxas, who embodied both light and dark and was symbolized by the celestial circle of 360 degrees. The Ikhwan al-Safa describe this main deity as being "Jirjas" or George, as in Saint George, and the introduction to the translation makes reference to Ibn-Washiyya's "Nabatean Agriculture", where he makes the equivalence between Saint George and Tammuz. The Abraxas like qualities of "Jirjas" are apparent in that his temple represents all of the signs of the Zodiac and all of the planets, with himself at the center. This is on pages 132-137 of the new English edition.

In this, he stands for the eternal sun, as well as for the intelligence that dwells within it. The translators of the Ikhwan al-Safa's book on magic reproduced description of the pose that the high priest of "Jirjas" assumes during initiation rites, and the description is of a seated figure that almost precisely resembles Eliphas Levi's drawing of Baphomet in its gestures. One leg is extended, while another one is bent. One hand and arm is raised, while another one points to the ground. Within the hands, three fingers, the thumb index and middle finger, are extend out, while the rest are not. All of these gestures represent the two sides of duality, of the positive and negative, the light and dark, up and down, left and right, united in the figure of the priest, who stands for "Jirjas", or Abraxas. This on pages 137-138

Abraxas, in this, is linked with Tammuz, being Tammuz represented on a higher level. Like Abraxas, Tammuz experiences both light, when he is freed from the underworld, and darkness, when he is imprisoned. The story of Tammuz as understood by the Sabians involved him experiencing torture and suffering, and living through it. Like Jesus, Tammuz withstands death and survives. The two appearances of Abraxas as a kind of Demiurge, a higher Demiurge, not a lower one, and as a person who endures torture and descends into the underworld, only to break the bond of death and escape, are similar to those of Jesus in his two forms, the first as the world creator and the second as the redeemer who was crucified and descended into hell, overthrew it, freed the captives in hell, and rose from the grave. This torture is the same as that experienced by the Anatolian Saint George, and Saint George was adopted by the Templars as a secret sign for Baphomet, who, in turn, they also understood as Jesus.

Jaako Hämeen-Anttila reproduces the sections of the "Nabatean Agriculture" of Ibn-Washiyya that deal with Tammuz, and that link him to Saint George in his book "The Last Pagans of Iraq". This is "Text 25", and goes from pages 226-231, with pages 229-230 relating Tammuz to Saint George. Interestingly, Ibn-Washiyya also talks about the same temple mentioned by the Ikhwan al-Safa, but he implies a separation of sorts between the sun god and Tammuz, with the "Idol of the Sun" in this temple reading the litany of Tammuz. However, the "Idol" that was reading the litany was most likely a priest, and it's very possible that the priest of the "Idol of the sun" doing this was the same priest described by the Ikhwan al-Safa as a priest of Jirjis himself.

Jesus, Baphomet, and Abraxas in this are all the same, with Tammuz being similar to the incarnate Jesus as the physical manifestation of the much higher deity. Tammuz also appears in the legends as a pair, with Ishtar, Venus, as his companion, and this parallels Jesus too, with Mary Magdalene first appearing as the parallel of Ishtar, and this later being changed to the Virgin Mary in practice once the Magdalene was considered too controversial. Simon Magus and his companion Helen were said to be imitating Jesus, and in this they were likely also imitating that who Jesus was imitating, Ishtar and Tammuz. The Sabians, venerating the planets and the gods who are connected to the planets as their main deities, would not have had a problem honoring Ishtar because she is the goddess of the planet Venus. In fact, it's a virtual certainty that Ishtar was honored by the Sabians in their worship of the gods connected to the planets.

Tammuz as life and death, as the life regenerated from death in the return of vegetation, and as Abraxas, resembles the two different parts that Baphomet splits into immediately, Death, in the north, and Life, the Green man or the Goddess, in the south.

The Templars have a link to Abraxas beyond just a proximity to Harran. They used an Abraxas gem as one of their official seals. In this, Abraxas appears in his traditional form with a rooster for a head, two snakes for legs, a scourge in one hand, and a shield in the other. This, too signifies that he contains duality united as one: the rooster crows in the morning, and is a symbol of the day, while the snake is associated with night and the underworld. The scourge is a weapon of offense and punishment, while the shield is one of defense. Day and night, the active and the passive, united into one figure. This was on one of the official seals of the Knights Templar, and very clearly has parallels with what the figure of Baphomet as outlined by Eliphas Levi.

However, this is only part of the doctrine that the Templars took back. Particularly, this part of the doctrine deals with the highest world, the Ideal realm, and says little about gnostic creation. The story of the gnostic creation of the world is supplied by the Nusayri sect, who we'll next examine, along with the doctrines of the Ismaili. These were combined with the doctrine of Abraxas/Saint George/the higher Demiurge as the god of the Eternal Sun.

Shia and Sunni

Both of these sects are united in their common Shi'ia background, and so before looking into these traditions directly, let's look at this branch of Islam.

In the wake of the death of Muhammad, two different groups emerged: the first saw his legitimate successors as those individuals chosen by the community, while the other saw the successors as legitimately stemming from the prophet's family, namely through his son in law Ali ibn Talib. The division became deeper than just who would lead, because the partisans of Ali believed not only that a specifically familial succession was appropriate, but that the members of the family received divine favor. The successors of Muhammad, the Imams, in this, were looked at as being able to give continued divinely inspired interpretations of the Quran, and to serve as God's representative on earth. The Sunni community denied these characteristics to the successors of Muhammad, seeing the traditions of the interpretation of the Quran that Muhammad himself made as the only canonical ones, and not seeing a semi-divine status in the chosen successors. The Quran itself, in both cases, was understood to be a complete revelation in and of itself, with the arguments shifting instead to how it was to be interpreted.

The Shia, Sunni, split, over time lead to a characteristic transformation of Shia belief. Either through believing that the household of the Prophet contained secret esoteric understandings of the Quran given through Muhammad, or through God himself in continued guidance, the Shia community became a focal point for esoteric interpretations of Islam. Part of this may have been related to the homeland of Shia thought, southern Iraq. Ali, as a commander of the invading army of Muhammad, conquered Mesopotamia and set up his base in southern Iraq, at the city of Kufa. Iraq, which was part of the Persian Sassanid empire at the time, was host to a great number of different beliefs, with the area being a melting pot between Babylonian, Persian, and Hellenistic culture, though the Greek influence was officially discouraged. Another potential explanation is the Shi'ia one, which is that the original Islam that was advocated by Muhammad was in fact esoteric, and the hidden esoteric doctrine was especially told to the immediate family of Muhammad and not shared with others.

That the Imams, the successors of Ali, were thought to give continued divinely inspired guidance certainly helped, especially in the case of the case of the sixth Imam Jafar al-Sidiq who was both a practicing alchemist, an Imam, and an influential Islamic legal theorist. Significantly, a split ensued within Shia Islam after the death of Jafar al Sidiq, with a group of people supporting the line of his first son, who was deceased, and a group of people supporting the line of his second son, who was still living. The first group, who, supported the son of the dead son of the Imam as the legitimate Imam became known as the Ismailis, or Seveners, while the second group continued on to recognize six more Imams, becoming the more orthodox Twelver or Jafari Shia group. The Twelver Shia are the group that are currently the ruling party in Iran, while the Ismailis currently do not form a majority in any country.

The Twelvers believe that, after Jafar al Sidiq, six more legitimate Imams succeeded him. After the last Imam died, the Imams went into "Occultation", which means going into a higher, hidden, spiritual reality, becoming known as the "Hidden Imam". He would return at the end of time as the Mahdi, and would perform a role similar to that of Jesus as narrated in the Book of Revelations, leading the final battle and the victory of good over evil. The way for this Occultation in pure spiritual reality was paved for by the "Minor Occultation" of the same last Imam, Muhammad al-Mahdi. In this, the last Imam went into hiding, being persecuted by the Sunni, and communicated his will to the Shi'ia community through designated secret representatives. This period of occultation lasted for seventy years. Before his death, he declared in a letter to them that he would be going into a greater occultation or hiding in spiritual reality and would only reappear at the end of time. He also said that no one would be a designated agent or successor for him in his state of Occultation.

Ismailis

The Ismaili line of succession was thought to have produced a total of twenty one alternate Imams, with the last one going into a similar "Occultation". The Ismailis became the focus for people who wanted to emphasize the esoteric doctrines associated with Jafar al Sidiq, and so became quite a bit more esoteric than the Twelvers, in general, although esotericism was strong in both camps. Though Iran is currently very legalistic, this should not be taken as representing Twelver Shia Islam as a whole. Ismailis would eventually adopt many aspects of Neoplatonism and Greco-Roman philosophy into their esoteric view of the world.

The line of succession in the Ismaili world is complicated by a split which occurred during the Crusades between the majority of the Ismaili community and a smaller but more famous group, the followers of Hassan-i-Sabbah II, successor to the group popularly named the "Assassins" in western history. The setting of this brings us back to the Crusades. At the time of the split, the Middle East had been rocked by serious internal change. The Ismaili lead Fatimid dynasty, centered in Egypt, had previously conquered most of the western Middle East, Lebanon, Palestine, as well as North Africa, even seizing Sicily, which was then under Muslim occupation. Into this scenario, the Turkish Seljuks injected themselves, conquering most of the Middle East outside of Egypt, including the lands under the control of the Fatimids. Though Christians and Muslims had lived side by side, though not equally, in the Middle East for centuries, the Seljuks were reportedly hostile to Middle Eastern Christians, which was the impetus for the start of the Crusades.

At the same time, the Fatimid Caliphate was seeking to regain its territory, and one of the people charged with doing this was Hassan-i-Sabbah, known as the "Old Man of the Mountain". Hassan-i-Sabbah created a network of network of fortresses in the Middle East in order to win back territory from the Seljuks. However, he also supported a rival claimant to the Fatimid Imamate, Nizar, and from that point the network of fortresses split from the control of the Fatimids and became an independent Ismaili state. Hassan-i-Sabbah, and the Assassins during his life, then, were opponents both of the Crusaders, the Seljuk state, and of the Fatimids, vying for control of the same territory.

Ismaili beliefs are important in that they, too, may have influenced the craft through the Templars. Because there is quite a bit of confusion about them, let's go through what they actually were and are. For this, I'm relying on Farhad Daftarys' "The Isma'ilis, Their History and Doctrines" as well as the "Encyclopedia Iranica", particularly the articles "Cosmogony and Cosmology vi. In Ismailism".

I should say, as well that in this, and in the treatment of esoteric Islam as a whole, I've been profoundly influenced by the work of Peter Lamborn Wilson, whose contributions to popularizing these ideas have been immense. Wilson has fallen out of favor for some of his ugly conduct and beliefs, but I believe in separating the scholar from the individual. I don't believe that it would be right to write Wilson out of my history, or pretend as if he hadn't been the pioneer in writing about the Ismailis, because of his actions.

To start with, both sources give the following set of beliefs for the initial Ismailis, that is to say the Ismailis as they were before both Hassan-i-Sabbah and the Fatimid state which he emerged from.

God created the universe through uttering the word "Kun", which means "to be". This word is made out of two letters, Kaph and Nun, and each of these letters stands for a spiritual being who helped to create the world. The Kaph stands for the Kuni, a spiritual being who is female in relation to that which is below her, but male in relation to God. In general, she creates the matter of the world. The Nun stands for Qadar, who is described as a vice regent to God, who in turn determines the destiny of everything. This may be interpreted to mean that the Kuni creates the world, while the Qadar sets the world into motion. Qadar is equivalent to the Celestial Adam, to Adam Kadmon.

However, in the creation of the world, the Kuni is aided by a series of angels. The two names, Kuni-Qadar, are, in turn looked at as being made of seven letters each, and each of these letters corresponds to an Cherubim angel which surrounds Kuni and

Qadar. These seven Cherubim also correspond to the seven Aeons of the phenomenal world that the Ismailis believe in, and to the prophets which are appointed to each of the seven Aeons. Next, out of Qadar, Kuni created three more angels, corresponding to Michael, Gabriel, and Seraphiel, who were to act as true spiritual intermediaries between the higher realm and the earth, with a particular job of instructing the prophets of each of the seven Aeons. Michael, Gabriel, Seraphiel, the Kuni and the Qadar form a Pentad. Simultaneously, Michael Gabriel and Seraphiel were the first three angels of a twelve fold emanation. The seven Cherubim angels also correspond to the seven planets, while the twelve lesser angels correspond to the Zodiacal signs.

The Encyclopedia Iranica says that after the creation, Kuni commanded all the spiritual creatures to prostrate themselves and pledge obedience to Qadar. Every being did this except Eblis, Satan, who was exiled to earth as a result.

Later, this cosmology was further developed, and so in Fatimid times it appears as the following. This line of thought is described as the "Persian School", and has more explicit, rather than implicit, Neo-Platonism in it. Here, God uses his divine word, or Amr, to create the 'Aql, or Divine Intellect. This is the source of light. It's the equivalent of the Ideal world, and exists in motionless perfection.

The 'Aql generates, in turn, the Nafs, the divine soul, which is equivalent to the god of the soul of the world, and of the psyche. Here, we have a division that echoes Neoplatonic psychology: the Divine Mind is the Intellect, that which is the mind in its fullest capacity, while the Nafs is the mind in its lower capacity of the vehicle of Reason. In this model, Reason is a subsection of the greater mind, and not the ultimate nature of the mind itself. The god of the soul of the world in Neo-Platonism was the god of Reason, while the god of the Divine Mind or Intellect was the god of the total mind, which preceded the god of the soul of the world in creation. The god of the World Soul is imperfect, which is related to its capacity for movement and change, which is necessary for it carrying out its tasks. These tasks include animating the planets and life on earth itself.

In a departure from normal Neoplatonism, it's the god of the Soul of the World which both creates matter and the sets the matter in motion. The 'Aql directs the generation of both. Through this, the 'Aql and the Nafs cooperate in the creation and setting in motion of the world. The creation of the world consists of the creation of the elements, of the stars, the planets, and ultimately the souls of humanity. The 'Aql is identified with the Pen, a cosmological idea from the Quran, while the Nafs is identified with the Tablet that the Pen writes on, another Quranic concept. As Daftary notes, the order in which the 'Aql and the Nafs are arranged appears to be a reversal of the earlier Ismaili concept of the Kuni and the Qadar.

Daftary outlines the role of man within this cosmological framework. The soul of man is derived from the substance of the Soul of the World. Therefore, it's imperfect, just as the rest of the creations of the Soul of the World are. Because both the soul of man and the world as a whole are imperfect, man wants to unite with the Divine Intellect. This is the place of rest and eternity, in comparison to the phenomenal world, which has movement, and so is imperfect and transitory. This is both salvation and the escape of the human being from the apparent phenomenal world to the true world of the Divine Intellect.

The Nafs is imperfect, and though there is no story recorded about a fall of the Nafs from perfection into imperfection, by human beings working to perfect their own fragment of it, their own souls, in their quest to approach the Divine Intellect, they help to move the Nafs as a whole to a perfected, repaired, state. Therefore, the quest for human salvation and perfection is also a quest that helps to repair the world, although "Repair" might not be the right word, in that the Nafs was purposely emanated in an imperfect way. Perhaps the "Perfection of the World Soul" might be a better way of describing the consequences of human action on the soul as it exists on a higher plane. This doctrine implies that before a person can unite with the 'Aql, the Divine Intellect itself, they have to ascend to the Nafs, the god of the Soul of the World, in order to go beyond it.

Daftary recounts that the path for this salvation is indicated by each prophet in each of the seven Aeons or Eras. Each prophet gives a different version of the doctrine which is appropriate for the age. The doctrine, in this, is a key to gnosis, in that it's the realization of the meaning of the doctrine, as well as the work for perfection, which leads the individual to the Divine Intellect. The doctrine includes the description of the true reality of the universe, including the nature of the Divine Intellect.

Very importantly, in Ismaili theology, time is not completely cyclical. Instead, there will be seven repeating cycles of history, then an end to history, the Qiyamat or Resurrection, brought about by the final prophet, the Qaim. Each of the seven previous cycles will have it's own minor Qiyamat, and the culmination of the whole will be the Great Resurrection. The prophets in this Ismaili thought had to undergo their own spiritual ascent; they were not simply endowed with spiritual knowledge, and when the Qaim undergoes his spiritual ascent and union with the Intellect, it will end time and open the door to more easy, direct, union with the Divine Intellect for a great mass of people. This brings us to the modification of Ismaili beliefs which happened under the son of Hassan-I-Sabbah, and that lead to the Nizari branch of Ismaili thought.

What became Nizari Ismailism started off with a belief that the Qaim had appeared, and that the realization and the opening of the doors to mass communion with the Divine Intellect had taken place. What happened was that Hassan-i-Sabba's son, after his father's death, declared that the end of time, and the event called the "Resurrection" or Qiyamat had transpired. Hassan II declared himself to be the "Lord of the Resurrection", an eschatological figure who was the embodiment of the revealed divine, and claimed that, secretly, he was a descendant of Nizar, and more legitimate than the other, more conventional, descendants of Nizar, and that for those who were capable of seeing the new, restored, earth, the Islamic laws of Sharia no longer applied, with only a simpler, purified code of behavior now applicable. This lead to a graded form initiation, where those who were at the top could realize this new state, while those who were not able to comprehend it were still bound by the Law.

It also meant that they could directly enter into the Paradisal state while incarnated on earth, something which is replicated by traditional witches at the Sabbat. Here, the famous words "Nothing is True, Everything is Permitted" have a double meaning. First, it means that the Sharia law no longer applies to individuals who have had the gnostic realization of the Divine Intellect, and that they only have to obey the purified laws of Paradise, of the Divine Intellect. Second, it refers to the imperfection of the phenomenal world. The phenomenal world is realized to no longer be the true world, to be true, and the immortal, unchanging, perfect world of the Divine Intellect is what the full initiates perceive and belong to. The initiates, in this, see the true reality that exists behind the reality of appearances, which corresponds to the parts of the Divine Intellect from which the phenomenal world is generated. This, strangely enough, brings some of Ismaili thought in line with Buddhist and Hindu doctrines, though Islam and Buddhism were mortal enemies because of the Buddhist rejection of a supreme being.

There is actually a book written during the time that the Nizari Ismailis were in Alamut called the "Haft Bab" which has recently been translated into English, as "Spiritual Resurrection in Shi'i Islam". There, it extensively quotes the words of Hassan-i-Sabbah II in arguing for his role as the Qaim. As part of this, it puts forward the doctrine of two worlds, the world of reality, or truth, haqq, and the world of relativity. One is the spiritual world, the other is the conventional world. The spiritual reality is the only true reality, and the author presents three grades of individuals: those in the land of discord, those in the land of gradation, and those in the land of unity. The land of discord is conventional reality, the land of gradation is the state of people traveling upwards to realize the world of truth, of reality, while those in the land of unity have reached the awareness of the divine world beyond the phenomenal world. Those in the land of discord, who aren't trying to improve themselves spiritually, are bound by Sharia law, while those in the land of gradation are still bound by it, but trying to get to a level beyond it, and those who have achieved union with true reality can dispense with it, though not with good conduct. It's assumed that those who have transcended Sharia law will still be good people.

It's very obvious in the treatise that Hassan-i-Sabbah II was looked at as God in human, incarnate, form. He's described as giving grace that will lead a person to realize the state of the Resurrection, the realization of the world of Truth, and part of the goal of the work is to present Hassan's own words so that they can lead the person to this realization as well. Hassan is looked at as the manifestation of the macrocosm on earth, as containing the entire spiritual universe within him.

The doctrine's antinomian tendencies lead to chaos, but eventually, as time went on, the doctrine stabilized into a less controversial form, with a simplified though still recognizably Islamic practice. This lead to the evolution of the current day Nizari Ismailis, who are guided by their current Agha Khan. He, in turn, is thought to be a physical portal through which divine reality can be perceived. In this, it's an especially blessed thing for a Nizari Ismaili to physically see the Agha Khan, because the act of seeing links him or her with the reality of the Divine Intellect. The Agha Khans are the descendants of Hassan II.

The Templars had documented contacts with these Ismailis, who were participants in a four way war between the Seljuk Turks, the Crusaders, the Fatimids, and themselves. It's very possible that the doctrine of a union with the divine Intellect, a return to Paradise, as the result of progressive inner esoteric work was communicated to and adopted by them.

Nusayri and Bektashi

Now, in the formation of esoteric Shia groups, the succession of Imams represents one axis, or one way in which many were formed, but another axis has to do with the regard that was given to the Imams, and to Muhammad's family, in general. This axis is that of "Ghulat" or "Exaggeration", with the focus being the deification of Ali, Muhammad himself, and Ali's family, such as Fatima his wife, Muhammad's daughter. The Ghulat sects were those who pursued this program of deification, ultimately leading to the identification of these figures, and each of the successive Imams, with cosmological principles that were derived from Neoplatonism, with Gnostic influence there as well. They have been treated extensively by Mooman in his "Shi'ite Extremists", where "Extremist" does not refer to political extremism but to exaggeration.

Some sects could be gnostic through the vehicle of Ismaili succession, others through Ghulat exaggeration, through both, or through another influence, such as pure philosophy. The Nusayri are an example of a Twelver Shia group that adopted Ghulat doctrines and used the exaggeration of the importance of Ali, Fatima, and other early Islamic figures to veil parts of the Neoplatonic spiritual universe. The Nusayri, in this, were not alone, with other sects such as the Bektashi dervishes in Turkey, and the general, related movement of the Alawites in Turkey also making the equation between deified human beings and the different parts of the Neoplatonic universe. The Druze partake of both streams, being an offshoot of the Ismailis that also adopted Ghulat ideas. However, I believe that the best candidate for gnostic Islamic influence on the Templars are the Nusayri.

The Nusayri inhabit Syria and Lebanon today, and, due to joining the colonial Syrian military and working their way up, are the current rulers of Syria. The family of Assad are Nusayri, as well as the ruling class in the country. Information on the actual beliefs of the Nusayri was scarce until fairly recently, when the fundamental writings of the group were first published in Arabic. These have been examined thoughtfully by Yaron Friedman in his book "The Nusayri-Alawites, An Introduction to the Religion, History, and Identity of the Leading Minority in Syria", as well as by Meir Bar-Asher and Aryeh Kofsky in "The Nusayri-Alawi Religion". It's these books that I'm drawing my summary of their beliefs from. In explaining their beliefs, I'm also going to make reference to parallel principles within the Bektashi Alawites.

First, lets start with the Bektashi trinity. For this, I'm relying on the book "Extremist Shiites" by Matti Moosa, as well as "The Bektashi Order of Dervishes" by John Kingsley Birge. The Bektashi Trinity is made up of the One, the Divine Mind considered in a passive sense, and the active intelligence within the Divine Mind. The Bektashi refer to the One as "Haqq" the Truth. This is the conventional God of Islam. Next is the Divine Mind, which is given the definition of the esoteric meaning of Muhammad in Bektashi thought. He is simultaneously the Perfect Man. Muhammad in this is the logos and the creator of the world as well. Moosa and others liken him to Jesus in his esoteric aspect. As part of this, he's also the ultimate reality, the true reality from which the manifest reality is derived. This is followed by Ali, who is the found of esoteric wisdom.

This esoteric wisdom which Ali possesses leads the individual to God, which is to say first to Muhammad as the original reality, and through him to God himself. This is linked to Ali through the analogy of him representing the secret, esoteric, essence within the doctrine of Muhammad. Here, Ali is parallel to the Holy Spirit, though, of course, this is denied by Bektashis.

The link between Ali and the Holy Spirit is made stronger by the constant emphasis on the wisdom possessed by Ali. The Holy Spirit itself is called Wisdom, or Sophia, in the Old Testament and in the New. In Catholicism four of the seven gifts of the Holy Spirit are Wisdom, Understanding, Counsel and Knowledge. This suggests that even today, though the role of the Holy Spirit as Wisdom might be forgotten in many Protestant sects, it still lives on. Not only that, but the association between the Holy Spirit and the female Wisdom only goes stronger the further east one goes, with the Syriac Christian traditions featuring the association the most strongly. These Christian sects were the ones that were present in the heartland of Iraq that gave rise to Shi'ism as a whole.

Now, God created what Birge refers to as the "Ptolemaic universe" through Muhammad, meaning various heavens with angels, then the planetary spheres, then the earth. He describes a downwards and upwards arc of creation, with the first being from the highest spiritual level down, and the upward being from the point of static earth up. In this, the various kinds of life are on the upward arc, in a kind of proto-evolutionist model, with man being on one of the highest rungs, and the man who has turned himself into the Perfect Man, and reached back into communion with the Divine Mind of Muhammad, being the top of the upward arc.

The Nusayri divide things up differently, and, though they're said to have a "Trinity" as well, what they really have is a quartenary. This is, in part, because of the origin of the Nusayris through the figure of ibn- Nusayr, their founder. Nusayr claimed to be the "Bab", or Gate, of both the tenth and eleventh of the Twelve Imams, and to have been a representative of the twelfth Imam, who later became the "Hidden Imam", while he was alive but in hiding. The "Bab" was the interpreter of the esoteric doctrine of the particular Imam, who in turn was the esoteric interpreter of the Quran. Nusayr claimed to possess the esoteric, true, doctrines that had been transmitted by the tenth and eleventh Imams, and advocated the divinity of these Imams. For this, he was excommunicated twice by the Shia community. His claim to be a representative of the last Imam during his period of hiding while being alive, the "Minor Occultation", was disputed by one of the Imam's representatives, who cursed Nusayr for claiming this.

Nonetheless, Nusayr cultivated an esoteric circle around himself, and the teachings of this circle were passed on and later elaborated on by other mystics, leading to the Nusayri faith. Nusayr's status as a "Bab" lead to the Nusayri incorporating a concept of a "Bab" or gate into their cosmology as a hypostasis.

The Nusayri "Trinity", which actually has four elements, consists, first, of God in his ultimate, transcendent form. This is followed by God in his capacity as a manifest world of light with an active intellect within it. These are interpreted as being different aspects of one being. This is known as the "Ma'na", the "Meaning", which is identified with Ali. The Ma'na generates the Isbm, the "Word", which is a subservient tool similar to the idea of the Logos, which Ali, as the Ma'na, uses to construct reality. This corresponds to Muhammad. Finally, there's the "Bab", the Gate, which Nusayri sources themselves equate with the Holy Spirit, and which is personified by the early Persian follower of Muhammad, Salman al-Farisi, Solomon the Persian. The "Bab", in this, is a gateway to the Ism, to the logos or the creative power generated by God in his manifest form of the Ma'na, which is personified by Ali. He's also the tool of the tool, assisting the logos, the Ism, in his creative duties.

In what may be an adaptation from Druze doctrine, which in turn may have received it from the Manicheans, the Nusayri Bab has five "Eytams" or Orphans, who in turn assist the Bab in assisting the Ism in the creation and maintenance of the world. In Manichean doctrine, these refer to five qualities of the mind of the Father of Light, as we shall see. The Five Eytams also regulate the world as it exists now, through things like lightning and winds. From these emanate a series of five other orders of angels or subgods, one from the other, who, in turn regulate successively more material phenomenon on the earth, with the last of the hierarchy governing different kinds of plant life. The creation of the human form itself is attributed by the Nusayri to Fatima, the daughter of the prophet and the wife of Ali, in her angelic or deific form. This basic cosmology sets the stage for the Nusayri account of the apostasy of the angels and the creation of the world.

The world of light was first created, populated with angels, and these angels were tested by God. Friedman relates two different versions of the testing, and of the structure of the world of light. In the first, which is relatively unstructured, God tests the angels obedience to him by appearing in a strange form, and when the angels refuse to recognize him, they become more material because of their sin. However, this didn't cause them to fall into incarnation. Instead, in this, Azazil challenged god's authority and rallied the angels against him. This was related to the creation of human beings, which the angels objected to, as well as to general arrogance about Azazil's position in respect to God. Azazil in this is the first created emanation below the level of the five Eytams. Azazil is clearly the Iblis of Islam, who refused to bow down to human beings when commanded by God. As a result of this disobedience, Azazil and the angels who supported him are expelled from heaven and forced to take on human incarnation. In this account, the descent to material reality is similar to that of the Cathar account. It's based on arrogance against God and disobedience, and is instigated by an angel parallel to Satan.

In a second account, seven heavens are created with seven Adams that lived in each of these levels. These levels are populated by angels. The angels of the seven heavens are tested by God, but the test was the process of incarnation itself. God decreed that the angels should depart from their heavens and take human form, but the angels refused to do so. Now, instead of voluntary incarnation, they're forced to incarnate in human form, with punishment added to their experience of incarnation. In this story, it was this first sin of the angels, refusal to take human form, that created evil spirits, and that eventually created Satan as the byproduct of sin compounding on sin. Satan in this rules the material world in ignorance and non-awareness of higher divine reality, which he cannot perceive. He, and his servants, persecutes the angels in human incarnation and cannot perceive their true angelic nature.

The angels who are now bound into human form are fated to reincarnate until they achieve liberation. In the Nusayri worldview, people can go downwards into animal, vegetable, and even mineral life as consequences of further sin in their incarnations. The Nusayri people consider themselves to be a people who are made up of the incarnated angels.

Next, with regards to the liberation of the angels and their return to the world of light, the Nusayri believe in cyclical time, where in periods of 400,000 years, seven messengers are sent from the world of light to earth bearing the keys to escape from the cycle of incarnation. Here, the same series of prophets appear in human form in each cycle, with each of the prophets being a particular high angel close to the source of creation. These prophets are considered to not really have taken on material form, but to only have apparently done so, instead preserving themselves as beings of light from the pollution of matter in disguise. They include both Adam, the Hebrew prophets and Jesus, with Simon Peter being seen as an incarnation of Ali, and Jesus being seen as an incarnation of Muhammad. In this, Peter represents the secret doctrine of Jesus. A version of Ali is also thought to live in the Sun, which is reported to be an image of the world of light of the Ma'na. The Manicheans had a similar belief.

Each of these prophets gave the same message veiled in the different religious traditions of their time. They also had a series of collaborators and sub-messengers or sub-prophets, holy people within these cycles who are considered to have been the incarnations of the Eytams and members of the lower orders of angels. The way out is to follow the mystic path of purification, ascent, and goodness, in order to achieve unification with the divine, and a return to this original state. The soul seeking this ascent needs to be guided by a higher soul, who, in turn, may himself be under the guidance of either an incarnate or non-incarnate higher guide.

Following the guide, going upwards, the Nusayri initiate will first work to ascend to a level where they have communion with the lowest order of the angels that are emanated from the Eytams, then successively move up the hierarchy until they reach communion with the Eytams themselves. From there, they ascend to communion with the Bab, who then allows them to have communion with the Ism, who lets the initiate have the final step of communion with the

Ma'na, with Ali himself as God. Accomplishing this liberates the individual from reincarnation permanently and allows them to transfer themselves to the paradise of the light world of the Ma'na after death.

With respect to both of the Nusayri cosmological origin stories, Friedman has identified their sources, and both of them are known. For the first tradition, he cites the "Umm al-Kitab", which is the "Mother of the Book" or "Book of the Matrix". This has been excerpted and translated in Barnstone and Meyer's "Gnostic Bible", and is also subscribed to by some Ismaili sects. The other tradition comes from the "Kitab al-haft wa-'l-Azilla", or the "Book of the Shadows", which has been translated by Mushegh Asatryan in "An Early Shi'ite Cosmology, Kitab al-haft wa-'l-Azilla and its Milieu", which was published in Brill's "Studia Islamica 110" in 2015. By "Shadows", the author is referring to the original archangels that in Nusayri cosmology were created by the Bab, which were "shadows" in comparison to the light of truth of God.

The "Umm al-Kitab" in Barnstone and Meyer's "Gnostic Bible" is very illuminating. First, it contains quite a lot of gnostic themes which either did not become part of Nusayri theology or that the people commenting on it have not included. The evil angel who appears as the instigator of the fall of the Angels is Azazil, the same angel who appears in the Book of Enoch as the leader of the Watcher angels. Here, he's Satan. Azazil also takes on some features of the Evil One in Zoroastrian and Manichean doctrine.

The part of the book which is reproduced in Nusayri doctrine starts on page 688. In the drama of the Fall, Salman, who would become the Bab in Nusayri theology, is contrasted to Azazil. Salman is only one of several high angels or beings, with others being Ali, Fatima who is Ali's wife, Mohammad himself, and Ali's sons Hussein and Hassan. These are, in turn corresponded to various cosmological principles. However, of all of these, only Salman participates in the story. As in the Nusayri story, God appears in the heavens in a concealed form, and tests the angels by seeing if they will worship him. Salman is the first that does so, and is praised by two other angels for doing so, who follow his lead and become his helpers. Then several successively larger choirs of angels follow in acknowledging God, first one composed of twelve great angels, then one composed of twenty eight. These naturally correspond to the zodiacal signs and to the mansions of the moon. After this, a larger group of 124,000 angels reluctantly, and waveringly, acknowledged God. The number 124,000 may possibly be linked to the Sun, in that 129,000 is the product of 360 * 360, with the square root of 124,000 being 352.1363. Salman will assume a role similar to that of Saint Michael the Archangel in leading the heavenly hosts against Azazil.

After this, Azazil refuses to acknowledge God. However, at this point, Salman has become the deputy of God because of being the person who first acknowledged him, and so six choirs of evil angels who refused to venerate God, and instead declared that they themselves were gods, fight against Salman and the good angels. The result of this battle was that the angels were imprisoned in a special isolated place within heaven created for this purpose, so that they could not corrupt heaven as a whole. Next, after a thousand years, God gives the angels another chance to acknowledge him. 124,000 do, and are released from captivity, but the rest don't, and start a new war. This process repeated, over and over again, with the angels falling successively through lower and lower spheres of heaven until they exit heaven entirely and come to the sphere that would become the Earth.

At this point, the book presents an alternate story of the creation of the world, and the creation of Adam. Here, all of the stones and creatures of the world were, in fact, the evil angels. Stones, plants, and animals are the spirits of the evil angels in a transformed state. This is reminiscent of the Lurianic Kabbalah. Finally, man is created, but initially not from the fallen angels. Pure humanity is created instead.

There were still some fallen angels who aren't transformed into static beings, who are instead of the element of Fire, and these fallen angels are asked to bow down before man. They refuse. They're punished in several ways. One of the ways is that some are condemned to become what could be called 'fallen women', that is to say women who are prostitutes and otherwise looked on as engaging in bad acts. After some are condemned to assume human form in this way, God creates a scenario where he forbids the remaining fallen angels from having sexual contact with their comrades who have assumed the forms of fallen women. This is described as being related to the test God gave about not eating the forbidden fruit from the Tree of Knowledge. The angels, of course, disobey, and when they have sex with these women the women give birth to humans of both sexes who have the souls of those who had sex with them. Through this, the fallen angels become incarnated into humans of both sexes. This is described on pages 714-719.

I should point out that between the initial failure of Azazil to acknowledge God and the final incarnation of the fallen spirits into human form, there are twenty six pages of gnostic descriptions of the progressive fall of the angels and the progressive creation of the earth, ending with the story of the incarnation of them in human form. Within these descriptions, the pattern follows of God offering these evil spirits the opportunity to repent, some taking this opportunity, and others not taking it, with God further condemning those who choose not to do so.

Some of these fallen angels who fell into human form similarly want to repent and return home, and the book gives instructions on how this can be done. This is treated on pages 719-725, which also discusses the cultivation of Gnosis and how Gnosis is delivered to the individual. Besides living by four principles, which are to acknowledge God, acknowledge the Imams, be good to other people and not to be worldly, the book recommends the pursuit of Gnosis.

All of this, on its face, is similar to Cathar doctrine. The Crusaders conquered Nusayri territory, in the Counties of Edessa, Tripoli, and the Principality of Antioch. The Nusayri, as heretics, were treated better by the Crusaders. I believe that it's very, very likely that Nusayri gnostic doctrine was passed onto the Crusaders, who realized the commonalities that it had with Cathar doctrine, and then brought this doctrine back to Europe, and mixed it with Cathar belief.

That the Crusaders may have found the Nusayri belief to be compatible with their own Christianity is suggested by the fact that the Nusayri celebrate the Mass, with wine, as well as the birth of Jesus on Christmas Eve. As said before, Jesus was seen as a messenger who preceded Muhammad. Fatima, the daughter of the Prophet who is considered by the Nusayri to have created the human form, is thought by them to have taken incarnation as the Virgin Mary. The

Mass is celebrated with a trans-substantiation of the wine where it becomes the essence of Ali, of the Ma'na. Instead of a small sip of wine, the Nusayri mass, according to Moosa, after honoring Ali, features successive toasts of the wine to various Nusayri saints and holy people. These include well known Islamic figures as well as more particularly Nusayri figures. Additionally, according to Moosa, the Nusayri identify the martyred Shia Imam Hussein as being Jesus, with his martyrdom echoing that of Jesus on the cross.

The Nusayri mass should be considered in relation to the Bektashi and Ahl-i-Haq Jam or Çem, a similar mass like assembly which features prayers, dancing, and a culmination of drinking wine that's considered to be part of the essence of God. The Çem ceremony has similarities not only to the Mass, but to the Witches' Sabbat as well, although it appears that, for the most part, nothing transgressive goes on during it. The Pir in the Çem, the spiritual leader of the community, stands in the center of the room and symbolizes the sun, while the other members of the community dance around him in a circle. The Çem itself was reputed by outsiders to feature transgressive behavior, though, like in many cases, this appears to have been exaggerated.

Similarly, with regards to the Nusayri, the idea that they were engaged in sexually transgressive practices is false. Particularly, they've been alleged to have worshipped a woman on an altar with spread legs, which was labeled the source of the universe. In reality, the Nusayri are somewhat sexist in their beliefs, in that they do not allow women to participate in the mysteries, and engage in divine ascent. They see being incarnated as a woman as punishment, with the only way for women to participate being to be reborn as a man. P.B. Randolph's ideas about the Nusayri, expressed in his "Ansairetic Mystery" document, which we'll be examining in volume 2, are similarly fanciful, and like the other claims based on slanders about the Nusayri composed by outsiders.

My belief is that Sabian, Nusayri, and Ismaili ideas combined in the Templar experience. Within this, I believe that the Sabians and Ismailis contributed an esoteric doctrine of what paradise, the world of light, the Divine Mind, actually was in practice, while the Nusayri contributed the model of the fall of the angels into matter and incarnation, and the Ismaili contributed a way of reascent. Putting them together, the Sabian Abraxas/Baphomet/Saint George could be identified with Ali and the world of light, the Ma'na or meaning of God. The astrological parallels between Abraxas and the complete circle of the sun, could be read into this Paradise, and the incarnation of Jesus as Tammuz could be associated with the descent of Ali, God, down to earth as a prophet to lead people back to the light. Significantly, though, the Tammuz myth has more in common with the traditional Christian idea of Jesus as being not only a prophet but the redeemer of the world as well, and so conflicts to a degree with the Nusayri idea.

I believe that the combination of Templar and Cathar beliefs, with the change of the Cathar belief into the inverse witch belief, was preserved within Knightly families in England, Scotland, and elsewhere whose ancestors had been Templars or who had gone on the Crusades. This would include some very important people. Additionally, the stories associating the Order of the Garter, linked to Saint George, to witchcraft, at least at one point in its existence, would have some foundation. This would be the Templar understanding of Saint George as a cipher for Baphomet, derived from the Sabians. Thus, a strange dynamic would take place, where witchcraft in the UK would be simultaneously popular and elite, with elite culture and popular culture mixing and influencing each other, with some families being protected by their status, and able to preserve knowledge. What's theorized, as a general principle, is that in many cases the people leading the witchcraft congregations were linked to more elite families, and escaped persecution, while, unfortunately, the more common people, including many women, who participated, took the brunt of the violence.

Manicheans and Zoroastrians

Another source for the secret Templar doctrine are the Manicheans. This is the group that I have the least conventional evidence for, but it's absolutely fundamental to 19th century Templar masonry. The link between the Templars and the Manicheans comes from a version of the origin of the Templars that's recounted by Marconis de Negre, the son of the founder of the Rite of Memphis, in his "The Sanctuary of Memphis or Hermes". This is an adaptation of the Ormus legend, which also appears in Mizraim and other rites. Ormus is supposedly a priest of some kind who teaches the Templars esoteric secrets. In the Mizraim legend, Ormus is an Essene and a Johanine, a follower of John the Baptist. Other variants include the idea that the doctrine that Ormus, and the group that he belonged to, was pushing was a synthesis of the worship of Serapis with that of Judaism. Serapis, in this, can be equated with Helios as the Eternal Sun.

The origin stories of the Rite of Memphis lists a priest of the Manichean's as being the instructor of the Templars in their secret doctrine. The Memphis version says that a Coptic Egyptian Manichean priest instructed the Templars, which might seem strange, but in the 20th century a book of Manichean psalms written in Coptic, used by Egyptian Manicheans, was discovered, and has subsequently been translated and published as Mani's "Kephalia", with this just being the direct transliteration of the Greek word for Psalm, which means "Heading", and which is used for Biblical Psalms as well. Mani himself is referred to as the "Son of the Widow" in both versions of the story, with this connecting him to Hiram Abiff. Mani was martyred, and his martyrdom in this is related in the legend to the ritual of the Master's degree in Blue Lodge masonry, though this is basically an esoteric reading of a much older mythos that originally didn't have anything to do with the Manicheans.

My belief is that Marconis was aware of the gnostic part of the Templar doctrine, and was aware of the Middle Eastern connection with regards to the doctrine, but did not know where it came from. The Manicheans were known to be dualists, and so Marconis made the assumption that they had influenced the Templars, even though, I believe, it was really other groups that had this influence.

Nonetheless, even though the Manicheans themselves were not likely a direct influence on the Templars, the beliefs of the Manicheans are fundamental to understanding all of the different gnostic sects, including both the Cathars and the Nusayri. Because of this, I believe it's very useful to go over what their beliefs actually were. Like Zoroastrianism, which we'll examine next, the Manichean doctrine forms part of the essential background for understanding the Nusayris and the Cathars. What did the Manicheans believe?

Actual Manichean documents have since been found, in the 1920s in Turfan, Xinjiang, Central Asia, now in China, in the dusty Tarim Basin, buried with the mysterious "Tocharian" people. They have been translated into English and published as "Gnosis on the Silk Roads", which, though out of print, is widely available in libraries.

The actual Manichean doctrine is summarized well by in the introduction to "Gnosis on the Silk Road", which this, in turn, is a summary of:

In the beginning there was the Father of Light, who lived in the world of light. The Father of Light generates five attributes, Reason, Mind, Intelligence, Thought, and Understanding. These exist as five primal deities or limbs. It would be very interesting to compare them to the five "Eytams" of Nusayri and Druze thought. The Father of Light also has three other attributes, Light, Power, and Wisdom, which, in combination with the general attribute of Reason, give him the name of the Fourfold Father of Greatness. These can be said to be inner attributes, as opposed to the more outer attributes of the Five.

The world of light is divided into five realms corresponding to the five attributes, and at the center of the five is the Father of Light, the Fourfold Father of Greatness. He is surrounded by twelve Aeons, in a circle. This is meant to be pictured as a deity surrounded by twelve other deities, three in each direction, on each side of him. These Aeons are both places, times, and deities, in one. The Father of Light also generated the Living Spirit as a kind of viceroy or executive helper.

Just as there is the good god, there also exists the evil god, who, like the good god, has existed since the beginning of time. There is no drama about the evil god being produced by a Fall. Instead, he has just always existed. This points to the difference between limited and full dualism within gnostic sects, something that also manifested in the Cathar system of belief, with authors such as the writer of the "Book of the Two Principles" arguing for complete dualism and against his more moderate brethren, the difference being whether evil came about through the defection of something good to the bad or whether it has always existed

The evil god originally lived apart from the good god, from the world of light, and he created his own counter-kingdom, with five evil attributes mimicking the five good attributes of the good god, and counter-Aeons that were populated by demons. Eventually, the evil god decided to invade the world of light.

Seeing that the Evil One was going to attack, the Father of Light generated a copy of himself, the First Man, who, like the Father, also had five subgods or attributes attached to him. These corresponded to the pure elements, and are the sons of the First Man. The Living Spirit, along with the Great Builder god, built a Paradisal parallel world for the First Man to rule over, and for the good spirits to live in who were going to fight the Evil One and his demons. This reflected the structure of the world of light as a whole.

The demons of the evil god attacked the First Man and his five attributes, and the First Man let the demons devour him, thinking that he could defeat them. Instead, the light of the five sons of the First Man was absorbed into the demons, and the First man himself was taken hostage by them and brought to the world of darkness.

After this, the Father of Light sent the Living Spirit on a mission to rescue the First Man, and succeeded in freeing him from the world of darkness, restoring him to the world that he had created within the greater world of light. However, there were parts of the light that had been seized by the demons through their eating of the five sons of the First Man, which were not freed. The Living Spirit then took these evil demons that had consumed the light, along with other material, and made the world with them, as a way both to contain the world of darkness and as a way to start the liberation of the light which they had consumed, allowing it to return to the world of light.

To achieve this, the Sun and the Moon were established, along with a pathway back to the world of Light, the Milky Way, referred to as the "Column of Glory". The Moon, in its cycles from newness to fullness and back again, liberates parts of the light from the earth, and transfers it to the Sun. The Sun then transfers the light to the Column of Glory, which returns it to the world of Light.

The Sun and the Moon, in this, also presented themselves as beautiful men and women to the demons of the world, which caused the demons to want to copulate with them. Particles of the captive light were extracted from the semen of the male demons and from the fluids of the female , and this light was returned to the Paradise that the Living Spirit had made, which the First Man ruled over.

Not wanting all of the light to be lost, the evil god and his demons decided to create humanity in order to keep the light imprisoned. The human soul would be a spark of this light, and it would transmigrate, reincarnating itself in person after person, and so would be continually held captive. The evil demon based the form of Adam and Even on two of the good spirits who had come to fight them, who they had seen. These good spirits live in the Sun and the Moon, respectively. They also enclosed bad influences or vices within human beings, to keep them reproducing, keep them chained to evil, and to keep the light from escaping.

Jesus the Splendor, who is similar in name to Jesus in Glory, descended to earth and instructed Adam on what the nature of his situation was and how to escape and return to the Paradise within the world of light. Unfortunately, through the influence of Eve, Adam did not obey the advice given to him, which included not reproducing, and so humanity continued to be imprisoned due to incarnation and disobedience. Jesus the Splendor is a purely spiritual being who does not suffer, and who reappears throughout time to offer help to humanity.

The more physical and personal instruction of humanity for liberation is done through the intervention of the Great Nous, or the Great Mind, aspirit who is an aspect of Jesus. Known as Vahman, from the Zoroastrian Vohu-Manah, he functions like the Holy Spirit in Christianity, in this case inspiring physical humans to serve as prophets, giving them the power to preach the message, and directly interacts with the minds of humans to bring them to an awareness of the truth. He is said to have five aspects or virtues, which are Love, Faith, Perfection, Patience, and Wisdom, which the soul which has been saved from matter and reminded of its heavenly origin will exemplify. Reforming ones own ethics and becoming aware of where the soul originally came from, in this, along with prayer, observing fasts, and other practices, liberates the spiritual man within and allows the person to be recreated as the new spiritual man.

Jesus the Splendor and the Great Mind, Vahman, are helped in their goal to save humanity by many other deities, particularly the Maiden of Light, who has a role similar to the Virgin Mary in Orthodoxy and Catholicism. Jesus the Splendor, Vahman the Great Mind, and the Maiden of Light are thought to live in the Sun and Moon.

As for the the end of time, it will not feature a reborn heaven and earth. Instead, Paradise is the part of the world of Light that freed souls go to, under the leadership of the First Man, and eventually after all of the light, and all of the souls, are removed from the world and transferred to Paradise, the now vacant world will collapse into itself and be destroyed. The souls, on the other hand, will continue to live in Paradise.

Within this we can see certain themes that will reappear: the First Man, who is parallel to the Neo-Platonic Demiurge, Jesus the Splendor, an incarnation of the First Man on earth, and Vahman, parallel to the Holy Spirit as a power of Jesus.

Would it have been possible for the Templars to have met Manicheans in the Middle East of the 11th and 12th centuries? The Encyclopaedia Iranica states that actual Manicheans may have survived in the Middle East into the 11th century. However, there's a bigger issue looming in the wings, which is that, even if the Manicheans did in fact exist until that time, the gnostic teachings that have survived in the Middle East fundamentally conflict with them.

My belief is that the Templars didn't actually encounter Manicheans, but instead encountered the Nusayri, as well as the Druze, and that this encounter became remembered in time as that of the Templars contacting "Manicheans". Interestingly, as in the story of the Eytams, there may really have been influence by the Manicheans on the formation of Nusayri and Druze theology, though they then also departed from the Manichean theology in significant ways. Nonetheless, Marconis' claim, and his incorporation of it into the origin story of Memphis, where the first teacher of the Templars was a Manichean, is in my opinion an attempted reconstruction of what happened, based on the knowledge of Templar-Cathar spirituality as it was received by him.

E.J. Marconis' belief in a Manichean origin of the Templars was not produced in a vacuum. Instead, it was preceded by a growing interest in Zoroastrianism that was promoted by the Chevalier Ramsay, who was the originator of the Knightly degrees in Freemasonry, the Templar degrees. Ramsay wrote the two volume "Travels of Cyrus", an educational book based on the life of the Persian king of the same name. We will examine Ramsay very closely later in volume 2. In any case, I believe that Marconis' statement, and the presumed sharing of this statement within the Rite of Memphis as part of the doctrine of the Rite, produced a surge in interest in Manicheanism, which, in turn, fueled even more interest in Zoroastrianism. Manichean documents were hard to come by, but the relationship of Manicheanism to Iranian dualism was known, and I believe that in the absence of actual Manichean documents beyond fragments, people turned to what was being published of the Zoroastrian religious texts to try to fill in the blanks.

As to the last of the Manicheans, outside of China and the Tarim Basin, they lasted the longest in Central Asia. They were chased out of Persia to present day Samarkand, and then to Tajikistan. Interestingly enough, the place where the last Manicheans lived in Tajikistan became a center of Ismaili thought, evangelized by the Fatimid Dai or emissary Nasr Khusraw. This branch of the Ismailis distinguished itself for being more mystical than most, and, among other things, it gained access to and used the "Umm al-Kitab", the "Mother of the Books", the same book which is one of the inspirations for the Nusayri story of the Fall. In fact, the present text we have of the "Umm al-Kitab" comes from this community, which preserved it in a Persian translation. Even more interestingly, it appears that it was this community that Gurdjieff spent time with in his travels, which became the basis for his idea of the "Sarmoung Brotherhood". There are Manichean aspects of Gurdjieff's work, which have remained largely unknown, such as his doctrine that people are "moon food".

This, the idea that the moon is slowly consuming the unconscious individuals in our world, agrees with the Manichean doctrine of the Moon steadily transferring the imprisoned light of the earth back to the world of light. It's given a negative implication in Gurdjieff's system, in that it's preferable to cultivate direct awareness of the divine instead of being moon food, but it's still present. Related to this, Gurdjieff's doctrine of being aware and of being present within ones self, of awakening, can be related to the gnostic idea of not being lulled into complacent behavior or unconsciousness by the Evil One.

This branch of Ismaili thought, though probably extinguished in Tajikistan itself due to its incorporation into the Soviet Union, persists in northern Pakistan. There, a religious figure, a Sufi Sheikh, known as Allamah Nasir Hunzai, has wrote extensively on spirituality, with many of his books being translated into English and made available for free on the internet through the "The Institute for Spiritual Wisdom and Luminous Science" at www.monoreality.org. With regards to printed books, two are available in English, his two volume "The Wise Quran and the World of Humanity", which, among other things, states that the Ismailis are spirits who have fallen into matter. Perhaps the legacy of the Manicheans lives on through Hunzai, though his doctrine is presented as a particularly mystical variety of Ismaili thought that's still located within the bounds of Islam.

Zoroastrianism.

We should now give an account of Zoroastrianism, the faith that is at the heart of many of these dualistic ideas. For this, my primary sources are the recent academic books "Zoroastrianism: an Introduction" by Jenny Rose and "The Spirit of Zoroastrianism" by Prods Oktor Skjærvø, as well as the 1956 edition of the "Bundahishn" translated by Behramgore Tehmuras Anklesaria, made available online by Joseph Peterson at Avesta.org. The following is drawn from this translation of the Bundahishn, with corrections drawn from the more recent translation by Domenico Agostini and Samuel Thrope.

Zoroastrianism is quite different than many think. Ironically, this is because of the influence of gnosticism, and the confusion between Gnosticism and Zoroastrianism. The basic cosmogony of Zoroastrianism is that from eternity, two principles have existed, a good principle and a bad principle. These were separated by a large distance, and each of them created their own kingdom, with their own hierarchy of creations. Ahura-Mazda represented truth, truthfulness, virtue, and goodness of all kinds, while Ahriman represented lies, deceitfulness, vices, badness, and bad behavior of all kinds. Ahura-Mazda or Ormuzd dwelled in a perfect realm of light.

Seeing that the Evil One would eventually launch an attack on the world of light, the good principle, Ahura-Mazda or Ormuzd, created seven spirits from himself in his world of light. These seven were emanations of his qualities. The seven spirits, in cooperation with Ormuzd, created different parts of an unmanifest, purely spiritual, world, which is the foundation of the manifest, visible, world.

The Evil One became aware of the world of light and launched an attack on it, but was repelled. He then countered by making his own, inferior, spirits, and his own lesser purely spiritual world, and with them launched a second attack on the world of light.

Ormuzd offered a truce to the Evil One if he would submit to him, but the Evil One refused. He then proposed an agreement with the Evil One where they would only fight for nine thousand years, after which whoever won would be considered the winner forever. The Evil One agreed to this. After that, Ormuzd showed the Evil One how he would lose, and this stunned the Evil One so much that he retreated from attacking the world of light for three thousand years.

Then, Ormuzd created the manifest world, on the foundation of the unmanifest spiritual world. To do so he created manifest versions of the spirits that he had created, and they participated in forming the different parts of the manifest earth. They were the Amesh Spentas proper, "Life-Giving Immortals", the six around the throne, who later became the seven around the throne.

The Zoroastrian Seven are:

1. Spenta Mainyu, Holy/Creative Spirit, direct representative of Ahura Mazda

   At the Right hand of Ahura Mazda
   2. Vohu Manah, Good Thought
   3. Asha Vahishta, Best Order
   4. Kshatrya Vairya, Well-deserved command

At the Left Hand of Ahura Mazda.
5. Spenta Armaiti, Life giving humility, goddess of Holy or Good Devotion
6. Hauwatat, Wholeness, perfection
7. Amurtat, Immortality

In response, the Evil One created his own versions of the manifest Amesh Spentas, and a manifest evil world.

The earth and all its creatures were created by Ormuzd in perfection.

Each of the Amesh Spentas participated in creating different parts of the perfect world:
1. Spenta Mainyu became the guardian of the first man.
2. Vohu Manah, created the sunlit sky and animals,
3. Asha Vahishta, created the sun and sunlit spaces, fire,
4. Kshatrya Vairya, created metals
5. Spenta Armaiti, created the element of Earth, and provides fertility.
6. Hauwatat, created Water
7. Amurtat, created Plant Life

The first man, Gayomart, was both a giant and shining in perfection. Gayomart was created by a conjunction of the perfect matter of Ormuzd's creation and spirit from the heavens. He was made of seven primal metals. He was accompanied by the primal animal, the Bull, Gōšurwan. The Sun and the Moon did not move in this perfect creation.

The counter-Amesh spentas of the Evil One saw the perfect earth, the creation of Ormuzd, and convinced the Evil One to lead an invasion of it, thereby ending the three thousand years of inactivity.

All of the features of Ormuzd's perfect creation were invaded and polluted. Each of the different parts of the world fought battles against the Evil One and his creations. The primal man, Gayomart, was put asleep by Ormuzd during the attack so that he could survive it. Upon waking, Gayomart saw a polluted, corrupted, world, and then fought against the Evil One. However, Gayomart was defeated.

The deceased Gayomart first emanated all of the seven metals that he was made out of from his body. Then, the seed of the first humans emanated from his body. The primal bull Gōšurwan was also killed. It was attacked by the Evil One's servants, and Ormuzd fed it a type of drug to put it out of its misery and give it a pleasant death. After its death, the seeds of all the good animals, and many of the good plants, emanated from his body. The seeds of human beings, like the seeds of all animals, were created from fire. Ormuzd created the spiritual body of man and united it to the material body that grew from these seeds. The first humans were pure in their thoughts, were committed to the truth, and acted with perfect virtue, but the Evil One saw this and polluted their minds with bad thoughts, the possibility of lying, and vices.

The first humans were initially in a good place within the corrupted world, but the Evil One took that goodness away and forced them to survive in the corrupt world. Within the corrupted world, they were taught how to make fire, a symbol of goodness and purity, by the good gods, and this helped them in their survival. These humans were the ancestors of all mankind.

The consequences of the invasion of the Evil One and his servants to the world was the introduction of things such as droughts, famines, earthquakes and hardship, as well as the thorns of plants, poisons, mountains, harmful animals, and desolate places. The good gods and spirits are still fighting the Evil Ones, and this can be seen in the cycle of the year, where the good spirits of fruitfulness and life are opposed by those of death.

The essence of what is to be done by humans within this state is purification, both of themselves and of the world. The world itself, though polluted by the Evil One and his servants, is not fundamentally bad. Neither is the body. Instead, the earth is a combination of good and bad which the actions of human beings, and of gods, can improve, purify, and make better. On the part of humans, this includes both virtuous actions, sacrificial rituals, and what could be called 'civilizing' behavior in relation to nature, and to other humans, such as partaking in the farming of vegetables and animals, and positive social organization. Above all, truth is the fundamental value by which people should live by, with lying, lies and deceitfulness of all kinds, being the fundamental feature of the Evil One and his servants.

Life is a positive value in Zoroastrainism, and fertility and reproduction are positive things. The world was intended to be perfect, and the purification of the world has as its goal the reversal of the pollution that entered it. What is good in the world will be extended. Once the pollution in the world has been removed, and the Evil One and his servants have been defeated, the world will return to the primal paradise that it once was. This will happen after a final battle between good and evil, lead by a messianic figure, the Saoshyant. The end of time will feature a resurrection of all of the dead as well, who will live in the perfected earth.

While there are many things that could be noted about this story, one which has a great deal of importance to the craft and to related doctrines is the specific character of the seven around the throne. Specifically, these seven are not identified with the seven planets. Instead, they are seven emanations of the qualities of the good god, which then become active powers in the world. In this, they are more like the concept of divine names in both Christianity, Judaism, and Islam. Particularly, in esoteric Judaism and Islam, the divine names are thought to be potencies through which God works in the world, with the action that they perform having to do with the meaning of their name. The temptation to identify the seven with the planets in esoteric doctrine is strong, but it's fundamentally wrong in relation to the primal vision, in that what's being described, with relation to the Sabbat, is far, far, beyond the character of the planets.

As to how these can derived, there are many different ways. Let me suggest, beyond essential qualities, that it's possible to relate these types of primal emanations to numbers as well, in a numerological sense, with the seven, or even a larger number of beings, proceeding from the source in ascending numerical order, each with the generative characteristics attached to that particular number.

The Zoroastrian seven were connected to Witchcraft and others through the rediscovery of Manicheanism and its relationship to Templar doctrine, and Templar masonry, in the 19th century, as we have seen. I feel, however, that Platonic ideas about the structure of the Divine Mind, and the generation of the different parts of it from each other in a procession, explain the structure of the seven much better than do the actual Zoroastrian attributions.

Joseph von Hammer-Purgstall and Baphomet

Misconceptions about Baphomet

The idea of a Manichean or Zoroastrian influenced Templar tradition was added to by a potential misinterpretation of something that the scholar Joseph von Hammer-Purgstall discovered. Hammer-Purgstall, in his writings on the Templars and their secret traditions, made reference to a drawing of a figure purported to be Baphomet as a world creator that's labeled "Bahaman", which is contained in ibn Washiyyah's book "The Nabatean Agriculture", and where it's labeled as the deity who is the biggest secret of the Sabians. The figure shows what appears to be a creature or god creating the world, though this is shown in the form of a figure making two different figures of concentric circles touching each other. This implies that "Bahaman" is the Demiurge, which in Hammer-Purgstall's world referred to the evil god of gnosticism.

"Bahaman" in this could be interpreted as a variation of the Persian "Vohu Manah", which is the Manichean "Vahman", and which originated as a deity in the Zoroastrian pantheon, the "Good thought". Vahman, in Manicheanism, as we have seen, is a tool and an assistant of the Jesus in his quest to liberate humanity, but is not a creator of the world. Similarly, in Zoroastrianism, "Vohu Manah" as "Good Thought", is a power of Ormuzd, but is only one of seven spirites that participate in the creation of the world.

I think that people, reading this interpretation by Hammer-Purgstall, jumped to conclusions, and, in fact, those who were actually sympathetic to Templar belief, and who did not think they worshipped the evil god, looked at it as a kind of breakthrough. What, though, was Hammer-Purgstall really looking at?

While the Nabatean Agriculture as a whole has not been translated into English, large sections of it have been in Jaako Hämeen-Anttila's excellent work "The Last Pagans of Iraq". There, the figure of "Bahaman" doesn't appear, but something else does. Though the illustrations are not reproduced, there are many references to a figure named "Dawànày" in the book. "Dawànày" is said to be a great leader of the Sabians who taught them how to create many magical pictures, that is to say how to make many talismans. Looking at it this way, the illustration that Hammer-Purgstall reproduces, purportedly showing the demiurge creating the world, can be interpreted as Dawànày drawing one of his talismans, with the talisman being one of the greatest secrets of the Sabians. In other words, it is likely not Baphomet at all, and the name most likely has nothing to do with Persian or Zoroastrian ideas, which makes sense considering that all of this was in the Semitic heartland, so to speak. Now this is the likely reality, but how was this misinterpretation understood by contemporaries? This identification, in my opinion, gave fuel to scholars to look at the Zoroastrian religion in trying to understand and reconstruct the Manichean influence on the Templars.

Zoroastrianism, in this, became an outward mask that was more socially acceptable to discuss, and more permissible to discuss, than the Manicheans, or the Templars. Other concepts from Zoroastrianism integrated into or discussed with relation to Masonry include the "Honover" which is the Zoroastrian Xvarneh, or Khvarenah, which is a mystical energy of anointing. This was taken by scholars and identified with the creative word, the Logos, of god in Christianity, and from that with the true meaning of the Mason's word, the Lost Word. In turn, this would be identified as the speech of "Bahaman" or "Vohu-Manah", Baphomet.

Interestingly, Albert Pike, in his commentary on the "Knight of the East and West" degree in "Morals & Dogma", though recognizing that "Vohu-Manah" or "Bahman" is a subservient spirit to the good god, nevertheless labels him the "Lord of Light". Similarly, Pike references Vohu-Manah in his commentary on the 26th degree in "Liturgies of the Ancient & Accepted Scottish Rite".

The focus on Zoroastrianism as a guide to Manichaenism, functioning as a guide to the Templar's beliefs, developed into a fascination on Indian religion when the relationship between Hinduism and Iranian religions became known. However, at this point, things become somewhat confused, because Hinduism is not dualistic, though there are linguistic and cultural relationships between Iranian and Indian peoples. This fascination lead to figures like Albert Pike thinking that the Vedas were the ultimate repository of truth for Masonic doctrine, and mysticism, which he explored in his last works, unfortunately using the term "Aryan", which was in common use, in discussing the subject. Pike's works are generally excellent, but the final turn, when he went from Iranian subjects to Hindu ones, was not productive.

Much more was found in Hindu doctrine which could be paralleled to both masonry and to the mystery religions of the west, but the connection to anything concrete which was transmitted from the near east to the west by the Templars, or any other historical group, was lost. It was at this point in the 19th century that we start to see the transition in high grade Masonry, including Memphis-Mizraim, from the older system to ideas that would flourish with the Theosophical society.

Going further into Hammer-Purgstall's conception of Baphomet, his basic idea, which he expressed in "Mysterium Baphometis Revelatum ", was that the Templars had been influenced by the Druze. However, his characterization of the Druze beliefs was far different than reality. First off, he refers to them as "Ophites", or serpent worshippers. This was not unique to him, but was derived from rumors about the Druze that their enemies had spread. Going from there, Hammer-Purgstall connects the "Ophite" Druze with the gnostic sect of Ophites, which, in turn, he says worshipped the evil god. Hammer-Purgstall very explicitly says that the Templars learned to worship the evil god, the creator of the earth, from the Ophites, and that Abraxas, among other figures, was actually a symbol for the evil god. He explicitly relates the god of the Templars to the evil Ialdabaloth. Within this characterization, he repeats many of the slanders against gnostic groups that the early Church presented, casting them as being true, and applies them both to the Templars and to the Druze.

This lead to a kind of halfway position on the Templars, one that partially validated their beliefs but got things wrong otherwise. It became popular in the late 19th, early 20th century, and can be found in the writings of the occult master G.O. Mebes. Although Mebes is very insightful in many aspects of his commentaries, which take the form of explanations on the Tarot that reveal esoteric truth, this was one commentary that was not accurate. While validating the idea of Baphomet, and repeating the idea that its name is a backwards rendering of "Temophab", which, in turn was an abbreviation for "Master of the Temple of the Peace of All Men", he nonetheless attributes Baphomet to the lower god, the Evil One. This is the opposite of the truth, as we have seen, with the reverse tradition putting Baphomet in the position of the true creator within the Divine Mind. This is particularly strange, because much of Mebes' commentary on the meaning of the "Peace of all Men" part of "Temophab" is quite positive.

Mebes work has appeared recently in English translation, and a condensed, plagiarized, version of his Tarot work can be found in the Polish expatriate Mouni Sadhu's book "The Tarot: A Contemporary Course of the Quintessence of Hermetic Occultism". Unfortunately, this idea has also been taken up by others who, with anti-Masonic sentiments, explain that Masons supposedly have "power" in the world because they worship the evil god in the form of Baphomet.

I believe this definition is from a composite of Hammer-Purgstall's work and Eliphas Levi's unfortunate mischaracterization of Baphomet. Levi's work, in turn may well have been partially based on Hammer von Purgstall's work itself. Levi's idea of Baphomet is that he occupies the position of the god of the Soul of the World, which has a semi-gnostic signification in his work.

To explain this, let's look at what the Soul of the World and the god of the Soul of the World is. In the Ptolemaic cosmos, above the earth is a series of concentric spheres corresponding to the planets. Beyond the sphere of the fixed stars lies the god of the Soul of the World. This god directs the Soul of the World itself, which is the animating force in the universe. It's the thing that causes motion and movement, that causes life. In fact, according to the Greek original, movement and life are identical, in that to have an anima, that is, a soul, is to be animate, moving. The Soul of the World corresponds to the level of the Aether which is above the fixed stars, and the Soul is the Aether itself.

The god of the Soul of the world directs the movement of the Aether, and, in fact, is usually considered to be a goddess. In the thought of some gnostics, the goddess of the Soul of the World was identified with Sophia, and integrated into the gnostic drama as a figure who decided to create (or to animate) without the permission of the higher gods. Alternately, the god of the Soul of the World is identified with the offspring of Sophia, Ialdabaloth, meaning that the Evil One is considered to be the one who is behind the movement and animation of the world. It appears that Levi, in his conception of Baphomet, saw him as a combination of the god of the Soul of the World and Ialdabaloth, albeit with the gnostic features being very lightly present. Baphomet for Levi directs the magnetic force of magic, which is also the life force. This is the Aether that makes up the Soul of the World itself. Levi somewhat confusingly calls this force also the Azoth, but in this I believe he's mixing up two different spiritual traditions, in that the Azoth is really something else entirely. Levi and his spiritual descendants, such as Oswald Wirth, believed that Baphomet had to be negotiated and gotten through on one's way of spiritual ascent, symbolized by the progression of the Tarot cards. This is far, far different than the witch conception of Baphomet.

Works Cited

Agostini, Domenico and Samuel Thrope trans, "Bundahishn". Oxford University Press, Oxford, 2020

Anklesaria, Behramgore Tehmuras, trans. "Greater Bundahishn" 1956, made available by Joseph Peterson at the "Avesta.org" http://www.avesta.org/mp/grb.htm.

Asatryan, Mushegh, "An Early Shi'ite Cosmology, Kitab al-haft wa-'l-Azilla and its Milieu", published in

Brill's "Studia Islamica 110" in 2015. Available on the author's Academia.edu page

Badakhchani, S. J. , "Spiritual Resurrection in Shi'i Islam", I.B. Tauris, London 2017

Bar-Asher, Meir M., Aryeh Kofsky "The Nusayri-Alawi Religion", Brill, Leiden, 2002

Barnstone and Meyer "Gnostic Bible", Shambhala, Boston, 2009

Barnstone and Meyer "Umm al-Kitab", translated in "Gnostic Bible", Shambhala, Boston, 2009

Birge, John Kingsley "The Bektashi Order of Dervishes" Hartford Seminary Press, Hartford, 1937

Callataÿ, Godefroid de trans. Bruno Halflants trans., On Magic I: An Arabic Critical Edition and English Translation of EPISTLE 52a (Epistles of the Brethren of Purity), Oxford University Press, 2012

Daftary, Farhad "The Isma'ilis, Their History and Doctrines", Cambridge University Press, Cambridge, 1999

Encyclopedia Iranica, "Cosmogony and Cosmology vi. In Ismailism" https://www.iranicaonline.org/articles/cosmogony-vi.

Encyclopaedia Iranica "Manicheans, general survey" https://www.iranicaonline.org/articles/manicheism-1-general-survey

Friedman, Yaron "The Nusayri-Alawites, An Introduction to the Religion, History, and Identity of the Leading Minority in Syria", Brill, Leiden, 2010

Gurdjieff, George "Meetings with remarkable men", many editions

Hämeen-Anttila, Jaako "The Last Pagans of Iraq", Brill, Leiden, 2006

Hammer-Purgstall, Joseph von "Mysterium Baphometis Revelatum", Vienna, 1818, Google Books

Hunzai, Nasir, "The Institute for Spiritual Wisdom and Luminous Science" at www.monoreality.org

Hunzai, Nasir, "The Wise Quran and the World of Humanity" Danishgah-I Khanah-I Hikmat, Pakistan, 2003

Levi, Eliphas, trans. AE Waite, "Transcendental Magic", William Rider & Sons, London, 1923, google books

Liddell, E.W. "Pickingill Papers", Michael Howard ed., Capall-Bann, Chieveley, 1994

Marconis de Negre, E.J. "The Sanctuary of Memphis or Hermes", Kessinger Publications, Kila MT., nd.

Mebes, G.O. "Tarot Majors", Shin Publications, England, 2020

Moosa, Matti "Extremist Shiites, the Ghulat Sects", Syracuse University Press, Syracuse, 1988

Mouni Sadhu "The Tarot: A Contemporary Course of the Quintessence of Hermetic Occultism", Wilshire Book company, North Hollywood, 1971

Pike, Albert "Knight of the East and West" degree in "Morals & Dogma", Kessinger publications, Kila MT. nd. Google Books

Ramsay, Chevalier Andrew Michael "Travels of Cyrus", 2 vols.. Woodward, London, 1727, google books

Rose, Jenny "Zoroastrianism: an Introduction" I.B. Tauris, London 2012

Russell, Jeffrey Burton "Witchcraft in the Middle Ages", Cornell University Press, Ithaca, 1984

Skjærvø, Prods Oktor "The Spirit of Zoroastrianism", Yale University Press, New Haven, 2011

Stoyanov, Yuri "The Other God", Yale University Press, New Haven, 2000

Wakefield, Walter, Austin P. Evans "Heresies of the High Middle Ages", Columbia University Press, New York, 1991

Wilson, Peter Lamborn "Sacred Drift", City Lights Publishers, San Francisco, 1993

Chapter 2
The Sabbat

The following is Neo-Platonic, based on the thought of Plotinus. The basic elements of this worldview are the One, the First Mind, and the deity of the Soul of the World, the world itself, and humanity. The One is the start of all reality, eternal and inaccessible. It generates the plan on which the world will be created. It emanates all of reality from it. The first emanation, which is the First Mind, is the visible manifestation of what's implicit in the One. It is the seat of the Ideals, and is self-conscious. The First Mind serves as the Demiurgos, the creator of the world. It takes the plans that the One has generated, and implements them, forging both the world, the Soul of the World, and ultimately mankind.

These creations exist in an inanimate, potential, form, within the primal chaos until the Soul of the World animates them and sets the motion of the planets and the earth. The churning of the universe brings the creatures of the world into manifestation from the primal chaos. The Demiurgos produces the souls of mankind as well, which are transmitted down into the bodies of humanity. The souls of humanity reflect the diversity of creation, and are a mean between the disembodied souls of the gods and daemons and those of animals.

The Sabbat of the Ages has several parts, and can be viewed several ways. First, looked at from the inside, the Sabbat, the Ideal realm, the first Fire, the Divine Mind, is the repository of all of the different forms that the world is made of. It is the millions-of-forms-of-being. These forms are alive and are in constant sexual union, combination, and recombination with each other. The energy of the first fire is also a sexual energy of a kind, corresponding to the will, but in a slightly different way than might be expected. On top of this primal fornication, the forces of the Sabbat are, or can be, organized into several discrete groups, with each of these groups corresponding to a subset of all of the Ideals within the Divine Mind. These are what Andrew Chumbley referred to as the conclaves of the Sabbat of the Ages, or the letters that make up the Azoetia. Within the world of the primal vision, the Sabbat as a general undifferentiated force manifests its consciousness in the personality of Tubal-Cain, who serves as the Demiurge. Simultaneously, the millions of forms of being are corralled into four forms, which are connected to Tubal-Cain as Baphomet, the Tetramorph, the Living Being and Paradigm. Baphomet/Tubal-Cain is both Living Being and Demiurge in one. The Living Being/Paradigm is a Platonic entity. These four forms are then replicated to include the transition points between them, leading to a total of eight forms. These eight forms correspond to the eight directions of the Circle. The Tetramorph is formed as a hieros gamos or sacred marriage between the Demiurge and the First Sun.

Plato describes how the four are generated in the Living Being in the "Timaeus", and it's very worthwhile to look at it. Fire and earth were created, and then air was created to be one mean between the two, to unite the two. This created a progression from one, Fire, to two, Fire and Earth, to three, Fire Earth and Air, which together describe a triangle. The triangle is a plain, but it is not three dimensional, so water needed to be added as another mean between Fire and Earth, in order for the figure to be expanded into the third dimension, which can be accomplished with the tetrahedron of four points. Significantly, if you assign numbers to the elements such that Fire is one, Earth is two, Air is three, and Water is four, and then add them together, you get Ten, the number of wholeness and unity. This means that all of the elements mixed together make up a whole entity, on another level, through a complete mixture. The four elements, taken together, are what make up the Living Being. This Being, in turn, is shaped by the Demiurge. The idea that the Demiurge and the Living Being are one means that the Demiurge, who is the conscious aspect of the First Sun itself, shapes the Living Being out of the stuff from which he is made.

The four and the eight are significant because, with regards to practical work, the model or the fundamental glyph that's related to the Sabbat and to traditional witchcraft, which is parallel to the Tree of Life symbol in other occultism, is the horizontal compass of the circle combined with the vertical axis.

Looked at in another way, the Sabbat has two parts. To describe them, I'm going to use the vocabulary that Henry Corbin uses in his analyses of Iranian Islamic Mysticism. This vocabulary, and the texts surrounding it, is most explicitly discussed in his volume "Spiritual Body and Celestial Earth". What we've just discussed, the aspect of the Sabbat which is the court of heaven itself, is referred to by Corbin as "Jabarut", the dimension of the Throne of God and the Cherubim which surround him. Below the world of Jabarut, however, it the dimension of the "Hurqalya". The Hurqalya is a pure, paradaisal, world, populated by unfallen angels who have not experienced sin, who are androgynous. This world, in Islamic mystical thought, is said to encompass at least three cities, Jabalqa, Jabarsa, and Hurqalya itself, from which the name for the whole is taken. In Islamic thought, these cities are made of emerald and have ten thousand gates each. The Sabbat itself, in this aspect, is a verdant, green, land of life, which exists underneath the midnight sun. By this is meant that the illumination of this part of the Sabbat is the aurora borealis itself, with the energy of the Sabbat pulsing with green and gold. This paradise is where the angels that later rebelled against God and were enticed to come to the earth by the Evil One came from, and returning to this place is the goal of the spiritual path. This is the true "Fairy Realm", which people occasionally go to. In other spiritual traditions, which don't incorporate the fall of angels, it may also be thought of as the original Paradise that Adam and Eve lived in before being expelled to the material world. It's where the people who escape from the cycle of reincarnation or captivity in the lower world live in after death. As for the relationship between this place and Jabarut, Corbin makes the comment that if you go far enough into these pure lands, this Paradise, you'll get to the place of the throne.

Note, though, in my opinion, the "Green Man" figures in European art refer to earlier symbolism regarding Tammuz and Saint George, in contemporary traditional witchcraft when mention is made of the "Green Man", it's often of the Islamic figure of Khidr. He is a kind of guide for the guideless, and his green aspect is interpreted as referring to his home in the Hurqalya, the green land. He's also paralleled to the witch god, who leads the way to the Sabbat, who we'll examine later.

This particular line of Islamic thought that Corbin puts forward is the product of the "Shaykhi" school of thought in Shi'ia Islam, which only developed in the 19th century, but which was based on the thought of medieval mystics such as Sohrawardi. In particular, what I've presented is drawn from both Corbin and his translation of a work by the founder of the Shaykhi school, Shaikh Ahmad Asai, who lived until the early 19th century. The Shakyhi school still exists. There are commonalities between Shaikh Ahmad's thought and Nusayri beliefs as well. Interestingly, there's a relationship between the Shaykhi school of mystical Islam and the origins of the Bahai'i faith. Disappointingly, the Bahai'is have little interest in practical mysticism, and little understanding of the cosmology that they have inherited from the Shaykhi school.

This division in the Sabbat can be seen in medieval Christian portrayals of it, which influenced traditional witchcraft. Particularly, the idea of the Heavenly Jerusalem as the Rest of the Saints the place where righteous individuals go after death, is reflective of this division. On the one hand, it's the place where Jesus, god, has his court, and is divided into foursquare. On the other hand, it's the place where, as a heavenly city, it is populated by people outside of the heavenly court itself. Here, the Heavenly Jerusalem appears as a combination of the cities of Jabarsa and Jabalqa with the court of the Jarabut at its center.

Additionally, the archetype of the Heavenly Temple, as the heavenly court itself, is dealt with extensively by Corbin both through the lens of contemporary, non-witch based, Templar spirituality, as well as through Islamic mysticism in his work "Temple and Contemplation". There, the court of heaven, the court of the Sabbat, becomes the Temple or Castle of the Grail, which is attended by the Grail Knights.

The mystical geography that Corbin and his Shaykhi and other sources attribute to the Hurqalya and Jarabut is applicable to the Sabbat as well: they say that both the Hurqalya and the Jarabut are to be found beyond the peak of the world mountain, called Qaf, which is the primal mountain that's thought to exist at the north pole. Here, there's a clear parallel to the mountains that the Witches' Sabbath is supposed to take place on, as well as Mount Sauvage, the Savage Mountain, which the Grail Castle is supposed to be located on top of. Here, however, to reach the pure lands, it's necessary to get to the top of the mountain and then to go beyond it. This praxis can be found in Chumbley's "Dragon Book of Essex", for example, where the primal mountain of "Al-Qaf Saba" has to be metaphorically climbed, and then once climbed, transcended in order to get to the next spiritual level.

We shall speak more about the climbing of this mountain in the comments about Internal Alchemy and chivalry, including the intersection between the esoteric contents of Wolfram von Eschenbach's "Parsifal" and the practice of the Toad Stone. Suffice it to say, for the moment, that there are two parts to this: first, the climbing of the mountain, with this corresponding to a particular type of spiritual work, and then going, or leaping, from the mountain into the world above it, which corresponds to Theurgical work. The Mountain of Qaf can also be equated with the "Venusberg" described in the medieval tale of Tannhäuser, which is a kind of cipher for the Sabbat, and the tale of the Fairy Queen, and the Fairy kingdom, as well, though this tradition conflicts in character with that narrated in Parzival.

The Sabbat can also be represented as a Rose, though other flowers, such as our Lotus example, will function as well. The link of the Sabbat as the Rose comes through the idea of each petal being an Ideal within the Divine Mind, and the Rose also symbolizes the female external genitalia exposed, which suggests birth, life, the coming of forth of many different beings. That the Rose can represent the Sabbat, Paradise, the Divine Mind is suggested by Dante's use of a white rose to represent the highest level of Paradise where the Saints dwell in his "Divine Comedy".

Hyperborea.

What I believe is that "Hyperborea" and the "Hyperborean" kingdom were ciphers for the Sabbat itself, which doesn't exist in physical reality. The use of the word "Hyperborea" in the "Magitians Discovered" volume one apparently was jarring for some individuals, who associate the word and traditions around it with Nazism and white supremacy. However, if you've read the works of the French scholar on Islam Henry Corbin, you've dealt with the idea of

"Hyperborea" in another form. Corbin, no doubt sensitive to the politics of the use of the word in the post-World War II world, and the abuses that the Nazis and their sympathizers had made of the concept, used euphemisms like the "Spiritual North" and the "Eighth Clime", but if you look in the texts at what this refers to, it's an imaginal kingdom that's metaphorically said to be at the North Pole. The "Climes" that are referred to are rows of latitude, going from north to south, and the eighth "Clime" is the highest latitude of them all, centered on the North Pole. Islamic mystics used this idea to indicate the same place which I attribute to the Sabbat of the Ages, to the Divine Mind, or, in some cases, to a world that was far lower than the Divine Mind itself, but still quite exalted above normal reality. The Imaginal, in Corbin's formulation, refers to the Barzakh, which is translated as "border", and is a meeting place of the divine, which emanates from the Divine Mind, and the earthly, an intersection of the two realms. It is the Hurqalya or world of vision, which contains different cities and centers within it. This is centered on the "Eighth Clime", which is the Hyperborean kingdom that's metaphorically said to be at the North Pole, in the "Spiritual North".

Hyperborea was thought to be a legendary paradisal realm, located at the north pole, which experienced endless light and where people experienced eternal youth. It was thought to be overseen by Apollo, which the Gothicists equated with Odin. That the pole also gets complete darkness for a long period of time was less important in the imaginations of people conceptualizing it, but the light and the midnight sun suggested to people its commonality with the Eternal Sun, the Divine Mind.

As being located at the north pole, Hyperborea was also the source of the four winds, connecting it with the aerial spirits. This connection between aerial spirits and that which is transcendent, as opposed to that which is lower, is an ancient one which is testified to by spells from the Greek Magical Papyrae, such as the "Consecration of All Things", which has recently been translated by Allison Chicosky as "The Secrets of Helios". A theurgic rite, the consecration calls upon Helios, who in this case stands for the Eternal Sun, the main god or container of the gods in theurgy. As the Divine Mind, the Eternal Sun contains the different intellectual gods such as the

Demiurgos. Within the litany of invocation, the rite calls upon Helios as one who rises from the four winds, which suggests that he rises from the Hyperborean source of the four winds. This is a concept which pushes the four winds beyond, and before, the planetary spirits, to be superior to them. This concept can also be found in public writings about Traditional Witchcraft, such as those by Shani Oates about the 1734 tradition of Robert Cochrane, where the Sabbat shows up as the "Castle of the Four Winds", which a person can do a ritual to get to.

The winds are referred to in Greek as Anemoi, literally as spirits, the word being the same as Anima, which is soul, from where we get the word "Animate", referring to beings that can move on their own accord. The winds, starting from the place of origin, can be said to be empowered by the heat, fire, and light of the First Sun. They carry life force of various kinds, which depend on where exactly they're coming from. This concept of relating the winds to life forces was taken up and modified in the 17th century, when the north pole was thought to have a giant magnetic stone at the top of it called the "Rupes Nigra", or black stone, that was the source of all magnetism. The north pole was also associated by 17th century figures such as Robert Fludd with the power of the Pole Star and the Big Dipper, who were thought to share in the qualities of magnetism, since they were always in the north, just as the north pole was.

We can see through this a metaphorical construction of a Hyperborean kingdom which is the place of the Eternal Sun, always light, with the Pole Star over head, which is the source of wind/magnetism, which influences the rest of the world. Because of its location, under the Pole Star, the kingdom would be circled by the constellation Draco, which is circumpolar, going around the polar regions. Draco, as we have seen, corresponds to the One, to the great Dragon Lord, just as the Eternal Sun corresponds to the Divine Mind which is the child of the Dragon Lord.

This symbolism, in turn, can be combined with that of the Heavenly Temple. Here, the Heavenly Temple sits on top of the World Mountain, which sits on top of the pole, and in the center of the Heavenly Temple runs the pole of the world itself.

The Neo-Druidic tradition of the 19th century identified the Temple of the Hyperborean Apollo with Stonehenge and other megalithic circles, as being earthly representations of the Heavenly Temple.

Because all this is the case, the idea that there was a Hyperborean people, which was especially connected with Nordic individuals, is completely false. The Hyperborean people are the gods and saints of the Sabbat, which is not identified with any particular race or ethnicity. The fall of the Hyperborean civilization, which some 20th century esotericists talk about, is, if anything, a materialization of the revolt of the Evil One against the Pleroma of the Sabbat. There, the Evil One lead the rebel angels against the Sabbat, and all were exiled to earth. The rebel angels that had been promised to be rulers were enslaved by the Evil One and forced to reincarnate endlessly in human form. They need to repent of their rebellion and ascend back to the Pleroma, to the Sabbat. Hyperborea itself still exists on the spiritual plane.

Coming back to Hyperborea, though, the relevance to "Magitians Discovered" is that Hyperborea, not in the mystical sense but as a legendary place, was identified with the name "Fiacim" by Edward Kelley in his scrying for John Dee, and the account of this scrying was included in "A True and Faithful Relation", published by Meric Casaubon. Our compiler of the 1665 material, I firmly believe, applied "Fiacim" as a ciphered reference to the Eternal Sun, which makes the three hunters that are summoned from the kingdom of "Fiacim" representatives of the Sabbat itself, and coming from it.

The volcano in the 1665 material, though it's represented as evil and is restrained, is another cipher for the Sabbat, in the form of the First Sun. The sunlike qualities of a Volcano are obvious, and Mount Hekla was one of many places associated with witches meeting for the Sabbat. These places are partially historical, partially non-historical and metaphorical. The meeting on top of a mountain, or in a volcano, is a metaphor for meeting at the top of the world mountain at the north pole, where the Hyperborean kingdom exists. Therefore, this is a cipher for Hyperborea as well, and Fiacim. The volcano rite involves summoning a parallel of the Sabbat, which, in turn, is Fiacim in Hyperborea.

The spirits that are linked to the work in the 1665 "Discoverie of Witchcraft" work treated in "Magitians Discovered" are primarily aerial spirits. These are spirits linked to the eight winds, and to the principalities, which in this case are identified as being 72 in number, which can be located around a compass rose, either in the form of 72 with each standing for 5 degrees, or in a double system of 36, where 36 stand for decans of the day and 36 for decans of the night. I prefer the 72 single spirits to the double 36 schema. In the 72 schema, there are 9 spirits for each of the eight directions, while in the 36 there are 9 spirits for each of the four directions.

This 72 number goes back very far, and is related to the 72 languages of man that the primal Ante-Diluvian language was split up into after the fall of the Tower of Babel. Here, each angel or Principality was linked to a people, who in turn spoke a language, who separated and migrated to a different place in the world. The Principality was the guardian spirit of the people. The people who represented the 72 were the workmen who built the Tower of Babel, who were first united in the work, then divided. What was the language that people spoke before the division, then? Because nothing is written of a change in language from the time before Noah to the time after the Flood, the primal language spoken before the division into the 72 would be the Ante-Diluvian language, which John Dee claimed to have received through his communications with the angels.

Within this schema, there is a connection to the inverse nature of Traditional Witchcraft. The inversion has to do with how the 72 can be pictured as the 72 Elders of the Temple around the High Priest, or around Solomon, or another entity, and this arrangement of Aerial spirits around a king has been taken by some to refer to the lower god, who is referred to here as the Evil One. Within this schema, the king of the 72, sometimes called Abraxas, is identified with the false god, with the 72 Principalities being some of the Archons that enslave humanity. The 72 Principalities, along with the aerial spirits that are assigned to the planets in order to be messengers of their influence, are in this contrasted with the pure celestial spirits, those of the planets and the stars, who in this schema, are thought to be representatives of the good god. However, certain forms of traditional witchcraft locate the 72 not on a lower level, but on a higher level, saying that, like Baphomet, they are actually around the highest manifest god, the true god, not the false one. The seventy two is associated with the Shem-ha-mephorash, the great name of God, and with 72 different names of God, which would be potencies.

These 72 principalities around the throne are thought to be servants of Nimrod, who is pictured as an embodiment of Baphomet, Tubal-Cain, with the idea being that the court of the builder of the Tower of Babel mimics the structure of the Divine Mind itself. The Tower of Babel is, in this, also linked to the Greco-Roman tower of the winds. It is also linked to Masonry, with Nimrod, or Nembroth, in this tradition being a master builder who was the heir and receiver of Ante-Diluvian knowledge, which he used in building the tower. A ruler of the world, Nimrod in this, was challenging the false gods' dominance over humanity, and over fallen angels, by building the tower. Implicit in this also is that the court around Nimrod prefigured the structure of the Elders and high Priest of the Temple in Jerusalem, built by Solomon, with the building of the tower of Babel perhaps influencing the Temple as well.

The Tower of Babel itself can be compared to the world mountain, with the Sabbat on top of it in the form of the court of Nimrod, and the building of the Tower can symbolically be connected to trying to recreate the world mountain and the connection between human beings and the true Sabbat which had been destroyed by the Evil One. In an inverse way, the top of the Tower of Babel, taken as a Temple, can be seen as a precursor of the Heavenly Jerusalem, the Heavenly Temple.

These 72 have also been associated in later occult tradition with the "Izeds" or minor gods of Zoroastrianism, who exist on a lower level than the Amesh Spentas, and who serve them. "Ized", in this, is an anglicization of a Persian term that originally goes back to the word "Yazata", which signifies a generic deity, and literally means "worthy of sacrifice" or worship.

To return to the Watchers and the aerial spirits, there's a good case to be made that the Watcher spirits originally were the Principalities, but that this had a different meaning. What's translated as "Watcher" can equally mean "Guardian", and as was outlined in "Magitians Discovered" volume 1, these were guardian spirits of towns and cities. These guardian spirits were literally called "Archons" by Iamblichus in his work "On the Mysteries". However, there's another tradition which identifies the Watcher angels with the Beni-Elohim, the sons of God, and these are identified with the Throne angels in the nine-fold angelic hierarchy. The Throne angels are the third order after the Seraphim and the Cherubim, and it's possible that the Watchers, could have come from this order, or that the Aerial spirits in their more exalted, older, higher, and more exalted, form, corresponded to the order of Thrones rather than to that of Principalities.

The 72 around the center of the Sabbat, could refer both to those powers which are still located up there as well as to those powers who decided to sacrifice themselves by descending to earth in order to teach humanity the truth about their condition.

With regards to the Fairy Faith, I believe that the Sabbat of the Ages is referred to in Robert Kirk's "Secret Commonwealth", though he might not have realized that this was what his informants were telling him. This information is included in volume 3 of "Magitians Discovered".

Sabbat and Sabbath

The Sabbat itself is related to the Sabbath, both Christian and Jewish.

The connection is that between the Sabbath and Paradise, the regenerated state, the unfallen state. In the Jewish Sabbath, no work is permitted because it's supposed to be not only a day of rest but of happiness and celebration. This Sabbath of rest, of holiday, is part of what informs the meaning of the Sabbat, where the Sabbat of the Ages is the place where the Saints have their own Sabbath—their rest. It's the rest of the Saints, and is paradise, the Heavenly Jerusalem, which in Christian thought will descend to earth at the end of time and be experienced by the righteous. Particularly, the idea of multiple Sabbaths can be found in Aelred of Rievaulx's medieval work "The Mirror of Charity", within an Christian context. In this, he states that there's a Sabbath within as well as a heavenly Sabbath, and that the individual needs to realize the Sabbath within through making the perfected and self-purified temple in order to realize the heavenly

Sabbath through divine contemplation. Here, these Sabbaths are linked with the periodic Jubilee years outlined in the old testament, and so linked with ideas of Paradise and of happiness, of Edenic restoration, if only for a time. The Sabbath of rest within happens when the self is rebuilt as a purified Temple. This has applications to Freemasonry as well, and points to the indebtedness of Masonry to medieval Christian mystical contemplation.

It is also related to the idea of the World Day conception of history, where, based on the Book of Genesis, the span of time governing the world from its beginning to its end was thought to consist of seven days. The seventh day, as the day of rest, would be the return of the world to the Paradisal state. This day would signal the negation of the Fall of Adam. Drawing on the Book of Revelations, this would correspond to the time when the Heavenly City, a version of the Heavenly Temple, would descend onto a new earth. These ideas were widespread in Christianity, and formulated in a slightly different form by Joachim of Fiore. In Joachim's system, the ultimate restoration of everything, where the Heavenly City descended to earth and Paradise was restored, happened on the 8th day, after the cycle of the 7 was completed, with the Seventh day being the Millennium of peace spoken about in the Book of Revelations, which preceded this.

In certain heretical sects, such as the "Heresy of the Free Spirit", it was thought to be possible to gain access to the Paradisal state before it had manifested on earth. Within the context of Joachimism, the seventh day was interpreted as leading into the eighth day, and so some of the features of the eighth day were thought to be available to pious people. The seventh day was the beginning of the "Age of the Spirit", and in this Age it would be possible for people to have direct contact with God without human intermediaries, instead relying on the Holy Spirit alone for guidance. Those who had achieved spiritual perfection could exist in this Paradisal state, where, through being completely submitted to the Will of God, individuals were no longer able to sin, and could engage in otherwise forbidden activity, such as sex, with one another if God willed it.

This is comparable, in some ways, to the Nizari Ismaili idea of realizing Paradise through esoteric work. The cycle of the seven also appears in Ismaili thought, where each world cycle has seven subcomponents, and after the complete world cycle has manifested, the world will be restored to its Paradisal state through the Qiyamat or great resurrection. However, Hassan-i-Sabbah II announced that the Great Resurrection had taken place, yet the world did not end, nor did it become transfigured. This was dealt with by claiming that, at the moment, this pure reality was only available for advanced adepts, but would eventually manifest in the world as a whole, complete with other apocalyptic events.

This meaning of the Sabbath as a taste of Paradise also influenced early Christians and can be found in Christian practice to this day, with the Agape meal between congregants on Sunday, the new Sabbath, Church service, and the kiss of peace, or shaking of hands, between neighbors that's practiced in Church services. The Agape meal, the Love Feast, clearly prefigures practices on the external, physical Sabbat of the craft, and the kiss of peace and greeting of the neighbors prefigures more involved practices within the craft. In these, through not only the kiss but through sexual union, the congregation moves from division into unity, from many into one. They experience and return to a Paradisal, regenerated, state, if only for a short time, with the delights of Paradise, food, drink, and love, being experienced on earth in a pure form.

This practice, engaged in by a larger group of people, is parallel to the rebirth of Baphomet within a smaller group of four people. Here, each of them assumes a god form which is an aspect of Baphomet, which forms we'll describe, and then engages in reciprocal, bisexual, intercourse with each other in order to bring the different fragments of Baphomet back together into one unity, creating the Divine Androgyne within the whole group. This can be reduced to two people, but the Quadriga, the fourfold working circle, composed of two groups consisting of one man and one woman, is the natural vehicle for it. Brother and Sister, uniting as one through the different combinations of homosexual intercourse, intercourse with another's partner, and intercourse with one's own partner, creates unity.

Baphomet

The figure of Baphomet itself has several forms. One of these is that of the Sabbatic Goat of Eliphas Levi, most likely based on the Abraxas seal. There are several others. What all of these forms involve is the presence of dualities united into one, as well as of the different potentialities of the world united into one. One account of Baphomet, related to the Templars, sees him as Janus, with one face turned to the left, being aged, and one face turned towards the right, being young. In this, Baphomet stands at the juncture of the new year, which is symbolically on the top of the circle of the year, and like Abraxas contains the whole of the circle of the year within him.

Another common figure is Baphomet as a Chimera, or a Sphinx. In this, Baphomet is pictured as a composite being made out of animals that correspond to the four elements. In these portrayals, it incorporates the features of a fish, a bird, a land animal, and a man, with the man standing for fire. The figure of the sphinx, as understood in 19th century occultism, also combined many of these animals, with it often being featured with wings. This portrayal of Baphomet is also adapted into Christian tradition by equating him with the Tetramorph or Cherubim of Jewish tradition. Here, the idea of a being composed of a lion, an ox, an eagle, and a man, are used as a substitute for the elemental animals. I believe that the original where this came from was Neoplatonic, and was from Greek pagan religion, not esoteric Judaism.

Originally, the meaning of Baphomet can be expressed as the fusion of the Neoplatonic "Living Being" or "Paradigm" with the Demiurge. The idea of Baphomet as Abraxas, and then as Tammuz, does not exclude this, since the pagans of Harran believed in a syncretic religion which incorporated core aspects of Greek thought along with Semitic paganism.

Baphomet, the Living Being, the Tetramorph, can also be identified with the Orphic Phanes, who breaks out of the Egg containing all the Ideals of the world which is overseen by Aion, the lion headed god of time and eternity. In this, the egg overseen by Aion is the Sabbat, from which Phanes, the Living Being, Tetramorph, emerges. There's also a parallel between the Orphic Egg and the Bull in Mithrism, with Mithras as Aion slaying the Bull in order to water the world with energy, which can be seen as both the Active Intelligence subduing the different parts of the Ideals within the Sabbat into the Tetramorph and as Phanes breaking out of the Orphic egg.

He can also be identified with Apollo as the god of the First Sun, who spreads fertility to the world from the First Sun. Here, the First Sun is also the Azoth as well as the Schamijam.

Baphomet, the Living Being, in this, is also the same as the Jewish Adam Kadmon, the primal man of light that contains all of the things of the world within him in the Lurianic Kabbalah. He is also Jesus, considered in his capacity as the Word that contains all Words, as we shall see, or as the Active Intelligence within the Divine Mind.

Works Cited

Aelred of Rievaulx "Mirror of Charity", Elizabeth Conner trans., Charles Dumont ed., Cistercian Publications, Kalamazoo, 1990

Chicosky, Alison ed, Cory Childs trans."The Secrets of Helios", Hadean Press, London, 2022

Chumbley, Andrew Azoetia, Xoanon, Hercules, USA, 2015

Chumbley, Andrew "Dragon Book of Essex", Xoanon, Hercules, 2014

Corbin, Henry, Nancy Pearson trans. "Spiritual Body and Celestial Earth", Princeton University Press, Princeton, 1977

Corbin, Henry "The Temple and Contemplation", KPI, London, 1986

Levi, Eliphas, trans. AE Waite, "Transcendental Magic", William Rider & Sons, London, 1923, google books

Madziarczyk, John, "The Magitians Discovered" vol 1, Topaz House Publications, Seattle, 2016

Madziarczyk, John, ed. "Magitians Discovered" volume 3, Topaz, Seattle, 2016

Chapter 3
The Heavenly Temple

Paradise, Jesus, Neoplatonism, the Sabbat

The notion of Paradise as both Jesus and the Neo-Platonic divine mind comes together from several different sources. Many of these, as with the sources for the Heavenly Temple, were discarded by Protestant theologians as being non-canonical or not really supported by the Bible. First, the identification of Jesus with the divine mind, emanated from the One, depends on several different readings: first, on the identification of Jesus with Wisdom, talked about in the Book of Wisdom, which, though excluded from Protestant Bibles outside of ones produced by Lutherans, is recognized by the Catholic and Orthodox Churches as completely legitimate. Wisdom, there, appears as a tool of God that he uses to create the world, which also possesses literal wisdom about the nature of things. Jesus, as the Word of God, who co-creates the world with God the Father, similarly has both connotations: a "Word" is a mental entity, like Wisdom, which is a series of insightful thoughts. Again, like Wisdom, Jesus co-creates the world. Additionally, the New Testament talks about having the "Mind of Christ", further suggesting the mental affinities of Jesus. Taken together, these ideas establish a case for identifying the pagan divine mind of Plotinus and others with Jesus as Wisdom. The pagan divine mind also includes the Demiurge as the creator of the earth, and the rest of the cosmos, and Jesus, too helps to create the earth with his Father, just as the Demiurge collaborates with the One to create the cosmos.

This aspect of Jesus as the creator of the world is reflected in the art of both Orthodox and Catholic traditions, with the figure of "Christ Pantokrator" or Jesus the all powerful, embodying this idea in the Orthodox Church and the figure of "Christ in Glory" reflecting it in the Catholic Church. "Christ in Glory" is, similarly,

Christ in heaven, in an undescended fashion. Jesus, as co-creator of the universe, existed before the universe, and before he incarnated into that same universe he existed in a heaven of some sort.

Similarly, Jupiter as the Demiurge can be directly paralleled to Jesus in his form as the co-creator of the world, very present not only through medieval Platonic Christianity but through Catholicism and Orthodoxy in general. Here, Christ is equated with Jupiter, and Jupiter, like Christ, serves as the Demiurgos, the Pantokrator, all powerful, Christ in Glory, the creator of the world. This goes back to the Timaeus of Plato, and in the Christianized tradition, Christ as Logos helps God to create the world, the Word helping to create the world with the Words that are within it, as Bonaventure might say.

Pagan sun mysticism is also brought into the picture through a quote from the brief pre-Christian writing the "Book of Malachi". Here, the coming Messiah is termed the "Sun of Righteousness", which reinforces the idea of the sun corresponding to the divine mind, which corresponds to wisdom, which is Jesus.

The first mind is equated by Plotinus with the sun, with the original, eternal, sun that the visible sun is based on. Whether through Plotinus or through another source, Saint Bonaventure in the 13th century extensively used this sun mysticism to refer to Jesus in his "Collations on the Hexaemeron", equating Jesus with the first mind and the eternal sun. It is also the divine sun, the eternal sun, as Bonaventure styles it.

Bonaventure develops many of these themes in his last work, the "Collations on the Hexaemeron". However, after introducing Jesus as Wisdom and sun mysticism, in the next "Conference" he's careful to transfer the quality of the eternal sun to all of the different members of the Trinity, saying that they're all eternal suns unto themselves, and that, collectively, these three make up one eternal sun. This is done through the idea of the circumincession of the different qualities of the members of the Trinity, which says that the qualities that exist in one of the members of the Trinity necessarily exist within the others in some way.

The first presentation of the Trinity is the vision of the Trinity as a whole as the divine, eternal, Sun, which is surrounded by nine choirs of angels. The fullest account of this model of the Trinity is in "Conference Twenty-One" of "Collations on the Hexaemeron", which is located within the section on the fourth stage of contemplation. God as Trinity is the Eternal Sun in his constant life giving power and influence. Within the idea of the Trinity as the Eternal Sun, Bonaventure makes some distinctions. On the top level, as the Trinity relates to the power of the Sun in a metaphorical way, Bonaventure says that the Father corresponds to Light, the Son to "Flashing" or Lightning, and the Holy Spirit to Warmth

Paradise and the Heavenly Jerusalem

The next move within this, which is that Jesus as the Divine Mind is not only an entity, but is actually Paradise, the Heavenly Jerusalem, Heaven itself, and also the place where the Saints go to rest before the end of the world, comes from a different source. Keeping in mind the idea of Paradise as the Divine Mind, first, let's look at this concept of Paradise without linking it to Jesus. There are two books that provide very good background into this concept. The first is "The History of Paradise, the Garden of Eden in Myth and Tradition", by Jean Delumeau, and the second is "Heaven, a History" by Colleen McDannell and Berhnhard Lang.

Delumeau devotes a whole chapter to the idea of Paradise as a temporary resting place of the Saints, "Paradise as a Place of Waiting". Here, he traces the idea back to the Apocalypse of Paul, which he relates had a very wide circulation in the west in the Middle Ages, circulating not only in Latin but in many vernacular languages, though being apocryphal. In this apocalypse, Paul is taken up to his third heaven, and this heaven is called Paradise and linked with the resting place of the righteous before the end of the world. Delumeau carefully charts this as a development that has its roots in the statements about Jesus about the world to come itself, which were then taken up by later authors and elaborated on.

McDannell and Lang chart the development of heaven as Paradise in the middle ages, pointing out the development of Paradise as heaven into Paradise as heaven as the Heavenly Jerusalem. Here, Paradise is associated with the Heavenly City, described in the book of Revelations, which exists somewhere beyond the cosmos, but will descend onto earth after the end of time. The Heavenly Jerusalem is the temporary rest of the saints, but what's experienced by them will be experienced by the righteous once the end of time and the final judgment has transpired.

However, there is previous precedent for Paradise being associated with the Heavenly Jerusalem. Particularly, the apocryphal book of the Bible 2 Baruch describes a Heavenly Jerusalem which is in Paradise. From the 2nd century, the book was written after the destruction of the second temple in Jerusalem, and in response to it.

The idea of Paradise as the Heavenly Jerusalem provides an essential linkage between Paradise as afterlife and Paradise as Jesus and the Divine Mind. Jesus is the head of the Church. The Church, which is made up of all of the faithful souls, is the Body of Christ. The Heavenly Jerusalem is the Church, in that Jerusalem is the sacred city that contains the Temple. Christ is present in the Heavenly Jerusalem. Therefore, the Saints within the Heavenly Jerusalem are part of the Body of Christ and the Heavenly Jerusalem itself is part of the Body of Christ. It is the Church Triumphant. It is also the Kingdom of Heaven, which Jesus promised his followers that they would inherit. Since the Heavenly Jerusalem is Christ, and Christ is Wisdom, and Wisdom is the Divine Mind, it figures that the Heavenly Jerusalem is the Divine Mind. Paradise is the Divine Mind, which is Christ, which is the Heavenly Jerusalem.

The Heavenly Jerusalem, the Body of Christ, the Eternal Sun, Paradise, the First Mind, all refer to the same thing. Additionally, in medieval Catholicism, one of the stages of ascent towards God was to gain the vision and experience of the Heavenly Jerusalem, which , depending on how one looked at it, would also mean union with Christ. After union with Christ in attaining the vision of the Heavenly Jerusalem, the mystic could then go farther and achieve union with the One, with God the Father. The First Mind was the first emanation from the One, and, standing within the first emanation, in union with it, the individual could turn their attention upwards to the One, and achieve union with it.

Paradise as an interchangeable term for the Holy City, for the Divine Mind, also has testimony from eastern Christian sources. Particularly, Ephrem the Syrian records his experience with ascents to Paradise in his "Hymns on Paradise". Ephrem lived slightly before Saint Augustine.

Also, beyond this, the idea of the Heavenly Jerusalem as an ideal plan for the forces of the world is linked to the practice of the "Paradise Garden", explored in the out of print book "The Garden of Eden, the Botanic Garden and the Re-Creation of Paradise" by John Prest and elsewhere. Like the Heavenly Jerusalem, the Garden of Eden was thought to be foursquare, since it had four rivers going out of itself, and these gardens were developed to reflect the sacred nature of this configuration.

The Heavenly City is,the foursquare city, is, in addition to all this, a microcosm of the world itself, split into four quarters, with the Omphalos or navel of the world at the center.Here, however, this microcosm is actually the plan on which the macrocosm is based, the Ideal world on which the physical world is modeled.This concept of the foursquare Heavenly City is, I believe, the source of John Dee's work with the four elemental tablets and the four watchtowers. I believe that his grand tablet, with the "Tablet of Union" at the center, is a representation of the Heavenly Jerusalem, and that he took this idea from the popular ideas about the Heavenly City that were circulating during his time. Jesus is located at the center.

That such a place can be both a location and a person can be explained by the following: one could look at Paradise as being the body of Christ, but at Christ's "I" or personality existing within Paradise as a separate entity. This would be a parallel to our "I" existing within our Mind, which, in the medieval, Augustinian, tradition, also included the storehouse of Ideals that were thought to be contained within the Memory.

Jesus as he is in and of himself, where he could be paralleled with the active force, or the "I" within the Divine Mind, appears, or can appear, not just as the maker of the world, but also as the Paradigm, with both roles combined into one. Jesus as Paradigm is suggested, again, by Saint Bonaventure's work, where, in the words of one of his recent commentators, he appears as the Word that contains all of the Words. These Words which make up the Word are the Ideals that Jesus uses in creating the world. This would be part of Jesus' Wisdom as well. In this, he would be Paradigm and Demiurgos in one. Following this, Jesus himself is the Paradigm or embodiment of the Ideals which are within him. This follows from the Word being the externalization of the Ideals which are contained in unmanifest form in the Father, the One. The role of the Paradigm, in this, would be transferred to Jesus in and of himself as part of the combined character of Jesus as both Paradigm and Demiurgos.

This idea of the Kingdom of Heaven as the Heavenly Jerusalem and as Paradise can also be found in the medieval "Treatise on the Spirit and the Soul", which had an enormous circulation, as documented by Bernard McGinn, who has recently translated and edited it. The treatise is contained in the book "Three Treatises on Man, A Cistercian Anthropology". This document, very importantly, links the Kingdom of Heaven, the Heavenly Jerusalem, of the Divine Mind to the saying of Jesus that the Kingdom of Heaven is within, meaning that the Microcosm within us is reflective of the structure of the divine mind. Two sections that discuss this are section 55, titled "The Names of the Trinity—The Life of Eternal Happiness" and section 60, titled "The Mind Must be Recalled to Heavenly things—Aspirations for doing this—The Glory of Heaven—The Joy of the Heavenly City". In turn, this idea, like most of the rest of the text, appears to have been influenced by Victorine spirituality, that connected with the Abbey of Saint Victor outside of Paris. Within this, Richard of Saint Victor was the main theorist of divine ascent and mystical union, and his influence is cited by McGinn on the book.

The mystical practice that Richard of Saint Victor that originated in "Benjamin Minor", also called "The Twelve Patriarchs", and that the writers of the Book of the Spirit and the Soul elaborated on, involves corresponding the different passions or emotions to different parts of a city, castle or fortress. These different passions and emotions are then set in order, turning them into virtues, and these virtues within the self form the building blocks of the castle or city within. Richard related the twelve patriarchs to the different passions and emotions that need to be transformed. This, I believe, was transformed by the authors of the "Treatise" to making the Heavenly City and the Heavenly Temple within. This has different symbolism from Richard's text, because his city has defensive fortifications that the Heavenly City does not have. The Heavenly City is typified by having twelve gates that also correspond to the twelve patriarchs, thereby making a transference of the passions from one to the other possible. See R.H. Charles' commentary on Revelations for an idea of how this could be done. Beyond the "Treatise", this image of creating an interior castle, or the Heavenly City within through reforming the passions became extremely popular, though the source of it is often obscured. Among others, Saint Bonaventure gives a general schema of how to construct the Heavenly City within using the Patriarchs as guides in his "Collations on the Hexaemeron", written over a hundred years after the "Treatise". Meister Eckhart, Johannes Tauler, and others of the Rhenish mystic tradition also used this as part of the image of building a Temple of the Holy Spirit within.

Within Richard's schema, the sanctified city contains the Ark of the Covenant, which is the subject of "Benjamin Major". This contains the living presence of God, and corresponds to the process of mystical, ecstatic, union with divinity which can be cultivated after a person sets their passions in order. The individual constructs the Holy City within themselves, then in constructing the Ark they call down the presence of the Holy Spirit into them, which in turn leads to a mystic union with God, where the person is correspondingly taken up to the divine presence. To use symbolism whose meaning we will introduce shortly, the Holy City corresponds to the horizontal dimension, while the Ark of the Covenant corresponds to the vertical dimension in this.

The tradition represented by the Book of the Spirit and the Soul may have flourished within the Cistercian Order of monks, and from there it may have escaped into the wild, so to speak. While there were many Cistercian monasteries in England before the dissolution of the monasteries, there specifically were two in East Anglia. Here, we're considering East Anglia to be made up of Cambridgeshire, Norfolk, and Suffolk. One of the monasteries, Sawtry Abbey, was in Cambridgeshire, and the other, Sibton Abbey, was in Suffolk.

The Grail and the Temple.

The grail mountain of Montsalvache represents Paradise, the Heavenly City, the Divine Mind, the First Sun, the Heavenly Temple, which we identify with the Sabbat of the ages. Those who succeed in lifting the grail from the depths back to the heights, to the top of the mountain, lift the stone of the angels back to its source. The grail in the depths is exalted unto the heights through the completion of both the alchemical work and the quest, as well as personal repentance. The grail knights on the mountain, the keepers of the grail, are those who have succeeded with the process and the quest, and who are now associated with Paradise, both in this world and in the hereafter.

The association between Paradise, and the Grail castle is made by Henry Corbin in his "The Temple and Contemplation". There, in looking at "Titurel", written as a prelude to "Parzival", Corbin looks at the jeweled grail castle on the top of Mount Salvache, and relates it to Islamic ideas on the Hurqalya and the Jaribut. These concepts we've already related to the Sabbat.

Though the "Younger Titurel", which is where the description of the Grail mountain and temple are, has been inaccessible for a long time, the relevant passages have recently been translated by John Matthews, and published in "Temples of the Grail", co-written by Matthews and Gareth Knight. Corbin also provides his own summary, as opposed to translation, of the text in "The Temple and Contemplation".

In Titurel, the Grail castle sits on a mountain of onyx, of black stone. The Temple on top of it is circular, with either twenty two or seventy two chapels on the edge of the circle. These chapels are octagonal, which was a sign of the the Templars, though it may also be a reference to the eight winds. The Temple is unique in that it's almost completely made out of precious jewels, with its ceiling being sapphire, for example. There are representations of trees with birds made out of gold and precious jewels. Rich jewels adorn all of the Temple, with even the windows being made of clear crystal. The floor itself is made out of precious jewels, which simulate a sea, complete with stones underneath them which are carved to represent sea creatures. In the middle of the Temple is a smaller model of the Temple that contains the Grail itself, which is carved from a giant emerald. Here, it's carved with signs portraying the victory of Christ over Satan.

Analyzing this, the emerald is that which has been lifted up. It's the emerald that has fallen from the brow of Lucifer which has been redeemed by the blood of the cosmic Christ, which has now been able to ascend, to rise to the pleroma of the Divine Mind from which it originated. The center is also the place of Baphomet/Christ. The jewels are the Ideas of the Ideal realm, which surround the central place of the active intelligence. The twenty two or seventy two chapels are the conclaves or subdivisions of the Ideal realm, bound by the Demiurge, and as such are extensions of the four square binding related in Plato's Timaeus. The artificial birds and foliage in the Temple suggest Paradise, the Garden of Eden. Corbin relates the stones to particular virtues which the individual can cultivate within themselves, and should cultivate, in order to reach the state of the Grail itself.

Corbin relates the Grail temple of Titurel to the Holy Temple model that ultimately comes back to Richard of Saint Victor. Here, the Temple corresponds to the body of the initiate, with the individual jewels corresponding not to Ideas so much as different passions, which when transformed make the Grail castle within. The Emerald in the center, in this, likewise corresponds to the Holy of Holies and the Ark of the Covenant, as the living presence of God. I should say that the construction of the Heavenly Temple within is an inherently Masonic venture, in that in the west constructing castles and temples involved cutting and placing stone, literal operative Masonry.

The Heavenly Temple idea is brought into contact with both the Free Spirit and the Grail mysteries by Henry Corbin in "The Temple and Contemplation". Interestingly, the Council of Vincennes, where the Templars were condemned, was also the council that condemned the Free Spirit as a heresy. Members of the Franciscan Order, who had known Free Spirit members, were asked if there was a connection between the two, and they replied that there wasn't. Perhaps they weren't as informed as they thought. Corbin points out the many times that the manifestations of the Grail were related to the time of Pentecost, the festival of the manifestation of the Holy Spirit, and relates this to the Age of the Spirit, with the reality of the Heavenly Temple being something that people in the Age of the Spirit can commune with. Significantly, in "Titurel", they state that the largest of the chapels at the edge of the rotunda is dedicated to the Holy Spirit. Here, the Holy Spirit becomes the Paraclete, and Corbin relates the power of the Holy Spirit to the blazing star of Freemasonry, the Shekinah, no doubt drawing from the "Rectified Scottish Rite" of which he was a part.

I should note that, with Corbin, the Heavenly Temple is associated with an image of the 'Aql, the Divine Mind and the true reality of Ismaili thought. I think that it can be equated with the 'Aql itself, instead of the image, with no qualifications, although the individual as a personal temple might be an image of the 'Aql, and not the Divine Mind itself.

20th Century Extensions

With regards to the idea of the Heavenly Jerusalem in relation to concrete witchcraft practices, it's writings connected to the East Anglian tradition that are most relevant. There are several books that, read in succession, will give a good picture of this. First, Nigel Pennick's work "Secrets of East Anglian Magic" is fundamental as a starting point. His nine-fold plot is the same as the Heavenly Jerusalem, though this is not made clear in the work. The nine-fold plot is also connected to the eight "Airts" or directions of the compass, and the circle.

Next is Pennick's "Secret Games of the Gods". Though on its surface has to do with things like board games, in reality it has to do with the inner meaning of the nine-fold plot taken as a holy temple, as well as with related ideas. These are treated in a largely cross-cultural aspect which does not say much about the Christian roots of the idea, but, within this, it goes very deeply into its inner meaning. This is remedied by John Michell's book "The Dimensions of Paradise". Though Michell also ties his idea of the Heavenly Jerusalem to questionable numerology, he introduces the idea of the Heavenly Temple in a way which people who have consulted Pennick's books will find familiar, within a Christian context.

Michell is known for writing "The View Over Atlantis" in 1969, which was extremely influential in relation to things like a renewed interest in standing stones and ley lines. In fact, the influence of Michell's work, particularly "Atlantis" on Nigel Pennick's work is very apparent, to the point where, in order to really understand where Pennick is coming from, familiarity with Michell's work is necessary. Michell's work is very profound on many levels, with the focus on numerology in some of them being an exception rather than the rule. For Michell's part, at least one of his later works, "At the Center of the World", shows a marked influence of pagan ideas, including those in common with traditional witchcraft.

Mention should also be made of Pennick's "Earth Harmony" which, while only having a chapter on the heavenly temple, nonetheless includes quite a lot of other very useful information. This work has recently been reissued under a slightly different name. In fact, "Earth Harmony", and "The View Over Atlantis" can and should be read together, and, in this, they can also be related to the Heavenly Temple. "The View Over Atlantis" has also been reissued in a revised form as "The New View Over Atlantis". Both books deal with what has been called "Geomancy", but what is really a western version of "Feng-Shui", with "Geomancy" in Europe properly relating to the system of divination of the same name. This science has to do with the flow of energy through the landscape and how different building configurations take advantage of, augment, or detract from this energy. Making the Heavenly Temple real, either through temporary ritual or through a more permanent construction, augments this energy, and helps with the healing of the earth. The Heavenly Temple is fourfold, and so the healing involves constructing a sanctified place with a fourfold symmetry on earth. This healing of the earth can be related to the victory of the good over the Evil One, through restoring the energies of that section of the earth to the primal form that they would have been in if the Evil One had not co-created the world. This is a kind of Theurgy.

Going further, also good in relation to this is Michell's book "At the Center of the World", which is a continuation, and expansion, of concepts in "Dimensions of Paradise". In this, he combines the symbolism of the pole or Omphalos with that of the Temple, integrating the vertical and horizontal dimensions together. This should be read in conjunction with the chapter "The Orientations of Patterns" in "Secret Games of the Gods", and, indeed, Mitchell and Pennick's ideas cross fertilize with each other in these works, implicitly and explicitly.

Here, the literal Omphalos, or navel of the world, the center of the Temple, is talked about in relation to sacred sites around the world. The Omphalos is linked, on the one hand, to sacred earth energies, and then to the cosmic axis, which unites the upperworld, underworld, and surface of the earth. Pennick adopts the fourfold pattern of the cosmic axis that ultimately comes from Iolo Morganwyg, which sees a further level of the "Ceugant" on top of the conventional upperworld and underworld. My interpretation sees these three worlds as being astrological, underworldly, earthly, with the fourth section, that of Ceugant, standing for the Sabbat itself, which, strictly speaking, is beyond these three. Within the greater discussions on this subject in Pennick and Michell's work, the earth energies are said to be arranged in alignment with the astrological energies, with the Omphalos in this sense being a stake in the middle of the ground that both subdues the earth energies and fixes the astrological energies to the earth energies in a similar way.

The three, which is the vertical axis, and the four, the horizontal axis, exist in union in the transcendent reality of the Sabbat itself, beyond the conventional three worlds. The Temple, with the axis going through the Omphalos at the center, is a version of this transcendent reality on earth. The Circle, in turn, cast for a particular purpose, is a temporary construction which echoes these more permanent Temples, having the same sort of division between three and four united in one.

The cosmic world pole also links the Temple to the concept of Hyperborea and the paradise at the world mountain at the north pole. Here, Hyperborea, the Sabbat, is oriented completely on the world axis. When earthly temples are constructed, and circles are constructed, with the same Omphalos and extension into the four, they're creating an earthly version of this visionary place as well.

Mention should also be made of Pennick's main deity, Termagant, who he describes in "Secrets of East Anglian Magic". Pennick interprets the name "Termagant" as Tyr-Magant, which he says means "Tyr, the great god", Tyr being the germanic deity of law, order and justice. Despite an apparent great difference between this concept and that of Baphomet, there are actually quite a bit of commonalities. First, "Termagant" entered the consciousness of Europe in the Middle Ages as a result of the Crusades. Here,

Termagant is a deity that Muslims supposedly worshipped, which was a concept applied to Baphomet as well. Beyond this, however, Baphomet, as ordering the material of the First Sun into the four elements of the Living Being similarly establishes the basic pattern of order which the world is based on. In this regard, he serves as a sacred king, which is something that can be applied to the concept of Tyr as well.

With regards to cross cultural comparisons, I should note that both Mandalas and Yantras are arranged as buildings with four gates, one on each side. In this, the Circle itself can quite literally become a Yantra or Mandala, echoing the primal structure of the universe as it represents itself within the dimension of the Sabbat.

Additionally, all of this ties into the use of Atlantis in at least one branch of traditional witchcraft, that expounded by Charles Cardell and the "Coven of Atho". This tradition has recently been examined, in great depth, by Melissa Seims in "Here be Magick, The People and Practices of the Coven of Atho". There, Seims relates that Cardell connected Atlantis to both Mount Olympus and, specifically, to the Heavenly Temple. Cardell referred to Atlantis there as the "Water City". Importantly, John Michell also links the Heavenly Temple to Atlantis in "The View Over Atlantis", although he would later write that Atlantis was a flawed version of the Temple, this leading to its destruction.

I believe that when Cardell, and other witches, talk about Atlantis and the fall of Atlantis, what they're really talking about is the gnostic drama that took place in heaven. Here, the Heavenly Temple, the Sabbat, is the place where the angels apostatized against God, taken as the One and Baphomet, and then descended to earth. In versions of this story, the war of the angels destroyed this heaven in its pristine form as well, causing it to "Fall". The "Survivors" of the "Fall" are then banished to earth, to the places outside of Atlantis. This is then combined with the story of the Watchers, which is a later event. Here, the Watchers, who in traditional witchcraft ideas came to help liberate the captive fallen angels, and help them to return to the Sabbat, are said to have come from "Atlantis", from the Heavenly Temple, and to have instructed people like the Egyptians in the arts and sciences.

These arts and sciences supposedly included the arts of megalithic building. In a completion of the circle, in some witchcraft beliefs, the repentant fallen angels, identical with the Atlanteans here, were thought to base these megalithic constructions on implementing the plan of the Heavenly Temple on earth, in order to restore the earth to proper functioning and health. Beyond this, these constructions were thought to be intended to allow communion with the Sabbat, with Paradise, the original Heavenly Temple, itself. Cardell's "Search for the Water City" is the search for a way to return to the Sabbat of the Ages.

Here, being of "Atlantean" descent is a code for witch blood. The mating of the Watchers with human beings, now thought to be the mating of "Atlanteans" with primitive humans, is the same as the primal mating of elemental beings with humans which introduced witch blood into humanity. This blood provides the opportunity for fallen angels to incarnate into people of the blood. When this is done, they can then repent and go through the process of redemption, of coming back to the Sabbat of the Ages that they left, and made war on, so long ago.

So, in this, Atlantis, and its fall, has nothing to do with the racialist interpretation that was applied to it by Ariosophist thinkers in Germany in the early 20th century, just as the similarly appropriated idea of Hyperborea has nothing to do with racism.

It's important to note that the only really unique thing in the association of Cardell and others of traditional witchcraft with Atlantis is the witch part. Speculations about Atlantis that linked it with various gnostic myths have been going on for quite some time, and, in particular, exploded with Madame Blavatsky's writings. Blavatsky and the Theosophical Society capitalized on the interest in Atlantis and other lost continents in the late 19th century, and they did what many people after them did: they projected myths and mystical ideas that had nothing to do with the latest obsession of popular culture onto those obsessions. For Blavatsky, it appears that the myths about the creation of the gods, about strife between the gods, and about the creation of humanity from various cultures were broken into pieces and linked to different lost lands, including Atlantis.

As we shall see, this process of reading ancient myths regarding transcendental reality into contemporary culture kept on going. The masters of Atlantis, the Watchers, became implicitly extraterrestrial in the channelled Egyptian teachings of Randall-Stevens, and they became not only explicitly extraterrestrial but in fact the occupants of UFOs in the thought of Brinsley le Poer Trench and George Hunt Williamson.

Works Cited

Saint Bonaventure "Collations on the Hexaemeron", Franciscan Institute Publications, St. Bonaventure NY, 2018

Charles, R.H. "A Critical and Exegetical Commentary on the Revelation of Saint John" vol. 2, Charles Scribner's sons, 1920, Google Books

Corbin, Henry "The Temple and Contemplation", KPI, London, 1986

Delumeau, Jean "The History of Paradise, the Garden of Eden in Myth and Tradition", Continuum International Publishing, New York, 1992

Ephrem the Syrian "Hymns on Paradise", Sebastian Brock ed. trans, Saint Vladimir's Seminary Press, Crestwood New York, 1990

Matthews, John ed. trans. and Gareth Knight,"Titurel", in "Temples of the Grail, The Search for the World's greatest Relic", Llewellyn, Woodbury MN, 2019

McDannell, Colleen, Bernhard Lang."Heaven, a History" Yale University Press, New Haven, 1988

McGinn, Bernard trans."Treatise on the Spirit and the Soul", in "Three Treatises on Man, A Cistercian Anthropology", Cistercian Publications, Kalamazoo, 1977

Michell, John "At the Center of the World, Polar Symbolism", Thames and Hudson ltd. London, 1994

Michell, John "The Dimensions of Paradise", Inner Traditions, Rochester VT, 2008

Michell, John "New View Over Atlantis", Hampton Roads publishing, Charlottesville, 2013

Michell, John "The View Over Atlantis", Ballantine Books, New York, 1977

Pennick, Nigel "Earth Harmony", Capall-Bann, Chieveley, 1997

Pennick, Nigel "Secrets of East Anglian Magic" Capall-Bann, Milverton, 2004

Pennick, Nigel "Secret Games of the Gods", Weiser, York Beach, ME, 1990

Prest, John, "The Garden of Eden, The Botanic Garden and the Re-Creation of Paradise" Yale University Press, New Haven CT., 1981

Richard of Saint Victor "The Mystic Ark", also known as "Benjamin Major", "Richard of Saint Victor", Paulist Press, New York 1979

Richard of Saint Victor ,"The Twelve Patriarchs", also called "Benjamin Minor"in "Richard of Saint Victor", Paulist Press, New York 1979

Seims, Mellisa "Here be Magic", Thoth Publications, Loughborough, 2022

Chapter 4
Jesus and Lucifer

Lucifer and the place of Jesus in the Craft.

Within his article "The Hidden Stone", Fitzgerald states that the fall of the stone of Lucifer redeemed the world, and transfigured it, and that this fact is one of the Arcana Arcanorum of the Cultus. While I can't claim to have direct knowledge of how this interpreted, I will say that this idea of the stone of Lucifer, and the fall of Lucifer, redeeming the world is another version of the story of Jesus. In this, Jesus is the original of Azra-Lumiel, or, I should say, Lucifer is the hidden, true, face of Jesus.

As in Cathar beliefs, by whatever term you want to describe it as, a figure from the world of light, an emanation of the Demiurge, incarnated or "Fell" to earth, sacrificed himself, harrowed hell and defeated the Evil One, then ascended back to heaven and merged with himself. The Evil One presented himself as the good god, as Jehovah, and Jesus as the unfallen Lucifer was an incarnation of the true god. The true Lucifer never "Fell" or was cast out from heaven in the Christian sense—this "Fall" was an intentional work of self-sacrifice for the greater good.

The "Fall" of Lucifer in this is the same as the willing crucifixion of Jesus, who took all of the sin of the world on himself in the process of Crucifixion and Passion in order to break the power of the Evil One. The "Fall" of Lucifer into the core of the earth, transforming the core into a stone, a Toadstone in this case, is identical to Jesus after the crucifixion descending into Hell and defeating Satan, setting those free who were captive in hell who were righteous. The fiery core of hell itself, at the center of the earth, is calmed and cooled.

Other traditions, beyond the one that we're discussing, in this, view the sacrifice of Jesus as the thing which endowed humans who aren't of angelic descent with a soul, though not a soul of the same kind as those of witches.

There are other traces of Christianity in the greater Sabbatic tradition, as represented in the Dragon Book of Essex and others, as well. Particularly, the figure of "Mahaziel" standing at the north of the circle is a version of Jesus. In this, Mahaziel, who in the practical work of this volume is also corresponded to the embodied Death and others, is the gate through which the energy of the Sabbat enters into the circle. In this, Mahaziel is the Shekinah, who is the Word of the Demiurge, the Great Architect of the Universe, in Masonic tradition. In turn, the Shekinah, as we've outlined, is thought in this Masonic tradition, associated with the Rose-Croix, to be the living presence of Jesus in the world. The individual should seek to unite with the Shekinah in order to gain access to the Divine Mind, which it provides a portal to. Mahaziel, the emissary and guide to the Sabbat of the ages, the Divine Mind, and facilitates the descent of energy from the Divine Mind into the circle. In the essay, Fitzgerald refers to the coming of the energy from the Sabbat into the circle as the manifestation of Azhra-Lumial, where, entering in through the north, through Mahaziel, the energy spreads to the seven other stations of the compass. This spread of energy to the other stations of the compass, which sanctifies them, is identified by Fitzgerald with the manifestation of the seven headed serpent or dragon of the Book of Revelations, an example of the inverse tradition of using originally condemned mythology for a good purpose.

Here, the power of the Word, too can symbolically be said to come through the power of various stars into the world, such as Sirius and the Pole Star, and from there to influence the material world.

Beyond this, the tradition in the Sabbatic Craft of the "First Sorcerer" is, in my opinion, a transformation of Jesus. Here, there's a departure from the Cathar belief: they appear to have believed in Jesus as a Docetic figure, which implies that he was purely spirit and not human at all. With regards to the First Sorcerer, taken to be Cain, this corresponds more with the Gnostic interpretation of Jesus as having the cosmic Christ or Chrestos descend onto him during his baptism. The First Sorcerer sees an influx of energy, of fire, from the Sabbat of the Ages onto him, and into his skull, his mind, which transfigures him and grants him knowledge. The First Sorcerer as the ancestor of all witches is venerated on altars in the symbol of the skull, and the same enlightenment that was granted to him is prayed for, and asked for in ritual, to be granted to the witch. This belief is similar to the modern gnostic idea that Jesus, though a great figure, was not the first to have realized the Christos within him, but that many figures, going back to the beginning of time after the Fall, realized it as well.

In addition, the veneration of Mahaziel as the Angel of Death, who is the gate, may, beyond the role of a psychopomp, also be a product of inversion—Jesus is life, so the opposite of Jesus may be the true Christ, which is an entity that embodies Death.

Alternately, Mahaziel is the bearer of the Creative Word, but is not the Word itself. The Creative Word, in this, appears to be a combination of the ideas of the Holy Spirit and of the Christian Word as Jesus, which have been collapsed into one entity and depersonalized. Mahaziel here functions as a psychopomp, transporting both people and energy, and is a gateway in that sense, a gateway for the energy to come into the circle.

Beyond the Sabbatic tradition there are other indications of Christian parallels in traditional witchcraft. In the letters of Robert Cochrane/Roy Bowers of the 1734 tradition, Jesus is referenced as an example of a dying and rising king. Beyond that, in a presentation of a "Midsummer Ritual", Cochrane writes that before the participants do the preliminary circle casting they should go through a rite of "Confession", "Expiation", and "Purification". Elsewhere, in the collection put together by Shani Oates, this process is elaborated on, with the "Expiation" consisting of being whipped with a willow branch three times and "Purification" consisting of an anointing.

This has obvious, though perhaps in the case of "Expiation" heretical, Christian parallels. Importantly, the use of a branch or rod for whipping someone in the process of "Expiation" parallels the use of floggers in Gardner's tradition for "Purification". This is also done prior to the members of the coven before entering the circle, although it is also done many times within the circle during the rites themselves. In Gardner's initiation rites anointing is also done after purifications.

Jesus Himself

In talking about how the craft partially comes from Christianity, it's a good idea to ask what Christianity actually is. By this I mean what Christianity originally was, before it turned into what we know of as Christianity today. I don't mean to suggest that Christianity today is universally negative, by any means. However, what it comes from is, in my opinion, quite different from how the Protestant tradition of Christianity in particular understands it.

There are two aspects of Jesus in Christian thought: Jesus the cosmic figure and Jesus the teacher. For this, I'm going to focus mostly on Jesus the cosmic figure. This role of Jesus, as the redeemer of both the world and of humanity, as the pre-existent Word or Logos that contributed to the creation of the world, is recognized and honored in Catholicism and Orthodoxy, but has been increasingly downplayed in Protestant theology. This is strange, in that the further east you go into the Orthodox world the stronger the role of Jesus as a cosmic figure becomes, with the lands in which Christianity was born being among those that place the most emphasis on this aspect of Jesus.

I believe that both of these aspects of Jesus were integral to Christianity as it originally existed. Jesus as teacher instructed people on the way to regeneration, and on the way to live a good and decent life, and on divine union. Jesus, in his more intimate sermons, which are recorded in the gnostic writings, may indeed have counseled people on more personal, mystical ways of regeneration and ascent to heaven. This human and approachable role does not outlaw the idea that Jesus also conceived of himself as the incarnate Son of God, as the Messiah , and as the co-creator of the world, the Greek pagan idea of the Logos. The difference, the disjunction, between Jesus the teacher and Jesus as cosmic figure may be explained by Adoptionism. This is the idea that Jesus was born as a human, but that at some point the cosmic Christ, Jesus as a cosmic figure, entered into this person and took him over. Adoptionists of various kinds disagreed on just when this transformation happened, with some seeing it as happening pre-natally, some after birth, and some at the point when Jesus was baptized in the river Jordan by John the Baptist, at which point the Christ entered into him through the descent of the Holy Spirit.

I believe that the original, cosmic, aspect of Christianity actually came from several sources. My position on this draws in part on Henry Corbin's analysis of Christianity in the essay "The Imago Templi in Confrontation with Secular Norms", published in his book "The Temple and Contemplation", but Corbin is not the only person to outline this scenario. Here, two types of Judaism are outlined: the mainstream Judaism of the Temple and a more dissident Judaism that's associated with the books of Ezekiel and Enoch. This Enochian tradition is more mystical, and features visionary journeys to the throne of God, or, more precisely to the throne of God's regent, who is called Metatron. Enoch, in being translated into heaven, is said to have become Metatron, who acts as an outer face for God, and God's servant, while also being the "Son of Man". I believe that Metatron, in this, is the model for Jesus, or, more precisely, for Jesus in his cosmic form as the "Son of God", who is also the "Son of Man". The idea of Metatron on the Throne is intimately tied into Merkabah mysticism. The Merkabah literally is the throne, which is combined with a chariot in mystical visions. The related Hekaloth, or palaces, refer to the heavens within which the Merkabah throne is located. The point of Merkabah mysticism is to ascend upwards to the Throne in spiritual form in order to achieve divine union with it. Metatron, as the vice regent of God, is a sub-God, of sorts, who can be considered to be like the son of God. This is the Primal Vision in early Judaic form, and is recorded in the little cited third book of Enoch, which deals with the Merkabah and Hekhalot almost exclusively. It can be easily syncretized with Greco-Roman conceptions such as that of the Divine Mind, as well as with pagan Semitic ideas such as the court of Marduk or Shamash, which may have influenced it.

The pre-Kabbalistic mysticism of the Merkabah and the Hekhalot, as it actually existed, in opposition to much more recent New Age conceptions that use the same name, intersects with the vision of the Sabbat. This is another example of a mystical doctrine that lacks the dualistic component but preserves the positive parts of it. The Temple that people ascend to with the Merkabah is the same as the Sabbat, as the Divine Mind. The Heavenly Temple of the Merkabah is described in the book of Ezekiel, and, in fact, the books of Ezekiel and Enoch have a deep connection to each other, both of them being part of this tradition.

This vision is not the whole of Christianity, though. Fundamentally, the story of Christianity is based on two different events: the Fall and the restoration from the Fall that's accomplished through the sacrifice of Jesus. To this was added later the final restoration of the world at the end of time. Jesus incarnates onto the earth and sacrifices himself in order to negate the sin of Adam. In this, I see several different themes coming together. First, to the Merkabah mysticism of Metatron has been added the Tammuz myth of death and resurrection. Tammuz sacrifices himself and descends into the underworld, only to emerge victorious afterwards. Jesus in his cosmic form establishes himself as a kind of universal Tammuz, who, instead of dying and rising in a cyclical fashion instead sacrifices himself once for the whole of the world, and of humanity.

This pagan Semitic idea is connected in Christianity to the apocalyptic tradition around this Enochian Messianic Judaism. Paradise was lost, and Jesus opens the door to the restoration of humanity to the Paradisal state in which they once lived. This is similar to the idea of the destruction and rebirth of the Temple, as well as to the notion of the occupation of Judea by foreign forces, who will be overthrown by the Messiah. The movement from a local fight centered on Jerusalem to a broader one that deals with the restoration of humanity itself is a unique adaptation of this theme by Christianity.

Paradise, here, is an ambiguous place, and state, one which has many different interpretations. For instance, it could be connected to heaven, to the Palaces of God himself as well as his Throne, or it could be a higher world that is nonetheless below the heaven where

God or Metatron exists. Similarly, there can be a multitude of interpretations on what exactly the fall from Paradise actually connotes, with many of these scenarios implying a fall into matter or into the material world. Nonetheless, the other end point, which was substituted when the end of the world itself did not immediately come, was outlined very succinctly in the Book of Revelations: the world itself would be transfigured into a Paradise. The Heavenly Temple, or the Heavenly Jerusalem, which would be the dwelling of Metatron, will descend onto a purified and transformed earth, and the reborn righteous will experience eternal life in a purified state there.

What, though, would a person have to do in order to merit this state in the afterlife? I believe that the Gospel of John provides the key to this. Though not the most comprehensive gospel with respect to recounting historical events, I believe that it serves, or was meant to serve, as a basic introduction to Christianity. The key is for the individual to imitate Jesus in a personal death and resurrection scenario of their own. In this, they die to the external world, the husk around their soul or spiritual seed is destroyed, and then they're resurrected from this state into that of the New Man. The Spiritual Seed is freed through the death cycle, and then the seed or soul becomes the root from which the New Man grows, until the restored, non-sinful, human being takes over. The individual then manifests themselves as the New Adam, living in a spiritually good, morally good, and virtuous way. This is an adaptation of the Tammuz myth to the individual. Here, the crucifixion of Jesus is key. The Gospel of John repeatedly indicates that Jesus prefigured his crucifixion in his teachings, and that what Jesus was going to do on the level of the world itself is what the individual should do on a personal level within themselves.

Connected to this are the Dionysian aspects of how Jesus presented himself. The Dionysian mysteries featured the god being dismembered and eaten in the underworld before being resurrected, and the Eucharist appears to be a replication of these ideas. Here, Dionysos, the god of ecstasy and wine, is syncretized with Tammuz. Jesus having a person consume specifically his body and blood as wine and bread is a type of communion with the sacrificial god who has been dismembered in the underworld, which then lifts the individual up to Paradise and communion with Jesus in his original, divine, form. The priests who affect the transubstantiation create the means for a theurgic communion with Paradise, with Jesus as the Divine Mind, through consuming the Dionysian flesh and blood of the god through the wine and the bread. There is also a parallel between the sacrifice of the seed, its regeneration, and the making of wine as well, in that the wine grapes have to be crushed, and then fermented, in order to produce the spirit of wine itself. The turning of the grape juice into wine can be seen as a resurrection of the the substance, and parallel to the resurrection of Dionysus after being dismembered. Also, lambs or goats were dismembered and consumed in the Dionysian rituals, so that Jesus as the lamb, as well as the scapegoat for the sins of the world, provides his "meat", through the wine and bread of the Eucharist.

Here, we have several parallel explanations of the process of spiritual transformation into the regenerated man: the parable of the breaking of the seed, from which something like wheat will grow, is parallel to an explanation of the bread of the Eucharist, while the idea of wine being fermented from grapes is an explanation of the wine of the Eucharist. The lamb and his sacrifice provide both blood and meat, wine and bread, which the person imitating Christ must also become, and he also must receive these from without, from beyond him, through taking the external Eucharist. This unites the prepared man or woman with the Divine Sun.

This doctrine of the new, spiritual, man replacing the old was elaborated in great detail by Saint Paul in his letters. Paul has come under quite a bit of criticism for his condemnations of immorality, particularly in the letter to the Romans, but people have ignored the doctrine of regeneration that he outlines in beautiful fashion after his condemnations. For instance, his letters to the Corinthians contain wonderful examples of this doctrine, as do many others, including his letter to the Romans. In my opinion, the notion that Johannite and Pauline Christianity are somehow at odds with each other is false. The letters of Paul support and elaborate on the teachings in the gospel of John, and, if we want to speculate about John the Baptist's teachings, Paul's letters may support the doctrine of John the Baptist as well.

People have noted for quite a long time that there are pagan elements in Christianity, including not just the dying and rising god but the Eucharist and other themes, and have taken these as being evidence against it. I would argue that these pagan themes were there from the start, and that they're integral to the Christian message, as well as to the self-conception of Jesus himself. Here, we should remember that one of the reasons that Jesus was not believed in his proclamation of himself as the Messiah was that he was a Galilean. This was because the people of Galilee had only recently converted to Judaism from semitic paganism. Within all of this, there's a possibility that in adapting the Tammuz myth to himself, that Jesus also had Mary Magdalene as a co-prophet, serving in the role of Inanna or Ishtar. Similarly, Simon Magus, in setting himself up as an imitator of Jesus with Helen as his partner may have been imitating Jesus and Mary Magdalene. The role of Mary Magdalene as Ishtar, acting as intercessor, may have been replaced by the Virgin Mary as a more acceptable model.

The idea of Jesus as Logos, as the Word, which may be an adaptation of the role of Metatron, in the Gospel of John is itself an indication that from the very start Christianity recognized the commonalities between its own doctrine and pagan ideas. This is why charges against Constantine that he corrupted Christianity by melding it with the doctrine of Sol Invictus are likely wrong, in that Christianity, in possessing the primal vision, likely saw Heaven, the Pleroma in ways that paralleled sun mysticism and Sol Invictus itself, though perhaps understood through a Semitic lens as Shamash or Marduk. Constantine perhaps was more aware of the true nature of Christian doctrine than people who have come after have appreciated. There are plenty of other of reasons to oppose what Constantine did, in that he used the manufacturing of Nicene orthodoxy to suppress gnostic variants of Christianity, which may have reflected the true initial doctrine to a greater degree. Within this, the orations of the

Emperor Julian the Apostate on the eternal sun, and his sun worship, may also have not been the complete departure from Christianity that they're often presented as.

There are other things to say about the early development of Christianity, such as that it's likely that some of the Gospels were falsified with regards to the sequence of events that lead up to Jesus' death. Particularly, it's very possible that the Gospel of Mark was composed in part to try to convince the Romans not to persecute Christians. In this, the final days of Jesus may have been rewritten to make the Jewish people, and not the Romans, out to be the instigators of Jesus' death. The Gospel of Mark was compiled during the times of the Roman persecution, and by painting Pontius Pilate as the good guy, as a surprisingly good figure, and by giving the blame to the Jewish people, the authors may have been signaling their fealty to Rome. This rewriting may have created two parties, or two more parties, within Christianity: the Church in Rome, which was committed to this altered doctrine, and the Church outside of Rome, which may have had centers opposing these ideas. Since this division would have happened during the time that the gospels themselves were being compiled, it would have taken place centuries before Constantine. The blaming of the Jews for Jesus' death is what has contributed to several millennia of persecution against them, on the understanding that they demanded the death of Jesus in opposition to the Romans, who really didn't see the problem with Jesus' teachings.

Coming back to the theme of paganism and Christianity, one of the consequences of Christianity being semi-pagan from the start is that many of the things that have been accused of being accretions to the basic Christian doctrine, like the integration of Greek philosophy and Greek theurgical ideas into Orthodox Christian thought, may not be so. Instead, they may be logical extensions of the syncretic ideas within early Christianity itself, and so, in an ironic twist, may be more authentically Christian than the Christianity which Protestant reformers have tried to construct. Plato and Christianity are not in opposition to one another, but are instead kindred spirits. Likewise, because Christianity in its early form fully partakes in the

Primal Vision, the variants of belief that we are discussing in this book, including variants of Christian thought, may not be as heretical as they might seem to be on the surface.

Figures such as Ephrem the Syrian, the writers of the Macarian Homilies, and Maximus the Confessor, also possessed this semi-pagan Primal Vision and wrote about divine union with it. The first two of these did so ecstatically, with Ephrem in his "Hymns on Paradise", literally recounting his mystical trips to Paradise, to what we would call the Eternal Sun. Maximus the Confessor was a later Greek Orthodox mystic who codified the notion of "Theosis", or Divine Union, in Orthodox thought. "Theosis" literally means Divinization, but it does not imply that a person will become a god. Instead, the process involves imitating the virtues of Jesus, which brings a person closer to the cosmic Christ. This is often followed by exercises in contemplation that effect a direct union between the individual and deity. Maximus, in particular, incorporates Neo-Platonic themes into his work, albeit partially through the Pseudo-Dionysos the Aereopagite.

Works Cited

Chumbley, Andrew "Dragon Book of Essex", Xoanon, Hercules, 2014

Cochrane, Robert, Shani Oates ed. "A Midsummer Ritual", "The Taper that Lights the Way", Mandrake of Oxford, 2016

Corbin, Henry "The Imago Templi in Confrontation with Secular Norms", in "The Temple and Contemplation", KPI, London, 1986

Ephrem the Syrian "Hymns on Paradise" , Sebastian Brock ed. trans, Saint Vladimir's Seminary Press, Crestwood New York, 1990

Fitzgerald, Robert "The Hidden Stone", "The Luminous Stone", Three Hands Press, Richmond Vista, 2016.

Maximus the Confessor, George C. Berthold trans. "Selected Writings", Paulist Press, New York, 1985.

Odeberg, Hugo trans. "3 Enoch or the Hebrew Book of Enoch", Cambridge University Press, Cambridge, 1928, google books

Pseudo-Macarius, "Fifty Spiritual Homilies and the Great Letter", Paulist Press, New York, 1992

Chapter 5
Madeline Montalban

Lucifer vs. Lumiel

Here, we'll compare the notion of Lucifer outlined here with the concept of Lumiel, which stems from Madeline Montalban's work. There are a number of different species of Luciferianism out there. What I've been presenting is a relative minority within this spectrum. Not all of these Luciferianisms are truly compatible with each other, despite superficial similarities. Though Madeline Montalban is very well known as a Luciferian, venerating her version of him as Lumiel, it's far from clear that her Luciferianism is similar to what I've described, which I believe is also subscribed to in some form by various traditional witchcraft lineages. Let's look at Montalban's beliefs.

For this, I'm depending on a number of sources. The most obvious source, the Order of the Morning Star, her magical order is not one of these. Ultimately, they would be the prime source for information on Lumiel, but they don't share this information publicly. Primary documents spelling out the beliefs in detail are also not available. Because of this, I've had to rely on a variety of secondary sources, as well as writings by Montalban that obliquely mention Lucifer or Lumiel and related topics. Many are less than ideal for giving concrete answers. However, in the process, I believe that I've made some important breakthroughs through following up on a reference one of these secondary sources made, which I'll outline.

Looking at these source, first there are Michael Howard's account of her beliefs, which are recorded in "The Book of Fallen Angels" and "Teachings of the Light" from "The Luminous Stone". While Howard's essay in "The Luminous Stone" is completely about Montalban's beliefs, "The Book of Fallen Angels" is more ambiguous territory. Though the core of it is based on her beliefs, Howard builds on these beliefs, perhaps trying to complete them or give a fuller account of things that were implied by them, but that she never spelled out. Because of this, it's at times unclear where Montalban's beliefs leave off and Howard's additions begin. There are also certain minor contradictions between what Howard says in these two sources.

These two are combined with material from David Goddard's "The Sacred Magic of the Angels", which is basically an unauthorized publication of much of Montalban's mail order course work, though it only includes a single reference to Lumiel, that being instructions on how to make a magic square for protection based on his name. That Goddard's work is really that of Madeline Montalban was asserted in a lecture I attended by Maxine Sanders, wife of Alex Sanders, founder of Alexandrian witchcraft. Maxine Sanders recounted that both she and Goddard were part of a group in the '80s that was working with Montalban's material, that she and Goddard had collaborated on this work, and that he decided to publish it without her consent. She also said that he deleted blinds that would keep people from hurting themselves accidentally, which she disapproved of. This story is also recounted in her autobiography, "Fire Child", which the lecture was connected to. Alex Sanders got access to the Montalban material in the '60s through someone unknown mailing their copies of the beginning lessons of the course work to him. Parts of it entered into the Alexandrian tradition through that.

On top of Goddard, I've consulted many of Madeline Montalban's articles on the tarot that have been reproduced by the website "Auntie Tarot", http://auntietarot.wordpress.com. These are from "Prediction Magazine", and the website has made them available for non-commercial use.

Beyond this, I've consulted several works by H.C. Randall-Stevens, who Howard very usefully points to in his essay in the "Luminous Stone" as being important to Montalban's thought, as well as Joscelyn Godwin's "Atlantis and the Cyclers of Time", which has a secondary account of Randall-Stevens' ideas. These writings, having to with Atlantis and Lemuria as well as much else, can be shown to have been very influential on Montalban's ideas.

Finally, I've consulted the recent video presentation "Madeline Montalban: Magus of the Morning Star" given by Julia Phillips, as well as the paper of the same name published in "Essays on Women in Western Esotericism". What were her beliefs?

The creator deity was considered to be bisexual, androgynous, both male and female. Lucifer, as Lumiel, is the first creation of this androgynous god, and the Elohim are formed afterwards. Lumiel is connected with intellect. Lumiel is appointed the angel of the earth, and angel of the intellect, while the Elohim are appointed angels of the other planets. Each of these Elohim were associated with a spiritual ray. There were also beings known as "Ray People", lesser angels, associated with them, who were also androgynous. Though it's possible that Montalban linked these "Rays" to the seven rays of Theosophy, this isn't explicit in the material. Adam and Eve were also originally created androgynous, lived on the astral plane, and did not possess a human form. Lumiel also created fabulous beasts on the astral plane.

The plan was that humans would be produced by a process of evolution. This process started with their form being more like an amoeba, and would develop through upwards through the lower forms of life, then into human form, and then into Ray People, angels, in the completion of the evolutionary process. According to Howard, while this process of evolution was going on, and was incomplete, Lumiel decided to speed it up, to speed up the evolution of humanity, and this was his crime.

This was done through having Adam and Eve eat of the tree of Knowledge, which caused the angelic consciousness associated with the "Ray People" to manifest in them before it was meant to. Howard says that their minds were unprepared for it. Lumiel was also responsible for splitting Adam and Eve into male and female, so this did not come about through a fall on their part. The eating of the fruit of the Tree of Knowledge caused Adam and Eve to fall from the astral plane into the material world.

Howard recounts that the fall of human beings into matter, and their split into two different sexes, also established the idea of "Twin souls", where people had their other half, their other spiritual counterpart somewhere in the world.

Lumiel's actions caused the war in heaven, and he was punished by falling from being an angel overseeing the earth to incarnating in human form. Lumiel is bound to reincarnate in human form, and to be punished in human form, until humanity has basically assimilated the higher knowledge and awareness that was infused into them, and has come to a more enlightened state. He's incarnated in many forms, recounted by Howard as including Quetzalcoatl, Tammuz, and Jesus. These are all figures identified with the "Dying and Rising God" in the tradition of James Frazier. Howard recounts that in the teachings of Montalban, human beings would similarly have to undergo a death and resurrection process, including suffering, in order to spiritually perfect themselves. Notably, Montalban states that Jesus was one of the incarnations of Lucifer.

In is essay "The Teachings if the Light" in "The Luminous Stone", Howard says that Lucifer was the Solar Logos, and the it was only after he had committed his crime this that he fell to earth. It may be that in this belief system, that as the Solar Logos, he was in charge of directing the general evolution of humanity as well. In describing the role of Lumiel, Howard links it to the Theosophical notion of Lucifer, quoting Blavatsky, who describes Lucifer as the Light in "Let their be light", and as the force of intellect, and associated him with fire as well. Notably, the "Light" in this has previously been described as Jesus by Christian tradition. Intellect, as well, is in Greco-Roman philosophy the first product of the One, and can be identified with the "Mind of Christ", in Jesus' aspect as Wisdom.

The presentation by Julia Philips about Montalban has an interesting slide where a page of Montalban's correspondence course is presented, where the "Fall" is talked about. There, all the entities of the earth are described as being incorporated into a system of precise guidance by the planetary angels, and that the Fall came about by giving humans the free will to disobey this guidance, which caused chaos to erupt on earth. Also, within Montalban's tarot columns, Lucifer is described as being mind without emotion, which she says is his downfall.

Tarot on Lucifer

Speaking of Montalban's tarot columns, in her column about the Horned god and the Devil card of the tarot, published in Prediction in February of 1967, Montalban presents a picture of Lucifer as the head of the Watchers, who came to earth. The seduction of women is presented by her as the result of the immense attractive beauty of Lucifer and the fallen angels. The aspect of Lucifer as "Horned God" is related by her to the equivalence of horns with rays of light that appears in some statues. For instance, some statues of Moses are unfortunately horned, because people misread the word for rays of light in the Bible as that of horns. This makes Lucifer one of the Ray People. She states that Lucifer does not actually hate mankind, but that mankind, in hating that which they're attracted to when they know they shouldn't, has demonized Lucifer for what they themselves feel—an attraction to him, which stems from his beauty, sexual nature, and angelic heritage.

In another Tarot column, titled "The Rayed God", published in Prediction in April of 1962, Montalban also talks about Lucifer through the vehicle of the Devil card in the Tarot. Here, there's less usable information, but Montalban is careful to say that Lucifer is not Satan, and, simultaneously is not Baphomet. She endorses the "Temophab" definition of the name of Baphomet, and implicitly links him with the astrological spheres, but says that he's been given a bad reputation. She also defends the Templars and others from the idea that the reason that they got ahead was because they worshipped an evil god, Baphomet in this case.

There's a final Tarot commentary having to do with Lucifer that's available on the "Auntie Tarot" website. This is about the 5 of Rods, and is titled "Love Must be Earned", from Prediction November1959. Here, Montalban includes her reference to Lucifer at the very end of the column. The connection between love and Lucifer here is the quality of illusion. The column talks about both love and love magic, with the latter being related to illusion. She states that after Lucifer fell into matter, he took a piece of his aura and "breathed life" into it. His aura was rainbow tinted. This produced "mirage & mist", who had sex with each other and produced Maya, or illusion. This is a variant idea to the main significance that she gives to Lucifer, which is that of a voice of reason who wants to lead humanity upwards, rather than a force that envelops humanity in illusion. This column is noticeably earlier than the others, so perhaps she hadn't formulated her Luciferian doctrines fully at that point in time.

Montalban also talks more generally about the fallen angels in her column "Daughter of the Mighty", about the "Empress" card of the Tarot, published in Prediction in March of 1961

Here, she talks about the Watchers as the "Mighty Ones", and says that their role is to protect the harmony of the universe. She says that the Watchers live in four Watchtowers and that they have the Empress as their female child. The Empress figure is similarly in charge of protecting the harmony of the universe. Perhaps the Empress here stands for the center of the four. She then talks about water in general, in relation to imbalances within the harmony of the universe, and about Atlantis, destroyed by floods. She says that she managed to reconstruct some of the ancient Atlantean language, but that it proved too powerful a magical tool, so she destroyed her work.

In Four Watching Kings, Prediction August 1965, about the four kings of the Minor Arcana, Montalban elaborates on the connection between the Watchers and the Watchtowers. She says that there are multiple planes of existence, and that four Watchers are placed on every plane, regulating them. On earth, these four Watchers correspond to the four Watchtowers, the four elements and the four directions.

Finally, in her column "The Watcher Within Ourselves", from the June 1963 edition of Prediction, Montalban links the Watcher to the spark of divinity within. This is related to the tarot card of the "Hermit". She refers to this as the "Secret Observer", and this has much in common with the Synderesis in the heart, or the Toadstone, which we'll discuss further. As a spark of divinity, she also describes it as a channel through which the divine can come into our self. It is the light that the Hermit carries in his lamp.

Randall-Stevens and Atlantis

Reconstructing things, it appears that many of her beliefs were a variation of the schema of creation outlined by H.C. Randall-Stevens. This individual claimed to be channelling an ancient Egyptian deity Osiris, who dictated to him the actual story of creation, as well as the truth of what happened on earth in its early years, including topics like Lemuria and Atlantis. However, simply looking at Randall-Stevens as an Atlantis devotee doesn't really capture what he, or his putative disembodied source, is doing in these writings.

We've seen how the Heavenly Temple, and Paradise, has been transmuted into Atlantis in the occult tradition. Similarly, with Randall-Stevens, what's really going on is that he's narrating a gnostic drama but is putting it in the concepts of his day. This gnostic tendency in Randall-Stevens' writings has also been noted by Joscelyn Godwin in his evaluation of his work. Here, the gods are overseers of particular planets, and all of the drama that would normally happen in the heavens, or generically in the heavens and the earth, is thought to take place in Lemuria and Atlantis. In reality, these are just somewhat random labels, and for the core of his story these places could be interchanged with any other name and you'd have the same ideas.

Now, looking at this, we can enrich the story that Montalban presents somewhat. His cosmology is as follows: There is a bisexual Father/Mother god who has a son. This Father/Mother god gave birth to a similarly bisexual individual, El Daoud, who is Adam and Eve combined into one being. This being is not a human, but the first of the Elohim, a ruler over the universe. The Father/Mother also gave birth to two other primal beings, Yevah and Eranus, who are Yahweh and Lucifer. These were placed in charge of the earth. Notice, this makes Adam/Eve or El Daoud the elder brother of Lucifer. El Daoud then gave birth to a number of other bisexual beings, who were the other Elohim, or great angels, who were the Ray People. As in Montalban's ideas, these Ray People were the ones that were created to tutor the evolution of life on earth from single celled organisms up to advanced spiritual beings. Ideally, these spiritual beings would become Ray People themselves, and be free, absorbed into the godhead. Yevah created life on earth, and so the human beings that evolved on earth are called Yevahic humans in the book. The center of life on Earth at this time was on the lost continent of Lemuria, where the Ray People collaborated with Yevahic humans.

Like in Montalban's ideas, Eranus sought to accelerate the evolution of life on earth. The exact process was somewhat complicated since he needed to convince Yevah to cooperate with him on this. Nonetheless, this cooperation was given, but the creations of Eranus were monstrosities. He also put a force field around the earth that cut it off from many higher influences. Some cycles of time transpired, with more drama, but within that another event of significance occurred, as Eranus, now named Sataniku, convinced one of the Ray People to split with her other half and to incarnate into a mortal body. This was a trick, a kind of punishment by Eranus, which presages his eventual corruption of the Ray People in general. Eventually, Lemuria itself was then destroyed, and this Ray person was freed.

However, before Lemuria was destroyed, Sataniku gave a speech that explains the origin of the Garden of Eden story. According to Randall-Stevens, what happened in the Garden of Eden is not what has been represented in the Bible. In several places, both in "The Book of Truth" and in "The Wisdom of the Soul" he states that the idea of Eve being tempted by evil in the Garden of Eden was a lie made up by Eranus/Sataniku. What actually happened is that Eve told Adam what Eranus was planning to do, as well as God's plan to punish Eranus by having him reincarnate over and over again as punishment for this. In his speech, Eranus states that he will mislead humanity into thinking that they're being punished because of what Eve did, and that they will be turned against Eve because of this. He states that he will promulgate a false religion next to the true religion of the Ray People, in order to confuse people and keep them from the truth. This is later revealed to be a version of Christianity which is suspiciously close to a parody of Catholicism.

After the destruction of Lemuria, Atlantis became the center of civilization and of life developing as it should, with the Ray People instructing the Yevahic humans. In Atlantis, Ray people voluntarily incarnated into mortal bodies in order to better teach the Yevahic people. Seeing that this gave him an opportunity to corrupt people,

Sataniku then evilly influenced both the Yevahic people and the Ray People, and, among other things, convinced them to mate with each other. In this, the souls of the Ray People forgot who they were and why they were incarnated. Also, though the incarnation of the Ray People in mortal bodies was originally meant to be temporary, as punishment their souls continued to reincarnate in mortal bodies. This is the ultimate fall of spirit into matter. It is also the story of the Watchers, of the Sons of God mating with the daughters of men.

These acts of miscegenation were followed by a long series of fights and conflicts between partisans of Sataniku, who believed he was the true God, and partisans of the good gods on Atlantis, which culminated with the island being destroyed by higher beings in the universe. Refugees from Atlantis, particularly those who had more of the heritage of Ray People within them, fled to places around the globe, including Egypt and South America, and established advanced civilizations there. There are now two different types of people in the world, or, more precisely, two different types of souls: advanced Ray People and more primitive Yevahics. This appears to have been merged by Montalban with ideas about witch blood and the Mark of Cain, this signifying descent from the Ray People.

It's apparent, within Howard's description, that Montalban is trying to reinterpret this story from a point of view sympathetic to Eranus/Sataniku. She also appears to have collapsed the two different stories of the acceleration of the evolution of mankind and the fall of man into one event, and also to have ignored the reinterpretation of the Garden of Eden story, substituting a more traditional account in its place. In light of this, there are many unanswered questions. The first one is how exactly did Montalban justify looking at this figure as a positive force? This is never outlined in the information that's publicly available. In the writings of Randall-Stevens, "Lumiel" is clearly satanic, and in fact heavily resembles the gnostic false god, the Ialdabaloth, constantly trapping and misleading otherwise good angels. In the "Book of Truth", this force presents himself as having the true faith, or a better faith, to the fallen people, and causes them to worship him in rites that are barbaric and mimic that of the true faith.

As for the good of helping to speed up evolution, from what Howard and others have written, it also appears that Lumiel lead the Ray People, who were on a higher level of evolution, downward, to be trapped on a lower level of evolution. In other words, this figure was responsible for the fallen angels being trapped in matter, which negates the good that wanting to speed up evolution would have done. Maybe Montalban interpreted this fall as a positive thing, but, fundamentally, this is the key sin of the Evil One. Perhaps the reason why this force isn't satanic is given in the unpublished lessons of Montalban.

However, there is a possibility that's suggested by the tone of many of the excerpts of Montalban's work in Howard's "Book of Fallen Angels", as well as the general treatment of it there. Let's say, for purpose of argument, that Montalban took Randall-Stevens' basic set of ideas and stripped a lot of the extra badness out of the figure of Eranus/Sataniku in order to make Lumiel. Instead of being a force which is completely evil, Lumiel could be an angel that wanted to help humanity in a Promethean way, and in the process made a bad choice and did a bad thing, was nevertheless was well intentioned in what he did. Like Prometheus Lumiel is said to be trapped in endless reincarnation as punishment. Perhaps in Montalban's system she felt that Lumiel's punishment was justified, and she approved of his intent, though she did not completely approve of his actions? If that was the case, Lumiel would be a romantic interpretation of Lucifer. Nonetheless, this still does not explain how tricking the Ray People, angels, into sinning, causing them to be trapped in the cycle of reincarnation within material reality was a good thing, or well intentioned.

Overall, Montalban's "Lumiel" has little to nothing to do with Luciferianism as I've described it. It also has very little to do with the Luciferianism presented in public writings associated with the Cultus Sabbati. There, it appears that the name "Lumiel" is used as a more socially acceptable way of saying "Lucifer", and that the underlying metaphysical significance has little to nothing in common with Montalban's beliefs.

Works Cited

Goddard, David "The Sacred Magic of the Angels", Weiser, York Beach, 1996

Godwin, Joscelyn "Atlantis and the Cycles of Time", Inner Traditions, Rochester VT, 2011

Howard, Michael "Book of Fallen Angels", Capall-Bann , Milverton, 2004

Howard, Michael ""Teachings of the Light" from "The Luminous Stone", Three Hands Press, 2016, Richmond Vista, USA

Montalban, Madeline "Horned god and the Devil card of the tarot", Prediction Mag., February 1967 https://auntietarot.wordpress.com/2014/02/19/angel-or-devil/

"The Rayed God",published in Prediction mag. in April of 1962, https://auntietarot.wordpress.com/2013/07/02/the-mystic-tarot-the-devil/,

"Love Must be Earned", from Prediction Mag. November1959 https://auntietarot.wordpress.com/2013/01/17/the-5-of-rods/

"Daughter of the Mighty", about the "Empress" card of the Tarot, published in Prediction Mag. in March of 1961, https://auntietarot.wordpress.com/2013/06/06/the-mystic-tarot-the-empress/,

Four Watching Kings, Prediction Mag. August 1965, https://auntietarot.wordpress.com/2013/11/23/the-magical-tarot-the-kings/,

"The Watcher Within Ourselves", Prediction June 1963, "https://auntietarot.wordpress.com/2013/08/27/the-mystical-tarot-the-wheel/"

Phillips, Julia and Amy Hale video presentation "Madeline Montalban: Magus of the Morning Star", "The Last Tuesday Society", https://www.thelasttuesdaysociety.org/event/madeline-montalban-magus-of-the-morning-star-by-julia-phillips/

Phillips, Julia"Madeline Montalban: Magus of the Morning Star" in "Essays on Women in Western Esotericism", ed. Amy Hale, Palgrave Macmillan, 2023

Randall-Stevens, H.C. "The Book of Truth, or the Voice of Osiris", Rider & co. London, 1927, Hathi Trust

Randall-Stevens , H.C. "The wisdom of the soul", Aquarian Press, London, 1956
Sanders, Maxine "Fire Child", Mandrake of Oxford, Oxford 2007

Chapter 6
UFO Literature and the Craft

Here, we have the final evolution of the transformation of the Watchers in relation to popular culture that began with their association with Atlantis: now, the Beni Elohim are transformed into actual aliens, who, in turn, are associated with Atlantis. Angels have here been replaced with space brothers. Specifically, the Watchers, and the gnostic drama surrounding them, has been transformed into aliens from Venus coming down to earth.

Brinsley Le Poer Trench is an example of someone with a probable knowledge of traditional witchcraft who presented it in other masks. Trench was an English aristocrat, Earl of Clancarty, and member of the House of Lords. Le Poer Trench is known for his many non-fiction works about UFOs and aliens, and speculations about how aliens visited ancient humans, influencing them. However, a strange thing happens if you view his works not through the lens of Ufology, but through that of traditional witchcraft. Le Poer Trench essentially takes the myth of the Watchers, and the idea of a Cainite bloodline, and transports it into an inter-planetary drama, with the Watchers now being literal aliens. Here, the association of Lucifer with Venus is transformed into the idea that aliens from Venus established the Cainite bloodline. These people are positively and explicitly identified as "Serpent people" and "People of the Serpent" by Trench, with this being linked by him to kundalini and magical serpent power , and to the magic of Hermes as well. Similarly, Jehovah is identified by Trench as a bad figure, with the Serpent People being the good ones. Normal humans, without the bloodline, were created by Jehovah.

My belief is that Trench was very much involved with Traditional Witchcraft, but saw the origin of it as ultimately being with extraterrestrials. In this, he states that these Luciferian or Venusian creatures created humanity as servants, ruled them, and had magical and psychic powers. Eventually, their civilization collapsed, and these Watcher like figures interbred with human beings, creating bloodlines that possess the magical powers of the original Luciferian Venusians. One can read his books, particularly "The Sky People" and "Men Among Mankind", with this in mind and derive quite a lot of knowledge from them, extracting the underlying knowledge and concepts from the mask that he placed them in. Atlantis is also mentioned by Trench as being linked to the Luciferian Venusian civilization.

He, however, was not operating in a vacuum. Particularly, he was drawing on the thought of George Hunt Williamson, who in turn combined ideas similar to those in the craft with a kaleidoscope of weirdness, including believing in Atlantis and UFOs simultaneously. Melissa Seims, in her book about the Coven of Atho, perceptively links some of Charles Cardell's Atlantean beliefs to Williamson, particularly to his book "The Road in the Sky". These include some beliefs which we will examine later, such as a connection between the megalithic civilization and the Watchers. There, we see a story close to that related by Brinsley le poer Trench: the Watchers were an extraterrestrial race, which Williamson calls "Els" after "Elohim". They used genetic engineering to create humans, who were developed from indigenous animals. The "Els" had spiritual powers as well, and they're referred to by Williamson as "Cyclops", with this relating to a supposed third eye that gave them power. They were, through this, also related to Cyclopean or megalithic architecture. This can, in turn, be linked to Atlantis. In this section of "The Road in the Sky", Williamson asks the reader to consult his work "Other Tongues, Other Flesh" for more information, and this is where it gets really bizarre.

To really understand all of this, it's necessary to look a little bit at UFOlogy in the early '50s. Kenneth Arnold had sighted UFOs by Mount Rainier in Washington State in 1947, and shortly after this was publicized a number of people started claiming that they had met these space brothers face to face. These people made up the "Early Contactee" culture, which George Hunt Williamson was a part of. This culture was far different than later UFOlogy. While the issue of UFOs and their nature is an open one, I think that the early contactee culture is almost completely explained by cultural reasons, as opposed to being explained by actually having contact with UFOs themselves.

In fact, I think that it's best to consider it as exemplifying the idea, associated with Jung, that popular culture basically incorporated the idea of the UFO into an already existing matrix of beliefs, beliefs that were either spiritual in themselves or had spiritual overtones. The people in the community that Williamson was a part of were people who, before UFOs came onto the scene, were interested in Atlantis, Theosophy, and more popular forms of occultism, including spiritualism. What happened is that they basically grafted the new UFO mythos onto these beliefs, and carried on like nothing had seriously changed.

It helped, perhaps, that one of the most public figures who claimed to have had contact with the space people was George Adamski, who had been involved in these very circles running the fraudulent "Royal Order of Tibet", which claimed contact with ascended masters and secret Theosophical teachings. Perhaps taking a cue from Adamski, most of the "Space brothers" encountered by the early contactees had quite a lot in common with the ascended masters of Theosophy. The early contactees certainly treated them as such. They were human, and brought the kind of messages of love and peace that are common in spiritualist and more white light magical circles. Sometimes this was more than a coincidence. Mediums in the spiritualist world, who may have previously channeled the spirits of Ancient Egyptian priests, now started to shift into receiving messages from these space brothers, with the content being similar, though now expressed in a more futuristic key. All this is not to say that these early writings are valueless, but that whatever value they have has no relation to their putative subject, UFOs, and instead lies in the esoteric and mythomaniacal traditions that they draw on.

Enter George Hunt Williamson. His work "Other Tongues, Other Flesh" is what you may have gotten if the mythomaniac Godfrey Higgins, known for the very strange "Anacalypsis", had been born in pre-WWII 20th century America and had come of age in the time both of beliefs in Atlantis and UFOs. He also believe in the lost continent of Mu, whose rise, fall, and putative language was channeled by James Churchward. The book is a kind of acid trip of comparative mythology and wild claims, at times reading like it was put together by an unmedicated schizophrenic. Yet, within all of this there are demonstrable retellings of the gnostic drama associated with the craft, regarding the Watchers. However, the ultimate origin of Williamson's speculations is a very disturbing source: the Ariosophist movement in Germany, particularly the thought of Jorg Lanz von Liebenfels and his "Theozöology".

Williamson was a disciple of William Dudley Pelley, who was an American Fascist who founded the "Silver League" or "Silver Shirts". Pelley was pro-Nazi, anti-semitic, racist, anti-catholic and more. He was also a spiritualist. Convicted of seditious conspiracy in the early '40s, Pelley was released from prison in 1950, and sometime later he adapted his spiritualist channelings to the new belief on the block: UFOs. What appears to have been the case is that Pelley basically added UFOs to an already racist belief system founded broadly on Theosophy and other currents. Though the explicit racism was dialed down in these publications, the space brothers were implicitly Aryan supermen, who came to this planet long ago and were once its masters. They were the Watchers, and had created humanity. Somewhere along the line Lanz von Liebenfels thought was integrated into this, and it was passed onto Williamson.

Liebenfels writes quite strangely about "Sodomy" between Aryan supermen and animals, which supposedly generated the majority of human kind, and Pelley, in his works for example in "Star Guests", similarly obsessively talks about "Sodomy" in this sense, as well as a "Sodomitic Civilization" that supposedly stemmed from these relations. You wonder just why exactly Pelley was so fixated on the subejct. For his part, Williamson is careful to not be explicitly racist, though readers may be puzzled about why he devotes so much time to the esoteric meaning of the swastika and its link to the space brothers. In fairness, however, much of his interpretation of the swastika links it to the turning of the constellation of the Great Bear through the seasons, which is also a central part of Gerald Massey's thought.

The chapter of "Other Tongues, Other Flesh" titled "The Migrants" recapitulates Lanz's theory of miscegenation between angelic beings and animals, updating it for the space age. Now, instead of bestiality, the super beings or Elohim experimented with mixing their genes with different sorts of animals, creating the fabulous animals of myths like griffins and giant semi-humanoid cats. This was the meaning of the mixing of the Sons of God with the Daughters of Men. All of this creation of semi-angelic, semi-bestial creatures was put an end to through the Flood, and only the hybrid that was based on monkeys was saved. Williamson extensively quotes the "Elder Brother" in this, who outlines much of the scenario. This "Elder Brother" is the supposed space brother that Pelley channeled in his "Soulcraft" writings, meaning that it's Pelley himself who is supplying the Nazi occultist aligned theory here. Williamson goes on to talk about the dilution of the Angelic or extraterrestrial blood which happened after the cataclysm, and about how further space beings came to guide humanity in order to breed them into a racially purer form that had more extraterrestrial blood in it, aiming to recreate the original super beings.

With regards to Lucifer, Williamson has two different takes. In the first one, "Lucifer" refers to a planet in the solar system which was ruled by black magic. This planet broke up, leading to a catastrophe that destroyed part of the earth. The souls of the evil black magicians of the planet Lucifer were banished to some place of outer darkness. In the second one, another group, the "Sons of Light" are highly advanced spiritual beings, extraterrestrials who Williamson also calls "Wanderers", who are incarnating on earth in order to lead humanity to a higher level of existence. Williamson hints that, if you're reading his book, you too might be a "Wanderer". This is very clearly the Theosophical idea of ascended masters updated for the post-UFO world. In any case, this melange of ideas, apparently prompted Brinsley le Poer Trench to create his own synthesis, which included much more craft based material.

Works Cited

Pelley, William Dudley "Starguests", Soulcraft Press, Noblesville IN, 1950, IAPSOP

Seims, Mellisa "Here be Magic", Thoth Publications, Loughborough, 2022

Trench, Brinsley le Poer "Men Among Mankind", Venture Bookshop, Evanston, 1963

Trench, Brinsley le Poer "Sky People" Tandem, London 1971

Williamson, George Hunt "Other Tongues, Other Flesh", Neville Spearman, London, 1965

Williamson, George Hunt "The Road in the Sky", Neville Spearman, London, 1973

Chapter 7
Doctrine

The following are my own positions, although I believe that many of them are echoed in the world of traditional witchcraft itself.

Questions of Evil.

Personally, I consider there to be a general evil God, who corresponds to the false, lower, more human resembling God, which is often vengeful, and a higher transcendent God, or series of gods. If a person or group recognizes the transcendent God in their practice, they're worshipping something good, if they recognize the other, they're doing something bad. Judaism, and Islam, for that matter, in their theology, conceptualize God in a very transcendent way, one which goes beyond many of these types of criticisms. This can be seen in their theological and philosophical ideas about monotheism, which are far removed from a vulgar conception. With regards to Christians, and this is very important as well, whether they worship the true god or the false god depends on this distinction. There are many Christians who are, in fact, in touch with the true, transcendent, God, and their Christianity is a valid path to the truth. On the other hand, there are Christians who worship a very anthropomorphic, vengeful, lower God, who venerate the Evil One even though they claim to worship the highest principals. This goes for the other traditions as well. The true divine is beyond anthropomorphism, and those who read scriptures literally mistake the image for the reality, and in the process venerate the Evil One, who is likewise image, a lie, instead of the true reality.

However, we should make a distinction here with regards to some aspects of Christianity. Some of the hellfire and brimstone in the preaching is a way of cultivating the "Fear of God" in people. This fear is basically an awareness that people have done wrong in their lives, and a concern about how this will affect their afterlife, which causes them to reform their lives and to act in better ways. This is separate from the type of demonization of individuals that I've mentioned.

There have been writers and groups that have abused the dualistic tradition associated with the Craft, who have taken Cathar ideas and used them to justify anti-semitism and white supremacy. Miguel Serrano's work is an example of this. His work is a complete distortion of these ideas, one which is not based on historical reality..

What the Evil One is

The Evil One is a spirit based purely on matter that dominates humanity and wants to keep humanity chained to the material realm, and to prevent it from ascending to the realms beyond the material, and even prevent people from having contact with the transcendent, which is the source of goodness. In this, the Evil One is allied to the most base, material, spirits, including underworld spirits who are demons, who are demonic. The Evil One encourages base behavior and dishonesty, selfishness and violence based on the passions. The demons of the underworld similarly encourage these things.

People on the earth, in civilization, who similarly want to suppress human freedom and human potential, who try to undercut the transcendent with base material concerns, may be allied to the Evil One. Of course, the nature of human freedom and human potential is somewhat subjective, with one person's idea of these things conflicting with another.

If a person is strong, and is allied to the good, to the Sabbat, the Divine Mind, the Eternal Sun, they can command, constrain, and dominate infernal demons, and by taking a superior stance towards them use them for their purposes in rituals. However, these are hostile creatures, which not only the Christian but the Greco-Roman world looked at as being corrupt, and wrong. They serve the Evil One.

With regards to those who, in a revisionist history, think that these creatures are someone not hostile, and that, in fact, they're nice and harmless, and that the people advocating for the transcendent and condemning them are wrong, these people are wrong in the extreme. Their philosophy, dictated by demons themselves, is an apologia to the Evil One, and is designed to limit human freedom and to thwart human liberation and human potential by denying people a connection to the transcendent. The demons, speaking through human interlocutors, who have advocated for a nicer, non-hostile, relationship with them are leading humanity astray, and are in fact the enemies of humanity. They literally serve Satan, and do Satan's work, as do the people who follow these teachings.

They ultimately serve the same cause as the conservative Christians who oppose love and who instead preach vengeance and hatred. Both of these groups serve the Evil One, one covertly, the other one openly. As has been said, the true gospel is the gospel of love, not of vengeance.

Actual Practitioners of Black Magic

There really are people that serve the Evil One in their magic and their practices. However, the concept of a group of black magicians existing, serving evil, either on their own or through something like that of a "Black Lodge" has been used in manipulative ways by many gurus. This includes Samael Aun Weor, who we'll look at later in volume 2. The same concept has been at the source of needless persecutions of people, such as happened during the "Satanic Panic" in the 1980s. Nonetheless, without buying into grandiose conceptions about there being some sort of war between a "White Lodge" and a "Black Lodge", there are people who in their magic do serve the Evil One.

The mark of these people is that they practice magic while denying the transcendent, even writing against ideas of the transcendent. Instead, they either have an atheistic perspective, or they have one which honors evil entities, such as demons, as somehow being "good", or at least not that bad. These are the people who honor the Evil One in their works, and their magic. While atheism is a perfectly fine philosophy, the combination of atheism with magic is another thing entirely. Magic itself is transcendent.

The existence of magic is evidence for the transcendent, and denying the transcendent, taking an atheistic position, while practicing magic perverts its nature.

Additionally, there are evil entities, demons, who do not want individuals to transcend the power of the Evil One, who want to destroy human progress and to ensure that people remain slaves to the Evil One instead of attaining freedom. People who deal with demons from a perspective of them supposedly being just misunderstood, and who deny the transcendent serve the cause of the evil, which can be seen in the consequences of their actions, and in the causes that they support. Here, it's the overall perspective that makes the difference, though, of course, basic morals and ethics also apply to whether something someone does is good or bad, in addition to their overall perspective. Related to the transcendent perspective is a basic commitment to truth, as opposed to lies. Though for spiritual purposes some people have described themselves as "companions of the lie", nonetheless, a basic commitment to truth is essential, as that which is transcendent is closer to the truth, while that which is associated with lies is linked to the Evil One.

The notion that these demons are just "Chthonic forces", forces of the underworld, is a false one. Evil is an infection within nature, and not an integral part of it. Underworld entities are distinct from demons, and it's a naive primitivism which associates entities which lie and cheat with natural processes. The Evil One, and the demons that serve him, are corrupters of nature, not nature itself.

The underworld is the domain of the dead, of the ancestors, not of demons. It is one of the places where people can go after death. The majority of individuals go to the underworld, or parts of them do, with another part of the soul being recycled, while the honored dead, the saints, go to the Sabbat of the Ages.

The Temple of Set

I should note that not all Left Hand Path organizations, or manifestations, honor the Evil One. In fact, the Left Hand Path offers routes that have nothing to do with Satan, even though Satanic manifestations of it have become popular lately. As an example of this, let me give my perspective on the Temple of Set. This group, though it came from the Church of Satan, is in my opinion, and I believe in theirs, not Satanic. They believe that the deity they're in touch with is the Egyptian Set, but beyond the change in name there appears to have been a change in doctrine too. Within the published writings of the Temple of Set there's a distinct gnostic content. Set is understood as serving a role similar to that of Lucifer, as promoting freedom for individuals, including personal thought. One of their documents relates Set to the serpent in the garden, with the apple offered freeing Adam and Eve from a lower form of consciousness. Set himself is pictured as a transcendent deity, who is opposed to Nature. In this, Set is considered to be an Isolate Intelligence, which is different from how we conceive things, but the opposition is there between Set, on the one hand, and Osiris, who is considered to be the lethargic accumulated power of the natural world and of human society, which keeps humanity back. Osiris, in this is similar to the Evil One, and Set, of course, destroys Osiris. However, we identify the Evil One not with nature itself, but with a corrupter of nature, with nature having the potential to be pure.

With regards to Isolate Intelligence, I feel that this is part of the way to the truth, but that it doesn't go far enough. The intelligence that's responsible for enlightenment is not isolate. Instead, it's been very close to many of the great philosophies of western and Middle Eastern thought, expressed through the writings of Plato, the Neo-Platonists, and others who have inherited the tradition.

With regards to the relationship between Set and traditional witchcraft, even though there are similarities between Set and the Opposer, Cain, there's been an enormous amount of "Dark Fluff" writings which completely distort this idea. Most of these writings have little, if any, value, and seriously misunderstand the witchcraft context which they presume to base themselves on.

The Reverse Masks and the Mystery religions.

Positive and Negative Masks.

The same basic reality, the reality of the Sabbat of the Ages and the craft, can be veiled in either a positive or negative way—it can be expressed in a way that's consonant with the highest positive religious realities of Christianity, Islam, or Judaism, or it can be expressed in a way which is dissonant to that. Today, ironically, it's more acceptable socially to use the negative mask than the positive one, but this cultural anomaly should not be taken to indicate the nature of the underlying doctrine, which, though positive, is ultimately itself. It should also not be taken to sanction Satanism, the praise of that which is lower while discounting, or ignoring, or opposing that which is higher. The higher is the origin of all souls, all witch souls, and is the place that we aspire to reascend and to return to.

That the complete emphasis on negative masks has lead people to misunderstand the mysteries, and to re-align individuals with the truth, the positive, that which masks the transcendent in a way supportive of the good, needs to be pointed out. Part of my emphasis on the very real role that Christianity has played in the development of the craft is an attempt to further this goal, and to counteract this tendency.

The Truth needs to be reaffirmed, with the mask of the Lie being far too strong a force for the majority of humanity to intelligently use. The mask of the Lie, in the sense of Cainite work, can only function when the Truth is known to the individual, and without possessing the Truth, those who engage in it will only lead themselves into illusion and destruction.

To put it another way, the inverse mode of the craft only flourishes when it's a current of spiritual dissent, within a greater society that affirms the good. When the inverse mask becomes dominant in society, and taken at face value, it becomes counter-productive. The inverse tradition was never meant to become the dominant force in society, and the majority of human beings are too ignorant to distinguish this mask from the truth.

The ideal state of things would be to have the pagan underlay of the craft appreciated as it is, without people falling for negative masks, or for that matter positive ones. If Christianity and related faiths fail, the replacement should be this type of positive paganism, not the beliefs of a sick society which takes the inverse masks as reality and so destroys itself with Satanism.

Ecumenicism and Masks in Traditional Witchcraft

It's unclear whether this was the result of the Templar influence, and through that Islam, or something else such as Manicheanism, but Traditional Witchcraft sees many different roads as leading to the same truth. The basic truth is the Sabbat of the Ages as the Ideal realm, the first Mind, generated by the One, and the experience of the Sabbat forms the "Primal Vision" that many different religious traditions can have knowledge of. If they have knowledge of the "Primal Vision" of the Sabbat, though it's expressed in their own terms, they're brothers of a certain kind. Many mystics have in fact discovered the vision of the Sabbat and have incorporated it into their works, including Christian mystics and Islamic mystics. In so much as their goal is to ascend to and unite with the Divine Mind, the First Mind, they're engaging in the same work.

However, our belief is that while the same concept, the Sabbat of the ages, may be expressed with different imagery and different language, that the craft preserves the knowledge of the Sabbat as it really is, without masks. In essence, we believe that behind all of these other mystical traditions is traditional witchcraft, and that the people practicing these traditions are unconsciously participating in the Craft, while people who practice the Craft are consciously participating in it.

With regards to universalism, I believe that the one reality of the Sabbat and the One, the Dragon lord, is behind every religion which has a true spiritual connection. The masks of religion are played out, with the adherents of Christianity, Islam, and others, praying to the masks of our gods and our gods answering in turn, using the masks which people expect of them.

Christianity, Islam, Buddhism

The unity of the esoteric traditions of Christianity, Islam, and Buddhism

These three religions, separated by so much, are nonetheless related in their esoteric forms through certain of these referring to the common reality of the Sabbat of the ages, under their own masks. This is because of their common Greco-Roman heritage. While the influence of Greek philosophy on Christianity and Islam is well known, the influence of Greek philosophy on Buddhism is less so.

I am not a scholar of Buddhism, but my belief is that Greek philosophy influenced the formation of Mahayana Buddhism through the Greco-Bactrian kingdom. This was a state that was part of Alexander the Great's empire, which was in current day Afghanistan and Pakistan, as well as central Asia north of it. It retained its Greek character and stayed intact as an entity even after the other parts of Alexander's empire were either retaken by the Persians or conquered by the Romans.

I believe that when Buddhism came to the Greco-Bactrian kingdom, that it engaged in a dialogue with Greek philosophy and theology, with the Greek mystery religions, and that the Mahayana esoteric Buddhism was produced as a result of these interactions.

Why I think that Mahayana Buddhism, which is more esoteric, was influenced by Greek philosophy is that the concept of a Buddha world centered on a particular Buddha, which is a feature, is very similar to the idea of the Sabbat, the Divine Mind, with the Demiurge at the center. These Buddha worlds are arranged in the form of a mandala, with the prime Buddha at the center and smaller other entities surrounding him, and this structure resembles the cells or conclaves of the Sabbat. Typically, the Buddha at the center of the Buddha world is the person that the practitioner has a personal devotion to.

Of the Mahayana practices that use these Mandalas and Buddha worlds, the one which I'm familiar with which is closest to the Sabbat is that of Mahavairocana, a form of Vairocana, who is the prime Buddha in Shingon Buddhism in Japan, as well as Tendai and Tien-Tai esoteric Buddhism. In this, Mahavairocana is the same as

Baphomet, Demiurgos, and the world that he inhabits is the same as the First Sun, the Sabbat, the Divine Mind. This place is referred to as the "Diamond Realm", and is shared by Vairocana with four other Buddhas. Together, they make up the "Five Tathagatas". These other four Buddhas are associated with the four directions, and the four elements, with Vairocana being the fifth in the center. Through this, these figures can be equated with the different points of the circle.

Other Buddhist denominations that are similar to this in concept include Pure Land Buddhism, with Amitabha being parallel to the Demiurge, and the Pure Land itself being the Sabbat, the Divine Mind. Through this, the devotees of Mahavairocana and Amitabha are unconsciously venerating our own figures as well, and share in the primal vision. The craft also has entities like Boddisatvas, in the form of people who have ascended to the Sabbat and escaped from the domination of the Evil One, who become saints of a kind, who can direct people still in the world.

The "Diamond Realm" can be identified with the 'Aql of Ismaili thought, the Divine Mind, and, within Alevi Shi'ite thought the "Diamond Realm" can be identified with Muhammad as the pre-existent reality, the Divine Mind itself. Following on this, Ali as the active intelligence within or with respect to Muhammad, from Alevi and Bektashi thought, can also be thought of as being Vairocana. We can also parallel the Nusayri conception of Ali with Amitabha and Vairocana, as well as with the Manichean Father of Greatness, and Ormuzd. Incidentally, we can also identify the unmanifest God in the Nusayri gnosis and the "Haqq" or truth in Bektashi gnosis, and Allah as the generator of the 'Aql in Ismaili gnosis with the Great Dragon Lord as the Neoplatonic One.

Part Two
The 19th Century

Chapter 8
The Megalithic Civilization

The standing stones of Europe, including Stonehenge, and various earthworks such as Avebury and Newgrange, have attracted an enormous amount of attention from esotericists. Today, we have much more reliable data on who exactly built these monuments, but before presenting that, let's look at the significance that was given to these objects by esotericists. Beyond equating their construction with the Celtic Druids, which was proven to be false in the 19th century, they were also equated with the works of a lost civilization. Particularly, that of the Ante-Diluvian civilization before the Flood. I believe that this is why Olaus Magnus, in his "History of the Northern Peoples" spends so much time documenting megaliths. The connection between the Ante-Diluvians and these monuments was encouraged by stories of the pillar of Hermes, or of Enoch. Supposedly, knowing that the flood was going to happen, this figure engraved essential esoteric knowledge on a pillar so that it wouldn't be lost. This pillar was equated with the standing stones or megaliths. What the contents of the pillar were thought to be varied, but one explanation was that it contained the "Emerald Tablet" of Hermes, which contains the famous formula "As above, so below", in explaining the way of alchemical transformation and divine ascent. There were other variants on this story as well, such as that two pillars were constructed and inscribed with this information, one made of bricks and one made of brass, and that in the flood it was the brick pillar that fell but the brass pillar that survived. These pillars are also the famous "Pillars of Tubal-Cain" examined in the book of the same name by Michael Howard and Nigel Jackson.

This idea of the megaliths, and knowledge inscribed on them, being from Ante-Diluvian times was seized on and integrated into Freemasonry. During the time when the stones were identified with the Druids, it was a reason for people to pursue research into them.

As outlined in "The Magitians Discovered" volume 1, the Druids were also given a clean pedigree by Annius of Viterbo, who identified them with having the good secret knowledge of Ante-Diluvian times that Noah had preserved. Annius hymned the Celtic Druids and their orders as preserving an primitive doctrine of monotheism and as being proto-Christian, and this provided more justification for esotericists to pursue researching them. Annius' approach in this was taken up by generations of Druidic researchers, who only gradually moved from the idea of Druids being crypto-Christians or monotheists to an acceptance and approval of their pagan ideas. The stones had a mixture of the positive, the good knowledge of the Druids, and the negative, the bad knowledge of the giants destroyed by the flood, associated with them.

There were legends, as well, such as that repeated by Geoffrey of Monmouth, and reproduced in "Magitians Discovered" volume 3, about evil giants having been in Britain before the virtuous Druids appeared. These giants were associated with Gog-Magog, and with a group of women who, supposedly fleeing Greece, came to Britain, copulated with bad angels, and produced these giants. This happened before, in Geoffrey's legendary history, Greeks in the form of Brutus of Troy, landed on the island, defeated the giants, and started Britain proper. The Druids in this would be descended from this later group that defeated the evil giants of the first civilization of Britain. This was derived from a common practice of the time of fabricating legendary histories for nations and royal families using epic poems such as the Aeneid of Virgil, which is where Brutus is drawn from. The evil giants, in this, too, were candidates for the construction of the megaliths. Both of these, the Druidic attribution, and that of the evil giants, would have great consequences for traditional witchcraft.

Olaus Magnus, who subscribed to the beliefs of Annius of Viterbo regarding esoteric knowledge transmitted by the sons of Noah, also incorporated an engraved stone containing knowledge into his "History of the Northern Peoples". This, though, wasn't the direct product of the Ante-Diluvian knowledge but was supposed to be the secret good knowledge transmitted by the sons of Noah, thought to be giants, down through their direct family. Some of these were thought by him to have founded a kingdom in the far north that corresponded to Hyperborea, from which the Swedish and Danish nations supposedly derived. For Magnus, the civilizing patriarch of the north was "Starchaterus", and the inscribed stone was the "Verses of Starchaterus" which he reproduced in his history, and which is contained in "Magitians Discovered" volume 3. These verses, in my opinion, are underwhelming, in that they're exhortations to virtue such as the importance of having a good diet, but the underlying concept remains. For Annius of Viterbo, the knowledge from Noah and his sons was the good aspect of the Ante-Diluvian knowledge, as opposed to the corrupt aspect which the giants who were destroyed by the Flood pursued.

However, before examining that, let's return to the megaliths themselves. Their creators were mysterious, especially after it was disproved that the Celts were responsible. With the Celts uncomfortably removed from the picture, authors flailed around to figure out who could be responsible, and if those responsible still existed. This lead to the manufacture of the idea that the fairies were actually remnants of the megalithic peoples, who were thought to be smaller and darker. Through colonialism, the British and others had discovered the existence of "Negrito" peoples in places like the Philippines, the Andaman Isles, as well as the presence of people who looked like they were African in Papua New Guinea and related islands. These were thought, accurately it turns out, to be descended from earlier waves of people to those places that were then over run by later migrants. This situation was taken by writers and applied to Britain and elsewhere, with Evans-Wentz in his "Fairy Faith in Celtic Countries" being a prime promulgator of it. There, the fairies were thought to be these people. This idea was also taken up by Pennethorne Hughes in his "Witchraft", where he identified witches with fairies and these with a relict population derived from the megalithic civilization, which still retained this civilization's knowledge and mysteries.

We know quite a bit about who exactly made the megaliths now, and the story does in fact intersect with the craft, in unexpected ways. For this part, I'm relying on the work of popular geneticist Razib Khan, a Bangladeshi-American writer raised in Oregon, who has done quite a lot of work to take knowledge of archeo-genetics that are buried in papers and bring them to a wider audience. Khan is not a racist in any way, shape, or form, and his work is not tainted by any kind of political agenda. Though his work has not currently appeared in book form, it's a virtual certainty that it will. As it stands, it's available through his online Substack, "Razib Khan's Unsupervised Learning".

According to Khan, the megalithic civilization was associated with the expansion of a group known as Early European Farmers out of Turkey. These farmers were pre-Indo-European. They expanded first to Greece, then the Balkan Peninsula, and to Italy, eventually reaching all of western Europe, including Ireland, Scandinavia, and Great Britain. They were the progenitors of the Etruscan Civilization in Italy, the Nuragic civilization of Sardinia, and were the ancestors of the Basques. They were present in Sicily as well, though they were subsequently displaced by many other civilizations. They were also one of the foundations of Greek civilization, and also of Roman civilization through the Etruscans.

Khan describes the population of ancient Greece as descended from three populations: these Early European Farmers, another group that came from pre-Indo-European Armenia and Eastern Turkey, and the Indo-Europeans. The Early European Farmers and the less known group from Turkey and Armenia combined and formed the basis for what's known as the Minoan Civilization, typified by the ancient palaces that were found on the island of Crete. This was succeeded by the Mycenean Civilization, which was an ethnically Indo-European group that had adopted the culture of the Minoans. Khan points out that the pre-Indo-European civilizations in Greece apparently resisted the invasions of the Indo-Europeans for quite a bit longer than the parallel cultures outside of Greece. This may be one of the reasons that Greek culture, in general, featured a mistrust of "Barbarian" outsiders. Italy also potentially shared a similar trajectory, with the Etruscans whose culture Rome was based on being members of the Early European Farmer group.

The Myceneans were the height of bronze age Greek culture, and they fell during what is generally known as the "Bronze Age Collapse". This happened around 1200 BC. The "Bronze Age Collapse" ushered in the Greek Dark Ages, and was most likely not directly related to the Indo-European invasions, but instead was due to piracy by various peoples in the Mediterranean. Out of the Greek Dark Ages emerged Athens and classical Greek culture.

The collapse of the Early European Farmer megalithic civilizations in various place was caused by Indo-European invasions, with the Indo-Europeans destroying the megalithic civilization and, alternately, adopting some of their agricultural practices. The Pelasgian culture of Greece, which was identified in later esoteric tradition with the Ante-Diluvians, was related to the Minoans and Myceneans, as were the Cabiri, who took on a very outsized significance in later work. This work includes traditional witchcraft where the Cabiric gods, as Ante-Diluvian figures, were directly incorporated into the work, identified with already existing principles. Among other attributions, Axieros, the Androgyne first Cabiric God, was identified with Baphomet, while his children Axiokersos and Axiokersa being identified with the subsequent division of the androgyne into male and female, signifying forms of the God and Goddess. This is briefly described by Paul Huson in his "The Devil's Picture Book", a book ostensibly about the Tarot but that actually also treats traditional witchcraft ideas within that context.

To come back to the megalithic culture, it can be argued that Greek mystery religions were partially derived from the culture of the Early European Farmer/Armenians of Eastern Turkey, and partially derived from Indo-European culture, both of which were present in the culture of the Myceneans. This general cultural mix in Greece would also have resembled that of the Etruscans, the culture which the Indo-European Latins who built Rome adopted as their own. These mysteries, I'm confident, are also ones that are at the heart of the craft, that are associated with the "Primal Vision". The Bull of the mysteries is the Sabbat itself, and the Serpent or Dragon is the One. Folk memories of these mysteries persist in the lore not only of the Basques, but in that of the Sardinians. These people are the lineal descendants of the Early European Farmers, of the megalithic civilization, as has been proved by genetic investigation. The Sardinian people created large stone forts, called "Nuraghe", which dominated the island, and which are representative of what was called "Cyclopean" architecture in the Mediterranean, thought to be constructed by the Giants in ancient times. Traces of the Sabbat can be found in Sardinian folklore, for instance in references in the book "Ashes", by Sardinian author Grazia Deledda, which portrays the sky as opening up on Saint John's Day, the Summer Solstice, and revealing a vision of Paradise as it exists in heaven.

The Early European Farmer lineage is still present within the peoples of southern Europe, with Greeks, southern Italians, Sicilians, and Spaniards in particular still having a significant amount of their genetic ancestry from these people. The Basque people also preserve a significant amount of this ancestry, and this may very well be why Basque mythology is very congruent with witchcraft beliefs: the same mysteries that fuel the craft were believed in by their ancestors as well. Basque witchcraft itself, in things like the Aquelarre or Akelarre, might reflect the beliefs of the megalithic civilization. As for the rest of Europe, the percentage declines as one goes north. With regards to the British Isles, there isn't much genetic continuity at all. A possible exception to this might be in Ireland, where in the very south of Ireland, the south of County Cork, descendants might still exist as the "Black Irish". Despite being derided as not real by authorities on the internet the "Black Irish" is a real thing, with a number of people in the United States with a documented genealogy of being purely Irish nevertheless having a mediterranean appearance. In this, the "Black Irish" would be descendants of the Fomorians, the people who the Celtic Irish defeated in settling the island., who were the Early European Farmers and the megalithic peoples. People have said that the Black Irish originate from Spain, and that may, in distant memory, be the case.

Additionally, research has poked holes in the idea that the Picts of Scotland were representatives of the megalithic civilization. Current research points to the idea that the Picts were northern Brythonic Celts, that is to say counterparts of the Britons, who became the Welsh and Cornish in the wake of the Anglo-Saxon invasions. The current Scots, who are descended from Irish peoples that invaded Scotland via the Highlands, would then have displaced a fellow Celtic language speaking group, and not defeated representatives of the megalithic civilization.

Nonetheless, though it's vaguely possible that megalithic knowledge and mysteries were passed on in part to the Celts, or influenced Druidic belief, there's no direct path there. Also, it's theoretically possible that bloodlines related to the priests and priestesses of the megalithic peoples somehow continued into their successors, but again, this is speculation.

To find the actual source of the mysteries of these people, one has to look back to Rome, Greece, and the mediterranean mystery religions. Basque mythology and witchcraft have been profitably studied, but the Sardinian myths and practices represent new ground to till and to research with regards to this issue.

With regards to the Flood, and to Atlantis, first, it's possible that the legends of the Flood were derived from an actual event. For example, the idea that has been floated recently in popular culture that relates the flood stories to memories of the end of the Ice Age, seems to be likely. However, if that's what the legend of the Flood came from, then the megalithic civilization developed far after it. Nonetheless, the later observations of the existence of a series of civilizations that had advanced agriculture and stonework that were no longer around may have fed into already existing Flood legends, informing the understanding of what existed before the Flood, in Ante-Diluvian times.

As for the historical Atlantis, which is often linked to the idea of a Flood, the city is said by Plato to have existed much later, in Athenian times. This is a fact that many Atlantis commentators forget, namely that Plato asserted that early Athenian civilization fought with the Atlanteans, who were trying to take over the whole of the Mediterranean. Historically, the civilization that Plato was talking about may have been based on that of Tartessos, located in southern Spain in the area of Andalucia around Seville and the Gaudalquivir river.

The Draconic Tradition Relating to the Megaliths.

Again, this is not something that I'm presenting as literally true, but as a tradition that grew up in the 17th through the 19th centuries. This tradition has, as one of its components, information from far beyond Europe. During exploration and colonization, Europeans came in contact with civilizations in Southeast Asia which venerated serpents. Not only that, some of the peoples in these places claimed to be descendants of serpent people, with the royal families of these countries specifically claiming to be descendants of them. Currently, the royal family of Thailand claims descent from a Naga or serpent being, for example. The Naga people of northeast India are another example of this. Unfortunately, these Naga people have since been converted to Baptist Christianity by missionaries. Not only did the Nagas believe that they were serpent people, but the dragon in particular was found by explorers to be generally venerated in Asia, for instance in China and Japan, in ways that were not found in Europe. Except in Wales, dragons in European tradition were usually looked on as bad creatures that needed to be destroyed.

Southeast Asia also featured both amazing, deserted, temples such as Angkor Wat, and megalithic constructions. Though the temples are better known, megalithic monuments are present in Laos, in the "Plain of Jars" as well as in Indonesia, where they exist in forms reminiscent of European megaliths. These standing stones are found as far east as Polynesia, for example on the island of Vanuatu, where new construction of megaliths continued into the 20th century. The megalithic tradition of Vanuatu, documented in the book "Stone Men of Malekula", featured several different rounds of initiatory sacrifices to the stones over long periods of time before a new stone could be considered to be completely put in place. Indonesia also featured an enormous amount of semi-ruined temples constructed according to esoteric principles.

European explorers and colonizers put these two facts together, and came up with a synthesis: there was a dragon civilization which built both the megaliths and the abandoned temples. The temples came from the megaliths as a continuation of that civilization. Not only that, but this draconic civilization was the same as that which existed before the Flood. In this, the Naga people, people of the serpent race, were considered to be the descendants of the Nephilim, the giants born from the mating of the children of Cain with the Watcher angels who had descended to earth. The story of the Flood was being increasingly questioned during the period of the 17th-19th century. One of the variant stories that was used to explain how archeology was discovering things that conflicted with the traditional story was that the Flood recorded in the Bible was only a local phenomenon. In this telling, it would have been possible for the Flood to have extinguished the Watcher civilization in Europe, but to have left it intact elsewhere in the world.

This logic was then applied to the standing stones of Europe. They, too, were said to be Cyclopean constructions by people from before the Flood, constructed by the Watcher civilization of the serpent bloodline. Geoffrey of Monmouth's story about the original inhabitants of Britain being giants that were descended from Greek witches mating with demons, in this, could be interpreted as really referring to a much earlier time period, the period before the Flood. Alternately, it could refer to a survival of Watcher angels in Britain, who were not destroyed by the Flood which affected the rest of Europe. The megaliths, Stonehenge and others, could then be interpreted as being constructed by the race of Cain, the serpent race. Witchcraft, in this, could be considered to be a continuation of this antediluvian serpent wisdom from the Watchers that was the fruit of the megalithic civilization.

Beyond this, the stone circles of Europe, in particular, were paralleled to these Indian and Southeast Asian temples. Because they were arranged to correspond to equinoxes and solstices, these antiquaries imposed a zodiacal schema on them, on their construction, and significance, with the stone circles of Europe resembling the zodiac and the cycle of the year.

Druids were also associated with Serpent worship, but, it should be noted that if they were associated with the Watcher civilization , that this would conflict heavily with the notion that they were innocent people practicing a kind of proto-Christianity bequeathed to them by the Prisca Theologia.

It's important to note that this line of thought was heavily discussed in fringe Masonic circles and in popular archeology in 19th century France. In fact, as we shall demonstrate in volume 2, the rite of Memphis in particular incorporated a great deal of this lore into its degrees. This was part of a larger rehabilitation of Cain within the traditions of Memphis and Mizraim which presented Cain's line as the good guys, and which endorsed aspects of the inverse tradition. In these French circles, the Antediluvians were also connected with the Cabiri.

Works Cited

Deledda, Grazia "Ashes", John Lane, London, 1908, Google Books

Evans-Wentz, W.Y, "Fairy Faith in Celtic Countries", Citadel Press, New York, 1994

Howard, Michael "Pillars of Tubal-Cain" and Nigel Jackson, Capall-Bann, Milverton 2003

Hughes, Pennethorne "Witchcraft", Penguin Books, London 1965

Huson, Paul "The Devil's Picture Book", iUniverse, 2003

Khan, Razib, http://www.razibkhan.com

"Razib Khan: Anatolia over 10,000 years", https://www.razibkhan.com/p/anatolia-over-10000-years

"Ararat's long shadow: Asia Minor's major impact on humanity", https://www.razibkhan.com/p/ararats-long-shadow-asia-minors-major

"Hittite Words, Byzantine Walls: what the West as we know it owes Anatolia's empires"
https://www.razibkhan.com/p/hittite-words-byzantine-walls-what

Layard, John "Stone men of Malekula", Chatto and Windus, London, 1942

Madziarczyk, John, "The Magitians Discovered" vol 1, Topaz House Publications, Seattle, 2016

Madziarczyk, John, ed. "Magitians Discovered" volume 3, Topaz, Seattle, 2016

Chapter 9
The Cabiri

Now, there are two main traditions regarding the Cabiri in 19th century British intellectual life, one which dominated the early 19th century in the UK and one that came to prominence in the late 19th century. The first strand was connected with George Stanley Faber, while the second was connected with the works of the French phallicists and astrotheists, most prominently represented by Charles François Dupuis and Constantin François Volney. Both of these traditions influenced pre-Gardnerian witchcraft. A third influence, not really constituting a school unto himself but very important, is François Lenormant, whose writings on the Cabiri combined French Astrotheism with more traditional symbolism regarding the Old Testament, the Ante-Diluvian realm, and the Watchers. All of these will be examined.

So who were these Cabiri and why did people think they were important? The Cabiri were pre-Greek gods from the isle of Samothrace in the Aegean sea. They were associated with smith work and with ecstatic rites. The Cabiri themselves were testified to in a number of fragmentary forms. In the most common division were arranged in the following way: Axieros, a bisexual god, gave birth to Axiokersos and Axiokersa, a male and a female god, and this was complemented by Casmillos or Cadmus, who is sometimes equated with Hermes. Beyond this, there are a number of variants, including one where the father of the Cabiri is a god named Sydyk and the Cabiri are seven in number, this being derived from the history of the Phoenician writer Sanchoniathon.

The Cabiri were looked to almost solely because they were labeled as the oldest gods by the Greeks. The vast majority of work in the 19th century which incorporates them into various schemas has little to do, or to say, about their actual mythology. Instead, they're fitted into one or another formalistic system, and used for whatever purpose the author has in mind.

The only main exception to this was the writings of the German Idealist philosopher F.W.J. Schelling, who fully engaged with the mythic meaning of the Cabiri in his essay, "Über die Gottheiten von Samothrake", or, "On the Divinities of Samothrace", which has recently been translated into English. Unfortunately, Schelling's work was also the least influential on the English speaking world. Godfrey Higgins indirectly cites it in a long passage in "The Celtic Druids", which summarizes a work by the French scholar Adolphe Pictet, titled,"Du Culte des Cabiris chez les Anciens Irlandais", which is largely based on Schelling's ideas. It also very vaguely and indirectly influenced parts of Gerald Massey's work through the untranslated french writings of François Lenormant, but in general its impact was nil. Strangely, Lenormant's direct writing on the Cabiri owes little to Schelling's schema. Instead, Schelling's ideas show up in his account of the Eleusinian and Egyptian mysteries, which is what Massey draws on. We will examine Schelling's schema in relation to Massey's use of Lenormant's writings on these subjects.

The interest in the Cabiri in the UK was initially produced by the reverend George Stanley Faber, who first produced an immense two volume work called the "Dissertation on the Mysteries of the Cabiri", and then later produced a three volume work titled "The Origin of Pagan Idolatry". Faber's account of the Cabiri has little to do with the historical Cabiri. Instead, it has to do with a putative belief system that sprang up after the Flood. Faber took the attribution of the Cabiri as the oldest of the gods and mixed it in with his story. Theoretically, any number of groups of gods could have been substituted by Faber for the Cabiri.

Faber's writings were influenced heavily by the ideas of Annius of Viterbo, though this was most likely through intermediaries, as well as by a contemporary who we haven't looked at, Bishop William Warburton. To fully explain Faber, we need to look first at Annius of Viterbo, and his rehabilitation of the Druids, then at Warburton. Annius arguably set the stage for the entire Neo-Druidic movement through this rehabilitation, and so his significance, while including Faber, goes far beyond him.

Druids and Cabiroi.

Annius of Viterbo made a name for himself in the mid-15th century by claiming to have discovered otherwise unknown writings by the Chaldean historian Berossus. Berossus was a real figure, and a number of short writings by him exist, preserved in Greek texts.

Annius' Berossus claimed to have written a history of the peopling of Europe after the Flood, and fittingly it was claimed that the texts were discovered in a monastery in Armenia, whose Mt. Ararat is supposed to be the resting place of Noah's Ark. The writings were forged in manuscript form. The story that this Berossus told was quite incredible, both literally and figuratively. What follows is a summary of his beliefs. For a more detailed account, interested readers can consult "Magitians Discovered" vol. 1, where Annius of Viterbo is discussed in more depth.

What Annius of Viterbo did was to take the Gods of Greece, Rome, and Egypt, turn them into heroes who were posthumously remembered as Gods, and to then associate these heroes with particular descendants of Noah. The belief that some pagan Gods were really heroes who had been posthumously deified was common both in the Renaissance and the Middle Ages, and can be found all the way back in the classical world. In Annius' work, the descendants of Noah spread across Europe, founding kingdoms, leaving, then coming back to restore those kingdoms after they'd degenerated, with their own descendants doing the same. Since people were thought to be very long lived during that time, the same heroes often traveled around Europe multiple times. Annius' Berossus focused much of his attention on Italy, Spain, and France, outlining the fictitious peopling of all of these by heroes bearing Greek, and sometimes Egyptian, names. For instance, Osiris shows up in Annius' history as a righteous son of Ham, and plays a positive role in restoring civilization to groups of people who have inevitably fallen away from their initial social state. This initial state of society in Annius' thought is one governed by the Ancient Theology, the Prisca Theologia, which was understood as the knowledge that Noah bequeathed to his descendants.

This knowledge was very important, and made Annius' Berossus something other than just another reputed historian. Annius' Berossus shows the descendants of Noah as having access to all of this knowledge, which included agriculture, astrology and astronomy, other arts, and true religion, and Annius explicitly links this transmission of the ancient theology with later pagan beliefs. The religious part of these beliefs was thought to be a kind of proto-Christianity that was based on monotheism. The beliefs of some of the pagans, in Annius' account, were really degenerated forms of the Ancient Theology. Because of this, some overtly pagan beliefs really were not anti-Christian, and instead contained a kernel of truth.

Annius argues this not in relation to any sort of Greco-Roman or Hellenistic paganism, but in relation to the beliefs of the Druids in France, and possibly the pagans in Spain. Now, a part of Annius' point in forging these documents, as far as can be determined, was to give the courts of France and Spain a heroic history, which eager court historians could incorporate into their pseudo-histories of their royal families. Such a thing had been going on for a long time, though mostly it was Aeneas and his crew from Virgil's "Aeneid", traveling westward after the fall of Troy who were the progenitors, as can be seen in Geoffrey of Monmouth's "History of the Kings of Britain". Annius added to that by providing a Biblical lineage to the royal families of these countries, which was more prestigious. He topped it off by stating that these countries, particularly France, were not primitive, uncivilized, states at the time the Romans conquered them, but were sophisticated societies that lived by a descendant of the ancient theology, though it was badly mutilated and corrupted.

Outlining this link between the ancient theology and the ancient Gauls, Annius spends link a lot of time describing the supposed founding, and recivilizing, of France. In this, it turns out that the Druids and their related order, the Bards, played a key role. The Druids were keepers of this theology and knowledge, albeit in a degraded form. The following is from a summary of Annius' works titled "The Travels of Noe" by Richard Lynch:

"Unto the kingdom of France after Sarron, came Drijus, Sarrons eldest son, unto whom Berosus ascribeth this title: Apud Celtas Drijus peritiae plenus. he began to raigne foure hundred and tenne years after the general deluge, which was about two hundred five &

fiftie years after the first foundation and inhabitation of the kingdom of France. he was deeply seene in principles of Philosophie, & very skilfull in many other sciences. [...] and that of his name came the sect of Philosophers, which were called Druydes, which were wondrous learned Divines, Augurers, Magicians, and Sacrificers: but such their oblations and sacrifices in these their days of blindnesse, were performed with such inhumane and ungodly fashions, with the effusion and shedding of human bloud in that lamentable and cruell manner, as is too strange to be reported"

"After the death of this king Drijus, his son (called Bardus) raigned in his place, & was the fift king of France. This Bardus was the first deviser and inventor of rimes, songs, and Musicke, of whome the Poets and Rhethoricians first tooke their sect, which were called also Bardes,"

This opportunity for a newly invigorated patriotic history did not go unnoticed in France, and neither did the claims of Druids for possession of the ancient theology. Guy le Fevre de la Boderie, a disciple of the mystic and orientalist Guillaume Postel, and a mystic himself, drew on Annius for his epic poem cycle "La Galliade", which was intended as a celebration of French history. In this poem, the Druids are placed in a very prominent position, following Annius of Viterbo's accounts of them. Guy le Fevre , on top of being an orientalist, was also a translator of numerous works by Marsilio Ficino into French. Interestingly enough, D.P. Walker, in his "Spiritual and Demonic Magic from Ficino to Campanella" says that le Fevre adopted this belief about the Druids in order to counter what he saw as pagan influences from French poets of his time. The reasoning was that the Druids weren't really pagan, but bearers of the ancient tradition, and therefore their heritage was more orthodox than the myths of the pagan Greco-Roman world.

Later, this reasoning would be noticed by antiquarians who wanted to be sympathetic to Druidic beliefs in Great Britain. William Stukely and others, from the 17th century onwards, were influenced by Annius' vision of Druids as crypto-Christians. If people in the 17th century thought that the Druids were really secret Christians who preserved knowledge from Noah in their traditions, as Annius of Viterbo argued, might it not have been permissible to seek out present practitioners of magic, thought to be descendants of the Druids, to see if they preserved some of this knowledge in their work and beliefs? In fact, if they did possess such knowledge, it might not only be permissible, but very necessary to do so. Not only that, but might not the people accused of being witches actually be people practicing this secret knowledge? I believe that considerations like these are why people sympathetic to the Druids from this perspective sought out, and contacted, both magical practitioners and witches. I believe that this contact had at least two phases, the first in the 17th century when these ideas first surfaced and then in the 19th century, when Neo-Druidism had a revival. The Druids in the 19th century revival were regularly said to possess the knowledge of Pythagoras as well, and in the 17th century they were also thought to have preserved knowledge of the mediterranean mystery religions through the supposed influence of the Phoenicians in Cornwall.

This latter comes from the book "Phaleg", or "Geographica Sacra, Phaleg et Canaan", by Samuel Borchart, which, unfortunately, has not been translated into English, but which exerted a large influence on British intellectuals. There, the Phoenicians were related to the pre-Germanic British through their influence on the tin trade. Tin was mined in Cornwall, and so a Phoenician-Cornwall-Druidic influence was somehow detected. Dubious linguistic associations also linked Semitic languages to Cornish and Welsh, to putatively show a connection. Here, the worship of Baal and others was thought to have been transferred to the Celtic lands of Great Britain.

I very strongly believe that academics did find witches and cunning men in the Celtic and English countryside, in Wales and Cornwall and in England itself, and, seeing their beliefs, interpreted them as being just these survivals. This mythology was then added to the originally existing craft mythology, which came from other sources. Here, we see an example of the high, educated culture and people who are aware of academic discourse that's not only literate but in Latin, and the low, people practicing craft traditions from a more humble background, with knowledge potentially percolating from one to the other.

Very importantly, not only were standing stones linked to Druids, and Druids linked to a pristine, ancient, theology, but in the early 19th century there actually came into being a Druid Masonry that built on both of these foundations, combining them with traditional Masonic themes. This would contribute, in my opinion, to a third combination of the craft and an outside, more elite, academic source—that between the Craft of the Wise and Freemasonry. We will treat of this in much more detail in volume 2 of this work. Also important, however, is that though the Druids and related peoples were thought to be virtuous pagans, this was not the only way to respond to these Ante-Diluvian ideas. It would also be possible for people to be interested in the darker side of these ideas and people, like the witches who were portrayed in the myth of Goemagog by Geoffrey of Monmouth, and to specifically try to make contact with them in order to learn this illicit Ante-Diluvian wisdom as well.

George Stanley Faber

To continue with Faber's influences, let's look at Bishop Warburton's "Divine Legation of Moses". This work, and its influence, have been examined to great effect in "Solomon's Secret Arts" by Paul Kléber Monod, an essential work on the history of the occult in the Enlightenment. Warburton's central idea was that all of polytheism was essentially a pious lie created by priests for teaching virtue, as well as natural science, and that the true beliefs of the priests were monotheistic. This monotheism was supposedly kept from the masses because they were considered incapable of behaving decently without the tales of the gods to keep them in order. Monotheism was only for the elite. Only those who became initiates of the mysteries had the truth about monotheism revealed to them. Polytheism, in his construction, was a civic religion, one that kept society together, and that promoted virtuous behavior, rather than an actual description of religious reality.

However, Warburton did something very interesting in order to try to prove his point: he tried to actually understand the myths from a more profound perspective than had previously been the case, before explaining them away. Before debunking them as being just tales which were conducive to virtue, Warburton examined them in ways that actually brought quite a lot of logic to them, and that in the course of analysis brought many facts about polytheistic religious thought forward. His work, then, like the "Discover of

Witchcraft" of Reginald Scot, could unknowingly serve a dual purpose—on the one hand, there was his stated thesis, on the other, in the process of trying to prove that thesis Warburton collected an immense amount of mythological and pagan material that would be useful for those interested who were actually sympathetic to polytheism.

For instance, as far as I know, the first printed source in English of the phrase "Hekas Hekas, Este Babeloi", the phrase of banishing that's still used in some traditional witchcraft circles, and is used in the Golden Dawn tradition, is in Warburton's "Divine Legation". This reference to "Hekas" precedes the Golden Dawn's use of it by many decades. It first appears in a section that focuses on Virgil's "Aeneid", and looks at the descent into the underworld that Aeneas undergoes as representing an ancient schema of initiation. Here, "Hekas" is a Greek equivalent to the Latin "Procul Este Profani", and is asserted to have been used in the Eleusinian mysteries. Although it's unclear what source he used for it, the phrase and its connection to the mysteries of Virgil was an idea that had circulated in Latin works for quite a long time before him.

With regards to its ultimate origin, the 16th century Renaissance scholar Barnabe Brisson states on page 2 of book one of his work "De formulis et solennibus populi Romani verbis" that the phrase was created by fellow scholar George Fabricius through twisting the words of the second hymn to Apollo by Callimachus, probably in Fabricius' commentary on Virgil. The Latin works that this phrase appeared in would, no doubt, be ridiculously out of reach for regular people in the United Kingdom, but through Bishop Warburton's "Divine Legation", which went through many different editions, and other works that drew on it, "Hekas Hekas, Este Babeloi" and its significance became more available for the slightly less elite.

To get back to the point, Warburton, in examining polytheism while at least taking it partially seriously, made a compendium of logically arranged lore that would be very useful for people trying to reconstruct polytheism itself. He made it socially acceptable to look at polytheistic doctrine by suggesting that the pious lie underlay all of it.

Both of Faber's works are basically an update of the ideas of Annius of Viterbo, with Faber applying them to the Cabiri, and in his later work applying them more broadly. Annius had said that in many cases the gods of mythology were really memories of patriarchs who were sons, and grandsons, of Noah, who had traveled Europe civilizing people and instructing them in primitive monotheism and the mysteries of nature. For Faber, the Cabiri were in reality Noah and his sons, with other gods being memories of the Ark and other objects.

For Faber, Noah's flood wiped out all previous traditions and knowledge that the world possessed. After the flood, Noah put forward a pure doctrine of monotheism. How, then, did the various systems of polytheism evolve after this good beginning? Faber theorized that the memory of the Flood would be something that was so important that it would have entered into the mythology of all the world's peoples. This included memories of Noah, his sons, and their wives, as well as memories of the ark itself, the mountain that the ark came to rest on, the dove, the rainbow, the sun that revealed itself as the clouds parted, and more. For Faber, the memory of the Ark was the beginning of mythology itself, a historical tradition that was passed on side by side with the monotheistic doctrine of Noah. From there, Faber theorized that polytheism came from people mistaking the various figures associated with the Ark and with the Flood with gods, so that not only Noah became a god, but the Ark itself, and all other animate and inanimate figures associated with it became venerated as gods as well. The Cabiri, in this, are the earliest representation of Noah and these other figures as deities.

On this basis, Faber proceeded to look at every pantheon of gods and every mythology that he could get a hold of, and equate all of the gods in them with either Noah, the Ark, Noah's sons, etc. In a kind of proto-phallicist argument, Faber associated the ark with female genitalia, and from there made the deduction that many female gods were really memories of the ark. The Sun, really important as it signaled the end of the flood, was also associated with a male god, with Noah himself. Jacob Bryant also preceded Faber with an extensive "Arkite" compendium.

Faber's two works, "Dissertation on the Mysteries of the Cabiri" and "Origin of Pagan Idolatry", were composed differently. The "Dissertation" is really haphazardly constructed and reads like a manic or schizophrenic episode, where, in a mythomaniacal way, the different pantheons of the gods are all inevitably reduced to Noah and the other symbols in a kind of free association. "Origin of Pagan Idolatry" is much more methodically constructed and argued, and is actually the better of the two works.

I should clarify that, in this, the term mythomaniac isn't meant to imply that the writings of these people have no value. Many times they do. It's a "Mania" in that these works are often disorganized, and their conclusions about symbols, though perhaps having spiritual validity in some cases, are nonetheless completely ahistorical. "Mania", in this, can nevertheless be a transmitter of esoteric knowledge. Some of those who are mythomaniacs may also have been actual maniacs, such as Edward Vaughan Kennealy, who on top writing the mythomaniacal "Book of God, or Enoch the Second Messenger" appears to have been mentally ill, and to have used his position as a lawyer to prosecute his enemies based on his mental illness.

Now, reading through this, and similar examples of "Mythomania" from the 19th and late 18th centuries, a reader may be tempted to ask "What's the point?" After all, Faber isn't a pagan, and he's specifically trying to explain why paganism was based not on theological reality but on a confusion of figures like Noah, his sons, and the Ark itself, for things like the Sun and Moon. However, there's method in the madness, method which in the end is very useful for those interested in pursuing the mysteries from a purer angle.

Faber, in attempting to demonstrate that all of the ancient mysteries were really based on Euhemeristic readings of Noah, his sons, and the Ark, where people and objects were conflated with gods, collates, reproduces, and arranges an enormous amount of useful mythological material. Though this is in a more confused form in his "Dissertations on the Cabiri", in his "Origins of Pagan Idolatry" his interpretation of what pagan doctrine consisted of is much more clearly spelled out.

There, before reducing all pagan doctrine to different aspects of Noah, his children, and objects like the Ark, he comes up with a kind of ur-Paganism, which he detects to be behind all the different pagan doctrines of the world. This ur-paganism consists of a male sun god, a female moon and earth goddess, and a hermaphroditic god. The hermaphroditic god is considered by Faber to be a later innovation made by the combination of the sun god with the moon goddess. The sun god has a court of seven people around him, which consist of Noah's wife plus the three pairs of Shem, Japheth, and Ham and their respective wives, making four pairs in total. He then introduces a kind of naturalism into it, saying that the pagan mysteries were about the descent of the soul from the soul of the world, and the soul's reascent into it, and that they also dealt with the mysteries of generation, that is, of reproduction and fertility, and the procession of the seasons. However, this theme isn't as developed as in the Astrotheist interpretations, with Faber's Noachite symbolism instead predominating.

On top of this, as part of the symbols, he identifies a primal cosmic mountain in all of these myths as the place that the Ark stopped at, and identifies the place of the post-Diluvian Paradise as being on top of this mountain. This is derived from the idea that the initial society that Noah established after the Flood was a perfect one, and so was Paradisal. Therefore, the stories of the gods enjoying life in a Paradise like Olympus were to him stories about Noah and his family in the place where the Ark stopped after the Flood, on Mount Ararat. The Paradise at the top of the mountain is the symbolism of the Sabbat, though Faber did not recognize this.

Faber also presents the idea in "Origins" that the gods of the pagans were the souls of the wicked people who had died in the Flood, who had returned as "Demons". Connected to this, he put forward the idea that pagan religion was a combination of this worship of these deceptive "Demons" with a veneration of the natural world, including the planets, as deities, which Faber termed "Sabeanism". People who may have been inclined to look at the Ante-Diluvian giants as good people may have read this in a very different way than Faber intended.

This work is also significant in relation to traditional witchcraft in several other ways: first, Faber in his quest to reduce all mythology to Noah and company devoted a large section to Celtic myths, which unintentionally helped those who were trying to connect traditional witchcraft beliefs with Celtic folklore. Secondly, in the process of doing this he linked the Celtic gods with the Cabiri, as part of his pan-Pagan unified vision. The Cabiri, here, became the original model on which the Celtic gods were based. We can go further than this, though.

Faber, in his "Origin of Pagan Idolatry" makes correspondences between his purified pagan representation of the Cabiri and various figures from Welsh mythology, who he identifies with Druids. These figures are taken from the Welsh Neo-Druidic movement associated with Iolo Morganwg, as well as from Faber's own reading of Welsh texts. There, he talks about two prime gods, Hu and Ceridwen, as the Father and Mother gods, Noah and his wife. These would correspond to the East and the West of the circle. He also, as part of his general pagan mythology he identifies the Caer Sidi of Welsh mythology with the top of the generic world mountain, which is the place of the Sabbat, and identifies Ceridwen and her cauldron with this place, with the Ark being the Cauldron. King Arthur is also identified with Noah by Faber.

Faber's primary source for his Celtic correspondences appears to have been Edward Davies' "The Mythology and Rites of the British Druids". Davies, in turn, was an admirer of Faber. In the introduction to the chapter in "Mythology" about the "Rites of Hu Gadarn", Davies recounts how while he was writing his book he found Faber's "Cabiri" series and rewrote portions of the text to incorporate Faber's ideas into it. Davies accepted the forged Triads of Iolo Morganwg as real, and mixed this Neo-Druidry, along with his own researchers into Welsh tradition, with Faber's ideas in his book. Davies' work has an outsized importance in relation to both traditional witchcraft and mythomania, in that his ideas show up both in "The Pickingill Papers", albeit indirectly, as well as in the work of Gerald Massey.

Looking more generally at Davies' ideas about the Druidic gods, we have the following. Davies centers his account on the supposed mysteries of Hu and of Ceridwen. In all of this, we have a compounding of myth upon myth. Hu Gadarn is a fictional character who was mostly manufactured by Iolo Morganwg in forged documents. Davies' approach is reductive. He doesn't create a full polytheism, and instead takes all of the gods from classical antiquity, and from supposed Welsh history, and collapses them into Hu. He admits and justifies this in his chapter on the "Mysteries of Hu". His chapter on the "Mysteries of Hu" can be summarized as "All gods are Hu, and Hu is Noah". Nonetheless, within this reductionism some very valuable equations are made between Hu and different pagan deities.

Besides being Noah, Hu is a sun god, as well as a general father figure and hero. He is a plowman, who uses oxen or bulls to plow, and so may have come to be associated with Cain as the originator of agriculture. In Davies' thought, the oxen also pull the chariot of Hu, associating him with Apollo. Hu is also Bacchus and Dionysos, as well as Osiris, in this. He's also associated with the Bull, which further associates him with Apollo, as well as with the serpent or dragon, which in the form of the Python is Apollonian as well. The three oxen said to pull his chariot are associated with the three sons of Noah.

His chapter on Cerwiden and her mysteries is less reductive. Ceridwen, or Kêd, as they call her, is the complementary moon goddess, who stands for the Ark itself, who is also Ceres and Isis. She's associated with a cow, as opposed to a bull or an oxen. She is labeled as the keeper of the mysteries. The mysteries are likened to seeds, and the ark, and the cauldron, is labeled the container of these mysterious seeds, which Davies interprets as the literal seeds of crops saved by Noah from the Flood. The idea of the Cauldron of Ceridwen containing all of the seeds of things, though combined with Arkite ideas, nonetheless captures some of the Cauldron as the Sabbat that contains the Millions of Forms of Being. In the myth of Cerwidwen and Taliesin, Taliesin, now empowered by the Awen, can perceive all of the seeds or things within the Cauldron. His knowledge of all the arts and sciences, which he boasts about, is given through the contents of the Cauldron.

Davies actually gives some credit to the idea that there was some depth and meaning to the Welsh accounts he cites beyond the idea that "Cerwiden is the Ark". Particularly, his analysis of the first part of the "Hanes Taliesin", dealing with how Taliesin got the Awen of

Ceridwen, goes further than the rest. It presents an interesting picture of initiation into the "Druidic mysteries". As part of this, his account of practically using the cauldron of Ceridwen for creating a kind of Awen that's used for anointing, consumption, and consecrating the ground has parallels in Cochrane's traditional witch practices, as does the mention of five herbs within the cauldron that are used to make the Awen, though this is mentioned in Welsh poems as well.

Significantly, though, the herbs mentioned in Davies work are not the same that Cochrane used. In Cochrane's work, the cauldron is kindled outside of the circle, and the contents of the cauldron are used to make the circle, through pouring them into a circular moat. In the Preiddu Anwen, a sword is raised to the cauldron, and this is echoed in Robert Cochrane's rituals where daggers are put into the cauldron before being put into the ground. Davies also makes good use of Serpent's Eggs or Dragon's Eggs, also known as Druid's eggs, which the Pickingill papers also say much about.

Nonetheless, for a supposed Celtic expert, Davies is ignorant about the literature that he writes about. For instance, in his analysis of the "Chair of Ceridwen" poem, he apparently does not recognize that it contains summaries of different stories in the Mabinogion. Instead of interpreting these as fragments from other well known stories, his reading of the poem is linear, treating the different sections as if they formed one coherent whole whose meaning is to be found purely within the poem, without reference to anything outside of it. On to this, the "Arkite" meaning of Ceridwen is imposed.

Faber himself adapted Davies adaptation of his ideas into his "Origins of Pagan Idolatry" in unique ways. Though obsessively Arkite, Faber was in many ways more creative and insightful than Davies, and it shows. Particularly, in Volume 3, of "Origins", Faber goes over the "Mysteries of Taliesin", which combines Davies' ideas about the mysteries of Ceridwen with that of many other mystery traditions. Here, he states that the mysteries, including the Eleusinian and Mithraic mysteries, were based on a person going into a dark cave where they faced trials and incubated, as it were, in silence, learning lore. They then faced the greatest challenge, which was being shut into a small ship and set adrift, like in the Ark. With this, like much of Faber's other work, it's necessary to separate the wheat from the chaff.

Faber likens the cavern to both the womb of Ceridwen, the Cauldron of Ceridwen, and this to the Macrocosm, and to the primal egg which contained the macrocosm. The initiate who was put into it stands for the Demiurge within the world egg. They emerge and break the egg. While in the egg, they absorb all of the wisdom which the Cauldron, or the Macrocosm, contains. Additionally, Faber corresponds this voyage to the "Preiddu Annwn", and sees Arthur's voyage with his seven men through the different castles as being different stages of initiation within the Cauldron, cave, or womb of Ceridwen, which is assimilated to a castle, or Caer Sidi, which symbolically contains the other castles within it. The trials that they endure are said by Faber to be imitations of that which the person would endure after death in the Underworld, and so undergoing these trials during life, and defeating them, would allow a person to ascend to the heavens after death, and not to be stuck in the underworld.

The person being set adrift in the small boat is said by Faber to be accompanied by a high priest or high Druid who took on the role of Charon, the boatman in Greek mysteries and myths. He was the embodied character of death, who guided the candidate across the river Styx into the greater life. This gestation, with its trials and tasks, is also linked by Faber with the dismemberment, reunification, and resurrection of Osiris. Additionally, the freeing of the person from the small ship at the end of the mysteries was equated with Faber with the entrance of the individual into Paradise, in that he saw Paradise as being a memory of the pure civilization that existed on Mount Ararat immediately after the Ark had come to rest. This Paradise, as said, was on top of the world mountain, which was interpreted as being Mount Ararat. When the person completed the voyage they were said by Faber to be seen as participating in the nature of the Demiurge, rising from the world egg into a paradisal reality, which Faber interpreted as making them into a being like Noah.

Faber's ideas had an outsized influence in the UK, so much so that more conventional accounts of the Cabiri, based on better history, were overshadowed until his basic worldview was discredited. Biblical chronology, such as that which recognized the Flood as a real event, had been under attack for quite some time, but in the 19th century enough evidence had accumulated to tip the scales against it. In educated society, at least, though people weren't sure what the actual history of the world looked like, they became confident that the Bible wasn't telling the whole story. With that change, the basis of Faber's thought was undermined, and it became more of an embarrassment than anything else. Even people who had supported Faber's arguments in print turned against them. For instance, in the beginning of his career, the Masonic historian George Oliver had incorporated a huge number of Faber's arguments in his "The History of Initiation", which dealt with initiation in the pagan world. His later work "The Theocratic Philosophy of Freemasonry", which touched on some of the same material, which he now labeled as "Spurious Freemasonry", removed all of the references to Faber. What replaced Faber's account of the Cabiri, both in Oliver's book and in the greater thought of society at large, was the French tradition, which is most precisely represented by Dupuis and Volney.

The French Astrotheist and Phallicist Cabiri.

This tradition saw the Cabiri as one more of many different permutations of seven as well, but it located them in a radically different framework. Unlike Faber, the people who founded the phallicist and astrotheist schools of thought in France did not accept the biblical framework of history. Instead, these people were products of the radical Enlightenment who rejected the idea of biblical history entirely. Volney, for instance, in his "Ruins" tells the story of the evolution of civilization from a kind of state of nature which resembles Locke and Rousseau's account, with Adam and Eve nowhere to be found. Similarly, these writers had no emotional investment in preserving a transmission of a pristine proto-Christianity from Noah, and didn't believe in it. The god of Volney was the deistic "Nature's God", who set things in motion but then retired and let nature take its course. Volney talks about God animating the world, but otherwise not intervening, but accepts the idea that the sun influences things seasonally and that the moon influences the world through tides. Dupuis' ideas were more pagan, and less skeptical, as we shall see.

The difference between the point of view of the Astrotheists and Faber can be summarized like this: Faber looked at the deification of natural phenomenon in order to preserve the prestige of Biblical figures like Noah, as well as of things connected to the Biblical worldview, like the Ark, while the French writers would say that these Biblical figures themselves were personifications of natural phenomenon. This is literally true, as Dupuis strongly argues that figures like Jesus were personifications of nature. In this way, Faber and the Astrotheists have a precisely opposite worldview from each other.

Because the basic Enlightenment framework that these writers were working within became dominant in history and science, including in England, as the 19th century wore on their work came to be more accepted while Faber's ideas were discarded. Importantly as well, Volney was a Freemason, a reported member of the Lodge of the Neuf Soers, or Nine Sisters, in Paris. Their doctrines represented the radical fringe of thought during their time, particularly in post-Revolutionary France, and their ideas fed directly into the formation of the Masonic rites of Mizraim and Memphis. The same ideas would later be incorporated by John Yarker into his "Arcane Schools", which presents ideas from Memphis degrees in a somewhat sanitized and concealed form. Ideas from Memphis, and Yarker appear in traditional witchcraft, such as the Cabiri themselves in their Astrotheist form.

There are two phases, or differences in opinion, within these writers, which can be seen in the contrast of Volney with Dupuis. The first tendency is a radical rejection of religion, and the use of astrotheism and phallicism as a naturalistic explanation of how religion came to be, with the goal of showing that religion is fundamentally false. This position is best represented by Volney. The other phase takes the idea of the stars and the powers of generation being the origins of religion as a positive thing, and constructs a kind of neo-paganism based on it. This is most clearly represented by

Dupuis. This neo-paganism proceeds from the Enlightenment theories of "Nature's God", and goes into the deification of nature itself, and into the rehabilitation of the pagan mysteries based on this identification.

Notably, both of these figures write that Christianity itself is just one more manifestation of the same sun-cult, the same astrotheist schema that motivates everything else. This ends up cutting both ways as well. In the case of Volney, and people similar to him, astrotheism provides the final nail in the coffin of claims of Christianity to a transcendental truth. In the case of people more sympathetic to paganism, the opposite appears to have been the case: Christianity's supposed basis on solar symbolism allows similar pagan ideas to be sanctified. This, too was a feature of Memphis-Mizraim.

In fact, we can summarize Faber, Volney, and Dupuis as being representative of the 17th, 18th, and 19th centuries: Faber was desperate to rescue the Biblical worldview from modern criticism, corresponding more to the 17th century than to the 18th. Volney, in looking to find a naturalistic and atheistic explanation for religion in astrotheism, was exemplary of the 18th century. Dupuis, in his pantheistic astrotheism, was a harbinger of the 19th.

Dupuis is an interesting figure. His "Abridgement", which we're treating here, was published in 1797, and its original French edition is labeled as being published in "An VI de la République", year six of the Republic. This year was in the time of the Directory, which was the period of the French Revolution after that of the Terror and before that of Napoleon. Dupuis, as is fitting for someone who thought that Jesus was a fictional character, mixes his at times quite sensitive and insightful analysis of pagan imagery with heavy anti-Christian sentiments. Though this is present throughout the work, the later part of his chapter on the "Mysteries" is particularly virulent, but this also shows where he was coming from intelletually.

Though Dupuis denounces Robespierre and his cult of a supreme being in this work, nonetheless, his religious ideals, such as they are, have some similarities to these. He states that he sees paganism as having been superior to Christianity because it venerated nature and the natural processes of life. These natural processes of life, including reproduction, are linked in turn to social virtues and to the ideal of fraternity, of people existing in a kind of social brotherhood living life in harmony with nature and with each other. Christianity is cast by Dupuis as being anti-social, as having the ideal of the individualist monk and nun, as well as the celibate priest, for its goal. The ideas of heaven and hell, particularly of hell, and of many different types of sins, are denounced, with a kind of pantheistic appreciation of the nature of the universe, and an appreciation of the natural urges of mankind, put in their proper place, along with social cooperation. Dupuis treads a very careful path in this, at once displaying great understanding of pagan thought, venerating the universe as holy, but also stating that the supernatural is not real. Nonetheless, his successors were not so careful.

For Dupuis, within this pagan pantheism, the observation of the seven planets, the twelve signs of the zodiac, and the four seasons of nature lead to a kind of formalism, where every account of seven, of twelve, or of four, is equated to one of these. Many schemas of gods, including the Cabiri, who were attested to both in the form of seven and of four, are placed into these schemas and made equivalent to each other. Here, the Cabiri too are honored as being the oldest of the gods, but they still were looked on in a formulaic way which did not have much to do with their essential character. These correspondences were also incorporated into esoteric Masonry.

Now, in looking at Dupuis and his revived pagan system, it's important to point out what it does not contain. Specifically, his pantheistic leanings mean that his school of astrotheism did not identify any sort of transcendent realm from which the phenomenal world originated. The gods were personifications of occult, but natural, phenomenon, and though the world may be thought to be alive, there was nothing truly transcendental in this worldview. In fact, Dupuis explains heaven and hell by deriving them from summer and winter. This separates him out from thinkers like Gerald Massey, who, though drawing on him, importantly make a distinction between a transcendent realm and the realm of nature. Other thinkers associated with Memphis-Mizraim, such as John Yarker, make similar distinctions.

Because Dupuis' revived pantheistic paganism is essentially a kind of deification of nature, it's not religion in the sense that corresponds to the old paganisms, which went far beyond this in talking about the creation and maintenance of the world. A fundamental feature of these original paganisms, such as Greek and Roman, is that there's a transcendental world, called the Divine Mind, or Mount Olympus, a heaven where the gods exist, and then there's the material world, which this transcendent world can and does influence. The transcendental world is also the origin of the material world. Though Dupuis' ideas were not fully pagan, they opened the door for thinkers of the time to smuggle some of the more complete pagan ideas back in.

Within "The Origin of All Religious Worship", the first four chapters are a veritable hymn to pantheistic paganism. Dupuis' astrotheist analogies are somewhat strained in his comparison of Hercules to the Sun, and the comparison of the travels of Isis to the Moon, but his analysis of Nonnus' "The Dionysiacs", comparing Bacchus to the Sun, has much more merit, and is valuable.

Particularly, though, Dupuis works by equating the seasons and the circulation of the sun with the Egyptian mysteries, namely the drama of Osiris, and with the mysteries of the vine of Bacchus and Dionysos, with Zoroastrian myths, and with Christianity. The way that he integrates Zoroastrianism into the schema is representative of the whole: Dupuis sees the creation of the positive Amesh Spentas by Ormuzd and their negative counterparts by Ahriman, as signifying the division of the year into cold and warm months. There were six main Amesh Spentas and six counter creations in one version of the story, and he links each of these to one sign of the Zodiac, with six of the signs being those starting from the Autumnal equinox, going into winter, and ending with the Vernal equinox, and six of them going from this equinox, through summer, into the other equinox. Ahriman's creations in this rule the winter months and Ormuzd's the summer months. Dupuis relates the change of the seasons to conflicts between good and evil, and heroic battles, and sees the Zoroastrian story as a coded heroic account of the sun vanquishing the cold of winter.

These heroic battles include the story of Zeus confronting Typhon, which Dupuis analyzes in his account of the "Dionysiacs". The heroic overcoming of a dragon, or of another monster, is the heat of the sun overcoming the cold. The defeat of the monster is at the winter solstice, where light starts to get the upper hand against darkness. The descent into the underworld in many stories is also equated by Dupuis with the weakening of the sun in the winter. The idea of a death, descent into the underworld, and a rebirth is paralleled by him with the autumnal equinox, the winter, and the vernal equinox, where the rebirth occurs.

Christianity

Here, in adapting the Christian story to this, Dupuis, and Volney following him, links the Fall in the Garden of Eden to the autumnal equinox. This, the beginning of the dark half of the year, begins to be vanquished by the rebirth of the light at Christmas, the winter solstice. The completion of the redemption of the world, the triumph of the light over the darkness, is linked by him to Easter, to the Vernal Equinox, and to the Crucifixion. Following this, we can identify the restored state which will exist after the second coming with Summer, which would be the same as the state that Adam and Eve were in the Garden before the Fall.

Similarly, Jesus himself, in his death, harrowing of hell, and resurrection, followed the four part seasonal model, even though most of it transpired within a few days. The "Harrowing of Hell" is a tradition found in Catholicism and Orthodoxy, but which, apart from a few sects, has largely been forgotten by Protestants. Jesus descends from Heaven on the summer Solstice, is killed at the autumnal Equinox, descends into the underworld, defeats Satan in hell on the Winter Solstice, and then is resurrected on the Vernal Equinox. His return to heaven, the Ascension, completes the cycle at the Summer solstice once again.

Dupuis is perceptive, in that he identifies the Heavenly Jerusalem with the pagan heavens, such as that described in Plato, and also identifies the Holy City with a picture of the macrocosm. Heaven is derived by him from a picture of the visible universe, as is Hell, and, as such, the Heavenly City is a replica of the macrocosm. It's not thought to really exist. Instead, for Dupuis, people observed the macrocosm, the solar system, and then imagined that there was a place that contained the entire contents of the solar system in an abstracted form, from which the actual city was derived. Dupuis goes into great detail talking about how the Heavenly City corresponds to the wheel of the year, and to the stations of the sun within it, as we shall see.

The Trinity, in this, is the thing which actuates and controls this city which is a picture of the macrocosm. Dupuis reasons that the first notion of a single god that controlled everything was taken from the idea of a unity of nature, and of natural processes, which, after being observed in the world, were projected onto another world beyond that of nature. This was transformed into a belief in a universal cause of all the effects in nature. It was the origin of "God the Father" who is also equated with Jupiter by Dupuis.

Dupuis likewise links the Holy Spirit to the presence of an apparent life force, or soul, within all creatures, which is considered to originate in God the Father, connecting this with the classical and Platonic "Anima Mundi" or animating Soul of the World.

Similarly, the Son is equated with the power of Reason or Intelligence, as it manifests in animals and within human beings, through the definition of Logos as not just "Word" but "Reason" or "Logic". Very importantly, this Reason is equated with light by Dupuis, and from that is equated with the Sun and the power of the Sun. From there, he points to many parallels in pagan cultures, from Greco-Roman to the Zoroastrian, which equate intelligence with the Sun. In this, the power of the Sun is the power which actuates the whole system of the world. He states that the Sun is like the mind of the world, with the world being not just the earth but the solar system as well. People transferred a version of the visible sun to a higher spiritual plane in their thought, making it a transcendental sun, and in this they also implicitly made it the actuator or activator of the macrocosm as it was portrayed in the Heavenly City. This relates, quite intimately, to Dupuis' claim that Jesus never really existed, and that he was only a figure who represented the physical sun as it traveled through the zodiac. Through this, the Christian Trinity is equated with the unity of nature, the life of nature, and with intelligence.

Dupuis' XIIth chapter, about the symbolism of the Book of Revelations, in especially important, in that many of the schemas of the four and the seven, and the twelve, which the Astrotheists and others, use, are ultimately related back to figures within this book.

Among other things, Dupuis comes up with his own four-fold symbolism of the Holy City, which stands as a representation of the macrocosm. The four-fold Holy City or Heavenly Temple corresponds, again, to the signs and to the four directions. Dupuis gives the following correspondences, which he states that he's taking from Dio Chrysostom. First, the four directions and four sides of the city correspond to the four horses of the apocalypse, and to the four elements. The first Horse, or direction, corresponds to Fire and to Jupiter, the second direction corresponds to Air and to Juno, the third direction corresponds to Water and to Neptune, while the fourth direction corresponds to Earth and to Vesta.

Fire Jupiter
Air Juno
Water Neptune
Earth Vesta

Within this, the Holy City as the wheel of the year means that at any given time, a different aspect of the city is activated. In the winter, the North is activated, then the East, the South, and so on. Implicitly, the zodiacal signs are also projected onto the Holy City, in the form of the winter six signs dominated by evil and the summer half signs dominated by good. The center point of the Holy City is where the forces that direct the circulation of life are pictured as residing, the Son in particular, with the Holy Spirit being the circulation of life itself, and the Father being the overall unity of the City, all gathered into one in the center. Dupuis links the triumph of the light at the equinox with the Holy City model, with the victory of light over darkness being represented by the whole macrocosm, with the symbol of the conquering force located at the center of it.

Lenormant

François Lenormant was the author of the work translated into English as "The Beginnings of History". He also wrote many more scholarly works on Mesopotamian magic and history, but "The Beginnings" is notable for being less strictly scholarly than these later works, instead reflecting more the beliefs of early 19th century

France. This work, relying on actual historical sources, relates the Cabiri to the Ante-Diluvians, to the family of Cain, and to metal workers. These ideas had been circulating in France since the turn of the 19th century, and, in fact, were incorporated into the degrees of the Rite of Memphis. The Rite of Memphis, in turn, preceded Lenormant's work.

Lenormant, though, is also very familiar with esotericism and mysticism, and regularly cites these in connection with the subjects throughout the book. Cain and Abel, in Lenormant's book are directly identified with the Cabiri as well. The tradition of Cain and Abel as the Dioscuri, Castor and Pollux, associated with the sign Gemini, as well as with Winter and Summer, which is present in Traditional Witchcraft, is found in Lenormant's book, in a chapter devoted to Cain and Abel.

The Cabiri themselves are singled out by Lenormant because of the reputed antiquity of their mysteries, as in Faber, though in this case Lenormant partially looks at the myths of the Cabiri and tries to make parallels between their story and that of others, instead of only using them as arbitrary cut outs without any particular characteristics of their own.

Within Lenormant's book, the Chapters IV, V, and VII, titled "The Fratricide and Foundation of the First City", "The Shethites and Qainites", and "The Children of God and the Daughters of Men" are the most important. The Cabiri are first introduced in depth in Chapter IV. The "Fratricide" in question is the murder of Abel by Cain, which Lenormant sees as having archetypal significance. Here, the slaying of one of the brothers is a human sacrifice linked to the laying of the foundation stone of the new city, to the establishing of the Omphalos or center of the city. In fact, the head of Abel is said to be the foundation stone of Cain's city of Henoch itself.

The Cabiri are linked to this in that they too were said to have killed one of their brethren, and so repeated the sin of Cain. However, as Lenormant says, the Cabiric brother killed is a savior figure who is then resurrected in the spirit, and then becomes a guide of the mysteries, with the other Cabiri serving him. This is tied by Lenormant to the sun, in a proto-type of the dying and rising god idea, which was later popularized by James Frazier, with this dead and resurrected Cabiri brother being paralleled by Lenormant to the sun in its seasonal changes. Lenormant states that Cain "must have been looked upon as a true Cabiros" by people who came in contact with the Biblical story. From there, Lenormant links Cain with Tubal-Cain, and Tubal-Cain with the smith god of the Cabiri, as well as with deities that were said to be the first Masons, in the sense of inventing the science of making sturdy bricks and of building with them. In this, both Tubal-Cain and Cain are artificers, one a designer and forger of metallic objects, the other an architect, designer of buildings. He states that from the children of these individuals, all the arts and the sciences followed, and that the Nephelim are examples of this.

Additionally, Lenormant points out that one of the Cabiri was called "Prometheus" and another "Aitnaios" by Pausanius. From there, he makes a parallel between Cain and Prometheus, and between Tubal-Cain and "Aitnaios", who is called by Lenormant a metal worker. Aitnaios is linked to the volcano Mt. Etna, and through that to Hephaesteus, the smith God. Aitnaios is also related by Lenormant to Henoch, the son of Cain who Cain's city was named after, and he links this to Aitnaios being in charge of initiations into the mysteries, which included all the secrets of manufacturing, building, and forging which the line of Cain established. He also associates two of the Cabiri with the constellation Gemini and with the Roman Dioscuri, or divine twins. These are then associated with the dark half and light half of the year. In this, the equivalent of Cain in the Cabiri is apparently thought to represent the dark half of the year, and the equivalent of Tubal-Cain is thought to rule the light half of the year.

From here, Lenormant links Tubal-Cain to the Cabiric equivalent of Abel, in a way which is somewhat confusing, and that contradicts the Biblical narrative, but that, nonetheless has its own logic. Tubal-Cain, in this, is Abel, the sun god who is sacrificed by Cain, then is resurrected, and then who, upon resurrection, becomes the Hierophant or guide of the mysteries, serving Cain, and teaching the people the different arts of building, manufacturing and forging. He's also still a demiurgic, forging, god in and of himself. The death and resurrection of Tubal-Cain, in this, is linked by Lenormant with the putative death and resurrection of Hercules, with all of this being linked to the sun's progress both through night and day and through the two halves of the year. Particularly, Lenormant interprets the seasonal changes to say that in the winter, Hercules/Tubal-Cain is slayed by Cain, and then is reborn later in the year, presumably coming to the peak of his power in the summer before falling once more. Lenormant also parallels this cyclical pattern to the death and resurrection of Jesus. Cain, here, also becomes associated with the Moon, in parallel to Tubal-Cain being associated with the Sun.

Conclusion

All of these definitions of the Cabiri can be related with even more precision to traditional witchcraft beliefs. We concretely know this because Robert Fitzgerald supplies the key in his essay in "The Luminous Stone", where he talks about the esoteric meaning of the Pole Star. Yarker, in his "Arcane Schools" talks about the seven Cabirs, and an eighth Cabir, these standing for the stars of the Big Dipper and the Pole. The eighth Cabir was associated by Yarker with Hermes and Aesclapius. Here, the seven stars of the Big Dipper stand for the seven points of the circle outside of the North, while the Pole Star itself standing for the North. The Pole Star, in Yarker's thought, is a portal that lets the energy of the "Mystery Sun", the Eternal Sun that stands beyond the stars, come into our world. It is source of the Shekinah.

Another way of corresponding the stars of the Big Dipper to the points of the circle is the following: the Big Dipper is divided into three and four, three stars in the handle of the Big Dipper and four stars making up the cup. The seven Cabirs of the circle are thereby divided into three and four. In traditional witchcraft practices, the division of the Big Dipper into three and four sometimes refers to the three of the vertical axis plus the four of the horizontal axis, with the Pole Star referring to the unseen power which animates both of these.

This correspondence of the stars with the Cabiri, and the Cabiri with the different points of the circle, is also the implicit background to a letter of Roy Bowers, aka "Robert Cochrane" to Joe Wilson, where the seven are talked about, and related to a ritual of self initiation where the person walks around a pillar with a skull on it in order to bring the energies of the stars down into the circle. The seven are also referenced in his work on the "Basic Structure of the Craft", where they're related to seven castles that Arthur encounters in the Welsh poem "Preiddu Annwn".

Finally, there are other writers who, despite similar mythomania, also seem to have had insight into what some of the actual mysteries were. One of the most important of these is Algernon Herbert, author of "An Essay on the Neo-Druidic Heresy in England". This is a work with insight, though it condemns what really is in line with the craft as being a heresy that was introduced into Britain by the Romans and that corrupted the Druidic doctrine. Similarly interesting is Herbert's large, several volume, mythomaniac work "Nimrod", which is also insightful. This is another work that provides a great basis for expanding a counter-tradition, with the "Nimrod" that Herbert condemns being usefully syncretized by him with a variety of gods from the Middle East. "Nimrod", in this, stands in the same place as Tubal-Cain within Herbert's cosmology, and is the king atop the Tower of Babel.

Another good mythomaniac is the more well known, though less insightful, author Godfrey Higgins, who, in this is good not for his "masterpiece" the Anacalypsis, which is very confused, but for his book "The Celtic Druids", which is a more measured piece of mythomania which similarly makes good connections despite its strangeness.

Works Cited

Borchart, Samuel "Phaleg", or "Geographica Sacra, Phaleg et Canaan", Leiden, 1692, google books

Brisson, Barnabe "De formulis et solennibus populi Romani verbis", 1754, Google Books

Davies, Edward "The Mythology and Rites of the British Druids", J. Booth, London, 1809, Google books

Dupuis, Charles François "The Origin of All Religious Worship" the "Abridgement", New Orleans, 1872, Google Books

Faber, George Stanley "Dissertation on the Mysteries of the Cabiri" vol. 1 and 2. Oxford University Press, Oxford, 1803, google books

Faber, George Stanley "The Origin of Pagan Idolatry", vol. 1, 2 and 3, F and C Rivingtons, London, 1817, google books

Herbert, Algernon "An Essay on the Neo-Druidic Heresy in England", Henry G. Bohn, London, 1838, Google Books.

Herbert, Algernon "Nimrod", vols. 1-3, Richard Priestly, London, 1828, Google Books,

Herbert, Algernon "Nimrod", vols. 4, Richard Priestly, London, 1829, Google Books,

Higgins, Godfrey "The Celtic Druids" Cosimo Inc., New York, 2007

Lenormant, François "Beginnings of History" Charles Scribner's Sons, New York, 1893, Google books

Lynch, Richard "The Travels of Noe" EEBO-Text Creation Partnership 2

Madziarczyk, John, "The Magitians Discovered" vol 1, Topaz House Publications, Seattle, 2016

Monod, Paul Kléber, "Solomon's Secret Arts", Yale University Press, New Haven, 2013

Oliver, George, "The History of Initiation in Three Courses of Lectures", Washbourn, London, 1829, google books,

Oliver, George, "The Theocratic Philosophy of Freemasonry in Three Lectures", R. Spencer, London, 1856, google books.

Pictet, Adolphe "Du Culte des Cabiris chez les Anciens Irlandais", J.J. Paschoud, Geneva, 1824, google books

Cochrane, Robert to Joe Wilson "#3 Transcript", "The Taper that Lights the Way", Shani Oates, Mandrake of Oxford

Schelling, F.W.J., "Über die Gottheiten von Samothrake", "On the Divinities of Samothrace", Frank Scalambrino trans, Magister Ludi press, Castalia, 2019

Scot, Reginald, John Madziarczyk ed. "Magitians Discovered, vol. 2". Topaz House Publications, Seattle, 2016

Volney, Constantin François de Chassebœuf,"The Ruins of Empires", Rossange Freres Booksellers, Paris, 1820, Google Books

Walker, D.P. "Spiritual and Demonic Magic from Ficino to Campanella", Pennsylvania State University Press,University Park PA, 2000

Bishop Warburton "Divine Legation of Moses", tenth edition, Vol. 1, Book II, pg. 254, , for Hekas, Hekas Este Babeloi, Thomas Tegg, London, 1846, google books

Yarker, John "Arcane Schools" Cosimo Inc., New York, 2007

Chapter 10
The Pickingill Papers

The Pickingill Papers are a very essential collection of writings. This chapter and the next examine them. The "Papers" are letters written by a diverse group of anonymous crafters, who bring together their various ideas through the common frame story of George Pickingill, cunning man from Canewdon, in Essex. The papers were passed onto E.W. (Bill) Liddell from a large group of people and then published in two places, "The Wiccan", and then in "The Cauldron", and have since been collected by Michael Howard and printed by the late, and much missed, Capall-Bann publishing house. If you read through them, in the first place you should forget about the historicity of Pickingill. An actual cunning man, he came to prominence through Eric Maple's very good book "The Dark World of Witches", where his story, and a putative photograph, appeared, but he appears to be a convenient reference point for the construction of a frame story within which information can be conveyed. Beyond that, I would say that the most important parts of the papers aren't the controversial big themes that they're known for, such as the claims that Aleister Crowley was initiated by witches and that the Golden Dawn founders were involved with witchcraft, or that Gerald Gardner was taught by Pickingill witches. I see those themes as distractions. Putting those claims aside, there are a number of the papers that are very forthright about their beliefs, to which more attention should be paid. However, with the letters concerning the big themes, as well as with the others, people should pay attention to the things that are seemingly referenced in passing, particularly to any names of authors or books that are referenced, because quite a lot is communicated in these seemingly innocuous citations.

Gardner

The most glaring of these is the reference to Pennethorne Hughes' book "Witchcraft". Within Hughes' book, he reproduces the French miniature of a witchcraft initiation, featuring the Saracen Square, that we'll discuss in detail. However, while the Pickingill papers examine this particular painting, what's unspoken is just why referencing Pennethorne Hughes is so important in and of itself.

The importance is that Gerald Gardner wrote in "Witchcraft Today" that the reason why he was writing a book exposing what he and his fellow witches were doing was because he had read Pennethorne Hughes' book and had been so repelled by it that he felt he had to set the record straight. Now, why was Gardner repelled by it? He was repelled by it because Hughes, especially in his beginning chapters, pictures witchcraft as a degenerate religion derived from both ignoble and noble sources. This, as we shall see, is not the whole story with Hughes and his book, or his portrayal of witchcraft, yet it was enough to set off Gardner, and in particular, for Gardner to come to the defense of witchcraft by presenting the theories of Margaret Murray as the truth. Gardner, in opposing Hughes' portrayal, made a full throated defense of the craft as incarnating Murray's matriarchal paganism, with his coven being a living example of the continuity of this underground matriarchal tradition. This claim, in turn, was to shape all of what Wicca would become, even though Gardner's own witchcraft rituals and practices generally had a much more nuanced take on things, and do not completely reflect, or support, what Gardner wrote in his non-fiction works. Similar statements can be made about the relation of Gardner's fictional works, "High Magic's Aid" and "A Goddess Arrives" , written before "Witchcraft Today", to his non-fiction works.

Gardner's advancing of Murray's thesis lead to the Alexandrian tradition, one step removed from Gardner's group, pursuing this thesis on their own, and eventually lead to Wicca escaping into the wild and combining with ideas that had little to do with the traditional craft. These ideas had more to do with current fashions in anthropology, and have lead to the situation we face today, where something called "Wicca" exists as a religion, but has little to do with the practices it claims to represent.

With this in mind, the Pickingill Paper author citing Pennethorne Hughes as someone who had found and reproduced an authentic pictorial representation of a witchcraft initiation is very significant. It points to this particular author giving the seal of approval, or at least a conditional one, to the writings of the very person that Gerald Gardner was reacting against in his introduction of Wicca to a public audience.

With that in mind, what does Pennethorne Hughes actually say in his book "Witchcraft"? As mentioned, the first few chapters are especially hard and demeaning, but once a person gets beyond them, they're rewarded with a far more nuanced and intelligent treatment of what the craft is than anything produced by the supporters of Margaret Murray. Particularly, Hughes preserves the notion that the craft was derived from mystery religions. Hughes' notion combines mystery religions from the Greco-Roman age and the Roman empire, with vestigial fertility rites, and traces the survival of this combination into the medieval world. This is correct, or at least much more correct than the Murray-ite thesis. It draws on an older stream of scholarship that looked at pagan mythology from a comparative perspective, one that, in a kind of debased form, was also believed in by Robert Graves. Hughes, however, is less prone to flights of fancy and mythomania than Graves is, and his work is much more anchored in reality. He talks about the transition from paganism to feudal Christianity, with the adoption of pagan deities as Saints, as well as pagan practices that were Christianized. Very importantly, Hughes examines the Cathars and other gnostic heretics, and mentions the potential links of the Templars to them. He also mentions paleolithic peoples of Great Britain, repeating the doctrine which we've examined, which linked these people to Fairies, and from there to witches.

Hughes, in distinction to the Murrayite thesis, kept the idea of a male character as the main god of the witches, which was in his mind derived from a horned god combined with several other less generic mythological gods of the pagans, including the idea of a Sabbatic goat and a man in black within this, with a goddess figure complementing him.

Hughes' rich examination and portrayal of a nuanced witch cult that derives from a number of different sources, from fertility rites, mystery religions, gnosticism, and others, maintaining an uneasy identity in combination represents the road not taken by modern Wicca. By choosing to link his beliefs to a rather fundamentalist interpretation of Margaret Murray's thesis, Gardner took more than a generation of seekers away from the sources that could have lead them back to the craft as it actually is.

Other works referenced by the Pickingill papers include those of Dudley Wright and Benjamin Walker.

Edward Davies and Dudley Wright

With regards to the Pickingill papers, there's direct evidence for Davies' influence, as well as Masonic thought, with Faber's thought being indirectly implicated. There, in a paper titled "Druidism, Freemasonry & the French Craft Connection", chapter seven in Michael Howard's collection, the author in explaining the officers of the circle in a rite, directs the reader to "Druidism, the Ancient Faith in Britain", by Masonic scholar Dudley Wright, written in 1924. There, in the passage cited, Wright connects Welsh mythological figures not only to Druidism but to officers in Masonic rites. He cites terms that come from Davies in this, and elsewhere directly cites Faber's "Origins of Pagan Idolatry" for support. Because it's actually recommended by a witch, this is good evidence.

The author of the papers list three officers: the "Cadeiriaith" in the East standing for the Worshipful Master, the "Goronwy" in the West standing for the Senior Warden, and the "Fleidwr Flam" in the South standing for the Junior Warden. Turning to Wright, the gods listed by him as corresponding to these officers are Hu or Hu Gadarn symbolizing the East and the rising sun the "Cadeiriaith", and Ceridwen symbolizing the west and setting sun and the dark goddess, the "Goronwy" , with a third officer standing for the sun at noon in the South, the "Fleidwr Flam".

These three unique titles are drawn from Edward Davies book "The Mythology and Rites of the British Druids", which, in a circular fashion, incorporates Faber's "Arkite" thesis into it. The "Cadeiriaith" is described by him as the chairperson in the court of King Arther, while the "Goronwy" has a function which corresponds to "Lord of the Water" and the "Fleidwr Flam" a function which corresponds to the keeper of a fire. The "Cadeiriath" is described as the son of the gatekeeper, or son of Janus, and Saturn, who is associated with Hu Gadarn. In this, what Dudley Wright and the Pickingill author would call the lodge or the circle is associated with court of King Arthur by Davies, which is then cast by him as existing within Caer Sidi. Caer Sidi appears here as a primal temple, one that Stonehenge and other standing stones are based on, as the place of Ceridwen, symbolizing the zodiac, or circle of the year. Caer Sidi as a Temple is equivalent to the sun in the zodiac. Davies represents the pattern on which the temple is based as being a circle of twelve standing stones, which he sees as the original pattern on which Stonehenge and related monuments are based. Stonehenge here is also associated with the sacred fire of Vesta, continually blazing, as a representation of the sun god.

Dudley Wright himself presents a picture of Druidic initiation that's drawn from Faber combined with Masonic ritual and other contemporary strains of thought on what the mysteries consisted of. He describes this initiation as consisting of an initial stage of being confined to a cave, after which the individual is put into a small boat which is like a Masonic coffin. Then, the individual is taken out of the boat, blessed with a hymn to the sacred phallic sun-fire, and then lead around a circle blindfolded nine times, while people in the circle try to frighten him with harsh sounds. He states that other ceremonies were done which, connected with this, were linked to the terrors associated with the elements, before the individual's blindfold was undone and they were exposed to the light. He also states that the officer who was the high Druid in ceremonies carried a ceremonial "Druid's egg", or serpent's egg set into jewelry.

Benjamin Walker and Others

Walker is someone who I consider to be a traditional witch who wrote works portraying witch beliefs in cryptic forms. In fact, out of several people who I believe were engaged in the same thing, Walker is in my opinion by far the most important. Unfortunately, the authors of the "Pickingill Papers" cite one of his lesser works, "Tantra". The works of Benjamin Walker that people should look at are "Man and the Beasts Within" and "Gnosticism". The latter work has far more information about actual tantric practices than his book on Tantra, and relates directly to dissident practices associated both with the Cathars and with traditional witchcraft.

"Man and the Beasts Within" is an encyclopedia format book with many small entries that, though innocuous on the surface, make many references to sex magic, trance states, witchcraft, and other occult themes. I would consider it a prime example of a mask that's used to veil the transmission of parts of the craft in public form. Walker even makes obscure references to a "new rite" and "old rite" of witchcraft, with this being presented in a matter of fact way with no further detail given. This work, which is in a convenient format, has been republished under many different names as an encyclopedia of the occult, though that's not really what it is.

Beyond Benjamin Walker, the Pickingill authors also reference the ill named "Satanic Mass" by H.T.F. Rhodes. Though it's named "The Satanic Mass", its first parts, which are the most important, deal with witchcraft, and are not at all Satanic. There, Rhodes connects the ceremony of the Sabbat to mystery religions and to gnosticism. Other useful books have made similar equations in their titles, which unfortunately may cause people to overlook them. One in particular is "The Satanic Cult" by Gerhard Zacharias. Originally published in German, and hard to acquire in English nowadays, much of the book actually has to do with the craft itself in its traditional or classic form. Within the world of German language publishing, it remains one of the occult books of the '60s that's been perpetually in print.

Another book that's mentioned in the "Pickingill Papers", albeit in Michael Howard's notes, that give an alternate interpretation to Gardner's "Witchcraft Today" is Michael Harrison's book "The

Roots of Witchcraft". Despite it being dedicated to Margaret Murray, Harrison extends the idea of the precursors of the craft into mystery religions as well. He also investigates the megalithic civilization, and relates it to the goddess theories of Marija Gimbutas. As part of this, he correctly identifies the Basque as being descendants of the megalithic civilization. Unfortunately, this identification is somewhat marred by his attempt to relate words recorded in Inquisition witchcraft records to Basque words, which leads to a hodgepodge of incoherent sentences. Despite that, though, the book is recommended.

Arianrhod

One of the unique claims in the Pickingill Papers is that the Welsh Arianrhod is one of the primal goddesses of Britain. Looking at the particular paper "The Goddess in Ancient Britain", chapter twenty in Howard's collection, where this claim is made, the author connects it to a book by James Vogh, alias of John Sladek, called "The Thirteenth Zodiac: the sign of Arachne". This book makes a sustained connection between Arianrhod, Ariadne, and Arachne, linking her to the labyrinth and spider webs. The book is strange, though, in that despite basically taking up where John Michell leaves off, it was apparently written by a person who didn't believe in any of it, and who wrote it in order to make money, as well as to demonstrate how gullible people could be.

Beyond the interesting, and perhaps real, correspondences that the author makes, he also makes many very basic errors regarding books, people, and dates, and puts forward an idea that there's some sort of underground "Arachne" current, connected to the supposed 13th sign. This 13th sign is linked to the tree alphabet popularized, or invented, by Robert Graves in "The White Goddess". This emphasis on a secret "Arachne" current goes into self parody. Nonetheless, there are actually real things in it, such as the opposition between Arianrhod and her son, with the son standing for Orion and Hercules, as well as Lleu Llaw Gyffess. This fits well with the idea of Orion/Hercules as the god of the East, and Arianrhod in her castle, as well as Ariadne in her labyrinth, standing for the West.

There's also an interesting argument, which, as with everything else, we don't know the author's intent behind, that connects the Druids to the Cathars, and both of them to witches. This, however, is combined with really bad history which connects the Waldenses, a Christian group that emphasized voluntary poverty, to witchcraft. It's not clear where all of this comes from, though it's possible that he came to it through the pseudo-account of the "Vauderie" in northern France. This was an inquisitorial account of a traditional craft group that falsely linked them to the Waldenses. I think that, to an extent, Vogh was just plagiarizing lots of other people's works and making random connections. Yet, even a stopped clock is right twice a day.

Significantly, the Pickingill paper that deals with Arianrhod also names Bride as a goddess, with Bride and Arianrhod being the light and dark goddesses of Britain.

Works Cited

Davies, Edward "The Mythology and Rites of the British Druids", J. Booth, London, 1809, Google books

Gardner, Gerald "Witchcraft Today", Citadel Press, New York, 2004

Harrison, Michael "The Roots of Witchcraft", Tandem, London, 1975

Hughes, Pennethorne "Witchcraft", Penguin Books, London 1965

Liddell,W.E, Michael Howard ed. "The Pickingill Papers", Capall-Bann, Chieveley,1994

Maple, Eric "The Dark World of Witches", A.S. Barnes & Company Inc., New York, 1964

Rhodes, H.T.F. "Satanic Mass", Citadel Press, Seacaucus, 1974

Vogh, James alias of John Sladek, "The Thirteenth Zodiac: the sign of Arachne", Granada Publishing, London, 1979

Walker, Benjamin "Man and the Beasts Within", Stein and Day, New York 1977

"Gnosticism, it's History and Influence", the Aquarian Press, Wellingborough UK, 1983

Wright, Dudley "Druidism, the Ancient Faith in Britain", Ed. J. Burrow, London, 1924, Google Books

Zacharias,Gerhard, Christine Trollope trans. "The Satanic Cult" by George Allen & Unwin, London, 1980

Chapter 11
Masonry and Massey

Pickingill and Conway: Knight of the Sabean Square

Other tidbits of information show up in the "Pickingill Papers" that intersect with a strange variant of the Rite of Memphis, which used Gerald Massey's thought. Not only that, but the parallels go much further, into several branches of traditional witchcraft. There exists corroborating evidence for the ideas in this Pickingill paper being shared among traditional witches of many different strands of thought, including a Welsh cunning tradition, and the Cultus Sabbati, with these possibly having overlap between them. This rite has to do with the constellation of the Great Bear, or Big Dipper.

The Pickingill paper that outlines this particular material deals with the French witchcraft miniature of something called the "Saracen Square". This is labeled as a French painting of a witchcraft initiation, and it featuring three women, two men, and a goat in the north. Their circle is drawn out on the ground in the form of a box or rectangle with some lines that go beyond it. The particular "Pickingill Paper" where this appears is titled "Medieval French Witchcraft", chapter four in the collection put together by Michael Howard, and originally appeared in "The Wiccan" in 1977.

The miniature appears in Pennethorne Hughe's book "Witchcraft". The author of this Pickingill paper calls this rectangle a "Saracen Square" and talks about how it was supposedly derived from the Middle Eastern mysteries of the "Saracens" or Arabs. While the phrase "Saracen Square" appears to have not been widely used, in a variant of the rite of Memphis there's a degree called "Knight of the Sabean Square". I believe that the Pickingill people intentionally confused some information in their papers, and so to call a "Sabean Square" a "Saracen Square" would be a possibility within reason.

Plus, technically, the Sabeans, a group that existed in present day Syria, are indeed Saracens, if this is defined as being Middle Easterners in general.

Some other things that are notable about this essay, which connect to our story is that, first, it extensively connects the miniature that it's discussing with Freemasonry and with Masonic ritual. In fact, it uses the miniature as a jumping off point for suggesting not only that the officers in a Masonic lodge are the same as the craft officers in the circle, but that Masonry and witchcraft have common origins. Not only that, but the "Saracen Square" is explicitly related to the practice of "Squaring the Circle", which is the focus of the "Knight of the Sabean Square" degree. Importantly, Gerald Massey, who is the source for much of this symbolism, doesn't write anything about Masonry in "A Book of the Beginnings". He does mention Masonry in the later "Natural Genesis", where he relates the word "Masonry" to the Egyptian "Maat" or "Truth", and in posthumous writings, but this and other references don't align with the symbolism that's used in this "Pickingill Paper".

The Saracen square is directly linked to Freemasonry by the author. They make a peculiar equation of the square and the circle, ascribing the Square to Life and the Circle to Form, and describing squaring the circle as reconciling these two. I think this is more obfuscation, and that, in fact, the Circle is linked to Life and the Square is linked to Form. The Circle, in this, is linked to the Goddess force while the Square is linked to the God force, as the Pickingill people outline, and squaring the circle reconciles the two forces with each other. Here, the God is what limits into form, and so is a kind of death, while the Goddess is that which provides life, which provides undifferentiated extensive life, and so is life itself. The two combined, the squaring of the circle, bind this Life into concrete reality.

Significantly, in Chumbley's "Azoetia", the Big Dipper or Great Bear is extensively talked aobut, with it being associated with the Goddess in her form as overseeing Decrease, as well as with the general process of the upwards flow of life from the circle to the Sabbat itself. This inflow of life to the Sabbat is presented by

Chumbley as the movement of that life to the Sabbat through the constellation of the Great Bear, which serves as a place of testing before the individual is let into the Sabbat itself.

If the equation between "Saracen Square" and "Sabean Square" in the Pickingill Papers hold, this could indicate that rectangles representing the cup of the Big Dipper were used in initiation ceremonies, which would equate well with Chumbley's attribution. Specifically, in the Azoetia, Chumbley attributes the stars of the Great Bear to deities that oversee the ordeals of initiation, and bringing down the stars of the Dipper to the earth in the form of the stations of the circle, could be a way of bringing the initiatory energies associated with the Dipper down to earth. These trials of initiation do not just have to manifest in the circle itself, where the person leaves the circle spiritually and goes to the Sabbat, but can be ordeals on the path which leads to that goal, which is a goal of those on the path of witchcraft as a whole.

The big dipper is also mentioned in the "Coven of Atho" material as a device to tell time, though its connection with the septagram, and seven principles, used by the coven is questionable. This sevenfold device may just relate to the seven planets and their characteristics, and not to the seven stars of the Great Bear.

I believe that the rite that contains the "Knight of the Sabean Square" relates both to Pickingill and to David Conway's work. This latter has to do with a Welsh cunning tradition by David Conway in "Secret Wisdom". Conway is the author of the better known "Magic: An Occult Primer". What, though, is the rite from which it comes from?

The Masonic Rite

This particular Masonic rite is strange because, though titled "The Egyptian Masonic Rite of Memphis", it's really a rewrite of that rite which was created in the United States in the late 19th century. It departs heavily from the established degrees of Memphis-Mizraim, and instead directly incorporates ideas, and content, from Gerald Massey's "A Book of the Beginnings". This content deals with Egypt, in particular with the constellation of the Great Bear and its seven stars. The rite appears to have been partially created as a scam to make money for its founder, but it has valid esoteric ideas within it.

Now, the incorporation of Gerald Massey's ideas into a Masonic rite, of whatever provenance, is doubly significant for traditional witchcraft in that Andrew Chumbley of the Cultus Sabbati was very influenced by Massey as well. I believe that this rite influenced several different traditional witchcraft groups, one of whom passed on this influence onto Chumbley as part of the synthesis that would become the Cultus Sabbati. Of course, this is an inference. I have not actually talked to members of the Cultus to verify that this is the case.

Let's look first at the history of the rite, then at the rite itself, then at the intersections between the rite and traditional witchcraft.

The History of the Rite.

The text of the ritual that I have is contained in "Collectanea, vol. 20", parts one and two, issued by the Masonic Grand College of Rites in the United States in 2008, and edited by Masonic scholar Arturo de Hoyos. Somewhat frustratingly, the two parts that make up the volume have no introductory material explaining where this rite came from. However, through looking at other publications associated with the Grand College of Rites, as well as at internal evidence, I believe I've found where it originated.

Here, the most important of these documents is "The Spurious Rites of Memphis and Mizraim", by William L. Cummings, written in the mid 1930s but republished by the Scottish Rite Research Society journal "Heredom" in 2001. This republication also features an update on what happened to the rites after the '30s, with this being that the American rites were dissolved and their rituals and authority transferred to the Grand College of Rites itself in the 1950s. Also important is an issue of the "Universal Freemason", an organ of the dissident "American Masonic Federation" published in August 1918, that talks about the splits in the U.S. lineages of the Rite of Memphis, as well as the more recent publication "Darius Wilson, Confidence Schemes, and American Fraternalism 1869–

1926" by William D. Moore of Boston University, published in 2013 in the "Journal for Research into Freemasonry and Fraternalism".

According to "Tabloid History: Rites and Orders Other than the Scottish Rite in America." in "The Universal Freemason", vol. XI num 2, August 1918, The Rite of Memphis was brought to the United States by Henry Seymour in 1862. Some time later, in 1865, Seymour, following the French Grand Orient, wanted to reduce the degrees in the Rite from 95 to 33, prefiguring, in a way, John Yarker's similar reduction for his "Antient & Primitive Rite". Seymour's associate Calvin Burt did not approve of this, and started a schism. Burt advocated for the rite to be preserved in its authentic form. Later on, in 1879-1880 Burt had a schism with a member of his rite, Darius Wilson, who went on lead his own version of the rite. The dissident "American Masonic Federation", which published "The Universal Freemason", was the alternative grand lodge that chartered Wilson's creations. I believe that the version of Memphis where the "Knight of the Sabean Square" appears is the one associated with Darius Wilson.

There are a number of reasons to think this. First, there's internal evidence within the documents suggesting that this later, variant, rite, is dependent on Burt's work. This comes in the form of some very uniquely spelled names of non-European gods in the ceremony for the granting of the 45th degree, Knight Consecrator, which also appear in the 43-45 degree granting ceremony of the variant tradition, the ritual being the same. These are "Vitzliputzli" and "Tetslipuca", unique variant spellings of the names of Mesoamerican gods. There's also the issue of the reworking of the rite itself. Burt presented his rite as being the authentic Memphis rite, in comparison to the altered later Seymour version. Because of this, I doubt that he would have severely reworked the different degrees in the way that they appear in the variant rite. Darius Wilson, on the other hand, may well have done this.

Evidence for this comes from William D. Moore's "Darius Wilson, Confidence Schemes, and American Fraternalism 1869–1926". There, he documents how Wilson, who joined many different fraternal orders, took several of them and created his own variants.

Particularly, Moore cites Wilson as creating a variant of the Odd Fellows called the "Good Fellows" and a variant of the Knights of Pythias called the "Chevaliers of Pythias".

Because of the nature of Masonry in the U.S., which is ruled for the most part by one Masonic establishment, containing two cooperating grand lodges, one for the Scottish Rite, one for the York Rite, with no competing authorities, Wilson was arrested for charges of fraud because he issued Masonic degrees without their permission. He claimed that an alternate grand lodge to these two, the American Masonic Federation, gave him permission, but unfortunately this was not persuasive. However, simply giving degrees without the permission of a grand lodge wasn't his only problem. As Moore's paper shows, he was also altering the signs and passwords of the rites, which is one of the reasons he was caught.

Moore's paper relates a story from a local Boston newspaper in the early 1900s, where a man who had just been initiated into one of Wilson's lodges very enthusiastically gave Masonic signs and passwords to his neighbor, whom he knew to be a Mason. The neighbor didn't know what he was doing, because the signs and words were completely fake, and this is one of the ways that Wilson's fraud was detected.

The "Standard History of Freemasonry for the State of New York", "Book XIII—The Rite of Memphis", also associates Wilson with creating the "Egyptian Rite of Memphis for the Cosmos" in 1881, with this being especially important, as we shall see. Wilson was also responsible for the creation of the "Royal Masonic Rite", which was a combination of Memphis with other material. Interestingly, the "Royal Rite" was only described as having a Chapter and a Senate, which matches the two manuals that we have for the variant Egyptian Rite of Memphis, which don't go further than the 45th degree.

The idea that Wilson was responsible for the creation of the "Egyptian Rite of Memphis of the Cosmos" in 1881 is particularly significant, because this alternate rite of Memphis includes material which was not published until 1881. Particularly, it includes sections from Gerald Massey's "Book of the Beginnings", which was published in that year. The compiler also used Egyptian texts from the Book of the Dead contained in "Egypt's Place in Universal History", vol. 5, by Christian Karl Josias Freiherr von Bunsen, published in 1867.

Allowing that Wilson may have rewritten or changed the Memphis material, this still leaves the question of how all of this could have gotten to Europe, where the Pickingill papers authors and Conway's Welsh teacher lived. I believe that the solution to this comes from Wilson's other fraternal interests. Back in the 19th century, many fraternal organizations functioned as life insurance companies, or provided other services based on mutual aid. Wilson was involved with many of these, and some of his alternative organizations were these types of groups. This includes his "Chevaliers of Pythias" as well as his "Royal Arcanum". This latter organization had nothing to do with occultism, despite its name, and its constitution deals with things like medical examinations to see if someone is fit for coverage. Moore, talking about these, points out that they involved ceremony, special dress, and ritual as well, though their purpose was not occult. He also reports that Wilson was so successful in promoting these organizations that he established branches of them in the UK and elsewhere. He cites an article about this that states that he established branches in London, Aberdeen, Liverpool, and Paris. Now, it may be that in marketing these fraternal organizations across the Atlantic, Wilson also made available other rites and organizations that he had access to for members. There appears to have been a significant financial motive in this, so it's possible that Wilson could have 'sold' chapters of his Egyptian Masonic Rite of Memphis to chapters of his life insurance fraternal organizations for a fee. On top of this, these fraternal life insurance associations appealed to the working class, since the elite in society didn't need them to get life insurance, and so this would make Wilson's Egyptian Masonic Rite of Memphis accessible to people in a social strata that may have not had access to John Yarker's "Antient & Primitive Rite", a social strata that included cunning men and women.

This dissident, semi-Memphis, rite, is testified to by A.E. Waite in volume II of "The Secret Tradition in Freemasonry". In an appendix, Waite references some of the degrees, particularly ones that are semi-alchemical, and rightly condemns them as being inferior and crude. He then applies this same criticism to Memphis as a whole, meaning Marconis' Memphis. This is unfortunate in that its grades do not correspond to those of Marconis' Memphis, and, in general, though some degrees are interesting, for the most part they're of a distinctly inferior quality to Marconis' work.

The Rite Itself

The series of degrees in the rite that concern us, that may have influenced traditional witchcraft, are outlined in part two of vol. 20 of "Collectanea", the "Senate" degrees of this rite. These are the degrees from 19 to 45. The 19th degree starts directly after the series of degrees associated with the Rose-Croix are completed. In reality, the unique, reworked degrees only go from 19 to 42, with 43-45 being granted in one ceremony which is directly taken from regular Memphis work. The 19th and 42nd degrees form the beginning and end of this part of the rite.

For our purposes, there are three sets of degrees that are the most important: the 19th degree, the 29-33 degrees, and the 34-41 degrees. Other degrees, such as the 25th and 26th, "Knight of the Sacrificial Fire" and "Knight of the Serpent of the Sun" might be tangentially important, but won't be examined here. As in the rest of Masonry, the degrees here are not stand alone, but instead are collected into sets which are governed by common themes. All of these are influenced by Massey, and have to do, either directly or indirectly, with the constellation of the Great Bear. The 19th is where the concept of the Great Bear as linked to initiation, and to spiritual progress, is introduced. The 28-33 degrees deal with the Great Bear as the keeper of seasonal time. In this, the Great Bear is most directly mentioned in the 31st degree "Knight of the Sabean Sqaure". The 34-41 degrees deal with the qualities of the seven stars themselves, with each of these degrees corresponding to one quality that in turn corresponds to one star of the Great Bear. Let's start by looking at the foundation, the 19th degree.

Knight of the Occident

The 19th degree is "Knight of the Occident", or "Knight of the West", but it's content is very unlike any "Knight of the West" degree which is found either in Memphis-Mizraim or in other Masonry. This degree is very extensive and serves as the initiation into the "Senate" or second series of degrees in this version of the Rite.

The name "Knight of the West" is linked to the "Western Lands" of the "Egyptian Book of the Dead", and deals with a ship that will take the person to these Western Lands. In the West lies the paradise of "Aah-en-ru".

The ritual itself is about picturing the candidate as a ship whose body is supposed to take them to Aah-en-ru, this being done through leading a virtuous life. The ritual relates different parts of the ship to Egyptian deities, with each part of the ship having a virtue attached to it. This likewise uses figures from Gerald Massey. Particularly, it includes the names for the seven Egyptian deities of the Big Dipper as being the planks of the ship that will take the candidate to Aah-en-ru. These are the same as the seven deities of the Great Bear in Massey. The ship itself is said to be the coffin, presumably of Osiris, which Massey associates with the Big Dipper as well. This degree of the Memphis rite also associates the boat with the "Mer-Kab" or Merkabah chariot, as the text itself says.

In addition to many Egyptian deity names, there's a quotation of an entire poem by Gerald Massey having to do with the sacred land of "Aah-en-ru." This poem appears on pages 174-175 of "A Book of the Beginnings", in a section titled "The Exodus". The spelling, punctuation, and everything else about the version that appears in the variant Memphis degree is an exact copy of Massey's work. We know that this is a poem by Massey, as opposed to something that appeared in a papyrus that he copied because Massey includes it as one of his creations in his book "My Lyrical Life, Poems Old and New", published in 1896.

The poem begins:
"To the paradise of promise in the AAH-EN-RU.
Who ploughed and sowed as mortals, and their furrows straightly drew,

They are gods that reap,says Horus,in the AAH-EN-RU.
The bark of Khepr bears us,with the good fruits that we grew;
Let them sweat who have to tow into the AAH-EN-RU. "

Aah-en-ru is paradise, and in the introduction to the poem Massey writes that "The AAH-EN-RU is a place of Plenty, a field of Rest, also the Heaven of the Gates, or Divisions, belonging to the Mythological Astronomy, whether Sabean, Lunar or Solar" and that the "The Sabean Heaven had seven gates". Elsewhere, he makes it clear that the the seven Sabean gates that lead to the Aah-en-ru are the seven stars of the Great Bear. The idea behind this is that through leading a good life, through implementing the virtues that are linked to the different parts of the boat, including the different virtues of the seven, a person can construct a boat or ark for themselves that will take them to the great reward of paradise after death.

The Degrees of Time

After this, there are two sets of degrees which are relevant to traditional witchcraft: 29-33 degrees,and 34-41 degrees. The first of these consists of
"Knight of Time",
"Knight of the Circle",
"Knight of the Sabean Square",
"Knight of the Double Headed Eagle",
"Knight of the Crown",
while the second series of degrees are based on the "Seven Properties of Nature", and so are titled "Knight of the First Property of Nature", "Knight of the Second Property of Nature", etc. with the final degree being "Knight of Infinite Space".

The first set looks at time and the cycles of the seasons, with the Great Bear being the ultimate time keeper, while the second series looks at each of the qualities of the seven of the Great Bear individually.

Cycles of Seasons

The "Knight of the Sabean Sqaure", the 31st degree, which directly incorporates the Great Bear into its work, is the most important here, but let's look at the context in which the "Knight of the Sabean Square" exists.

This degree is in the middle of a five degree series, which starts with the "Knight of Time", goes through the "Knight of the Circle" to the "Knight of the Sabean Square", then goes to "Knight of the Double Headed Eagle" and "Knight of the Crown". None of these are traditional degrees.

"Knight of Time" describes three forms of reckoning time: One using the Pole Star and the Great Bear, one using the Moon, and one using the Sun. The reckoning of time using the Pole Star is described as the oldest reckoning of time. This follows Massey's conceptualization of things. The Four seasons as an analogy for life are introduced, and linked to the four directions.

"Knight of the Circle" relates the cyclical passage of time to both the Circle and to Eternity, with the Circle being related to the Ouroboros snake. It talks about the perfection of the circle and asks the initiate to imitate this perfection.

In the "Knight of the Sabean Square", the reckoning of a year through the revolution of the Big Dipper around the Pole Star is called the Sabean Circle. This degree introduces the concept of the squaring of the circle, and relates the squaring to the square shape of the Great Bear. The Square in this is related to 90 degrees, and the squaring of the circle is likened to the imposition of four of these squares, four of the dipper of the Great Bear, onto the circle in cyclical form. These four are linked to the four stations or seasons of the year. The year, and the world, is described as being divided into upper and lower, and then left and right, with these echoing both the directions and the seasons.

In this, the four stations of the year form a swastika, and the Sabean Square in this is formed from the projection of the arms. The idea of squaring the circle is present throughout Masonry, and refers to the work of spiritual perfection, which in this case means making the material, the person, like the eternal, the circle, through squaring it with work. In the Pickingill Papers, the "Saracen Square" is also discussed as a means of squaring the circle. This can also mean bringing the eternal down to earth.

The degree of "Knight of the Double-Headed Eagle" appears to be consecrated to Thoth as the Pole Star around which the Great Bear rotates. The password of the degree is "Tahuti". However, the content of the degree talks about a "Double Ibis", which looks in two directions, and in this Thoth is linked with the figure of the "Double Horus". The degree is connected with the two horizons, or equinoxes, and to the rising and setting sun, and it describes this as the axis of Osiris-Horus and Osiris-Isis, along with other dual figures, and with duality itself. Massey also links these to the double Horus in "Book of the Beginnings" and to Horus and Set. This makes up the first part of the four which are squared by the Great Bear, the left and right of the Equinox.

Finally, "Knight of the Crown" looks at the upper world and the lower world, described as heaven and earth, as a complement of the two horizons, the other two directions, upper and lower, of the squaring of the circle, symbolizing the solstices. Together, the left and right of the previous degree and the upper and lower of this degree make up a cross, which cross is the fourfold cross of the Great Bear.

The idea of a Sabean Square, and of the Pole Star and the constellation of the Great Bear being significant is, in fact, found in the original Rite of Memphis, along with Yarker's Ancient & Primitive Rite. It's likely that in constructing their pseudo-Memphis rite the compilers were looking at actual material from the original rites. Particularly, the 47th degree of Memphis titled "Knight of the Seven Stars", is a good candidate for the source material for the "Knight of the Sabean Square" degree and for the others around it in this pseudo-Memphis rite. This degree features an analysis of Ursa Major's rotation around the Pole Star.

The Degrees of the Seven

Next, we have the series which goes through seven "Properties of Nature", ending with "Knight of Infinite Space", which is the end of these unique degrees. We know that these seven properties of nature correspond to the seven stars of the Great Bear because they're listed as so in "The Book of the Beginnings", vol 2, where they're described as the "Taas". In that book, they're not alchemical principles per se but instead are related to the elements. They're also directly related by Massey to the Cabiri through his reference to them as the "Sons of Sydik", with "Sydyk" being the father of the Cabiri. In his later book, "Natural Genesis", Massey relates the "Taas" to the seven vowels (in Greek), and to the seven tones in the musical scale. We shall have much more to say about the origin and nature of these Taas.

The seven properties are "Matter", "Cohesion", "Fluxion", "Coagulation", "Accumulation", "Station", "Division". Now, there's a natural division of these into three and four. The three are composed of Accumulation, Constancy, and Division, while the four are composed of Matter, Cohesion, Flux, and Coagulation.

The way that these are presented is related to the formation of the earth. This departs quite a bit from Massey, or at least is a large addition to Massey's work.

The variant Memphis 34th degree, "Knight of the First Principle of Nature", relates "Matter" to the primal chaos from which everything arose. The lecture of the degree relates matter in this sense to darkness, and contrasts it with the light and perfection of the Aah-en-ru. Next, in the 35th degree, "Cohesion" is presented as the anti-thesis of the chaos of unordered matter, in this case referring to the beginning of the formation of the earth. The 36th degree, "Fluxion", defines itself as a kind of medium between cohesion and chaos, describing a state of nature where atoms come together, but are still hot and energetic enough that they flow instead of being totally static. Finally, the 37th degree, "Coagulation", is the complement of "Fluxion", also between cohesion and chaos, where that which is liquid is congealed into that which is solid.

As for the three, "Accumulation", the 38th degree, refers to the general progress of the formation of the earth, which has gone through all of the previous states. "Station", the 39th, is related to inertia, namely to the inertia of the earth and of all planets after they've been put into place, and into orbit. "Division", the 40th, is linked to the initial division of the primal chaos into various elements. In this, it's a complement of "Accumulation", or a different way of looking at the same, in that the process of "Division" here is linked to the development of the earth, from chaos to differentiated elements, which is an "Accumulation" of progress. Within all of this, within all of the seven, there's an implicit suggestion that the seven are forces that have co-created the earth, an idea which shows up in Theosophy, where the seven are related to the seven Elohim as co-creators, among other currents.

"Knight of Infinite Space" takes the individual beyond the seven properties, and beyond the four stations of the Great Bear. The degree states that the person who has received it has explored all of the four stations in the four directions and wants to go beyond them. Infinite space, here, is defined precisely as that, going into what astrologers call the Firmament, where the stars live, with the lecture talking about the vastness of space in a very modern way. This leads directly into the last degree, "Knight of the Judgment"

Knight of the Judgment

The 42nd degree, "Knight of the Judgment", features a very long and elaborate ceremony where the person reenacts the questioning that a soul undergoes in the "Egyptian Book of the Dead". These are the statements of the "Negative Confession". These are also the questions that a person gives before they're allowed to enter paradise. The individual who enters into this degree faces a simulation of the final test at the end of their lives which will lead them to Paradise, which lies behind and beyond Infinite Space. This is the goal of the creation of the self as a ship, the entrance into the western lands, to Aah-en-ru. There are no particular secrets given in this degree. Instead, when the candidate has passed the tests, the initiator commands him to retain the purity which he has demonstrated in reaching this degree for the rest of his life.

Conway and the Welsh tradition.

The next major tradition that appears to draw on this material is the very interesting cunning tradition that is related by David Conway in his books "Magic without Mirrors" and "Secret Wisdom", and that forms a substrate of his most famous book "Magic: An Occult Primer". In "Magic without Mirrors", Conway gives an extensive account of his education as a youth by a cunning man. Notably, Conway never refers to this tradition as witchcraft, though there are obvious parallels between it and traditional witchcraft practice.

Conway is from Aberystwyth in central Wales, and the tradition concerns a Welsh cunning tradition that he learned from a "Mr. James" in Tanrallt, Wales, who he became a kind of apprentice to as a young man. Though "Magic Without Mirrors" talks extensively about his experience with Mr. James, the particular material that links this tradition with the Pickingill paper, and with Wilson's Egyptian Masonic Rite of Memphis is contained in the chapter "First Steps Along the Path" in "Secret Wisdom". This chapter, published many years before "Magic Without Mirrors", talks about Conway's experience with Mr. James.

Conway is Welsh and the cunning tradition that he relates is rooted in Welsh culture. The link between this tradition and medieval Welsh poems and other material is given in more detail in "Secret Wisdom". Unfortunately, "Secret Wisdom" is for the most part about other types of mysticism, and though Conway's relationship with Mr. James is treated in depth, this Welsh material is examined more in passing. However, he makes reference there to a Welsh tradition which talks about seven different worlds and seven different levels of consciousness, which worlds, in other traditions, are related to the different points of the compass. This tradition is supposed to go back to one related to Taliesin and Owain Glandwyr, a national hero of Wales who lead a rebellion against the English in the 15th century., and to be related to the Druids.

There, in "Secret Wisdom", Conway recounts that Mr. James believed in a system of seven "Cantrefi" or worlds, four of which were manifest, three of which were not, which corresponded to seven different states of consciousness. A "Cantrefi" is a medieval Welsh way of dividing up land. This, James related to a Welsh tradition claimed to be associated with the Druids that came from Taliesin, that was also participated in by Owain Glandwyr. These were related to the seven parts of the Welsh kingdom of Dyfed, which are literally seven Cantrefi, as well as to the seven stars of the Great Bear, the same stars that the "Knight of the Sabean Square" deals with.

This is all well and good, and suggestive, but the thing that concretely links it to the alternate Memphis rite are the alchemical correspondences that Conway presents for the seven stars and the seven "Cantrefi". These are "Matter, Cohesion, Flux, Coagulation, Accumulation, Constancy and Division". First off, these are not conventional alchemical correspondences, but, more importantly, these seven exactly match the seven principles from seven higher degrees of this alternate Memphis rite. After looking into it, the only place where these seven principles occur is in Massey's work, and in the work that he based the "Taas" on. It's not a conventional way of dividing up either alchemical principles or elements.

Beyond this, Conway reports that the individual in Mr. James' system was supposed to subdue the seven Cantrefi, and in this "Square the Circle", the same language used in the "Knight of the Sabean Square". Here, the individual Cantrefi are the circles that need to be squared. The subduing of the Cantrefi are related by Conway to the actions of one Llwyd ap Cilcoed, who appears in the third branch of the Mabinogion. He has enchanted the kingdom, making it disappear. This story symbolically can be taken to refer to dominating the ancient kingdom of Dyfed. However, looking through this story, it appears that Llwyd ap Cilcoed is not the person who is tested, but Manawydan, and that Llwyd is the antagonist. Manawydan has to complete a series of tasks to restore the ancient kingdom of Dyfed, after Llwyd ap Cilcoed has enchanted it.

As said, Conway never refers to Mr. James' system as witchcraft, or to Mr. James as a witch. In fact, in "Magic Without Mirrors" he states that the closest that he ever got to being a witch was being offered to get in contact with some Alexandrian Wiccans in London by a mutual friend who knew them. The subduing of the Cantrefi may be linked to the work in the seven Sabbats that is outlined in the Dragon Book of Essex, where these multiple Sabbats are linked with the directions of the compass. The Draconic tradition in the Cultus Sabbati has been linked with the Welsh part of the craft that Chumbley was an initiate of. The seven can be linked to the different points of the compass in non-Draconic working as well. It would be interesting, as well, to substitute the Sephiroth pathworkings that Conway uses in "Magic: An Occult Primer", with the Cantrefi. For ideas about how this might be done, the reader should consult the grimoire section of this work.

Other Potential Links Between Conway's System and Witchcraft

Looking at Conway's "Magic: an Occult Primer", there are some aspects of it which do suggest parallels with witchcraft, even though Conway is adamant that this is not what was being done. One of the largest is the process of the "Kabbalistic Master Ritual", one of the two "Master Rituals" given in the book. Here, the working process starts out in a fairly conventional way, with the casting of a Lesser Banishing Ritual of the Pentagram. However, after the basic circle has been cast, something unique happens: the individual starts to travel mentally through the astral plane, and this is done through the ritual anointing of ones self with ointment. Looking at the ointments that Conway gives, all of them have ingredients that overlap with the traditional witches ointment. He gives a recipe for that as well, though it's more poisonous and less balanced than the other two. The Kabbalistic master ritual directs the individual to open a door to the astral plane, identified with the moon, then recite a brief confession of ignorance, ceremonially anoint themselves with the ointment, then step into astral plane itself. They're then directed to go to the specific sefira and, once they're there, to will the energy of the sefira and the god associated with it down from the astral plane into a triangle of evocation which they've set up. Later, the energy is taken into the circle itself from the triangle, and at the climax of the rite this energy in the circle joins with the magician, who has worked themself up into an ecstatic state, whereupon the desire that they have is imprinted onto this god energy. Once done, the god energy departs from the individual and then is thanked and dismissed from the circle.

This is very different from Golden Dawn style magic, as well as from neo-pagan magic in general. If we substitute the idea of Cantrefs and the Sabbat for Sefira, the process of putting on the ointment and traveling to the particular Sefira can be interpreted as putting on the ointment and going to a particular conclave or subdivision, of the Sabbat itself. These would correspond to the Cantrefs of Mr. James. Once there, the god energy of the conclave or Cantref would be sent down to earth, into the triangle. Then, it would be allowed back into the circle and allowed to possess the magician in ecstatic union. Here, the possession and ecstatic union would be parallel to a process of calling down energies from the Sabbat that correspond to the godforms of the sacred letters, who then possess and unify with the individual who has called them down, for various purposes. The sacred letters, in turn, correspond to the directions of the compass. These are the powers of the Sabbatic conclaves. Conway gives advice on how you can integrate sexual activity into the possession, with the possession happening during sexual activity but before orgasm, with the imprinting of the desire onto the entity that possesses you happening during orgasm. Orgasm, in this, would be interpreted as a direct sacrifice to the gods of the letters.

Notably, "Magic: An Occult Primer" makes use of material from the 1665 edition of the "Discoverie of Witchcraft", discussed in "The Magitians Discovered", though the source of it is not indicated. These parts are to be found in the footnotes regarding malevolent of "kliphotic" rituals oriented towards the North. "Magic without Mirrors", which is a more personal memoir, is also good for many reasons.

To come back to the Pickingill Papers themselves, interestingly, David Conway's book "Magic without Mirrors" also sheds some potential light on the claims in the Pickingill Papers about "Cunning Lodges", places where the aristocracy and cunning people met and worked together. Michael Howard, who both published the original Pickingill Papers in "The Cauldron" and who edited the collection of them published by Capall-Bann, has written in "Children of Cain" that despite extensive searching no evidence of these associations have been found. "Magic without Mirrors" provides evidence that, at the very least, there were contact between aristocrats and cunning people.

This comes from a story that Mr. James, told about a local lord who invited both him and Aleister Crowley, and potentially other occultists, to an event on his estate. Mr. James was given a book of Crowley's poetry by Crowley himself, which he produced as proof of his experience. This may have been an act by a lord who either thought it would be entertaining to bring occultists to his estate, or maybe transgressive, or it could signal that this lord in particular had an interest in occultism. If one person did it, maybe as an example of aristocratic a-morality, perhaps others did as well throughout time. This doesn't prove that "Cunning lodges" existed, but it does undercut the idea that there wasn't any contact between the aristocracy, who would be well educated, and popular practitioners of magic.

Besides documenting Conway's apprenticeship with Mr. James, it also provides testimony debunking Alex Sanders' claims to have been initiated into witchcraft by his grandmother. Conway apparently knew Alex Sanders' grandmother, who lived in Wales, and gives a more objective account of her, which is that she was a spiritualist medium who was said to be able to talk to fairies. He maintains it's possible that there was something that Sanders learned from her, but that whatever it was, it wasn't "Alexandrian Witchcraft", which is largely a copy of Gerald Gardner's beliefs.

Other Correspondences

Now, there are very interesting correspondences between this and between letters and documents produced by Robert Cochrane of the Clan of Tubal-Cain. First, in his "Basic Structure of the Craft", Cochrane talks about a similar seven, called seven worlds, four of which are manifest, three of which are not. These are, in turn, related to the four horizontal directions, and implicitly to the three vertical directions. They're also related ambiguously to stars, though and Cochrane elsewhere relates the seven to the Great Bear. The four directions are related to four castles, and elsewhere, in a letter to William Gray, Cochrane relates the castles, and through them the seven, to the Welsh poem "Preiddeu Annwn", from the "Book of Taliesen", which Robert Graves included in "The White Goddess". There, king Arthur goes through these six or seven, according to how you want to count them, castles in the underworld, giving his experience of them.

Notably, that the tradition associated with the Cultus Sabbati, one of whose roots lies in Wales, also makes use of symbolism from Gerald Massey may not be a later affectation, or mask. Instead, it may draw on the pre-Gardnerian tradition itself. The seven stars of the Big Dipper are linked by Andrew Chumbley in the Azoetia to seven sisters that oversee the trials of initiation. Put another way, the trials of initiation can correspond to seven challenges given to a person, which can then be linked to the conquering of the seven Cantrefi, and the conquering of the seven castles in the " Preiddeu Annwn" of Cochrane's tradition. Here, as well, the seven stars of the Great Bear, with the Pole Star, are the portal to the Sabbat, which can be equated with Aah-en-ru. Robert Fitzgerald, in his essay "The Hidden Stone" in "The Luminous Stone", specifically links Gerald Massey's ideas with the Sabbatic tradition, states that Massey successfully reconstructed the "Draconic Tradition and, in this, links the seven stars of the Big Dipper with Gerald Massey and with the craft in general.

Elsewhere, in the grimoire section, I've linked these stars with Caer Arionrhod as a place of testing that a person needs to go through before reaching the Sabbat itself, and with the castle of the west of Ariahrhod, Hekate, Ononshu. Arionrhod appears in the Mabinogion as well, and casts a number of spells on her son, Lleu ap Gryffes, which are similar trials that have to be overcome. Besides this last, which is my own reconstruction, I would say that there's a substantial amount of material shared between this alternate version of Memphis, the contents of the Pickingill letters, the tradition related by Conway about Mr. James, Robert Cochrane's Clan of Tubal Cain tradition, Gerald Massey, and the Cultus Sabbati.

There's much more to be said about the Taas, about the seven, by looking directly at Massey's work, and this is precisely what we're going to look at next.

Works Cited

Bunsen, Christian Karl Josias Freiherr von "Egypt's Place in Universal History", vol. 5, by, published in 1867. Google books,
Chumbley, Andrew Azoetia, Xoanon, Hercules, USA, 2015
Chumbley, Andrew "Dragon Book of Essex", Xoanon, Hercules, 2014
Cochrane, Robert "Basic Structure of the Craft", Cochrane , "Taper that Lights the Way", Shani Oates, Mandrake of Oxford, 2016
Conway, David "Magic without Mirrors", Createspace Independent Publishing, 2011
Conway, David "Secret Wisdom, the Occult Universe Explored", The Aquarian Press, Wellingborough, 1987
Conway, David, "Magic: An Occult Primer", The Witches' Almanac, Newport RI, 2016
Cummings, William L. "The Spurious Rites of Memphis and Mizraim", written in the mid 1930s but republished by the Scottish Rite Research Society journal "Heredom" in 2001, with updates.
Fitzgerald, Robert "The Hidden Stone", "The Luminous Stone", Three Hands Press,Richmond Vista, 2016.
Hoyos, Arturo de ed. "Collectanea, vol. 20", parts one and two, issued by the Masonic Grand College of Rites in the United States in 2008
Howard, Michael "Children of Cain", Three Hands Press, Richmond Vista, 2011
Liddell,E.W. "Pickingill Papers", Michael Howard ed., Capall-Bann, Chieveley, 1994
Madziarczyk, John, "The Magitians Discovered" vol 1, Topaz House Publications, Seattle, 2016
Massey, Gerald "A Book of the Beginnings"vol 2, Williams and Norgate, London, 1881, Google books
Massey, Gerald "My Lyrical Life, Poems Old and New", First Series. Watts and Co., London,1896, google books
Moore, William D. "Darius Wilson, Confidence Schemes, and American Fraternalism 1869–1926", published in 2013 in the "Journal for Research into Freemasonry and Fraternalism", available from author's Academia.edu page.

Ross, Peter, "Standard History of Freemasonry for the State of New York", "Book XIII—The Rite of Memphis", 1899, Google books

Scot, Reginald, John Madziarczyk ed. "Magitians Discovered, vol. 2". Topaz House Publications, Seattle, 2016

Seims, Mellisa "Here be Magic", Thoth Publications, Loughborough, 2022

Thomson, Matthew McBain, "Tabloid History: Rites and Orders Other than the Scottish Rite in America." in "The Universal Freemason", vol. XI num 2, August 1918, IAPSOP

Waite, A.E. "The Secret Tradition in Freemasonry, Volume II", appendix, Rebman Limited, 1911, google books

Chapter 12
Gerald Massey

Finally, another figure who has been influential on the craft in certain ways is Gerald Massey, one of the last mythomaniacs. We know that Massey has been influential because members of the traditional craft have said so. Similarly, going through Chumbley's Azoetia, you can find god names and other concepts that are drawn from Massey's work. It appears, as has been narrated before, that Chumbley did inherit some of the concepts of Massey from his own tradition, and that his use of them is not purely a mask that he's putting in place to communicate concepts he's not allowed to explicitly talk about. This tradition appears to have started itself on Massey's "A Book of the Beginnings", but to have been expanded with information from his later works, particularly "Ancient Egypt, the Light of the World". For this analysis, I've looked at all three of his major works: "A Book of the Beginnings", Massey's first work, "The Natural Genesis", his middle work, and " Ancient Egypt, the Light of the World", this last being published posthumously.

Massey, writing from the end of the 19th century into the beginning of the 20th, drew on a great many previous mythomaniac sources, as well as Theosophy and contemporary archeological findings. However, his work is not archeologically accurate, but is instead a continuation of the quest for an underlying spiritual truth posited to exist behind all the myths and legends of the ancient world. His work is not historically accurate, but it may be spiritually accurate, as is the case with many of the writers that we've looked at. Massey's work shows him to be very aware of, and tuned into, the "Primal Vision".

Massey is the last mythomaniac in the sense that he was the last one whose work received serious attention, with his last books being published in 1907. There were others, notably Robert Graves and

Alfred Boyd Kuhn, but Graves' "White Goddess" got recognition largely because of the respect that Graves' previous work, such as "I, Claudius" commanded. Alfred Boyd Kuhn's work was largely ignored, and even today is much less known in esoteric circles than that of Massey. What happened after Massey's time was that archeology and the translation of primary source documents progressed to a point where the type of synthesis that the mythomaniacs were advocating no longer became tenable.

Massey's Framework.

Gerald Massey makes so many correspondences in his books, between words from every language, between these words and Egyptian deities, and between all of the above and other deities, that it could be argued that a person can basically pick and choose from his works and come up with any concept they want, in that it appears to be a conceptual word salad without any particular structure. However, I believe that there's a method to the madness, and that it's possible to derive some basic contours to his thought without being overly torturous.

First, let's be clear about Massey's method. He'll take words from Egyptian, English, Maori, Akkadian, Latin, and Greek, and make equivalences between them based on putative similarities in spelling and pronunciation. If the spellings and pronunciation won't fit, he'll force them together through saying that the pronunciation is different from the spelling, or that the pronunciation can be conceived of in another way. However, though it would be very easy to poke fun at him, there is really insight in his works, in amongst all the non-insightful correspondences. Also, and quite crucially, his thought developed over time. The book which appears to have been most influential both on the pseudo-Memphis system of Masonry developed by Darius Wilson and on the Welsh cunning tradition associated with Conway's "Mr. James" is "A Book of the Beginnings", which, as the title implies is the start of Massey's work. His last work, "Ancient Egypt, the Light of the World", which I believe Andrew Chumbley significantly drew on, shows quite a bit of evolution and clarification of his ideas.

The thing to remember, when dealing with Gerald Massey, is that, fundamentally, many of these god names, Egyptian, Celtic, Semitic, are just ciphers that are applied by him to underlying astrotheist ideas. The structure of these astrotheist ideas is what underlies all of his thought, and it provides the underlying order within the general chaos of Massey's seemingly random associations of words and gods.

Additionally, Massey recognizes three different ways of reckoning time in the past, stellar time, lunar time, and solar time. This is important because, fundamentally, Massey is basing his ideas on a kind of Astrotheism, where the stars that were used to tell time were turned into deities. However, he does not develop three pure systems, one being stellar, one being lunar, and one being solar. Instead, he develops alternate stellar symbolism for each of them, with the symbolism of lunar time being a synthesis of stellar symbolism and lunar symbolism, and his schema of solar time being a similar combination of the stellar and the solar. What you get are three different stellar pantheons with a similar underlying structure.

Initially, all of these are counter-intuitively linked to the seven stars of the Great Bear and the Pole Star, but in his last writings he separates them out into several constellations. Nonetheless, for about two thirds of his works Massey identifies every group of seven in mythology with the stars of the Great Bear, with an eighth connected to the Pole Star.

Welsh Mythology Through an Egyptian lens.

"Book of the Beginnings"

Though most people know that Gerald Massey focussed on Egypt and Egyptian mythology and religion, many fewer realize that he made correspondences between Egyptian, British, and Welsh mythology and traditions. This linking is especially prevalent in "A Book of the Beginnings", his first major mythomaniac work. "A Book of the Beginnings" is fundamentally about the beginnings of all cultures, including the British. Massey believes that Egyptian culture is the primal origin of all of the world's cultures and mythologies. Throughout the book, he devotes chapters to "proving" how Welsh and English terms are really derived from Egyptian, how English and Welsh folk celebrations are really pagan Egyptian celebrations in disguise, and finally how Welsh mythology is really Egyptian mythology in disguise. In analyzing the folk customs, he relies on a combination of chance correspondences between words due to alliteration, as well as Astrotheist arguments that see most, if not all, of English folk festivals and customs as being part of a fertility cult oriented paganism. As part of his general analysis of folk customs, he also references accounts of the witches' Sabbath in multiple places, and imposes his Egyptian interpretation onto it as well.

Massey's fusion of Welsh mythology with Egyptian mythology goes quite a long way to explaining how Egyptian ideas got into Andrew Chumbley's work, in my opinion. These ideas most likely come from the Welsh tradition that contributed to the formation of the Cultus Sabbati. I believe it's possible to work backwards from public statements and works by Cultus members that reference Massey's Egyptian myths, and to connect them to the Welsh myths that Massey linked them to. In this way, I believe it's possible to get to what lies behind the mask of Egyptian mythology and terms that Chumbley and others put forward.

The basic structure of "Book of the Beginnings", into which Massey fits these Welsh sources, is an Astrotheist model that's centered on the revolution of the Big Dipper around the pole as being indicative of the sun traveling around the earth in the geocentric model. This stellar idea is thought by Massey to be the original on which the later solar model was based. Within this, the Big Dipper is identified with the Ark of the Sun, the Solar Bark or ship of Egyptian religion, within which the sun god Ra travels around the earth every day. The Big Dipper has seven components, and these are corresponded with seven gods. Though Massey spends a lot of time speculating about different figures such as Horus and Seth, which could be related to the seven gods, he doesn't give a systematic meaning to the seven gods in this work. That systematic meaning would only be presented in "Natural Genesis", where he breaks the seven up into a group of four and a group of three. The seven "Taas" are mentioned in "Book of the Beginnings", but they're not systematically looked at.

Now, looking at the Welsh material, chapter or Section 8 of the book, "Egyptian Deities in the British Isles", is the most substantial part of this analysis, in that it relies on more than purely coincidental correspondences, though these are still present. This, I should say, is one of the parts that contains part of the system that "Mr. James" of David Conway's works presented to Conway. For this part, Massey looks mostly at Welsh poetry, seeing this as very reasonably having some type of continuity with pagan beliefs, and from there with putative Egyptian beliefs which underly it. However, Massey is not looking at these works from a completely isolated perspective. It's important to keep in mind that Massey took the same liberties with Welsh mythology that he did with Egyptian, and that on top of this he also recognized neo-druidic material from Iolo Morganwg's school as being genuine, something which is now known to be false. He also drew on other Neo-Druidic commentators such as Edward Davies.

You'll remember that Davies adapted Faber's "Arkite" thesis to Welsh mythology. Davies reduced all of the male characters in Welsh mythology to one god, who was Noah, and did something similar with references to ships and the Ark. Part of what Massey is doing is to take those synthetic figures and take them apart. Ironically, Massey comments on page 315 of volume 1 of this work about Davies' "wearisome references to the goddess Kêd and her ark", which, considering Massey's own repetitions in his equation of various mythological figures with each other, is quite an amusing statement. Let's look at some significant parts of this chapter, then.

Like most of Massey's work, the entire chapter is chaotic. However, a basic astrotheist story can be detected. Here, Ceridwen, equated to the Egyptian Tawret, or "Ta-Urt-E", as Massey says, is the ground of being which generates the Sun. The Sun is seen as having both a dark and a light part, the dark part corresponding to Ceridwen's son "Affagdu", the light part corresponding to the neo-druidic figure of Hu Gadarn. This figure, which is Abraxas like, corresponds to the eternal sun in the transcendent dimension. The power of the First Sun manifests itself through the Pole Star, which is mercurial in character, and corresponds to Thoth. In turn, Massey corresponds Thoth to the character of Gwydion from the Mabinogion. This Gwydion was a powerful magician. Thoth is looked at by Massey as the vehicle of the Word, which is emanated by Hu. The Word, in turn, manifests in the world as the life giving solar force.

This force manifests through the seven stars of the Great Bear, though Massey in this work does not give many details about just how this works. The seven stars of the Great Bear revolve around the Pole Star, and their orientation around the Pole Star signals the different seasons. In this, picture the Pole Star as the center of the circle, with the different stations being the east, west, north and south points of the circle. If you make four copies of the Great Bear, and align each of them to these stations of the circle, you have a swastika, which is in Massey's opinion the primal origin of this sign. The travel of the Great Bear, in this, also corresponds to the distribution of the life force from the transcendental realm to the material realm. This distribution of life force follows the cycle of the physical sun. From here, the distribution of the life force through the seasons follows the Astrotheist model.

The Great Bear is interpreted as being the ship of Thoth, which carries the physical Sun in its journey around the earth in the geocentric model. In this, the ship of Thoth and his seven companions battle the forces of darkness. Here, Thoth, despite being corresponded to Gwydion, is also corresponded to King Arthur, with the seven stars of the Great Bear corresponding to Arthur's seven companions in the poem the "Preiddu Annwn", or Spoils of Annwn, the underworld. This is a poem where Arthur and his companions travel through six different castles, gaining objects, with the Cauldron being a prime one. Using Massey's symbolism, the recapture of the Cauldron can be equated with the recapture or victory of the solar life energy in the cycle of the year, the Cauldron of Ceridwen corresponding to the source of the Eternal Sun itself, from which Affagdu/Hu is generated. Other, later, interpreters of the poem, particularly Robert Cochrane, no doubt had very different interpretations of this.

The Astrotheist model is fairly standard: the northern Solstice is simultaneously the darkest part of the year and the beginning of the general inflow of life. The rebirth of the light at the northern solstice sets the action of the year in motion, as the sacred king attacks the darkness and finally conquers it at the vernal equinox. After conquering the darkness, the king establishes his kingdom, which flourishes at the summer solstice. Next, the powers of darkness start to reassert themselves, and they get the upper hand at the autumnal equinox, before reaching their peak at the northern solstice, whereupon the cycle begins again. Massey tells this story in a confusing way, using figures from the Mabinogion and other Welsh poetry, as we will see.

He also relates the figures at the station of the Vernal Equinox and the Autumnal Equinox to the two aspects of the Sun god Hu. The Vernal equinox corresponds to Hu himself, the light aspect of the sun, while the Autumnal Equinox corresponds to the Affagdu or dark aspect of the sun, the sun at midnight. The light aspect is the conquering hero, while the dark aspect is the negative force, with these also corresponding to Horus and Set. However, these figures are two sides of the same coin, and so Set, in this, is not truly evil, but is instead just another force in the cycle of life.

Massey corresponds these two to a number of different twin figures that appear in English and Welsh folklore, and he expresses the cycle of the year using different figures from Celtic myth. We will consider each of these different parts, namely Ceridwen and Hu, the motion of the sun, and the nature of the seven, as well as the role of the pole, in more detail.

The first, main, story which tells the cycle of the Sun, is that of Pwyll and Arawn. This comes from the Mabinogion. In the original story, Pwyll is king of Dyfed, and Arawn is king of Annwn, the underworld. Pwyll is hunting in the woods and sees a group of dogs chasing a stag. He orders his hunting dogs to chase the other dogs off, and to bring the stag down themselves. Then, a man appears who introduces himself as Arawn, king of Annwn. He declares that Pwyll has greatly insulted him by claiming the stag for himself, but that he can make it up to him by doing him a service. Arawn's kingdom is being constantly attacked by a man named Hafgan (or Havgan), and if Pwyll will go down into his kingdom and slay him, they will be even. To do this, Arawn enchants Pwyll to resemble him, and so Pwyll takes his place as the king of Annwn for a year, until he gets the opportunity to slay Hafgan. This being done, he returns to his own kingdom, where Arawn has been imitating him, through magic, for a year. Pwyll is then known as both the king of Annwn and of Dyfed for the year he spent as king there.

Now, Massey relates this to seasonal change, and to the conflict between Horus, Osiris, and Set. He relates Arawn to Osiris, Hafgan to Set, and his war with Hafgan to the winter. Pwyll, as Horus, goes to war with Set/Hafgan, and defeats him at the Equinox, thereby liberating the kingdom not only from Hafgan but from winter, and ushering in a new era of fertility for the kingdom.

The second story of the Mabinogion that Massey threads into this, and makes into an equivalent with the first, has to do with Manawaydan and Pwyll's son Pryderi, in opposition to an evil sorcerer. In the original Mabinogion story, Pryderi is a king of the seven cantrefs of Dyfed as well, but offers Manawaydan his kingdom, and becomes his companion. During the story, an evil sorcerer casts a spell over the land, a mist which causes every person and city in it, and every farm animal, to disappear. This mist is referenced in Conway's account of Mr. James' ideas about Dyfed. At first, Manawaydan and Pryderi subsist by hunting wild animals, but eventually they leave the kingdom to find places to work and to earn a living. They become craftsmen, and in a series of tests they become very good at their crafts in particular cities, so good that the other craftsmen expel them, forcing them to move on. They make saddles, shields and shoes. After this, they return to Dyfed, and, surviving on hunting wild animals again, one day they find a wild boar who leads them to a castle which they've never seen before.

Pryderi goes into the castle, and inside finds a large golden bowl. He touches the bowl and is immediately stuck to it and paralyzed. Manawaydan does not go into the castle. He cannot find a way to save Pryderi, so eventually he leaves Dyfed and again goes to another town, becoming a craftsman once again, making shoes. The same thing happens to him which happened before, with the fellow craftsmen becoming upset at his skill and driving him off. This time, though, he takes a bushel of wheat and goes back to Dyfed, determined to plant it and start farming.

He plants his wheat, and his wheat grows, but the night before the first row is ready to harvest someone comes and takes it all. The same happens on subsequent nights, until Manawaydan sits out at night to see who's stealing his crops. He sees a large group of mice come, and though he's unable to stop them, he manages to capture one. After this, Manawaydan is resolved to hang this captured mouse as punishment for stealing his crops. Many people in the story observe him planning this and remark on how treating a mouse like this is excessive and cruel, but he proceeds, only to be interrupted at the last moment by a Bishop who not only pleads to him to stop, but promises him that if he does stop he'll lift the curse on Pryderi as well as the curse on the land. The Bishop reveals himself to be the sorcerer Llwyd ap Cilcoed, who has cast the spell on Dyfed, and who has also sent mice to take Manawaydan's crops. He reveals that the mouse is his wife in a transformed state. She's pregnant, which made her slower, which is the reason why Manawaydan was able to catch her.

The reason for this curse has to do with a previous story of the Mabinogion, which is not relevant to Massey's interpretation. Within this, the important parts for Massey are that the land was cursed, it was enveloped in mist, and that the actions of Manawaydan saved it. Massey equates the kingdom of Annwn with Dyfed. The mist here is equated with winter, with the lifting of the curse being equated with the Vernal Equinox. Llwyd ap Cilcoed is Set, Manawaydan is Horus.

This is linked by Massey to the first story most fully through the character of Seithennin. This figure in Welsh mythology was a person responsible for some type of barrier against the sea, which kept the land from flooding, but because of his drunkenness he neglected his work and allowed the land to flood. Through dubious linguistic associations, Massey links Seithennin both with Satan, Set, and seven, the seven kingdoms of Dyfed. Massey links this drowning of the kingdom to the enveloping Dyfed in mist in the Mabinogion. He further makes a parallel between this and the sinking of Atlantis. So, Seithennin is a Set character responsible for destruction, is opposed to Horus, who is the positive king who defends the kingdom against evil.

Massey also links Seithennin to the Egyptian Khnum through Khnum's connection with water. Khnum is a goat headed god, and Massey goes further and explicitly links him, and by implication Seithennin, with the goat at the witches' Sabbat. After making this identity, he takes it one step further by linking both Horus and Set with the Sabbatic Goat, with the goat encompassing both light and darkness. Here, Set/Khnum/Seithynen, stands for the back of the goat, while Horus stands for the front, and the "Osculum Infame", the obscene kiss on the buttocks or anus, is seen as honoring Set/Khnum/Seithynen. This makes up the full, Abraxas like, character, similar to that of the combination of Affagdu and Hu Gadarn.

Putting this together, we get a fuller picture: Seithennin let in the water that flooded Dyfed, leading to it sinking. Arawn, the king of Annwn is the king of the flooded Dyfed, which is Annwn. Seithennin is Hafgan, who is his enemy. Pwyll/Manawaydan, goes to war against Hafgan/Seithennin/LLwyd ap Cilcoed, and defeats him, thereby causing the water to recede. The water receding is also the end of winter, and it happens at the Vernal equinox.

Finally, Pwyll and Pryderi are linked, through dubious linguistic similarity, by Massey with Prydain, or Britain itself, taken as signifying both the seven lands of Dyfed and the fertility of the land in general, which manifests through the growth of crops. This association makes Pwyll, Pryderi, and Prydain sun gods, forms of Hu in Massey's telling, with Prydain taken as the manifestation of the power of the sun of Hu on earth. Though not integrated into complete cycle of the myths, the figure of Prydain completes the cycle of the year. Additionally, at the very beginning of the chapter, Massey says that Christ is a form of Prydhain. I interpret this as saying that Prydhain is the Astrotheist Christ, whose birth, death, and resurrection are linked to seasonal change, and that as the embodiment of the land he also undergoes different trials corresponding to this change.

The wheel of the year, in this, appears to start with Seithennin releasing the water in the west in Autumn, thereby ushering in the dark half of the year. Arawn, the king of the sunken province, calls out to Pwyll for help at the winter solstice, in the North. Pwyll then fights against Seithennin/Set, eventually overcoming him at the point of the Vernal Equinox, in the East. Finally, the kingdom is restored and enjoys its fertility and the production of crops at the Summer Solstice, as Prydhain, in the South. If we were to continue with this cyclical interpretation, you could say that after Prydhain experiences this prosperity, Seithennin releases the waters yet again, flooding the province, necessitating the intervention of Pwyll once more. Applying all of this, we get a compass of the year with the following four points:

Seithennin in the West,
Arawn in the North,
Pwyll in the East
Prydhain in the South.

Seithennin's association with the West is commented on by Massey himself.

On top of this, the Neo-Druidic character of Hu Gadarn can be equated with Pwyll in the East. This draws on Edward Davies' "Arkite" interpretation of all of this. Davies drew on forged Neo-Druidic manuscripts which associated Hu Gadarn with a magical creature called the "Avanc" or "Afanc", which he labels a "Beaver", and so can be looked at as a "Magic Beaver". This beaver is related to the cause of the flood of a lake, perhaps by destroying a dam, and so Hu Gadarn is said to have drawn the magic beaver out of the lake with oxen, thereby preventing a new flood from occurring. The Afanc is related here to Set, as well as to Seithennin, with Hu Gadarn being related to Horus. So you have a duality here of Seithennin opening the floodgates in the West and Hu Gadarn hauling the magic beaver out of the waters and stopping the flood, at the station of the East. Maybe after this Seithennin returned the magic beaver to its home, where it went back to its nefarious ways, continuing the cyclical pattern.

However, I don't think that a completely cyclical interpretation was how all of this was used in the system of the Cantrefs that Conway describes Mr. James as subscribing to. Instead, I think that the drama of the year was a background for the individual taking on the role of Pwyll, or Manawaydan, and subduing the various Cantrefs, thereby liberating them. Here, there's just one cycle: a fall, a fight, liberation, and the enjoyment of said liberation. The fight for the liberation of the Cantrefs is a fight for mastery of all of the seven.

Also, and this is very important, the four points of the year here do not correspond to any of the Cantrefs themselves. Instead, this cycle is something put on top of them. If the particular Cantrefs were given associations with Celtic gods in the various traditions associated with them, this was most likely not drawn from this chapter of Gerald Massey.

Going back to the stellar correspondences, if the four seasons correspond to the Great Bear in its four configurations, then the center point of all of this is the Pole Star. This point is the source of the life energy which the Great bear in its four configurations distributes to the earth. This point Massey variously attributes to either Thoth, or to King Arthur, with Thoth in turn corresponding to Gwydion, from the Mabinogion. Gwydion is a magician, and is related by Massey to Mercury, and Arthur is cast by Massey as being Solar-Mercurial, combining both characters in one. What unites all of these different attributions is the idea that the Pole Star corresponds to the logos, to the creative word, which is cast by Massey into different forms: on the one hand, the creative word, as a word, is connected to Thoth and to Mercury, on the other, the creative word is the power of the Sun and is a solar logos, which both manifests and sustains the world with life energy, and so is connected with Hu.

With all of this, it's clearer if the center is first thought of as the sun itself, in its absolute form, which in going through the different seasons rises in its energy, peaks, declines, and meets its depths, before rising again. The association of this point with the logos or word just takes this relationship and moves it back one step: now you have the solar god, who exists in a different plane, whose voice or tool is the solar logos. The solar logos speaks or channels the power of the solar god into this universe, and from there that power obeys the same cycle as the physical sun itself. The physical sun, in this, is actually secretly supported by the Pole Star and by the solar logos, which channels said energy from the hidden sun in a different plane of existence.

Arthur, as a form of Thoth and a channel for the sun, also emerges in Massey's correspondences as the leader of the Great Bear. Here, the seven stars of the Great Bear are identified with the seven companions of Arthur from the "Preddeu Annwn", who travel through six Caers or castles and subdue them. Here, Arthur is the same as Pwyll. This story, too, can be identified with the seasonal change of the Great Bear, though the number of Caers in the poem are more than four. In fact, in Natural Genesis Massey will make a comparison, between the six Caers and the Zodiac. He attributes each of the Caers that Arthur travels through to two signs of the Zodiac, with his transit through all six of them consisting of a full circulation of the wheel of the year.

Thoth, here, is the announcer of the Sun god, Hu, the god which in turn is the child of the Celtic goddess Ceridwen in Massey's cosmology. Gwydion, in this, takes on the combined form of the sorcerer and Anubis, a magician in the cast of Woden as well as a god of the dead and a psychopomp leading the dead to the blessed lands. In Massey's Egyptian terms, he is a synthesis of Thoth and Anubis, with Set thrown in as well. Gwydion is described by Massey as being "The Word", the manifestor and announcer of the gods, and, like Thoth, and the inventor of letters, as well as a powerful magician. He's related by Massey to Woden, in the sense that Woden discovered the Runes (pg. 363-364). He's also identified with cutting, in his capacity as the one who inscribes the Runes, and through this, with the power of opening. Massey also gives the opposition of Set/Horus, or Pwyll/Seithwynn to several other pairs of mythological and folkoric figures, namely Taliesin himself and "Tom and Jack".

Taliesen here is a solar figure. The transformation of "Gwion the Little" to the sage Taliesin is linked by Massey to the Solar overcoming the Lunar, and to the birth of the sun after gestation, by Ceridwen. In the original story, Gwion the Little accidentally gets three drops of the Awen from Ceridwen's cauldron on him, empowering him. After a chase drama of transformation where he runs from Ceridwen, he turns into a grain of wheat, which is eaten by Ceridwen, impregnating her. He emerges from this as the newly empowered sage Taliesin. Massey sees Solar significance in this.

Massey also links Taliesin's original state, as "Gwion the Little" to the dark phase of Affagdu, with the light phase of Hu Gadarn standing for Taliesin after he emerges transformed. Massey's Taliesin, in being linked to the light and dark sides of Hu Gadarn, is also linked to the East and the West, with the Affagdu, aspect being in the West, and the more properly Solar aspect of Hu Gadarn being in the East. His form of "Gwion" is linked to lunar world of the West, the setting sun, while his form of Taliesin is linked to the solar world of the East, the rising sun. In this, Taliesin is also Jack of the Green, or the Green man, mentioned before. This, again, is also related to Set and Horus.

Jack of the Green also appears in another series of folk songs and myths analyzed by Massey, particularly "The House that Jack Built. This is the same as in the poem which Robert Cochrane also talks about. However, Massey's interpretation of this appears to be quite different from that of Cochrane, who based much of his interpretation on Robert Graves' comments on the poem in "The White Goddess".

Here, in Massey's interpretation, we have "Tom, Hu, Jack", as a British triad. In this, Hu besides being a sun god, splits into two different aspects, Tom and Jack. Tom is connected with the Egyptian Tum as the sun at night, the sun in the underworld, and the sun in winter. Jack is the sun at its fullest, which Massey describes as being full of life and associated with May Day, with summer, and is associated with an Egyptian god Kak. These two are also equated with Set and Horus, on the horizon of the two Equinoxes, because Massey, in his unique logic, shifts the significance of the story from the Solstices to the Equinoxes. In fact, he says that the Equinox attribution of Tom and Jack preceded the Solstice interpretation, which is a degeneration of the first.

Troy Town.

The Seven Cantrefs

On page 312 of vol. 1 of "A Book of the Beginnings" in the chapter titled "Egyptian Deities in the British Isles", Massey makes direct reference to what David Conway relates as Mr. James' belief about the Great Bear and the seven Cantrefs of Dyfed, stating that they correspond to one another. This is after a sentence relating both of them to the Troy Town maze, or classical labyrinth, which, if you count from the outside in, has seven rings. This maze is found in Cornwall. The discussion about the Troy maze is contained in a section on Troy as a version of the Holy City. London is described as "New Troy", with the original city being over the water and destroyed, and the original London is said to be ruled by Baal as a

Sun god. This is related to the story of Geoffrey of Monmouth which sees Britain as being founded by refugees from Troy, which Massey sees as being a story based on Egyptian concepts which were latinized.

There's quite a lot here. As said, I believe that these seven, as corresponding to the seven stars of the Great Bear, were the subjects of seasonal change, and did not correspond here to the points of the seasonal circle themselves. The inner logic of the seven is distinct from the seasonal schema in this presentation. The seven stand for land that's variously flooded, made inaccessible, then redeemed from the flooded water, making it fertile once again, before the cycle repeats itself. This is the change of the seasons expressed in the language of water and flooding. Going off Mr. James' account given by Conway, though, it would appear that each of the Cantrefs, each of the seven, within the individual, was seen as naturally sunken and occluded at birth, and that it was the goal of the individual to resurrect the particular cantrefs from their watery depths through spiritual effort. This action is squaring the circle, making the potential actual. Massey's equation of the seven with the seven rings of the Labyrinth and Troy Town, gives us an idea about how this might come about, as well as what the ultimate goal would be in subduing the Cantrefs. This ultimate goal is going from the seven to the eighth, which is the Pole Star, the gateway to the Sabbat. The goal is the Sabbat itself, the center of the maze, the Holy City.

To start with, the Troy model sees the seven as concentric circles leading to a center. These are said to be equivalent, and to correspond to the Great Bear. Doing the work is a progressive movement through the concentric circles to the center, but seen as movement through the turns of the labyrinth. In this, if you're using the Troy Town maze to get to the center, every turn that you go through, every reversal in direction, gets you into another of the concentric circles, until you arrive at the center, the eighth part, which similarly is the Sabbat.

There's a very interesting parallel to the Troy Town maze which is present in the Charles Cardell "Coven of Atho" material. As we shall see, they have five principles which can be arranged in a cyclical fashion, around a a fourfold circle, with the point of north standing both for the start and the end of the cycle, making five. These five principles are simultaneously pictured by them as corresponding to five concentric circles, with the end point being in the center. Based on Cardell's like of Atlantis, I believe that these circles were thought to describe the organization of the City of Atlantis, which links it with the Holy City model. The ringed nature of Atlantis is described in Plato's account, and like Troy it's a city over the water where the ancestors are supposed to have come from. Going through the five rings, and the five principles, which lead from birth to death, is, then, the same as going through the outer parts of the Holy City to its sanctum sanctorum, its holiest of holies. This would indicate that the movement through the Troy Town maze is similarly a journey through seven rings of a city which leads to a holy center. We can picture the journey from birth to death as one where the stage of just being born is the biggest circle, and where the subsequent stages of life form smaller and smaller concentric circles until, at death, we return back to the center. The journey through the stages of life from birth to death, then, becomes the path through the maze the leads to the spirit world of the center. This, in turn I interpret as the Sabbat. The concentric circles, in this, can also then be identified with the stations of the wheel of the year.

Again, with all of this, I believe that the literal identification of this with Atlantis (or with Troy) is a reinterpretation of something which is much older through a contemporary lens, and that the underlying concepts don't really depend on believing that Atlantis really existed or functioned in this way. Significantly, Massey also links Atlantis with the seven provinces of Dyfed, though he talks about the "seven caves of Atlantis", and so does not conceive Atlantis as being made out of concentric rings.

Within Massey's world, there's a transcendent manifestation of the Holy City, or Atlantis, and then seasonal change is viewed as the cyclical flooding of land in the material world which is the complement of Atlantis, Britain in this case, and its subsequent overcoming of the flood in the summer. The flood is equated with winter and the decrease of the life force in the land, while being freed from the flood is equated with summer, and with the coming forth of the life force in the land.

With regards to the seven kingdoms of Dyfed, though Massey's overall presentation of Celtic mythology is confused, you can detect a seasonal pattern regarding them in his writings. Here, it's the seven kingdoms themselves that go through seasonal change. This follows from the idea of the big dipper acting as an indicator of the seasons, with its orientations changing in the winter, spring, summer, and fall, these four combined resembling a swastika. Massey makes this equation by combining two stories of the Mabinogion into one, with an additional minor Welsh story also serving as glue linking them together.

In Massey's telling, Baal, the Sun God who is supposed to rule over new Troy, is identified with the neo-Druidic "Hu Gadarn", who in this case takes over the role of Atlas and Baphomet. The maze also links all of this to the goddess of the West, described in the Azoetia as Ononshu and linked to the seven stars of the Great Bear in that work, who oversees the ordeals of initiation. These ordeals lead to the Sabbat itself, with the ordeals in this case being parallel to navigating the labyrinth to the center. The Great Bear, in this, points to the Pole Star, which is a portal to the Sabbat itself, which is beyond the stars. Within the seven, the four are most likely the outer rings of the labyrinth, while the three are likely the innermost rings.

Easy instructions on how to draw the Troy Town maze can be found in Nigel Pennick's "Secret Games of the Gods". Drawings of the maze can be used as meditative tools, with it not being necessary to construct a real one, though versions of this construction have been integrated into various ritual constructs, like some of the double ouroboros rituals in the "Dragon Book of Essex". In these, the labyrinth serves as the second circle.

Seven Taas

Let's look at the context within both "A Book of the Beginnings", "Natural Genesis" and "Ancient Egypt" where the principles of the "Taas", the seven elements used in the pseudo-Memphis rite, are located in. The seven Taas are the seven qualities that are associated with the seven Cantrefs of Dyfed in the system outlined by Conway's "Mr. James". These "Taas" are consistently identified by Massey with the Lunar schema, with Thoth being connected with them as the Pole Star. Thoth, in turn, is called by Massey the "Living Word", with the Taas being the speech of Thoth. He explicitly links the combination of Thoth with the seven Taas with an eight spoked diagram which will be familiar to people knowledgable of traditional witchcraft, connected with with the spokes of the compass, the wheel of the year, on page 140 of vol. 2 of "Beginnings". Here, Thoth the revealer is the eighth in the compass that completes the seven.

However, Massey's later writings, particularly those in "Natural Genesis" suggest that the three and the four do not actually correspond to seven points on the compass, but instead correspond to the vertical dimension and to the horizontal dimension. In this, the four correspond to the cardinal directions in the horizontal dimension, while the three correspond to the three stations of the vertical dimension: above, below, and center.

The eighth figure of Thoth actuates and activates the system of the seven, as a link between the transcendental dimension and the manifest one.

We can get very specific here about how Massey relates all of this to both principles and to other gods. The seven Taas are given as "Matter", "Cohesion", "Fluxion", "Coagulation", "Accumulation", "Station", "Division".

These can be broken up into four and three: "Matter", "Cohesion", "Fluxion", "Coagulation", standing for the cup of the dipper, and "Accumulation", "Station", "Division", standing for the three stars of the handle.

In this, Matter can be linked with Water, Cohesion with Fire, Fluxion with Air and Coagulation with Earth. Matter is linked with Water as being the primal chaos, Cohesion is linked with Fire as being the first manifest, and organized, form of matter. Earth is linked with Coagulation as a combination of Fire and Water, while Fluxion is linked with Air. This follows from the ultimate source of the "Taas", a writing by François Lenormant which we shall examine next.

Water—Matter
Fire—Cohesion
Air—Fluxion
Earth—Coagulation

Now, as for the three principles of Accumulation, Division, and Station, it's best to look at the source of all of this, Lenormant's writings. Massey adapts these three to his own symbolism of Set, Horus, and Shu, but Lenormant's work is the foundation on which that is based, and it helps to illuminate the logic behind it.

Lenormant's Taas

Where exactly did Masssey get the seven "Taas" from? The list appears in James Bonwick's "Egyptian Belief and Modern Thought", published in 1878, and Bonwick, in turn, cites a familiar name as the source: François Lenormant. The source is a large monograph, not about Egypt but about the Eleusinian mysteries, printed in "Histoire et mémoires de l'Institut royal de France", volume 25, published in 1861, and titled "Mémoire sur les Réprésentations qui avaient lieu dans les Mystères D'Éleusis". It's co-written by François Lenormant and his brother Charles. It was also published as a stand alone volume. The page number for the Taas in the collected volume is 433, while the page number in the stand alone volume is 91.

Lenormant cites a chapter in Lepsius' edition of the Egyptian "Book of the Dead" for his source for the Taas. In his citation, he states that he believes that the the abstract principles that he and his brother have associated with Eleusis can be found in Egyptian texts as well, and, after listing the seven principles, he says that they'll provide proof of them later, presumably in another work. This work was apparently never completed or published. Lenormant cites chapter 17 of Lepsius' edition of the Egyptian book of the dead for this. Lepsius' edition is not a translation, but is instead a print of the Egyptian hieroglyphs themselves. However, following his numbering system, we can correlate this page with Budge's translation, where it appears under Plate VII. Using Budge's 1895 edition of "The Egyptian Book of the Dead" , Plate VII is treated in section "Plates VII-X", which starts on page 276, and runs to page 291.

Looking there we get a surprise: This is the same section that Massey cites for the four gods and the three gods, for the original seven gods of the Great Bear that he treats at great length. The names of the gods, though translated somewhat differently by Budge, are the same. From the Budge translation: "The holy ones who stand behind Osiris, even Mestha, Hapi, Tuamautef, and Qebhsennuf, are they who are behind the Thigh in the northern sky." The "Thigh" in this is the Great Bear. Massey most likely read Lenormont himself, in that Bonwick's book does not make these associations with the seven qualities. There's nothing in the passage that suggests a correspondence between these gods and particular elements.

It appears that the link between these gods and the seven "Taas" is something that Lenormant himself came up with. Additionally, since he was trying to explain Greek pagan thought through this, arguing that the original source of these ideas was Egypt, I think that Lenormant adapted the Greek elements to these figures, adding Accumulation, Station, and Division to the three that were left over. Lenormant, though, was not just randomly assigning elements to these beings. Instead, he was basing his correspondences on another system. Lenormant's work on the inner meaning of the Eleusinian mysteries is based on Schelling's concept of the Cabiri. This was outlined in a published speech by Schelling called "Über die Gottheiten von Samothrake", which has been translated into English as "On the Divinities of Samothrace". Let's go into Schelling's ideas.

Schelling's original system of the Cabiri identifies the four Cabiric gods as Demeter, whose Roman equivalent is Ceres, Persephone, the Greek version of Proserpina, Dionysos, and Hermes. There are three non-Cabiric gods attached to these, although Schelling only explicitly names one, Zeus. The myth attached to them is not one that goes from the top down, but from the bottom up. The Cabiric deities in this correspond, first, to the underworld, and then ascend up from there. This bottom up progression is one of the distinctive features of Schelling's system, whose presence is a give away that the author is drawing on it.

Ceres or Demeter is the great void, identified with desire and craving, which generates Persephone or Proserpina, who is a positive emanation. This emanation is associated with a pure flame by Schelling, as well as with magic, and is labeled by him as the ground of all manifest nature. Dionysos comes next, and is presented as her husband, and as someone who tames her pure flame, as a restraining influence who serves as a medium between the unmanifest Ceres and the manifest Persephone. He is labeled by Schelling as the lord of the Spirit world. Hermes, or Casmillos, appears as the fourth as both an intermediary, messenger, and herald, between the lower gods and the upper gods, as well as the lord of both Dionysos and Persephone. These upper gods are, in a sense, generated from the lower gods. Schelling cites "El" or "Zeus", Jupiter, as being the next god in the series after Hermes, as being the one whom Hermes serves. Implicitly, if the idea of seven Cabiri is accepted, there would be two other gods beyond Zeus. Here the likely candidates for these two gods are Cronus or Saturn and Uranus or Caelus, who are the father and grandfather of Zeus, respectively.

The context in which the seven of Schelling appear in the brother Lenormant's work deals with the creation of the world through the creation of several different figures. They change the correspondences around, but the underlying logic survives. This process of the creation of world is described by the Lenormants as coming through a process that they refer to as "Double Incest". Derived from Greek philosophy, this process starts with passive matter, the Mother, Ceres, Water, generating an active matter, or Fire, Jupiter, the Son. Then, these two combine or have "Incest" with each other, and generate a third principle, which corresponds to Coagulation or Earth. This principle is linked to the Greek Proserpina by Lenormant. After this, the Son, Jupiter, the Fire principle, who has now become the Father principle of Earth, has sex with Proserpina, his daughter, and generates a fourth principle, Dionysos, which corresponds to Fluxion or Air, and to the general life force. We could restate all this by saying that the Mother, Water, generates the Son, Fire, and then the Fire unites with the Water to generate Earth or "Coagulation", then the Fire unites with this Earth to produce Air or "Fluxion". This is close, but not identical, to the way that the elements are generated in the account of Plato in the Timaeus. It leads to a system of

Water—Ceres, Matter
Fire—Jupiter, Cohesion,
Earth—Proserpina, Coagulation
Air—Dionysos, Fluxion

Going by Massey's correspondences, this would equate to

North—Water, Ceres
South—Fire, Jupiter
West—Earth, Proserpina
East—Air, Dionysos

This explanation of Lenormant's begins on page 428 of the collected volumes, or page 86 of the stand alone edition.

Next, Lenormant explains the three. He has freely adapted Schelling's ideas to his elemental schema, but, here, Dionysos, now taking the place of Hermes as the last of the Cabiric gods, also serves as a gateway between the lower gods and the higher. The higher gods, in this, are related by Lenormant to the Astrotheist gods of the seasons.

Dionysos, as air, or Fluxion, is implicitly linked by Lenormant with the general life force, or spirit, and his account of the final three members of the seven is a reenactment of the seasonal mysteries, according to Astrotheism. After the Fluxion is born, it is torn apart by the Titans, signifying Division death and also implicitly winter, and thrust into the earth. This can be related to the death of Osiris, with the Titans standing in for Set.

Accumulation, in this, is correspondingly associated with the coming together again of Osiris' parts. This resurrection, the coming together of the parts, corresponds to the spring. Lenormant makes Apollo, the god of the sun, responsible for gathering Dionysos' parts back together, which is associated with Accumulation and growth linked to life and to the health giving force flowing from the Sun. Here, Apollo is parallel to Horus, as the enemy of Set, even though in the original story it's Isis who does the collecting of Osiris' parts. The sun warms the corpse of Dionysos in the winter, causing it to regenerate, Accumulate, and to be resurrected. The completed rebirth of the rebuilt Dionysos corresponds to the quality of Station.

The last part of the process, that of the literal resurrection of Dionysos through the reassembling of his parts, is said by Lenormant to have been represented in the Eleusinian mysteries by the solar phallic Hierophant as Apollo engaging in a Hieros Gamos or holy marriage, a sex act, with the priestess of Ceres, or of the Earth, who in this case signifies the tomb of Dionysios, and who contains Dionysos within herself. A person dressed up in the costume of a gigantic penis symbolizing Mercury, an "ithyphallic figure", is said by Lenormant to preside over the sex act. The priest has sex with the priestess, and through this the sun symbolically impregnates the earth, who then gives birth to the reborn, reconstructed, Dionysos in the spring. Lenormant presents Venus as the symbol of this Hieros Gamos. The sacred sex act is portrayed by Lenormant as being the climax of the Eleusinian Mysteries, and the great secret that the initiates were forbidden to reveal.

Continuing our correspondences,

Titans/Set—Division, underworld
Apollo/Horus—Accumulation, sky
Reborn Dionysos/Osiris—Station, surface of the earth.

Air—Dionysos, Fluxion
Earth—Proserpina, Coagulation
Fire—Jupiter, Cohesion,
Water—Ceres, Matter

The Inner Significance of Massey's Three and Four

Natural Genesis

Massey recognizes both a transcendent dimension and a material, manifest dimension. Within each of these is a vertical and a horizontal axis. The vertical axis is linked with the number three, while the horizontal axis is linked with the number four. In the transcendental realm, the vertical axis is that of the core gods themselves, while the horizontal axis is that of the paradise where the honored dead go, as well as the secondary gods. The transcendent dimension is most like the vertical axis, while the manifest dimension is most like the horizontal axis. The transcendent dimension is the source of life and light which manifests in the material dimension. In this, the horizontal axis in the manifest world is defined in an astrotheist way, with the stations of the four related to the four seasons and to seasonal change.

However, Massey adds a unique twist to all of this by associating seasonal change with the motion of the Big Dipper. This is unique in that the seven stars of the Big Dipper are, in turn, given the significance of the three and the four themselves, of the vertical and the horizontal axes, so that what you have is a system within a system. The Big Dipper, in this, contains a replica of what exists in the transcendent dimension, a model of the three and the four, but it changes with the seasons itself. Perhaps its best to think about the system of the three and the four as it manifests in the Big Dipper as being a framework, as being a model of the transcendent , which is put into motion through the change in the orientation of the Big Dipper through the different seasons of the year, such that the star corresponding to the east is most especially activated during spring time, the star of the south is most heavily activated during summer, and so on. In this, the process of seasonal change is diffferent from the material that the seasonal change is imposed on.

Let's look at the three first. The vertical dimension is described in the Celtic chapter in "Book of the Beginnings", and then more fully developed in "Natural Genesis".

Ceridwen appears as the vertical dimension in Massey's work. She is said to be the genetrix or generator of the world by Massey, to be Cybele, the Magna Mater with a thousand breasts, as well as the sow and Astarte. She's related to the Egyptian Ta-Urt , or Tawret, by Massey, which leads to the linguistic association of her with As-ta-ur-te, which Chumbley also uses for her in the Azoetia. She's also related to the dragon, though it's unclear in Massey's work if the dragon is a figure that's also beyond her, and that she's a manifestation of, or whether she herself is the dragon entire. I find in looking at things that it's more logical to see Ceridwen as a manifestation of the Dragon, of the One, than as the dragon in total. Hu, Ceridwen, and the Dragon live in a separate dimension, a transcendental dimension, which manifests its power in the physical world through the voice of Thoth at the Pole Star.

She contains within her the Sabbat of the Ages in the form of the Cauldron of Ceridwen. This is understood as either the womb or the heart of the goddess. Ceridwen as the great Dragon, would generate the Cauldron that contains the Sabbat, whose parts form the focus of the vertical dimension, but would nonetheless be separate from them. She would be connected to the primal serpent behind all of the action, the Neo-Platonic One. This would be embodied by the constellation Draco, the circumpolar constellation, which encircles the true center or hidden true pole, where the ultimate Sabbat, the ultimate reality of the gods, lies.

Her child, Affagdu or Morfan, is contained within her cauldron, as a black god who later becomes a sun god. Affagdu becomes Hu Gadarn, who is also Baal, the sun God who figuratively rules the Holy City. Massey directly connects this figure to the Witches' Sabbat, saying that the witch god who appeared at the Sabbat was shining from the waist up and rough and hairy like an animal from the waist down. In this, he embodies the conjunction of opposites, Affagdu and Hu Gadarn combined, as Baphomet. He is also labeled Aten or Atum, the Egyptian sun god, by Massey.

The idea that Affagdu, who is black and deformed, becomes a sun god is taken from Davies work. It heavily departs from the original story of Taliesin, and undermines it in many ways. Massey states that Affagdu gets the Awen, while in the original it's Taliesin himself who gets the Awen. Davies, though, through equating Affagdu with another character, Elphin, presents Affagdu as being the waters of the deluge, and Elphin as being the rising sun which manifests after the deluge has subsided. The rising of the sun after the deluge is equated by Massey to the reception of the Awen by Affagdu. From there, we get the idea of a dark and a light Affagdu, which Massey integrates into his work as two different phases of the sun god, one of the sun in winter, and the other of the sun in the summer. Through this, he becomes a god who has both light and dark characteristics, and so is Abraxis like. Also, something to be noted is that in Massey's telling, Ceridwen has no husband, and instead conceives Affagdu from herself without a mate, something that departs from Welsh myth and from Davies. Here, the three consist of Affagdu as a dark god, Hu Gadarn as a light god, and the light and dark combination of the two as the third god.

Massey describes the solar god turning into a cat for the witch, and similarly into a cat at the witches' Sabbath on page 323 of vol. 1 He describes the witches assembled giving the cat the "Osculum Infame", infamous kiss on the anus, then extinguishing the lights and having group sex.

In "Natural Genesis" Massey develops this process of the formation of the three more explicitly. There, you have the dragon goddess also generating a light and a dark god as well, but this is represented differently. First, the vertical dimension consists of three distinct beings, which Massey gives several correspondences for. One of the primary ones is to see the dragon goddess as generating first Set, the dark god, then generating Horus, the light god, after which they combine with each other to make Shu, the god of breath, who is the generator of the Logos. This logos manifests in the material world through the Pole Star, whose god is Thoth, with Thoth being the vehicle of Shu and of the Logos in the material world. Within this, you have the same components as with the Celtic version of Ceridwen: a light and a dark god, parallel to Affagdu and Hu Gadarn, who combine to become a bisexual light and dark god, Shu in this case, who is like Abraxas and Baphomet. These three also correspond to the three Taas of Division, Accumulation, and Station, with Set being Division, Horus being Accumulation, and Shu being Station. I believe that Massey may have been influenced by kabbalistic ideas in his formulation of the three here. This thought sees the three as corresponding to the primal mother letters Shin, Aleph, and Mem, with Shin being fire, Mem being water, and Aleph, placed between them, being air.

Backing this up, Massey relates these three to primal acts of God portrayed in Genesis. Massey relates the Light to the light of Genesis, and the Dark to the Water of Genesis. Shu, Air, in Massey's telling, can be seen as a combination or son of this Light and Darkness. The air that moves across the water, creating the world, in this, can be interpreted to have been generated by the action of light on water, creating mist or air, breath. The breath here, can also be linked to the Word, the creative Word which is Thoth or Hermes. This is the creative word as the product of the combined Affagdu/Hu Gadarn solar god figure who incorporates both light and darkness into himself in an Abraxas like way. That breath would be an imitation of the primal spirit that generated both the light and the darkness, both Set and Horus.

Massey also corresponds these three with the three phases of the moon, in a series of passages that evidently had great influence on the Azoetia, in that the same terminology of the Red, White, and Black goddesses used by Massey also show up in that work. These goddesses are said in the Azoetia to make up the body of the great goddess, who is Ceridwen, who Chumbley labels as "Iuno" or Juno, the wife of Zeus, the great mother goddess of the Romans.

In "Natural Genesis", from page 530 on, Massey provides details about these three lunar goddesses. Here, the three are linked with the Ceridwen. She herself is the goddess that has produced the seven, including the three. The structure of the three is reported by Massey to be the following: There is one goddess who is a replica of Ceridwen, who is Hermaphroditic in this aspect, a combination of light and dark. Next, there's a goddess that incorporates the positive, light aspects of Ceridwen, and finally a goddess who incorporates the dark aspects of Ceridwen. Massey labels these the Red, White, and Black goddesses.

The way in which the Red goddess is a replica of Ceridwen is also suggested by Massey in passages after those cited: Ceridwen splits up into the White and Black goddesses, then these two goddesses combine to make the Red goddess. The Red goddess' hermaphroditic nature is brought about by the conjunction of the two other goddesses, and so she's the product of the reunification of the two forces of light and darkness, who Ceridwen initially splits into. In this, she's an image of the goddess, rather than a direct manifestation of the goddess herself.

Here, the Red goddess can be linked with the goddess of the full moon in Chumbley's thought, while the Black goddess is linked with the goddess of the waning moon, and the White goddess is linked with the waxing moon. The Red goddess, goddess of the full moon, echoing Ceridwen, contains a version of the cauldron of Ceridwen within her. This is the Sabbat itself, with the full moon standing in for the Eternal Sun in this. Here, she's a combination of increase and decrease, of Accumulation and Division, being Station, in the seven Taas that Massey has established, and that Darius Wilson incorporated into his pseudo-Memphis rite.

The White and Black goddesses easily correspond to Set and Horus in their aspects. Horus becomes the waxing moon, Set becomes the waning moon, and Shu becomes the median between them, the Full moon. Through Massey's unique symbolism, the Red goddess as between the White and the Black is referred to as the goddess of the "dual horizon", with this language also showing up in the Azoetia.

This has relevance to different patterns of action that the Azoetia describes in relation to the three as they manifest within the body. However, the order in which these are used in my schema of internal alchemy, and, I believe, in the Azoetia, is different from what's implied in Massey. In Massey's schema, Set, Division, the Black Moon, would be the lower center, connected to the Underworld, while Horus, the White Moon, Accumulation, would correspond to the higher center, with Shu, the Red Moon, corresponding to the Heart center. In the correspondences that I use, the White Moon corresponds to the lower center, the Black Moon to the higher center, and the Red Moon to the Heart Center.

Nonetheless, the idea of this primal combination of the different centers remains: you combine part of the lower center with the higher center to make the hermaphroditic force that corresponds to the heart, the middle center, and then you slay the hermaphroditic image in order to liberate the essence that the image corresponds to. Within internal alchemy, this corresponds to liberating the essence which exists within the secret chamber of the heart, which contains a replica of the Sabbat itself. Once liberated, this essence can not only ascend to the mind, but to the objective Sabbat that exists in the transcendental realm, and that can from there call down the original essence to the individual. The energy liberated from the Sabbat of the Heart can also be used to speak forth the Logos from ones self as a word of magical creation.

The three are also corresponded to the three fates by Massey, Clotho, Lachesis, and Atropos. In this, we can see the middle fate, Lachesis, who deals with the course of a person's life, as corresponding to the full moon, the Red Moon, and to Being, to existence in the present moment. This is in contrast to Clotho, who oversees beginnings, and manifestation, who can be corresponded to the waxing moon, and the White goddess, and Atropos, who oversees endings, and decrease, who can be corresponded to the waning moon and the Black goddess. The full moon can be taken to represent the Sabbat itself, the First Sun, with the fragments of Being being the fragments of the First Sun itself, the Ideals that exist within it. The symbol that Massey associates with the three goddesses is a "T" like character, is also the one used in the Azoetia to signify the same concept. We shall, in the grimoire section, correspond these concepts to the three different parts of the primal vision of the transcendental realm.

To conclude, looking at it from an esoteric perspective, it would be most logical to link the three of the Taas to the "Tria Prima" of Paracelsus—the alchemical principles of Salt, Sulphur and Mercury. However, Gerald Massey in no way does this. The three are linked to the Tria Prima in later tradition however, by Chumbley. We will treat the Tria Prima in the chapter on the Toadstone, and interested readers should skip ahead to read it.

Suffice it to say that the three centers can be related both to Mercury, Salt, and Sulphur as well as to Set, Horus, and Shu, to Life, Death, and the combination of the two, and to the White, Black and Red goddesses. Accumulation can correspond to the principle of Life, which can correspond to the principle of Horus. Division can correspond to the principle of Death, and with that to Set. Station can be conceptualized as the coming together of the two, the restoration of what previously existed before the split into duality, which would be the combination of Life and Death into one as a Baphometic bisexual deity.

In Chumbley's symbolism, Mercury stands for the Lower Center, and for Life, the White goddess, Horus, and Accumulation. Salt stands for the Head Center, Death, and for the Black Goddess. Sulphur stands for the Heart center, the Red Goddess, and is the outer image of the Azoth. By combining the Mercury and the Salt, and then applying it to the Heart center, the secret chamber of the Heart that contains the Azoth within the human being, which is the secret aspect of Sulphur, can be accessed. For more details on these terms, consult the Toadstone chapter.

Gods of the Four Quarters

Compared to the gods of the three, the gods of the four are fairly straightforward. They correspond to the elements, and there isn't any sort of drama which Massey reads into their relations with each other The language of the Taas is replaced here with more conventional symbolism. Massey provides two sets of names for each of the four in "Natural Genesis".

Nun—Water, Green, North, Matter
Child Horus— Air, East, Blue, Fluxion
Khabsenuf— Fire, South, Red, Cohesion
Seb—Earth, West, Green or Grey, Coagulation

and

Hapi—Water, North, Blue Matter,
Amsta, (man)—Air, East, Green, Fluxion,
Kabhsenuf—Fire, South, Red, Cohesion, ,
Tuamutef—Earth, West, Grey, Coagulation,

The pantheon with the more familiar gods is, in my opinion, based on the one with the less familiar ones. Here, Seb and Nun appear in their traditional aspects as the earth and the water. Following this is a very different attribution of Horus the Child with Air. Massey explains that, in this, the figure is linked to human blood or life force, which is linked to air or breath. This is an adaptation of the figure of Amsta, standing for Man in the other pantheon. The final figure, Kabhsenuf, is linked with an Hawk by Massey, and through its association with Horus and the Sun it is corresponded to Fire. Kabhsenuf also comes from the other pantheon.

The other pantheon, Amsta, Khabsenuf, Hapi, Tuautmutf, appears in the pseudo-Memphis rite as well, and is directly derived from the passage of the "Book of the Dead" which Lenormant also drew on. These cross quarters are not given Celtic correspondences by Massey, unfortunately. These are given the directional correspondences of the North for Nun or Water, the East for the Child Horus or Air, the South for Kabhsenuf and Fire, and the West for Seb and Earth. These four constitute the paradisal realm around the vertical axis in the transcendental realm, the castle around the vertical axis which is its core.

These seven, in one of the few passages where they're described as "Taas" in "Natural Genesis" are listed as corresponding to the seven vowels of the Greek language, and as the seven words or principles of Thoth. The extra Greek vowels are the eta and the omicron, standing for the short "e" and the short "o".

With regards to colors, Thoth, as the Word or revealer of all of the seven could be pictured as being a combination of all of the other colors.

Put together, the vertical axis and the horizontal axis have the following correspondences:

Darkness, Set—Down, Black, Division
Light, Horus—Up, White Accumulation
Breath Shu—Center, Golden, Station

Sut—Darkness, Division, the Depths, Black, Black moon goddess
Horus—Light, Accumulation, the Heights, White, White moon goddess
Shu—Air or breath, Station, the Center, Golden, Red moon goddess, also Thoth, Word

Nun—Water, Green, North, Matter
Child Horus— Air, East, Blue, Fluxion
Khabsenuf— Fire, South, Red, Cohesion
Seb—Earth, West, Green or Grey, Coagulation

Hapi—Water, North, Blue Matter,
Amsta, (man)—Air, East, Green, Fluxion,
Kabhsenuf—Fire, South, Red, Cohesion, ,
Tuamutef—Earth, West, Grey, Coagulation,

The Watcher Angels as "Taas"

Massey also identifies the Taas with the seven Beni Elohim, and this is then connected with the seven Watchers, in that Massey says that they were also the "seven of revolt". In "Ancient Egypt" Massey lists these seven Watchers as "Azazyel, Amazarak, Armers, Barkayel, Akebeel, Tamiel, and Asaradel". This list is drawn not from the R.H. Charles translation of the Book of Enoch, which is regarded as the most up to date translation of its time, but a previous one, "Nagar Kānsu. The Book of Enoch the Prophet" translated by Richard Laurence, published in 1838. Laurence gives the following attributions to the seven: Azazyl teaches men to make swords, armor, and other things forged, as well as how to use stones and cosmetics. Amazarak teaches sorcerers and people who use roots, and is another name for Semijaza. Armers taught how to counter sorcery. Barkayal taught astrology. Akibeel taught divination. Tamiel taught Astronomy. Asaradel taught the significance of the Moon's phases. These are also related by Massey to the seven spirits around the throne of the Merkabah. No further correspondences are made by Massey with these names. However, we can divide these into a three and a four as well.

Azazyl, Amazarak and Armers are a group of three, and Barkayal, Akibeel, Tamiel, and Asaradel are a group of four. Amazarak and Armers, teaching sorcerer and counter sorcery, form a natural opposition, with Azayzl teaching how to make weapons being a third between them. Azayzyl in this also corresponds to Tubal-Cain as a blacksmith, though I believe that later writers have made quite a mountain out of this mole hill about this, one which misses the point about Tubal-Cain being the Demiurge.

Here, Amazarak or Semijaza would be equivalent to Set, Armers would be equivalent to Horus, and Azazyl would be equivalent to Shu in Massey's thought.

There are also common oppositions in the other four. Barkayal and Tamiel form a pair, dealing with Astrology and Astronomy, as do Akibeel and Asaradel, who deal with divination in general and with the significance of the Moon's phases. Barkayal and Tamiel deal with the observation of things which are higher, while Akibeel and Asaradel correspond to things which are lower, comparatively speaking. There may be a correspondence here between Akibeel and the Earth, Asaradel with Water, Tamiel with Air, and Barkayal with Fire. Alternately, Tamiel and Barkayal may have the reverse significations.

Tentatively, we can make the following associations:
The three:

Amazarak/Semijaza—Set
Armer—Horus
Azazyl—Shu

The four

Barkayal—Fire
Tamiel—Air
Asaradel—Water
Akibeel—Earth

Ancient Egypt

Massey's models changed over time as well. Particularly, in his posthumous work "Ancient Egypt, the Light of the World", Massey adds the constellation of Orion to the mix, which corresponds to the East in the fourfold circle. This move away from a system purely centered on the Big Dipper leads to a system which is echoed in Chumbley's Azoetia and in Sabbatic publications in general. Instead of the action of the year being centered on the rotation of the Big Dipper around the Pole Star, you now have a four fold system, where North is signified by the Pole Star itself, East is signified by Orion, South is signified by Sirius, and West is signified by the Big Dipper. These make up the stations of the wheel of the year. Within this system, both the Big Dipper and Orion are still thought to have seven components, but these are demoted in significance. Orion is read to be made of seven stars through the equation of the three stars of the sword with one star. Within Chumbley's work, the seven stars which make up these two constellations are thought to correspond to servitors which aid the powers of the East and the West, respectively.

Another innovation by Massey is the introduction of the "Heptanomis" in this work. This is a departure from the schema of the transcendental realm as outlined in "Natural Genesis". Here, the seven Pole Stars of the "Great Year", one complete zodiacal age in the procession of the equinoxes, are corresponded with the seven, as opposed to the seven being corresponded to the generic horizontal and vertical axes. This presents some complications, but, equally, it's important, as Chumbley very obviously incorporated these ideas into his Dragon Book of Essex and related work, using the identical term of "Heptanomis". Notably, the dragon work described by Chumbley is the next stage beyond that of the Azoetia, which is what we're dealing with here for the most part. The Azoetia itself is much more structured according to the interpretation which attributes the seven to the vertical and horizontal axes. Before looking at how Chumbley incorporates the schema of "Ancient Egypt" into the Azoetia, lets look for a moment at the parts that influence the "Dragon Book".

Heptanomis

Massey describes the Sabbat in terms that by now will be familiar to readers. He talks about a paradise that's underneath the Pole Star, which is surrounded by the circumpolar stars. In the appendix to volume two, where he compares Egyptian mythology with Christian, he compares this paradise with the Holy City, the Heavenly Jerusalem, described in the Book of Revelations. Additionally, the paradise under the Pole Star is paralleled with the top of the holy mountain, with the mountain of creation. In this, he also describes the mound of creation as being surrounded by an "Emerald Dawn", or an "Emerald Tree of Dawn". Ra, the sun god, presides on top of the mound, in the Heavenly City below the Pole.

Around Ra are seven gods, which in the craft is translated into the seven around the circle, with the concealed eighth behind. These seven gods are also described as seven lands, like seven aeons.

Talking about the procession of the equinox in relation to the Pole Star, he notes that in the course of the great year, where the rising of the sun at the vernal equinox has gone through all of the signs and has come back to the start, seven different stars will have served as the Pole Star. He relates the seven stars to the seven which was originally around the single pole. This leads to a system of thought where the seven become seven paradises, with a central paradise uniting them, each under a different Pole Star, with the central Pole Star, as it were, being hidden. These seven paradises most likely correspond to the seven "Cantrefs" of the Welsh tradition, which also corresponds each of them to one of the seven stars of the Big Dipper.

The expansion of the Sabbatic system into that described in the Dragon Book of Essex echoes this. There, the Eternal Sun and the Sabbat under the pole are particular manifestations of a much greater Sun and Sabbat. Once the Sabbat itself, in the present form, is communed with and mastered, the next step is to expand ones contact to all of the different manifestations of the Sabbat, as they have occurred throughout history. This means as they have occurred under the different Pole Stars of the great year. The thing which unites all of these different Pole Stars and Sabbats, the thing which provides the ultimate circle or boundary for them, is the constellation of Draco, the Dragon.

The Dragon, here, is the Neo-Platonic One, which is often portrayed as a blackness which is beyond all concepts, black not because it's negative, but because it's beyond conventional description. The One, here, is silently in the background behind the Sabbat, and the various plural Sabbats, but through communing with these replicated Sabbats as they've existed throughout history, the presence of the Dragon can be detected, and worked with. It is the system behind the Sabbatic system, the stars behind the Sabbat and its Pole Star, as well as behind any other particular astral correspondences to the Sabbat. The dragon work consists of detecting, communing with, and joining ones self to this underlying force.Ultimately, it's the One, the Dragon, which powers and creates the various Sabbats themselves. The One as the Dragon has several divine attributes or names, which in the system created by Chumbley correspond to different parts of the body of the dragon. In uniting ones self to these divine names or attributes through combining the parts of the dragon with ones self, communion with and union with the One is achieved. The dragon and its force, as will be talked about, also creates the initial stone from which the Sabbat emerges as a flaming sun.

Massey also, in the section of volume two called "The World's Great Year", relates Stonehenge to the sevenfold pattern, and states that the "Palladium" or protection stone of the Romans, was a version of the world mountain, on top of which is Paradise. The "Xoanon", it should be noted, is this same Palladium. The "Palladium", in turn, is related to Stonehenge and to the seven around the throne in the Heptanomis. The particular stones of the henge are further related by Massey to the "Heptanomis of Atlantis", or the Pole Star of Atlantis, which "sank in the deluge". Atlantis, like Hyperborea, here becomes a paradise, and a place of the Sabbat. Atlantis is identified further by him with the civilization of the Cyclops, and with Cyclopean architecture. As we have seen previously, this is a reference to the megalithic civilization, which was equated with the Ante-Diluvian civilization of the Watchers and the children of Cain.

Ancient Egypt in the Azoetia

Chumbley adapts the new stellar framework outlined in "Ancient Egypt, the Light of the World" in the following way: the seasonal forces are split into a force of manifestation of the life energy which comes from the transcendental realm of the Sabbat to the earth, and a force of demanifestation, or of the withdrawal of this life energy, a pulling back of the life force from the earth to the transcendental realm of the Sabbat. This is first represented in a dual way, with Horus standing for the force of manifestation and Set standing for the force of demanifestation. This is then broadened into a four-fold schema. Set is associated with the Big Dipper and Horus is associated with Orion. Each of these constellations is pictured by Massey as having seven components within them, which echo the seven of the horizontal and vertical axes.

Chumbley adjusts the duality of Set-Horus in the Azoetia a bit. Massey equates Set with Anubis, the Egyptian god of death, in the form of "Sut-Anu" or "Sut-Anup". It appears to me that it's the Anubis form, that of the guide of the dead, which Chumbley first draws on in his concepts in the Azoetia and elsewhere, with the Set archetype being secondary. Anu is equated with Set by Massey, and Sut-Horus, or Set-Anubis and Horus, are also related by Massey to the twins in the sign of Gemini. Anubis-Horus, then, is another way to signify the coming forth and going back of energy from the Sabbat of the Ages to Earth.

This going forth and coming back of energy is united to the wheel of the year and the change of the seasons. Horus, here, and the constellation Orion, symbolizes the energy going forth from the Sabbat to the Earth. This energetic influx starts at the winter solstice. At the spring equinox, the incoming life force overcomes the darkness, and at the summer solstice the incoming life force reaches its peak of manifestation. Similarly, after it has reached its peak of manifestation, the force of demanifestation starts. This is corresponded generally to Set and to the Great Bear. Starting from the summer solstice, at the vernal equinox the power of demanifestation or the withdrawal of life from the earth to the Sabbat overcomes the force of the manifestation of the life force. At the winter solstice, the force of the withdrawal of life to the Sabbat reaches its peak, after which the positive influx of energy and life force starts once again. I should note, again, that this is Chumbley's adaptation of Massey, and does not likely represent in its god names the underlying names of the tradition that he inherited.

Chumbley uses the same word for Orion, the East, and the manifestation of life, that Massey does: Sah, which corresponds to Horus. In Massey's work, the Sahu are honored dead that have ascended to the constellation of Orion. "Sahu" is linked to the word for mummy, and Orion is labeled here the constellation of the mummy. Horus himself becomes a Sahu in Massey's recounting when, after battling the Apep serpent in the underworld, he emerges victorious and rises out of it. This is identified by Massey, on pages 189-90, with the fertilizing rays of the sun inundating the earth and vanquishing the cold of winter, with Horus emerging from the earth at the vernal or spring equinox.

Massey pictures this cycle of seasonal change as the battle of Horus around the circle of the year as well.

Something that Massey talks about, within this idea of seasonal change and Horus, is a distinction between a celestial serpent and the lower serpent Apep, or "Apap" as Massey calls it. The celestial serpent, who corresponds to the constellation Draco, is a positive force for Massey. It surrounds the circumpolar stars. Apep, however, is the negative serpent who lives in the underworld, who Horus seasonally battles. Massey references this on page 320 of volume one. This recalls the duality of serpents in James Morgan Pryse's thought, where the serpent of the earth is evil, but the serpent of the cosmos is sacred and divine, which we shall examine in much more depth in volume 2 of this work.

Massey talks about two Horus' associated with the "two horizons", these being the Autumnal and Vernal equinoxes. Here, at the Autumnal equinox, Horus is born, and goes into the underworld fighting the evil serpent Apap. At the Vernal or Spring Equinox, Horus wins against the serpent, and is reborn as Horus Sahu, associated with the constellation Orion.

This is related by Massey to Jesus' resurrection, with the time in the underworld being the "harrowing of hell". This harrowing is given a seasonal interpretation, with Horus in the underworld fighting the forces of coldness as the Sun god, and emerging victorious with the "rebirth" of the sun at the vernal equinox. This pattern of Horus descending into the underworld, fighting, and emerging victorious, ascending into the sky, is also identified by Massey with Jesus, his descent into the underworld, and his ascension. In fact, Massey spends a huge amount of time trying to demonstrate that Horus was the god that Jesus was originally based on. When Horus is referred to as Jesus, it's in the form of "Iu-Sa", which means Jesus. For instance, on page 735 of volume two, in the section called "The Jesus Legend", Horus is called the Iu the Sa. In the appendix to volume two, there are several pages that are devoted solely to listing the parallels between Jesus and Horus.

Horus/Jeus/the Word, signifies here the force of the eternal sun going forth into the earth, through the medium of the visible sun, fertilizing and fructifying it. Set-Anubis represents death and the guide of the dead, who leads the energy back from the earth to the

Sabbat itself. The going forth of energy is symbolized by the constellation of Orion, while the going back of energy is represented by the Big Dipper.

Because of the correspondence of the outflow and inflow of energy with the wheel of the year, this schema naturally leads to four stations. The extra two stations are provided by the Pole Star, which is connected with Set and with the Great Bear, and with demanifestation, and Sirius, which is associated with Horus, Orion, and with the power of manifestation. These four stations can be corresponded to the four in the following way: Set in the North, Horus in the East, Isis in the South, and Nephthys, the wife of Set in the West. Here,

North—Pole Star, Set
East—Orion, Horus
South—Sirius, Isis
West—Nephthys, Great Bear

Chumbley adapts this symbolism in the Azoetia in the following way: he puts "Ononshu" at the Autumnal Equinox and Horus at the Vernal Equinox. "Ononshu" is equivalent to Nephthys, as a female form of Set-Anubis, of death, and is associated by Chumbley with the big dipper. She's also associated with Hekate, and other goddesses, as we shall see. "Sah" Horus is associated with the constellation Orion, and with the hunter. In this, there's a parallel with Nimrod/Nembroth as the great hunter. The Pole Star in the north, corresponds to Set-Anubis, Mahaziel, himself, while the south point is represented by the star Sirius, and Isis, the goddess of the force of life and manifestation, the mother of Horus and the goddess of fertility. This is not given in the Azoetia, but in the Dragon Book corresponds to Rahab, who is a version of the Red Goddess. Here, the two constellations point to the respective stars. Therefore, they're helpers, in a sense, of the stars. Nephthys the wife of Set is the helper of the Pole Star, and Horus is the helper of his mother Isis, Sirius.

Here, there are two intersecting categories: that which brings life, that which brings death, male, and female. Death, signifying energies going out from the earth to the Sabbat, is represented by the male Set-Anubis and the female Ononshu, in the North and West of the circle, respectively, while life, the force going from the Sabbat to the earth, is represented by the male Horus, or "Sah", as well as the female Isis, with these standing for the East and the South. Within the circle, Anubis/Death represents energy that goes back to the Sabbat in its pure form, while Isis represents energy goes forth into the world in its pure form. The stations of the North and the East are male, and those of the South and the West are female. North corresponds to Set, or to the synthetic figure of Set-Anubis, or to the much more synthetic Set-Thoth-Anubis,

The force of Manifestation rules the first half of the year, and the force of Demanifestation rules the second half. In the seasonal sequence, the force of manifestation or of the life force corresponds to the East and to the South. The life force goes forth from the Sabbat to earth, starting in the East, with the power of Horus, and manifesting fully in the south, the summer, with the power of Isis. After the life energy peaks with the manifestation of Isis in the South, it starts to decrease, corresponding to the power of Nephthys in the West, before coming to its lowest state of power with Set-Thoth-Anubis in the North. This is echoed in the fourfold horizontal axis of the circle, where each of these figures, albeit with other names, plays a similar role. In this, the north, corresponding to Set-Thoth-Anubis, also serves as a gate for the power of the Sabbat to come from the transcendental realm into the earth.

Thoth, here, plays the role of Mahaziel in the north of the circle as the gateway of energy, of the word, from the Sabbat to the Earth, and is identified with magic, in the sense of the First Sorcerer. Though Thoth is about going forth, in Massey's multiple pantheons, the Pole Star in relation to the Great Bear is also associated with Sut-Anpu or Set-Anubis as the god of the dead, who facilitates people also going back to Paradise. Mahaziel, in the way he's described in Sabbatic publications, combines both of these characteristics, that of Thoth and Anubis, with a dash of Set: the force of demanifestation that can also serve as the gateway for the force of manifestation to come through into the world. I believe that this was an adaptation from earlier beliefs which did not use this symbolism. Thoth in this can also be equated with the Welsh figure Gwydion, who Massey equates both with Set-Anubis, Odin, and Thoth as the inventor of letters.

Isis, it should be noted, is corresponded by Massey to Sirius already, from the "Book of the Beginnings" onward, with the correspondence coming from the appearance of the heliacal rising of Sirius in Egypt, which heralded the flooding of the Nile. The flooding of the Nile brought new earth and new fertility to the land, which was used in the subsequent year by agriculture. Heliacal rising refers to the star rising with the sun at dawn, with this happening during the "Dog Days" of late summer, named for the dog star, Sirius.

Coming back to the sevenfold symbolism, each of the two constellations can be organized into seven stars. This makes for three sets of seven: the first set being the primal seven in the First Sun, in the Sabbat itself, the second seven in the Big Dipper, and the third seven in the constellation of Orion.

Speaking practically, the two sets of seven associated with the constellations of Orion and the Great Bear correspond to two configurations of the circle as it relates to either manifestation, the coming forth of energy to the circle, or to demanifestation, the going back of energy from the circle to the Sabbat.

Within the circle, within magic, there are operations that involve drawing the energy down from the Sabbat, and there are operations that involve going upwards to the Sabbat. There are also operations that involve a mix of these two. For the purpose of drawing down energy, the seven stars of Orion, plus Sirius, can be corresponded to the vertical and horizontal axes of the circle plus the eighth point, which is the source of energy that empowers the two axes. For the purpose of going back up, from the earth to the Sabbat directly, the seven stars of the Big Dipper, plus the Pole Star, can be corresponded to the same. Here, the eighth point is that which sends energy through the gate of the North of the circle. For operations which are a combination of these two, both sets of stars can be drawn down, and called up, with these two sets meeting in the middle.

Ancient Egypt, Creation.

Massey's "Ancient Egypt" is also important in that it outlines his correspondences between his Egyptian concepts and those of the book of Genesis. Interestingly, he assigns the role of the creator to Kheper-Ptah, who creates the seven Elohim, the seven gods of the circle, from him, who serve as co-creators. Bringing this into our symbolism, here, Kheper is not understood as being created from nothing, or to be purely self created, but to instead be the concretization of the divine mind into the active intelligence. In this, Kheper is the Active Intelligence within the Divine Mind, the First Sun. Ptah, in Massey's work, creates with the divine word. The Word itself, in this, is attributed by Massey to Wisdom, which is equated with the Egyptian Maat. Kheper-Ptah, in this, despite being created from the Nun, lives in a transcendental dimension, the supercelestial paradise of Massey, which is the original from on which the physical world is formed. He's also described by Massey as being Biune or Bisexual, calling to mind descriptions of Baphomet.

Kheper-Ptah, in speaking the Word and creating the earth, recreates in manifest form in the material world that which exists in the transcendental world. The seven Elohim who help him, correspond to the seven directions of the horizontal axes, and are already present within the paradisal realm.

Each of the elemental forces help in the formation of the corresponding elements in the manifest world, with the earth co-creator helping the element of earth to manifest and so on. Massey relates these seven Elohim to seven craftsmen as well.

These seven are also corresponded by Massey to basic animal forces and forms, which he elaborates on in his account of the supposed development of gods and symbolism. These seven, as we shall see, form a kind of primal pattern which is replicated in the body, and, particularly, is replicated within each of the centers of the vertical axis of the individual. Here, the heart or middle term of the vertical axis is the anchor for the four, but, equally, a smaller version of the seven exists within the head center and within the lower center, the sex center. In this center, the seven form the series of the "Primal Atavisms" of Austin Osman Spare, which can be called up for ritual work. In Massey's description, six of these primal forces are pre-human and animal, with the seventh being human and capable of speech.

Works Cited

Bonwick , James "Egyptian Belief and Modern Thought", C. Kegan Paul & co., London, 1878, Google Books

Budge, E.A. Wallis "The Book of the Dead, The Papyrus of Ani in the British Museum", British Museum, London, 1895, Google Books, Sacred-Texts.com

Chumbley, Andrew Azoetia, Xoanon, Hercules, USA, 2015

Chumbley, Andrew "Dragon Book of Essex", Xoanon, Hercules, 2014

Davies, Edward "The Mythology and Rites of the British Druids", J. Booth, London, 1809, Google books

Fitzgerald, Robert "The Hidden Stone", "The Luminous Stone", Three Hands Press, Richmond Vista, 2016.

Gantz, Jeffrey Mabinogion, Penguin, London 1976

Guest, Lady Charlotte, "Hanes Taliesin" in "The Mabinogion", Bernard Quaritch, London, 1877, sacred-texts.com

Higley, Sarah "Preiddu Annwn", online edition, Camelot project, University of Rochester USA, https://d.lib.rochester.edu/camelot/text/preiddeu-annwn

Laurence, Richard, "The Book of Enoch the Prophet", Oxford University Press, Oxford, 1838

Lenormant, François and Charles"Histoire et mémoires de l'Institut royal de France", volume 25, published in 1861, and titled "Mémoire sur les Réprésentations qui avaient lieu dans les Mystères D'Éleusis", Google Books

Lepsius, R., "Das Todtenbuch der Ägypter", Georg Wigand, Leipzig, 1842, Google Books

Massey, Gerald "A Book of the Beginnings" vol 1. and 2, Williams and Norgate, London, 1881, Google books,

Massey, Gerald "Ancient Egypt, the Light of the World", vol. 1 and 2., T. Fisher Unwin, London, 1907, Google Books

Massey, Gerald "The Natural Genesis", vol.1 and 2., Williams and Norgate, London, 1883 , google books,

Pennick, Nigel "Secret Games of the Gods", Weiser, York Beach, ME, 1990

Schelling, F.W.J., "Über die Gottheiten von Samothrake", "On the Divinities of Samothrace", Frank Scalambrino trans, Magister Ludi press, Castalia, 2019

Seims, Mellisa "Here be Magic", Thoth Publications, Loughborough, 2022

Part Three
Practice

Chapter 13
AOS Witchcraft, Chaos Magic, Massey, Chumbley

The Focus of Life.

"The Focus of Life", a work that Spare published in 1922, is the work of Spare's which Chumbley appears to draw on the most in the Azoetia. The style of many of the invocations and passages within the Azoetia echo the "Focus". For instance, Spare speaks of "The abyss Self projecting from non-existence the procreatrix I", a very Chumbleyan turn of phrase. "The Focus of Life" can be summarized by saying that Spare there explores the intersection of sexuality, creativity, the self, and ecstatic states powered by sexuality. It's a text that's both experiential and an account of dreams. The relationship between sexuality, sexual energy, and self development is portrayed again and again: sexuality and sexual acts, either autosexual, that is to say masturbation, or otherwise, the experience of sexual energy and the actualization of desire, brings forth hidden aspects of the self to consciousness. Through pursuing sexual activity, autosexual and otherwise, these hidden aspects of the self are brought to the surface, and this breaking through of these aspects of the self manifests as a great coming forth of creativity into the conscious mind. The creativity reflects the contents of the inner self, which manifests first in self knowledge, and which from there can be directed to artistic or other creative ends, such as writing. This rush of creativity coming from the breakthrough of these inner aspects of the self into the mind, powered by sexual activity and exploration, leads to ecstatic states of consciousness as well.

Within Chumbley's work, these breakthroughs are identified with remembrances of the primal vision, with the different aspects of the self which are activated being sections of that primal vision. By this I mean sections of the First Sun, the Sabbat of the ages, and of the different cells or subdivisions which make up the Sabbat. These are the cells which are the figures around the throne. Ultimately, they relate back to the seven-fold and eight fold division. Spare's account, and style, which is taken up by Chumbley, differs from outside and more abstract accounts of similar things in that it's a view of what this is like from the point of view of a practitioner, as opposed to someone just rationally describing it. In fact, Chumbley pointed to this very feature, the experiential nature of Spare's writings on various topics, including the witches' Sabbat, as being a large part of the unique value of Spare's writings.

This process is pictured by Spare in the context of the difference between the Self and the I. The Self is the totality of the individual, while the I is the very present current focus of the consciousness. The I is the active part of the self, the ego which thinks and does things. Through this practice of meditation on the feeling of sexual desire during sexual activity, the Self brings forth new contents to the I. The Self, in this, can be said to be empowering the I. This is a kind of empowerment which corresponds to Life. Again, this can be done through things like an open ended, free meditation, that takes place over an extended period of masturbation, where orgasm is approached and then backed away from, and where focus on a sexual object is interspersed with free association. The build up of sexual energy and sexual ecstasy over a long period of time with this brings the knowledge and self insight up into a frenzy which culminates in the release of orgasm.

This same type of power or empowerment can also be realized in a way which corresponds to Death. Within the sexual act as well, the experience of orgasm also powers the realization of these selves, in the ecstatic experience of release as a "small death" , with the visions that can come from this if the preparation for orgasm has included a significant amount of meditation during the sex act.

This self-pleasuring and auto-sexuality is self love, as defined by Spare. Self love, in this, leads to self empowerment and self knowledge, self realization, creativity, and ecstatic states. All of this is linked to the first "Aphorism" in "The Focus of Life", called "The Effort of Remembering in the Valley of Fear". The "Valley of Fear" here is conventional life, the life that a person is born into , as opposed to the fuller life that they've experienced before incarnation.

For Chumbley, this knowledge is that of the Sabbat, the Ideal realm glimpsed by souls before they're made to forget. For Spare, this fuller life is expressed by him as a succession of incarnations of animal selves spanning the evolutionary chain from protozoa to human, all of which still exist as unconscious residues within the self. The realization of all of these animal selves and their potential within the person makes them, in a way, a Chimera, a combination of all the different animals in one, Baphomet, in other words, expressed in the language of the elements as opposed to Levi's particular formulation. Ultimately, both Chumbley's interpretation and Spare's converge, in that the ultimate product of realization is the same. By realizing the different aspects of the self as the different cells of the Azoth, the Divine Mind, the person makes themself into a synthesis of all of the deific and energetic forms that the Azoth contains, and this is precisely what Baphomet as the Living Being and Paradigm is. Baphomet here is, as has been said many times, a combination of the active force of the Demiurge with the Living Being or Paradigm, and the individual who realizes themselves as Baphomet recreates this—the vertical axis of the circle is the axis of the Demiurge, which corresponds to the "I" and to the power of the "I" to direct things, the "Autochthonic I", while the horizontal axis, the "Aetheric I", corresponds to the cells which are realized and then attached to the vertical "I". The vertical "I" in this also corresponds to the "Active Intelligence" within the Divine Mind. A further combination of Spare and Chumbley can be seen through corresponding the different animal selves of Spare with the type of deific forms of the seven that are described by Massey.

Within the process of the implicit selves being realized and going forth through sexual stimulation, the creativity that results is on the border between an experience of the selves and trance possession, with the creative products of art, writing, or other media being on the verge of automatism. Within Chumbley's system, this aspect of things becomes clear: the heart, the container of the model of the Sabbat within the individual, contains elemental forces and energies which are the basis of these implicit selves. These elemental forces and energies within the heart correspond to the objective elemental forces and energies which are present in the macrocosm. They correspond to the elemental forces and energies that are part of the objective divine mind, the objective Ideal realm, which exists beyond the planetary spheres. Therefore, the realizations of the "selves" that correspond to these forces rides the boundary of possession by the objective forces themselves. Similarly, the ecstatic states experienced after orgasm during the auto-sexual meditations echo the objective mystical states of communion with the objective Sabbat. These can be attained through the destruction of the "I" which happens during orgasm, and in the manifestation of that contained in this "I" on a higher level which follows, this "higher level" in some cases, but by no means all, being the same as the Sabbat. There are many levels of reality which the destroyed and then sublimated "I" can manifest in during the experience of post-orgasmic trance, and the Sabbat itself is the highest one, with levels within the astral and the mental existing below it being much more commonly experienced. Ultimately, the Sabbat itself is beyond both time and space, at the center of the greater reality of which the mental and astral realms are subsequent layers placed upon.

Here, in the experience of the charged orgasms, we see the iconoclasm, which we will get into much more detail in the grimoire section. The experience of meditation during masturbation charges the "I" with the power of the implicit selves, makes it an idol, and the moment of orgasm breaks that idol in an iconoclasm which liberates the consciousness from its physical constraints, allowing the whole complex of energy to sublimate and manifest. This is parallel to the destruction of the sigil at the end of the work, or the destruction of the circle after a spell is cast. The essence, the quintessence in this case, the Azoth of the heart, the energy of the high Sabbat of the ages, which is the sexual energy of the implicit selves brought to consciousness, is freed from its material container, and goes to wander in the world.

Spare links the ultimate sources of the Self to the primal atavisms, and to the lower center, so that what we have is a system of two poles: that of the "I", which corresponds to the Head, and to Belief, and that of the "Self", which is rooted in the lower center, and corresponds to Desire. The primal atavisms of the lower center, that of Desire, are brought up into the mind, into the realm of Belief, through the action of Will. This corresponds to the middle center, what we've called the heart center. The Will is the force which realizes the potential selves, the primal atavisms, and turns the potential into the actual. This is related to the realization of Kia. In Spare's thought, the Will appears to be primarily instrumental.

Importantly, in "The Focus of Life", the Self is described as "Zod" while the I is "I", which is useful in deciphering several chapters. The third chapter, "Ikkah Speaks of Himself", is really I-Kah speaks of himself, with the "Kah" being the Ka or soul of Egyptian theology, which can correspond to the general life force which is involved with both the Self and the I. Similarly, the chapter "Zod-Ka speaks of Ikkah" is the Self, the "Zod" aspect of the soul, speaking about the "I" aspect of the soul. Zod, the Self, in this, is the background on which the "I" exists. The Self, in Spare, can be identified with the lower center, the I with the head center, and the "Ka" with the Heart center in its external form.

Belief, in Spare's system, is both a tool and a curse. If the lower center corresponds to the primal atavisms, the work of the head center, in directing the power of the primal atavisms, once they are realized, into particular magical pathways is both hindered and helped by Belief. Here, Belief refers not just to conscious belief but also to the general background of beliefs that are just below the level of consciousness. Beliefs can prevent a magic ritual from either working or taking place at all, in that if you don't believe that something can truly be possible, your mind will prevent the energy which you've called up from from flowing in the direction you want it to flow. To counter this, Spare advocated deconstructing ones Beliefs, so that when the energy was called up it could be directed towards the realization of any Belief that a person wanted. This could be done in one of two ways, a direct way and an indirect way. In the direct way, the Belief would be the goal of the spell, asserting that whatever it is, is true, according to one's empowered Belief, with this symbolized by a sacred letter. For the indirect way, the force of Belief would be channeled into a sigil and then repressed.

The deconstruction of beliefs, which in immediate practice Spare described as going into a "Neither-Neither" state, creates a type of flexible energy that the mind can make use of which Spare called "Free Belief". This energy, this mental flexibility, can be used to direct the energy that's been called up, with a greater amount of "Free Belief" giving the mage a greater capability to control the energy.

Stephen Mace, in "Stealing the Fire from Heaven" describes the "Neither-Neither" process as taking a belief, a thought, or a feeling, that a person is having in the immediate moment, and then conjuring up its opposite, then combining one with the other to destroy both. This can be applied to strong emotions that one is having. Mace points out that the energy that's freed through this destructive process can, in and of itself, be used to charge sigils, and this is very valid.

Though Spare's "Neither-Neither" process was an immediate practice, deconstructing dogmatic beliefs and limitations on a deeper level creates a greater capacity for the generation of "Free Belief" when you need it. A person who is more flexible in his or her belief system will be more able to direct magical energy according to their will when they need to. This process forms the basis of much of Chaos magic as well as the background of my own development of some of Spare's ideas, which we'll examine now.

Some Extensions

The following are my own additions and interpretations of Spare's ideas. In my schema, there are three parts of the mind, the "I", the Ego, and the Self. The "I" is the current point of consciousness that a person uses to navigate the world, it's the commander behind the dashboard of the mind. This part of the mind is not personal. Every "I" is interchangeable. It's the Ego and the Self which are personal. The Ego as I interpret it is the layer just beyond the I which we show the world, the "Persona" of Jung, where some of our personality is located. However, the Ego or Persona is largely formed in reaction to outside influences, and therefore does not embody the true Self. The true Self lies in a layer below the Ego or Persona, and is the seat of the deeper, more authentic, aspects of our personality.

This definition of the Ego owes much to Buddhism, but to bring it back to psychological ideas, what I'm referring to as the Ego actually possesses the characteristics of both the Freudian Ego and the Freudian Subconscious, with the Subconscious being interpreted as another layer of the support which the Ego provides to the I. In this, the Ego as I use the term would be behind the "I", and the Subconscious would be behind the Ego, providing a deeper layer of support for it. The Ego in this is partially conscious, while the Subconscious is almost entirely unconscious, although it shares many features with the Ego.

Spare, very notably, does not use this terminology, and instead labels the I the Ego, so that there's a duality in his thought between Ego and Self. However, what I label as Ego is talked about by Spare, albeit indirectly. I see the Ego as containing, among other things, our personal beliefs, or Belief. These beliefs, which are part of the personality, can limit or extend us. Spare talks quite a bit about transforming belief, and about using the transformation of beliefs to make change in the world, particularly when the mind that has the beliefs has been empowered by sexual atavistic energy. The Ego, then, can be conceptualized as the thing that changes when belief changes.

To proceed, I believe that the Ego is something that exists between the I and the Self, and is largely negative. It's a false conception of what and who people are, and the coming forth of greater insight and awareness of the many selves from the unconscious mind is done at the expense of the Ego. The Ego, in this, must be destroyed in order for the commerce between the unconscious selves and the I to fully and completely manifest. The petty attachments and Egoistic selfishness of life are much different than the two poles of Self and I. Alternately, because actual permanent destruction of the Ego is a hard thing to obtain, it must be completely modified and its power overthrown. For this, in my opinion, Buddhist meditation is recommended, in that ego attachments, in the technical Buddhist sense of attachment, can be managed and worked on through this work. Attachments include things like jealousy and greed, grasping for things. Details are in the Toadstone section, but I would recommend simpler Theravada techniques like Insight Meditation and Vipassana in opposition to the more complex Mahayana techniques, which present deific forms. The Buddhists, both Theravada and Mahayana, believe that the Ego, the "Form" or Rupa, can never be fully eliminated while a person is incarnate. Indeed, as we shall see, complete annihilation of the Ego would prevent a person from functioning normally. Ego death, here, means not the destruction of the "I", or the destruction of the parts of the psyche that unconsciously support the "I" in its functioning, but instead means the suppression of that which prevents the true self from manifesting. This is the meaning of the term with respect to psychedelic drugs, for instance, some of which can affect this for a week or so, letting the inner, sometimes more innocent, Self to come through.

The modification, destruction, or suppression, of the Ego for the benefit of the coming forth of the different aspects of the Self also has echoes in Jung's notion of the difference between the Self and the Ego, in that the Self is the real reflection of the true self, while the Ego is a kind of Persona or mask that we show the world. The modification of the Ego in order to have the different aspects of the Self come through would also, in Jung's perspective, lead to a more integrated conception of the Self, in combination with the "I". Interestingly, and very relevantly, Jung's maps of the fully integrated Self are mandalas, that is, collections of entities or circles surrounding a central circle. If Jung's Self corresponds to the heart center, then Jung's Shadow, which has to be integrated into the Self, corresponds to the negative aspects of the lower center, associated with lower Desire.

Wilhelm Reich, too, intersects with this schema, in that his idea of the organic core of the Self, is that which is linked with during sex, and which is that which orgasm restores ones connection to. This organic core of the Self lives underneath the character armor, which we can equate here with the Ego and the Subconscious (as opposed to the Jungian Unconscious). It may be better to say that the Character Armor is behind the Subconscious, just as the Subconscious is behind the Ego, and the Ego is behind the "I". By loosening the character armor, the life energy of the organic core of the human being is more able to cross over into the psyche, and the individual manifests better mental health through this. In Reich's conception, the idea of the "Id" is not present in the way it is in Freud's thought. Instead of atavistic, and possibly violent, "Ids", Reich has more benevolent drives emanating from the central organic core of the person, which drives are the product of a positive sexual life energy. Reich's organic core, in this, more closely resembles the secret chamber of the heart than the lower conception of the Ids as base desires, though, of course, these two conceptualizations can come together. In this, Jung's mandala of selves, or aspects of the Self, is what is located in Reich's organic core, particularly in the heart center, and coming to sexual communion with the organic core facilitates the exploration and realization of the Selves connected to the Jungian mandala.

This process of remembering the selves, and of modifying the ego, overcoming the character armor, integrating the Jungian split selves into unity, corresponds to what Peter Carroll refers to in his "Liber Lux" as "Liberation", this document being contained in "Liber Null". This is one of the five modes of magical action that he elaborates on in this document. Here, what I refer to as the Ego is linked to beliefs, and to rigid morals that are the outcome of limiting beliefs. These limiting beliefs interfere with the commerce between the Self and the I, as Spare outlines in "The Focus of Life". By undoing ones static system of belief and by making our interpretations more flexible, the kind of dogmatic moralism that takes the energy of the Self and directs it, canalizes it, into dead paths and dead ends is destroyed. However, Spare, in writings in "Zos Speaks!" is careful to point out the problems of letting one's "Ids" run things. Liberation from stultifying belief through different forms of destruction of belief and reconstructions of belief does not mean letting your basic drives and desires control you, and overwhelm you. Though Spare has an opposition to the excesses of Reason reminiscent, and perhaps derived from, William Blake, he does not actually advocate throwing all of Reason out, or ones life being controlled by primal atavisms.

This type of liberation is also connected to what William S. Burroughs outlines in his non-fiction interview book "The Job". There, he points to a kind of control system of society which manifests in the mind through key words, which are rooted deep in the subconscious mind. These words are the basis of automatic reactions, that are then used by people in society to control and to direct others. These words imprinted into the subconscious, that we're not directly aware of, are the same thing as the Beliefs of Spare and are connected to the top of the Character Armor of Reich. They're also at the level that can be accessed through hypnosis, and so part of what Burroughs is getting at is a kind of ever present social hypnosis through which social institutions exercise control. It's important to remember that Freud's discovery of the Subconscious mind came through his practice of therapeutic hypnotism in this. This is also the "Reactive Mind" of Dianetics, which Burroughs references many times in the interview, though I consider both Dianetics and Scientology to be very poor examples of techniques that lead to liberation. A much better model of hypnosis and psychology can be found in Melvin Powers' "Self-Hypnosis: Its Theory, Technique and Application". Burroughs applied his "cut up" technique to try to deprogram people, by rearranging social texts designed to trigger words in the reactive mind, which would ordinarily create stereotyped responses within the general state of hypnotic trance that exists within society. By rearranging the propaganda texts, the trigger points of stereotyped beliefs are undermined.

In "Liber Lux", the advice that Carroll gives for this type of liberation is largely negative, consisting of breaking, blaspheming, and otherwise profaning one's belief systems. In the section of "Liber Nox" called "Random Belief", he advocates putting on different masks of belief in order to change one's concepts in a more positive, flexible, way. These two, the destruction of belief and the taking on of new beliefs for the purpose of liberation, are complementary. This type of primal masking, and primal breaking, is also present both within Chumbley's work and within traditional witchcraft in general. In this, different faiths that have contact with the primal vision can be pursued in order to reaffirm contact with the Sabbat itself. Through pursuing different modes of work according to these different faiths, the original, primal, doctrine as it exists both within the individual and within the macrocosm can be reconstructed. The primal experience of the seven, of the compass around the throne, can be experienced within one's psyche, and understood within the outside world and within the macrocosmic Ideal realm. By putting on masks, pursuing the truth, then breaking and discarding those masks if they become limiting, and putting on other ones, the "Pattern beneath the plow" becomes visible, so to speak. This turn of phrase, as I use it, means the underlying pattern behind both the psyche and objective reality itself, which exists behind and beyond all beliefs. Through iconoclasm and intentional masking, the person can realign their psyche to the original state of things that existed before they, of necessity, absorbed the beliefs of their environment, from their time and place which they were born into. Correspondingly, they can also learn how to better commune with the macrocosmic reality of the Sabbat in a way which is not limited by the beliefs of that same time and place in which they find themselves. They can also manifest a purer copy of both of these within ritual, where the psyche and the macrocosmic reality come together in an image created through the ritual which is a representation of both of them. Yet, approaching this is, in a very real way, a kind of "Self Undoing", where the false beliefs are stripped away to reveal the pattern in the organic core of the Self.

Something to note with this is that, though in the more recent chaos magic world, there has been a focus on changing beliefs, the connotation of belief in Spare also goes deeper than this, to affect behavior and ways of acting as well. The type of flexibility that's being advocated by Carroll and others should not be purely intellectual, but affect one on a deeper level as well. This is how belief, and "Undoing" belief, can intersect with undoing character armor. The psychological repressions, fears, complexes, and fixations that are reflected in the character armor have to be undone for the flow of energy from the Self, or from the organic core, to the "I", to be increased. For this, various changes of belief which have personal psychological consequences, for example personal mask making which has psychological relevance, are indicated. If a person is very anti-Christian, for example, because of personal issues, perhaps a good mask would be to become a practicing Christian, studying and following Christian mysticism, which could help to overcome this psychological programming. This would contribute more to personal liberation than to just take on beliefs that are comfortable, or that are just extensions of what the individual already believes. True flexibility of belief, if it's also going to have the effect of flexibility of character armor and ultimately personal liberation from imposed constraints, does not come from following the easy path that you've been pursuing. Similarly, Peter Carroll, in "Liber Nox", in the section on "Transmogrification", makes reference to physical changes, physical actions, that a person can do in their lives, to facilitate liberation. These include things like radical changes in location, occupation, and way of life. All of this also goes into Left Hand Path territory, and for more details on this, I recommend the writings of Don Webb, of the Temple of Set, for advice. Particularly, "Uncle Setnakt's Essential Guide to the Left Hand Path" is a good work. This type of liberation was also part of the original orientation of Thee Temple ov Psychick Youth, and of Genesis P-Orridge, before other concerns and the selfishness of stardom overwhelmed it.

Part of this challenging of the limits, too, is present in Chumbley's works as the role of the "Opposer" or of Death. I believe that focusing on the "Death" aspect is the much better way of treating this, in that using the name the "Opposer" brings into it a lot of unnecessary associations which can be counter-productive. Death, in this, means iconoclasm or breaking, which includes not just physical things, and orgasm, but the sacrifice of beliefs and way of acting and thinking as well. The point of the iconoclasm is to liberate that which has been trapped within that which is being sacrificed. This is pictured as the liberation of the Azoth or Essence from the Form which contains it. The Azoth is the primal energy of the Self. On the one hand, there are vessels for the Essence which are chosen and consciously implemented, on the other, if we apply this to the psyche, there are beliefs which we've been born into and conditioned into which are not chosen. These trap the Essence, the Azoth, in ways which we may not want it to be trapped. The iconoclasm or destruction of these beliefs changes this, and, in ways like we've been discussing, can change the character armor and the ego as well.

The energy which has been liberated by this process was referred to by Spare as "Free belief", free energy that can be applied to whatever a person wants to apply it. Freed belief, in this, can also allow a person to perceive the "Pattern under the plow", the primal mandala of the Self, and the energy that's freed can be used to create effigies, beliefs, and other material which reflects that primal mandala of the Self while existing within the greater world. This type of free belief, and the freed sexuality coming from it, is described in the "Focus of Life" in terms reminiscent of Freud's idea of "Polymorphous Perversity", and is labeled by Spare as "Unmodified Sexuality". This is the state of the Sabbat itself, as well as the eternal fornication of liberated nature in the external world, nature in its pure, uncorrupted state. This can be linked to the idea of taking pleasure in everything, in all of the states of the millions of forms of being that the different masks of belief and different atavisms give access to and embody, these corresponding to desires as well.

Interestingly, though "The Focus of Life" deals primarily with masturbatory sexuality, it also references women and heterosexual sex in particular ways. Women appear in the text as externalized parts of the self which Spare has had congress with, or parts of the self that have been projected outwards onto the women. He speaks in many places about taking the women back into the self as part of his self-sexuality. Here, we can make an equation of the women with the Hand, with the "Aetheric I", spread around the "Autochthonic I" of the I and the Eye. The women in this form part of the self-mandala, each revealing a different section of reality. They represent refractions of the Self found in others. With this, we have something quite different than the current, very fashionable, discourse about "The Other". One can know the self and the different selves within the self through knowing others. Presumably, this happens in the other direction as well, in a complementary way. In taking women back into ones self, what Spare is indicating is that he has accidentally, unconsciously, projected part of his self onto these women, and is bringing this part of the self consciously back into him, in order to become a more fully integrated person.

At the end of "The Focus of Life", Spare reduces these different loves to one love, to one woman, the primal love, so to speak. This is related to the first love, and to the first Desire. Here, he Wills to recollect the Belief in the primal woman, the primal love, which activates the primal Desire. This activation, consummated in orgasm, leads to the rising of ecstasy from the Self to the "I", which transforms the "I" into an "Atmospheric" state, this being the ultimate source of the "Aetheric I" in Carroll and Chumbley. The "Atmospheric" state is an ecstatic state experienced as something within the aura, as the Belief externalized. It's indicated that this is a type of hallucinatory reality where the energies that power the Beliefs are experienced as something distinct from the "I", where the selves, so to speak, are experienced as gods around the "I" which it can interact with.

What we see in this is that, through knowing the "Other" in the form of a single woman, who represents primal Belief, we can know ourselves in a single, most powerful, primal way. The first love calls up the first desire, which culminates in the first Ecstasy, which involves a primal Self coming forth from the unconscious and empowering the "I". This can practically be adapted to work with a physical woman, as opposed to just the recollection of first loves in auto-sexual reverie.

However, the notion of Self and Other here, is different from what is claimed by people who are fixated on trendy Critical Theory, in that the Other is herself a woman who, though different, is not completely alien.

Here, the woman as Other is a different version of the same Self that the man possesses, and, overall, the Self of the man and of the woman combine to be a third thing, a third type of Self that's all encompassing. This greater Self is in its being bisexual, having all the possibilities of the Sabbat taken in its male and female aspects within it, as the First Mind. This reconstructed third mind is androgynous in this, and corresponds to Baphomet, in his manifestation as Paradigm or Living Being, containing all the possible selves of the Divine Mind within him/her. People who believe that women are the ultimate "Other", alien to male consciousness, should probably get out more and meet more actual women. Alternately, this can also be pursued in a homosexual way. Here, Self and Other are more pure personal orientations, rather than genders. Presumably, as well, from the point of view of the woman, the man is the Other and she is the Self, she is the Eye and he is the Hand.

Interestingly, the idea of a "Third Mind" is referenced in a book of the same name by William S. Burroughs and Brion Gysin. They describe it as a "complete fusion of subjectivities" that leads to a new entity. The authors elaborate on this "Third Mind" as an "unseen collaborator" a "superior mind", and a "new author". The "Third Mind" was produced by the collaboration of Burroughs and Gysin. The authors state that they got the concept from a quote from Napoleon Hill's "Think and Grow Rich", which references the idea of an "invisible, intangible force", a "Third Mind", that's produced by the collaboration of a group of people. This would appear to be a kind of group consciousness created by collaboration between people.

Wilhelm Reich and Self-Undoing

On a more basic level, Reichian therapy locates the character armor in muscle memory, and physical exercises which undo this muscle memory can contribute to the breaking of the built up Egoic forces, though true Reichian body therapy is not comfortable, nor is it meant to be comfortable. Reich saw work with the body as complementary to work with the mind, which in our context is the work of Belief. There is a direct parallel between this idea and that of Spare's "Death Posture". In its original form, this had three phases. Stephen Mace, in "Stealing the Fire from Heaven" gives a good summary of it: the first phase was getting into a meditative state through gazing into a mirror. This was followed by assuming a deliberately uncomfortable and contorted position for a short period of time in order to liberate their mind and their bodily psychic energy from conventional restraints. The posture hurts if you pursue it, and can't be sustained for long periods of time. This was followed by lying down on the floor in a "dead" state and feeling ones self unified with the universe. This follows the Reichian model of creating tension through body work and breathing, and then releasing it, feeling a oceanic, more integrated feeling afterwards.

More details can be found in Mace's book, which also discusses in specifics Spare's idea of "Neither-Neither", the process of questioning and confronting Beliefs in order to liberate ones self from their domination, which, in the process, frees up psychic energy which can then be devoted to magical acts. In general, "Stealing Fire from Heaven" is an excellent analysis of Austin Osman Spare, but it can be hard to find. Mace's "Shaping Formless Fire" covers similar ground, and is more available.

Coming back to Reichian work itself, though the most well known book about this sort of "Undoing" is Christopher Hyatt's "Undoing Yourself with Energized Meditation", a much more detailed version of this work can be found in Jack Willis' "Reichian Therapy for Home Use". This covers the same territory, albeit without the magical elements. Willis has made this work available for free on the internet, at https://reichiantherapy.info, although there is also a printed copy of the work available.

Hyatt's "Undoing Yourself with Energized Meditation" is valuable, but only a fraction of the work actual deals with the physical process of "Undoing". This is contained in chapters 10 and 11. This amounts to around twenty pages, as opposed to the several hundred pages of instructions which Willis gives. A fuller version of these same two chapters, without the juvenile attitude of the rest of "Undoing Yourself", is found in Hyatt's "Secrets of Western Tantra". This work is divided into two parts. The first part, which outlines a Reichian framework plus exercises, including exercises involving non-penetrative sex, is very good. The second, which implements a Golden Dawn ceremonial magic framework is, in my opinion, much less so. Hyatt also gives solid advice regarding a general philosophy of sex, and relationships, so to speak, in the theoretical framework of the first part. Notably, Willis' work deals purely with the individual, and does not contain instructions for sex work of any kind.

"Undoing Yourself" has another gem within it, however, which is its twelfth chapter. Chapter 12 is titled "On the Invokation of Eris: Chaos as Prerequisite to Change " This chapter is by a writer using the pseudonym ©.D. Rose Hart(wo)man, whose philosophy and terminology has a surprising amount in common with that of Peter Carroll. This is an illuminating read, particularly the last sections of it, which synthesize various ideas of Chaos magic with ritual and personal liberation. With regards to more general questioning of beliefs and "deprogramming", which don't involve body work, Hyatt's work "The Tree of Lies", reissued as "To Lie is Human, Not Getting Caught is Divine", can be useful.

There are some limitations to the Reichian material from Willis and Hyatt, namely that neither work gives a good introduction to the Reichian framework itself. Both Hyatt and Willis learned their therapy from Israel Regardie, known more for his magical writings and for being a one time secretary of Aleister Crowley. Fortunately, Regardie wrote an introduction to Reichian body work and therapy in the late '50s, which goes into great depth about what it is and the theoretical background on which it's based. This work was unpublished until recently, and is now available in two different editions, put out by rival publishers, one titled "New Wings for Daedalus: Wilhelm Reich, his Theory and Techniques", the other one simply titled "Wilhelm Reich: His Theory and Techniques". Reading this work helps to illumine the purposes behind different practices that Willis and Hyatt presented to the reader but do not fully explain. Within the book, the chapters that are most directly linked with the practical work are those titled "Method I" and "Method II". "Method I" outlines the breathing pattern, while "Method II" presents examples of the same sorts of "Undoing" exercises that are found in Hyatt and Willis. Particularly, practicing the breathing method after orgasm can lead to remarkable effects. These can include some of the benefits of Ego suppression that psychedelic drugs can induce.

Strangely, despite writing an entire book, "The Art of True Healing", dealing with the circulation and use of healing magical energy, which he says suffuses the universe, Regardie rejects Reich's notion of Orgone. This is a specific Prana like energy that is held in muscles and which contains, or is linked to, specific memories and parts of the character armor. This is doubly mysterious considering that even in his late writing "Healing, Prayer and Relaxation" Regardie explicitly refers to an atmospheric life energy, and gives instructions on how to absorb it into your body. Hyatt and Willis, and Hyatt's students, apparently follow this denial of Orgone as well, with one of Hyatt's students writing in a new introductory essay to Regardie's " New Wings for Daedalus" that Reich's belief in a life energy was a "psychotic delusion" on his part. I can see why Regardie, who was a professional chiropractor, might want to shy away from publicly talking about Orgone, but why would his successors still publicly reject the idea?

An important final note for the study of these documents is that, at the heart of all of these accounts of Reichian therapy are breathing exercises that are undertaken in a very specific posture. This is perhaps not immediately apparent in Hyatt's accounts.

For a Reichian perspective that recognizes Orgone, Wilhelm Reich's writings are the place to start. Although Reich's writings are vast, the best introduction to his whole thought, including Orgone, is the dual book "Ether, God, and Devil & Cosmic Superimposition".

Also, as far as recommended reading goes, renowned psychic and remote viewer Ingo Swann deals with Reich and sexual energy quite extensively in his excellent work "Psychic Sexuality".

Another practice associated with Reich is Rolfing. This is a deep tissue massage which has an emphasis on the abdomen and pelvis. It appears that in the beginning there was an awareness that this massage would liberate emotions and memories in the process. However, these days Rolfing tends to market itself purely as a physical therapy practice. The idea of going to a Rolfer for personal fulfillment and exploration might be met with skepticism by the practitioner.

With regards to other Reichian and semi-Reichian practices, Charles R. Kelley, who headed the "Radix Institute", and who was a student of Reich, maintained a belief in Orgone, and integrated it into his practice. He also made what I consider to be great advances in understanding Character Armor, connecting it with "Purpose" as well as with trauma. A variety of his works are available, though they contain no practical instructions, in that his Institute trained people to do the manipulations for others as therapists. His major work is "Lifeforce...the Creative Process in Man and in Nature"

In a way, Kelley provides a very valuable correction to some of what we've been going over, a correction that was also noted by Austin Osman Spare. Kelley didn't believe that all Character Armor was wrong. Instead, he believed that available life energy was channeled by people in certain ways according to their goals and purposes, and that this was the origin of Character Armor, what we've been linking to the Ego. When this is established in an excessive way, which can happen due to much of the formation of character happening during childhood, it can cause serious issues, which undoing can help. However, Character Armor in this, along with the Ego, is linked to basic directed functioning of individuals, and to a level of necessary repression of instincts without which we can't function as adults. The Ego itself, though it can be weakened, and should be, cannot truly be eliminated without crippling a person's capacity to function as an adult human being. This brings up a danger of undoing, which is important to point out.

If you undo yourself too much, Kelley argues, you regress to an infantile state where you lose self control. It's possible to strip away too much of the Ego. Simple liberation itself, pursued without anything else, can lead to a negative outcome. This can happen not just for individuals, but for a culture as well. Kelley countered this tendency with his emphasis on "Purpose". While undoing excessive Character Armor is sometimes necessary, it's also sometimes necessary to build up Character Armor in order to channel one's life energy for a particular life purpose. This life purpose, chosen by the individual, is key to giving life meaning. It's a type of partial order within chaos, but not a complete negation of it. Instead, it's a type of direction within chaos. A positive, constructive, direction complements liberation done by destroying constraints. This overlaps with Spare's idea of directing your energy for a particular goal once you've liberated it. After all, if you're practicing magick, you want to accomplish things, you want to realize goals, not just experience either a chaos or a communion with the universe. Spare too commented on the dangers of repressing too little by pointing out that you shouldn't let your ids control you, but that you should control them, despite the benefits that can come from realizing different bestial parts of yourself through activating primal atavisms.

This qualification also applies to general skepticism and undoing of beliefs. Some beliefs, those which we don't choose but that are imposed on us, can be oppressive, but after we take ownership of determining our own beliefs, we can find ones that we believe are true. Those beliefs are not oppressive, but come from our own core values, from what we think is important in life. These beliefs can be so strong that a person would be willing to make serious personal sacrifices in order to live according to those beliefs, and to advance them in the world. In my opinion, it's good to have values and beliefs like that, instead of just floating away with a general skepticism of all beliefs. The destructive phase of questioning beliefs can be productive, but at some point you have to define what you're for, not just what you're against.

I believe, as well, that Hyatt's promotion of skepticism of beliefs was not intended to lead people a mushy semi-belief in everything. Instead, I believe that it was intended to let a person choose the beliefs that they really cared about, after the programming of beliefs that they'd inherited was questioned and taken down. As he says repeatedly in his "Tree of Lies", "Become who you are, there are no guarantees". To become who you are, you have to define what you actually believe and care about, because that defines who you are.

Another book by a follower of Reich who also believes in Orgone may be useful: Elsworth Baker's "Man in the Trap". The book is the most complicated of all the books listed, approaching the more complex works of Reich's such as "Character Analysis", and is nearly at that level. Nonetheless, it contains both practical advice with regards to each of the muscular sections that supplements Regardie's work as well as general observations on the life energy and the process of armoring which have immense value. Baker stated that he was chosen by Reich to continue his work once Reich went to prison, after having worked beside him for eleven years, and for a long time after Reich's arrest and death this was the only book available dealing with these ideas, and so was the standard book. In my opinion, Kelley's theoretical framework goes beyond Baker's, but, on the other hand, Baker's work goes over many areas which Kelley doesn't treat at all in "Life Force". Much of the work deals with Reichian psychoanalysis, as well as topics for practicing psychiatrists.

Finally, a possible source for some of Reich's ideas on Orgone is Felix Auerbach's "Ektropismus, oder die Physikalische Theorie des Lebens.", "Ektropy, or the physical theory of life", published in 1910. This work deals with the concept of "Ektropy" as the opposite of "Entropy", and Auerbach's "Ektropic" forces are concentrated in life and life energy. Orgone was said by Reich to be anti-Entropic, and so is Ektropic by definition. There are many parallels between the two men's work, yet it's not known if Reich was aware of Auerbach's book, or if he drew on it. Ektropy can also be translated as Extropy, which in the form of the Extropian movement has quite a lot in commen with Auerbach's ethos. This ethos also shares common ground with Russian Cosmism.

W.E. Butler

Austin Osman Spare, though influenced by witchcraft and a great thinker unto himself, did not create his system of magic in a vacuum. Particularly, his use of psychology in magic, and his psychological perspective, is paralleled by the writings of Golden Dawn initiates who are part of the "Western Mystery Tradition", such as W.E. Butler. In the United States, many individuals are very familiar with the core Golden Dawn documents from Israel Regardie's publication of them, but the writings of British Golden Dawn initiates that describe their general understanding of magic are less known.

Butler was an initiate of Dion Fortune, but his two major books, "Magic: It's Ritual, Power, and Purpose" and "The Magician: His Training and Work", are not rehashes of Golden Dawn material available elsewhere. Instead, they talk about magic in general, and the experience of performing it, and can be adapted to any system, Witch, Neo-Pagan, Chaos magic, within reason. In fact, Butler's works were regarded as foundational for UK occultists in the '60s, '70s, and '80s, and its influence can be found in many writers you wouldn't expect. I would argue that the Chaos magic movement, on top of using Spare, also used ideas from Butler without the corresponding Golden Dawn beliefs. Equally, terms from Butler and the "Western Mystery Tradition", such as the "Sphere of Sensation", referring to both the aura and to the literal reach of our perceptions, show up in Chumbley's work.

Butler, in his "Magic: It's Ritual, Power, and Purpose", puts forward a model of evocation which has quite a lot in common with Spare's idea of Atavistic resurgence. There, the magician is supposed to send specific images to their subconscious mind. These images will resonate with images in the collective unconscious, and cosmic energy will be gathered to bring these archetypal images out of the subconscious and into the waking consciousness. Here, an equation is being made between the collective unconscious and the sexual-elemental realm of the lower center, where Spare's "Primal Atavisms" live. These archetypal images are god forms, and the energies which will be evoked, from the personal psyche, are god energies with a variety of characteristics. Now, these god forms either flood the personal psyche itself, empowering it, or the energy, in Butler's opinion, can be channeled into some place outside of the psyche where with the help of incense or other materia, it can assume a physical, manifest, form, whereupon the magician can interact with it. The energies can also be redirected outside of the self and interacted with in a purely psychic form as well, through inner vision. A major difference between Spare and Butler in this is that Butler uses Kabbalistic images, which in ritual are supplemented by using colors and correspondences within it which reinforce the imagery, whereas Spare uses sigils, but the meaning is the same. Butler even talks about the individual using the Kabbalah to establish their own personal language for interacting with the higher realms. Here, the self-programming or learning of the different colors and correspondences of the Kabbalah, the adoption of this particular symbol set, allows the deep psyche of the individual to be more efficiently accessed through symbol and ritual. This basic principle can be detached from the Kabbalah and instead applied either to a person's wholly individual symbolism, or to other types of symbol sets, like those involved in witchcraft.

Butler elaborates on his thought in general in "The Magician: His Training and Work". There, he also presents a more nuanced account of magic as a whole. There, the powers that are called up from the collective unconscious into the mind can also be projected outwards and upwards, towards the highest point of the cosmos. In doing so, the higher cosmos can echo those energies and send their version of them back down to earth, accomplishing feats of magic this way.

Magic, according to Butler and others, is the art of affecting changes in consciousness according to will. This in itself is an incomplete statement about what Butler and others of that school believe. A better summary would be the following: magic is the art of affecting changes in consciousness according to will, and by applying images through your subconscious, energies are brought up from the microcosm. These energies then change your consciousness, which then changes the aura, and sends these same energies out to the macrocosm. Then, the macrocosm answers this by sending the corresponding energies down, which then influences the greater world. Depending on how you conceptualize the microcosm and its energies, this can mean atavisms from the collective unconscious, energies from the secret sun within the heart, or energies from the various parts of the body, among other possibilities.

Butler's use of Jung's "Collective Unconscious" concept in this is very interesting. Spare would no doubt say that the Collective Unconscious is located in the lower center, and that the various Atavisms are part and parcel of it. However, there is another possibility, which is that in the three center model that we've been working with, the Collective Unconscious is located in the Heart center, where the true Self lives. In this model, the primal atavisms of Spare would be located beneath the level of the Collective Unconscious, and much of the realization of different aspects of the Self would be entangled with realizing archetypes of the Collective Unconscious that live in the Heart. These two could, of course, be combined, with the primal Atavisms of Spare, from the lower center, empowering the Archetypes of the Collective Unconscious in the Heart, so that when they're drawn on an empowered, synthetic form comes through.

Chumbley in Relation to Massey and Spare

Chumbley, in the Azoetia, draws on both Spare and Massey, and melds them, in a way, into one. Much of the schema from Massey shows up in the Azoetia's drawings. Lets look at this melding.

Chumbley in the Azoetia has a few drawings where he breaks things down into four forms: the Sidereal, the Deific, the Linear, and the Fetishistic. Parts of this schema are used in many drawings, although it's only in a few that all four appear. The Sidereal drawings are of pure energy, which is the energy of the Sabbat, which comes down to earth through the stars, which are the Aster that the word Sidereal refers to. The Deific drawings are those that have Egyptian animal gods in them, which in turn are an adaptation of the pure energy of the Sidereal drawings into symbolic animal form. These are Hieroglyphs. The linear level consists of drawings that are the reduction of the hieroglyphic pictures of the gods into sigils, in part, though I believe that much more is going on here in the composition of the sigils than just that. Also, the linear level involves letters and the manipulation of letters, which the hieroglyphic or deific level does not. The Fetishistic drawings are representations of physical objects that are composed of animal parts like skulls combined with vessels and other objects which are supposed to embody the Sidereal and Deific energies in physical form. This represents four levels, from the most abstract to the physical, and I believe that it can be corresponded to Chumbley's four-fold symbolism of the Eye, the Mouth, the Hand, and the Phallus, of which we'll discuss much more in the Grimoire section of this work.

Massey outlines three of the four levels in the first chapters to "Ancient Egypt, the Light of the World". These are what corresponds to Chumbley's Sidereal, Deific, and Fetishistic levels.

To start out it's important to note that Massey starts from a non-anthropomorphic standpoint in analyzing gods and myths. In book I of "Ancient Egypt", he makes the point that the original gods were elemental powers, and that these elemental powers were first imagined as corresponding to animals. The animals were chosen because, in some way, their behavior mimicked the action of the elemental forces. Similarly, Massey states that before writing was established, people communicated with each other about these elemental forces through imitation: by syllables that echoed the calls of the animals, by hand gestures that imitated their actions, and by dances where people mimicked the actions of the animals as a whole.

In Massey's reading, myths and tales that show different animals interacting with each other are representations of physical phenomenon observed in the world. The animals, in this, are embodiments of the phenomena, and their interactions are the interactions of the different physical elements with each other. This can be abstracted to apply to spiritual phenomena and spiritual elements as well, or to the esoteric or spiritual significance of physical phenomenon, like the changing of the phases of the moon, or the interaction between the sun and the earth through the seasons. Glorified ancestors also could become gods, and be portrayed in the same way in Massey's schema.

Magic, too, is talked about by Massey in this. Here, ritual is done to imitate the actions of animals, which actions, in turn, symbolize the actions of the elements. By imitating the actions of the animals in real life in ritual, the actions of the elemental forces that they represent are put into play, and are set to act in the world. Massey recounts that rituals were also used to communicate and keep alive accounts of the interactions of the different elemental forces in the world, with this not necessarily having an overt magical intent. For Massey, these rituals, which include especially dances, were the way for tribes to preserve this knowledge before actual verbal myths had been made. These ideas were applied by Massey to all symbolic rituals that pre-modern people carried out, from manhood initiation rites to hunting rites. In this, people put on the skins of the animals that they wanted to imitate, with masks representing the animals, with other physical material from the animals being present in the outfit. He also recounts that people could, through donning the mask and doing the rituals, enter into a trance state where they communed with the elemental force of the animal nature itself.

For Massey, magic, in this sense, is done through the manipulation of elemental energies by means of mental constructs, by means of mental power, as he says. The mental constructs are the symbolic correspondences of animals to the elemental powers. However, these mental constructs are based on real physical characteristics that the animals have, and so there is a physical aspect to it. This physical aspect is present in physical fetishes and spells with physical components, but the magical power in these works through symbolism. He talks about the medicine worked with fetishes as being fundamentally mental in this sense, having to do with physical associations given to animals and their characteristics, with the medicine depending on this mental energy and symbolism, as opposed to chemical powers.

Fetishes, as physical objects, are presented as the remnants of the sign language, with charms, amulets being given the soul of the different animal energies that they're constructed out of. The ensoulment of the fetishes gives them the elemental power or soul of the god. They could be said to be a more permanent form of what's pulled down to the individual when they're masked, in costume, and performing rites as the gods. Here, the material could be a permanent representation of the relationship between the elements that was portrayed during the dance or ritual. Massey argues that the more abstract fetishes and amulets were originally derived from concrete parts of animals, such as bones and feathers, teeth, and dried parts, which were thought to embody and symbolize the elemental powers. The fetishes themselves, for Massey, are ideographs, or hieroglyphics, in physical form.

For Massey, too, the hieroglyphs were derived from portrayals of the animals, who in turn represented the characteristics of elemental powers. Pictorial hieroglyphs preceded conventional letters, which, in turn, are abstracted pictorial hieroglyphs. Sigils, as an accumulation of hieroglyphs that are arranged for a particular purpose and then abstracted, can be seen as a type of written fetish, meant to ensorcel the different energies being represented into itself for a specific purpose. Sigils, of course, can be combined with physical material to create more traditional fetish amulets as well.

Though Massey presents as complex system for how tribes derived their identity, ultimately he links the idea of elemental powers symbolized by animals to the origin of souls. In this, the elemental powers were thought to be the fathers of children, and so the children are supposed to have taken on the totemic emblem of the animal whose spirit child they were supposed to be. According to Massey, the people who enacted the rites of transformation, transformed into the animal form of the element which their soul belonged to, using masks, skins, and other physical material. They might then turn into other creatures or powers not of their soul as well. These animals, in Massey correspond to the seven, to light, darkness, fire, water, air and earth, and so the elemental powers and the heritage of spirit children are just that—spirit children of elementals, like in the "Comte de Gabalis".

This was the origin of totemic tribes by legendary ancestors. Eventually, within the seven, the idea of being conceived from one of the elements gave way to the idea of being conceived by blood, the seventh member of the heptad, and this signified being ensouled and descended from a human being instead of an elemental spirit. Later, Massey makes a distinction between people thought to have a soul that originates from elemental spirits and people thought to have a soul derived from previous humans, with witches being in the category of those who are descended from elemental spirits. This is then related to the Book of Enoch and to the Watchers, and to their descent to the daughters of men. The Watchers, in this, are elemental spirits, but elemental spirits that are simultaneously corresponded with the highest parts of the court of heaven—the seven around the throne, located in Paradise, on the top of the world mount, under the Pole Star. Souls, or some souls, pre-existed in the form of elemental spirits there.

Coming back to Chumbley and Spare, as far as I can tell, though he touches on the subject, Massey doesn't have a concrete theory of alphabets and scripts, instead leaving off his theory with hieroglyphics, so this fourfold idea seems to be a combination of Massey and Austin Osman Spare's ideas, along with those of Chumbley himself. In this, you can see a progression, from the abstract graphs of the Sidereal energy being transformed into the animal hieroglyphics as symbols, and these in turn being turned into the different letters of Chumbley's "Alphabet of Desire", which represents those same types of energies within the grimoire of the Azoetia. However, that's only a very bare, and not really satisfactory, description of what's going on. Chumbley's sigil workings are a subject unto themselves, and go far beyond what we're discussing. Sigils can be letters of an alphabet of desire, and/or glyphs that encode and express the nature of elemental powers unto themselves, or they can also be formed through a combination of these and the reduction of conventional letters, as Austin Osman Spare outlined, to name just a few of the possibilities.

In "Zos Speaks!" there's a very interesting piece by Spare titled "Language — words in general and particular". There, Spare relates his theory of the origin of language. He states that the first words represented emotions, by which he likely means Desires. Writing evolved to express these Desires, first with what could be called hieroglyphs, then with more abstract signs. Other words evolved to coordinate these words, which means the evolution of grammar—subjects, verbs, objects, articles, to tell what the words of Desire were being directed towards. Spare brings this up in the context of the language which the unconscious responds to, with relation to asking the unconscious questions and getting back answers. This method of asking questions and getting back answers is a form of sigil magic, and the intent appears to use the language of the primal atavisms, corresponding here to Desires, in order to elicit a response from the unconscious. Again, here, the link of language with Desires and atavisms within the individual can be linked to Massey's idea of language as reflecting external elemental energies and powers, which too were first represented by hieroglyphs, of animals in his case. Similarly, Massey provides an underlying structure for the atavisms that's not present in Spare's work.

Chumbley seems to have mixed Austin Osman Spare's ideas of powers as "primal atavisms" with Massey's notion of gods as embodying similarly primal elemental forces, which become primal spiritual forces in the course of his description of them. The primal forces of Massey, which are located outside of the individual, are corresponded with the primal atavisms of Spare, which are located within the individual. In Chumbley's work, and, I believe, in traditional witchcraft in general, there's a fundamental pattern to the atavisms. They're linked to the eightfold plot, and to the sevenfold set of spirits around the throne, around the lord of the Sabbat, in paradise. These are the components of the horizontal and vertical axes that we've been discussing.

Coming back to the four levels of Chumbley's art as a whole, there is a way of looking at the Witches Tetragrammaton which Chumbley links to Gerald Massey's work. This schema is different from the one that we shall present in the grimoire section. This schema can be looked at as four levels of concretization. Here, the pattern is different, being Eye, Mouth Hand, Phallus. In this, the four levels start from internal visualization and move through the more concrete speech, to the more concrete writing, to the most concrete act. Here, the Eye relates to the pure energetic patterns, which are seen, the Sidereal energies; The mouth refers to the Totemic or Deific aspects of the energies,which are invoked, which are represented by Hieroglyphics. The hand refers to Sigils and alphabetic, linear, diagrams, which are drawn. The Phallus refers to the Fetishistic or physical matter that corresponds to the energies, which are taken from animal bodies and from inanimate matter that corresponds to the energies, and can refer to the powers taken on permanent manifestation or earthed. It also refesr to concrete ritual actions, taken with or without objects.

Aesthesis.

In Austin Osman Spare's terminology, found in the "Logomachy of Zos", "Aesthesis", refers to the deep sensations of desire, as well as to external sensations. These could be called internal and external sensations. Though the word literally means "Sensations", emotions, too, are internal sensations. The representation of these basic elemental desires or Atavisms by deific forms in the mind is the "Apotheosis of Sensations". However, as noted before, Chumbley departs from Spare about the specific location of these sensations. Therefore, the "Apotheosis of Sensations", which Chumbley talks about quite a bit, is a much broader concept than what Spare is referring to. The deific animal forms, and representatives of sensation are linked to the heart and to the seven fold plot of the circle, with the seven primal elemental deities residing there. This is an "Apotheosis", making something into a deity. The emotions, the "Aesthesis", in turn, are linked to the "primal atavisms" or elemental forces within the lower center and heart.

Desires, here, in Spare, are linked with these atavisms, with the "Aesthesis", and with magical states. This suggests heavily that in Chumbley's work the sigils of the Alphabet are themselves linked with primal states of Desire, or states of consciousness linked to Desires, as well as with different deific connotations. Particularly, in Chumbley's work, the emotional states, states of consciousness, or states of desire, of the seven, are linked with different types of "Ecstasis" or ecstatic states of consciousness. "Aesthesis", the deep inner sensations linked to desire, and in that to the primal energies of nature, symbolized by animalistic characteristics, leads to "Ecstasis", ecstatic states where the mystical energy felt as an emotion is experienced more fully as a whole state of consciousness. This state of consciousness corresponds not just to the emotion, but to the mystical meaning and reality of the particular member of the seven which is being experienced. For Chumbley, it appears that the same sort of deep yearnings or desires, that were located by Spare in the lower center are attributed to him to the heart center.

With this, you have some overlap between ideas that are present in Peter Carrol's work in "Liber Null & Psychonaut". Here, in "Liber Nox", Carroll presents his own "Alphabet of Desire" based on

Spare's work, which is a mandala like mapping of emotions corresponding to primal atavisms that are present in the psyche. Carroll's mandala is based on two sets of three opposing emotions: Love, Desire, and Sex, on the one hand, and Fear, Hate and Death on the other. The desires in question are very primal and in line with the lower center. In Spare's vocabulary, these types of things would be identified with "ids", desires which exist within the Freudian Id, which is the unconscious source in Freud's thought of the most primal, animalistic, drives and desires.

Here, I should add, with regards to the basic desires, that the "Ids" are connected to the lower center, where the Toad Stone, the angelic soul, is also located. The Toad Stone there, is a thing of stability among these rather vicious drives. These drives have been categorized as, and associated with, demons of various kinds, in various works such as Frater U.'. D.'.'s "High Magic" project. That might be metaphorically true, but the Stone, the angelic soul, is not one of them, which means that if you go down deep enough into your psyche, you reach not just these primal forces but a part of your being, a part of your "Self", which is not part of them, and which, when seized, can be used to order and to discipline them.

The sigils in Spare's work are also sexual, with the alphabet of desire being made up of signs that are labeled as sexual. This corresponds to sexuality as a deep kind of atavistic desire. This also carries over to Chumbley's thought, though in a transferred form. Again, instead of referring to the lower center of desire, the sexual energies relate to the Sabbat itself, and to its representation within the heart. The energies of the First Sun, the Ideal realm, are in fact sexual life energies. Nature's eternal fornication, as Spare said multiple times, the life energies of the eternal sun copulating and relating to each other in millions of ways and in millions forms of being. This same life sexual life energy is the energy of the will, the vital life energy, and also the energy of love. Here, there's a mixing again of Massey and Spare, as well as traditional witchcraft ideas in general, in that Spare's sexual atavistic energy becomes the elemental energies of Massey sexualized. These same forces of natural fornication are located by Spare in the lower center of body.

In the section "The Heaven of Aaos", in "The Focus of Life", Spare talks about this sort of eternal fornication, and the Sabbat, which is entered through activating the Desires within the lower center of the human body through sexual ritual, in other words, by communing with the external fornication through activating the internal forces of fornication: He describes himself as a resurrected god in heaven, and speaks from the perspective of Baphomet: "I am the Iconoclast of Logos: The sun-satyr of Chaos!"

Spare also refers to a "Chaos" in his "Zoetic Grimoire of Zos", however, this chaos is likely somewhat different than that Chaos magician interpretation of it. This chaos is a feature of the witch's Sabbat itself, which is a protean form of all the Ideals coming together in profusion, before being ordered by the Opposer. Indeed, one way One way to conceptualize Chaos is as the Sabbat, in its protean form of all sexuality, with the idea of a globe of fire, the First Sun, being chaotic in the nature of the archetypes, the Ideals, floating within it, which fornicate constantly. This is not the only way to conceptualize this. Chaos, as used by Carroll, in Liber Lux, does have some overlap with the Sabbatic concept. However, other writings by Carroll, including those outside of "Liber Lux" that are also contained in "Liber Null and Psychonaut", define Chaos in other ways that do not align with this, and subsequent Chaos magick writings have further taken the concept away from this idea, so that it's not very common in Chaos magick writings today.

Part of the other definitions of Chaos, in Chaos magick, appear to come from at least one dissident student of William G. Gray, author of many fine books including "Magic Ritual Methods" and "Inner Traditions of Magic". Though a fine magician, Gray appears to have been caught up in a paradigm that saw a Cosmic and a Chaotic (or anti-Cosmic) current doing battle with each other, in a way that, looked at generously, could be connected with gnosticism. The Cosmos, and the Cosmic Plan, was supposed to guide everything to a higher state of existence. However, his writings against Chaos and the agents of Chaos extend into a support of a kind of cultural conservatism with regards to society that appears to have been restrictive and limiting, and somewhat paranoid. This includes condemning discordant music and culture. Notably, though, Gray explicitly says that Chaos and Cosmos do not stand for Good and Evil.

In the era of the late '70s, with the punk rock movement in full swing, it's easy to see how people could look at Gray's editorializing on the dangers of Chaos with regards to culture and life and say, "You know, Chaos sounds good to me, let's go for it". Gray saw the Cosmos and the Cosmic plan as the gnostic good guys against the agents of Chaos, but it's possible to invert this, and to see the excessive order of what he was advocating as being something that serves the cause of the Evil One, with Chaos being part of what can free humanity from its gnostic prison. Just as too much Chaos can threaten things, so too can too much Order. For more details, consult the last chapter of Gray's "Magic Ritual Methods".

Other Uses of Aesthesis

However, there are ways that Chumbley uses "Aesthesis" in the Azoetia which aren't related to emotions. One way, in particular, is the formula to attain communion with the different sabbatic energies represented by the cells and the letters of the sacred alphabet. Here, the sensations are those attached to the five senses. The process of doing this is to picture the letter in your mind, then will yourself to "hear" the sound of the letter, to "smell" the letter, to "taste" the letter, and then to "touch" the letter. After doing this, bring all of these together into one, so that you simultaneously perceive the letter with all five of your senses. This opens up a door to the pure energies of the letter, which come forth from it in what Chumbley refers to as "Telaesthesis".

This is a term that Spare originally used for the coming together of all emotions in "The Zoetic Grimoire". This process of opening the door to energies through this five-fold picturing can be done with any sigil, though it works better if the sigil that you're using is something that corresponds to an entity or state of being in the external world, rather than to an abstract active desire or wish connected with a spell. This is a tried and true method. Another way of working it is to picture a pentagram with each of the senses as points, and in getting the various senses of the sigil, go from one point to the other of the pentagram, until after going through the various lines and states you can picture them all at the same time. This use of the pentagram for contemplating or communing with an underlying principle is present in various traditional witchcraft traditions, and can be found in such places as the "Iron Pentagram" of the Feri work, where the correspondences aren't to senses but to other five fold aspects of the underlying principle, which is realized through contemplating its outward aspects.

Additionally, there's a commonality between this five fold pattern liberating the center and the five fold pattern that Peter Carroll outlines in "Liber Lux". There, Divination, Enchantment, Invocation, Evocation, and "Liberation" , are listed as five points of a pentagram whose center is Gnosis. The idea there, I believe, is that through repeated practice of all of the five points or paths, the central coordinating idea behind all of them, Gnosis, is realized. This would be the essence of magic itself.

Carroll's "Liber Null", containing "Liber Lux" and "Liber Nox", was published before many reprints of Spare's work were published. Influences on this are potentially Kenneth Grant's summaries of Spare's works as well as the original writings such as the "Book of Pleasure". The introduction by Kenneth Grant to "Zos Speaks!" as well as many writings by Spare contained in this, line up very well with Carroll's presentation of Spare, even though this was published in 1998, almost two decades after "Liber Lux" and "Liber Nox" were first published.

Aetheric I and Autochthonic I

These two terms are featured by Chumbley in the Azoetia and other writings. Using Spare's terminology, "Zos" is the Autochthonic I, which is the body as corresponded to the three centers, the vertical axis. It's linked to "Zod", but contains more. "Zod" appears to mean the core of the Self, while "Zos" stands for the greater area of the vertical dimension as a whole, the different centers of the body. The word "Autochthonic" means indigenous or original, something that is rooted, or is generated "from the ground", without any other interference.

The "Kia" is the Aetheric I, the I that's extended to the eight horizontal directions. This is the place where the different selves are extended out from the body. The name of this concept appears to be a combination of Spare's idea of the "Atmospheric I" with Peter Carroll's ideas about the Aether, which are outlined in Liber Null. Though Spare defined "Kia" in several different ways, including as a kind of ultimately unknowable Tao like force, Kia, in this sense, can be thought of as the ultimate sphere of all possibilities which the different selves within the person can participate in. Through this, realizing these selves is realizing Kia, but like a circle, it can never be squared. Instead, the goal of full realization can only being endlessly approached. This profusion of possibilities is linked to the horizontal axis. In "Zos Speaks!", and in his introduction to "Images & Oracles of Austin Osman Spare", Kenneth Grant labels Kia the Hand, and associates it with the Will, with action and actualization, and Zos with the "Eye", as related to comprehension and to Imagination.

Peter Carroll talks about his own definitions of Kia, Chaos, and Aether in the first part of "Liber Lux", contained in "Liber Null & Psychonaut". There, the Kia is what we've referred to as the Self which underlies the waking consciousness, with Carroll putting quite a bigger boundary between normal consciousness and this than we have. Kia is identified with the life force, and actualizes itself through the Aether which surrounds a person in their aura. Because of this, the Atmospheric I could also be called an Aetheric I, since the Aetheric energy, here, is the vehicle of the Atmospheric I. Kia, here, very importantly, is again linked with the idea of actualization, where the possibilities inherent in Kia have to be realized through doing, with this doing taking place, at least in part, through the manipulation of the Aether that constantly surrounds an individual. This suggests a deeper division between the "Autochthonic I" and the "Aetheric I": the "Autochthonic I" is the original I that we're endowed with, while the "Aetheric I" is something which we have to consciously realize in order to make function properly. Importantly, Carroll also says that a kind of primal chaos exists within the individual, which exists as part of the Kia. He states that along with the Kia being actualized in the Aether around the individual the potentialities of chaos within are actualized as well.

Chumbley, as part of the magical community of the UK in the '80s and '90s, participated in the Chaos magic community, certainly knew Carroll's work. Among other connections, he published some of his first writings in Chaos magic journals, and the first edition of the Azoetia was typeset by Ian Read, who is a member of Carroll's "Illuminates of Thanateros" or IOT

Within the human body, "Zos" is the Eye, while "Kia" corresponds to the Hand, which projects the compass of the eight directions from itself into the world. "Zos", in one sense, corresponds to the body, while the "Aetheric I", "Kia", corresponds to the Aura, and ultimately the eight of the compass are projected out into the personal aura of the individual, and from there outwards beyond the personal aura to the boundaries of the circle. In another sense, "Zos" is the interior of the body, while the "Aetheric I" is connected to the exterior parts of the body, particularly the four parts which correspond to the witches' tetragrammaton. Grant labeled Zos, the Autochthonic I, female, because of its passivity, while labeling the Aetheric I male, because of its connection to actualization. This is the reverse of other concepts of the horizontal and vertical axes, though it's not clear if Grant would have agreed with this symbolism. In this other attribution, the horizontal axis, the Hand, surrounds the vertical axis, the Eye, as a vagina surrounds a phallus, extending its power into the world.

The "Aetheric I" does not just exist when a person self consciously projects something into it. It is also not simply identified with the inner Selves. Instead, the "Aetheric I" works with both the Ego and the Selves, as I've defined them, and does this continually in an unconscious way. The aura reflects the unconscious belief structure of the individual, and this belief structure which is unconsciously projected onto the aura structures the reality around the person. By aligning the "Aetheric I" consciously with a specific set of attributions, you can gain control over what the aura is transmitting and affecting in the world. Through modifying the belief systems connected to the Ego, and working to realize different aspects of the Self, the Aetheric I can be consciously altered to do this. In the context of witchcraft, this process would start with reorienting the aura, the "Aetheric I", to the directions of the compass, with their attributions.

This can be linked to the atavisms and to Spare's magic in the following way: though he does not explicitly say this, it can be inferred from his writings that by using sigils in a rite, you activate the atavistic Desires in your lower center, which are the "ids". These desires then ascend into your head, and then alter your mind and your Aetheric I, transforming your structure of belief, which is reflected in your aura. Your aura, now changed, acts as a talisman to attract things which otherwise would not be attracted and repel things which otherwise would not be repelled due to this new configuration of belief within it. This works through both sending out waves and altering reality on a basic level. As said, however, this uses the model where the lower center predominates, and is the force associated with the Selves.

Also, within the context of Spare, we can relate the "I" to the Head, the "Zod" to the Selves that inhabit the lower center, and the "Ka" to the middle center. The Ka, here, is linked to the Will and to the process of willing within the complex of Will, Desire, and Belief. By an act of will, the Selves in the "Zod" become realized in the horizontal dimension of the Aetheric I through the Ka, the life force that exists at the heart center. The selves in "Zod", the primal atavisms, become actualized as part of Kia through this.

Memory and Recollection

One of the main differences between Spare's sigil work and the other kinds of representations is that the sigils are not supposed to have an obvious meaning that can be recognized by the conscious mind. Instead, they're supposed to encode meaning that can be recognized by the subconscious memory. The subconscious memory can then call forth the corresponding atavistic elemental forces from itself and then cause the wish that the sigil encodes to manifest through these forces.

Here the mind, and the memory, is primary. I believe that, in Chumbley's work, the model is that we all have a vision of the Sabbat, of the Ideal realm, within ourselves, though it's there unconsciously. This replica of the Sabbat, the Divine Mind, is a version of the Microcosm within. In similarity to the Platonic story, we perceive the truth of the Ideal realm in the time between lives, but when we're incarnated we forget it. Remembrance can be stimulated through sigils, which, in reality, activate these unconscious Ideal forms and bring them to the surface, these forms being the same thing as the Elemental energies of Massey or the Atavistic energies of Spare. Chumbley often writes that nothing is learned, everything is remembered.

"Inspiration", as a form of remembrance, can come from the awakening of the Forms within the heart, as well as through whispers from exterior spirits. Following inspiration in this leads, or can lead, to a progressive awakening to the truth and to the experience of the Ideal realm, which is the Sabbat itself.

I believe that Chumbley ultimately located the version of the Sabbat, and the compass, in the Heart, but that Spare located it in the lower center. These two are not mutually exclusive. As part of this, I believe that Chumbley used Spare's term "The Great Watcher Within" in a similarly different way: for Spare, it's a part of the greater self that's located in the lower center, around the Toadstone, while for Chumbley it's in the Heart, in the secret chamber of the heart. We shall go over the three centers in more detail in the next chapter, but a version of the Sabbat, a version of the compass, may to a certain extent be present in each of these three centers. In this though the Heart would be the primary center, the sex center would also have a version, one perhaps more directly tied to Spare's version of the "Primal Atavisms" in a more directly sexual and animalistic way.

The secret chamber of the heart is activated and accessed through the coordination of Desire, Will, and Belief. The sigilic forms activate the corresponding parts of the eightfold plot which exists within the secret chamber of the heart and bring them to the surface, to consciousness, though through indirect means. These are the same forces that are projected out into the "Aetheric I" of the aura, or into the circle, during work within the circle. The heart is the "Great Watcher within", and within the image of the First Sun within the heart is our own personal version of Baphomet, who is literally a great Watcher within.

Azoetia Notes

These notes are based on the "Book of Preparation", the first book of the Azoetia

Chumbley in the Azoetia refers to the central pillar of the three as the "I" or Eye, and as Death, while the extension of the three into the four directions, or into the eight directions, is referred to as the "Hand", or the Self, and Life. How this is derived is essential to understand: the central pillar consists of the Toad Stone in the depths, the Heart and the secret chamber of the heart in the middle, and the Head, the space of rationality and thought in the height. Within the drama of the Sabbat as it exists beyond time and space, the Heart, the Sabbat itself, is generated from the seed of the Toadstone. Next, the active intelligence is generated from the heart of the Sabbat itself, with this corresponding to the Head and to Reason.

The Active Intelligence, which is the Demiurge, then takes the material of the Eternal Sun, the Sabbat, which is at the level of the Heart, and shapes the world with it. There are several stages to this, but the essential thing to note is that this action is described in the Azoetia as Cain shaping this material with a knife, as Cain killing Abel, with Abel being the undifferentiated First Sun. In this, the shaping is itself destructive, and so can be related to "Death". Also, the First Sun, or Abel in this case, is referred to as the Goddess by Chumbley, meaning that the God, the Demiurge or Cain, dismembers the Goddess and shapes the world from her flesh. The God, in turn is an emanation of the Goddess, and so this is a shaping from his own flesh as well. A good parallel can be made here between Mithras and the Bull, with the Bull being the Goddess and Mithras, the slayer of the bull, being the God. Here, the bull can be equated with the primal cow from which the world is formed, the goddess as First Sun containing all the ideals of the world.

The God is identified with the "Eye" in the sense of the "Eye" being related to rationality and to the Evil Eye. The Evil Eye, in turn, is thought to emanate rays from itself which are destructive to what they fall upon. In this, the rays of the Eye are like a knife, and they kill, or can kill. By likening the vertical pillar to the Eye, to Death, and to the God, Chumbley is focusing on the top section of the pillar.

Chumbley, in discussing the individual's experience of the external Sabbat, being the Sabbat as Dreamt, identifies the "Dreaming I" with the heart consciousness of the individual. This is the level of consciousness of the individual which exists below Reason, which is freed from the constraints of Reason in the dream state. This heart consciousness is also the original consciousness of the Sabbat as it exists within the secret chamber of the heart, and Chumbley identifies a monad as existing within it. This monad is what I've previously described here as the Synderesis, the unfallen spark of divinity which people possess. In the Azoetia, Chumbley makes this monad one the foci of the whole magical experience, it being the literal center of both the vertical pillar and of the horizontal circle. This monad is the heart of the first letter.

Waking Reason, in this, can interfere with the heart consciousness, but the Dream state unchains it. The heart and heart consciousness is the "Ever Open Eye", which is also the Dreaming "I". Literally, the heart is an ever open consciousness because it never goes to sleep, instead pumping blood twenty four hours a day. Reason corresponds to waking consciousness, the Toad Stone corresponds to sleep, while the Heart and the secret chamber of the heart correspond to the dream state and to the trance state. Here, too, in the interplay between life and death, with regards to the circle, from one point of view the earth is dead until the Hand of the Self, the energy of the Sabbat, is extended into it in its four directions.

Banish nought, but re-align all...so says Chumbley. This is based on the idea that the eight-fold plan of the circle, reflecting the four elements, and the primal seven or eight, is the perfected plan of the universe. Because it's the perfected plan of the universe, a return to this order is a return to perfection, and so re-aligning the energies in the circle with this primal pattern brings things back to order. This is based, in part, on the projection of the Temple, the Heavenly Jerusalem, onto the Circle, with the Heavenly City being the model of perfection itself. Here the eightfold plot becomes the foursquare city. This has much in common with magic rituals and rites that seek to restore the world through repeating the original process of creation that lead to the world as it is. Through re-enacting the primal creation, the primal, and most healthy, arrangement or alignment of the energies is put into place, with the rite binding these energies once again into their proper form. Casting the circle and drawing down the energies for the circle from the Sabbat itself, in this, is a restorative rite unto itself, parallel to creating a mandala which exhibits a perfected form of existence, and is Theurgical in this sense. Personally, I feel that it's better to banish negative entities as well.

At the end of the "Book of Preparation", Chumbley gives a diagram of three and four lines combining, making seven, being complemented by an eighth. Though there are many different ways of interpreting this, and different ways of applying it, one of these is as follows: the three, the vertical axis, is extended through the four cardinal directions of the circle....after which, the power of the Sabbat itself is drawn down into the four cardinal directions, from the North empowering the image of the Sabbat that has been made on earth. Though in Chumbley's diagram the four correspond to the cross quarters, this does not have to be the case, and, in reality, the operation which uses the cross quarters in this way is much more complicated. The four, in this, can more easily be related to the cardinal directions. The person, standing for the vertical three at the center of the circle, externalizes the four from himself, constructing an image of the Sabbat within the circle, and then calls down the power of the Sabbat itself to consecrate and empower the circle. The empowerment is the hidden "Eighth Ray" which, as we shall see, we can picture as coming into the circle through the gate of the North cardinal direction. This is the formula of Ingress. The Sabbat that this energy is drawn down from, I should make clear, is the same Sabbat that people go to in dreams and in other work, and which is contained within the heart in a microcosmic version.

Sex and Sex Power.

Sex and sexual energy is important in traditional witchcraft, and my read of it with regards to the gnostic background is as follows. Sex was not responsible for the fall, and sexual desire is not inherently sinful. However, sex and sexual desire can be directed upwards towards the divine, or downwards, in ways that link people closer to material reality. Within this, I believe that what makes the difference between them is the relationship within which the sex exists. Continence is not the way of directing the sex instinct upwards, unless one chooses. Sex can either manifest in the individual, or between individuals. In the first case, manifesting through auto-sexual acts, masturbation, it can be easily directed towards the higher. The second is where more difficulties lie. Here, especially in heterosexual relationships, the quality of the relationship itself determines whether or not the sexual instinct is being directed to something higher or to something lower.

What I would call a high quality relationship, where the two people who enact it are not necessarily in love, but where they care about each other, and are not simply interested in one another for their body, is productive to sexual acts that ennoble and lift up a person. Relationships founded more purely on lust, with the denial of the other's personality as an issue, or on exploitation, lead a person downwards. This includes temporary, casual, relationships that have these characteristics.

The conjunction of man and woman is complicated by many issues, psychological differences, the possibility of procreation as a result of the relationship and its possible consequences, which are not present for homosexual relationships. There, particularly in gay male relationships, it's much easier to mutually engage in an uplifting sexuality while having casual relationships. This is partially because of the lack of psychological differences between two men, and partially because the question of procreation is not important. I don't have direct experience in how the relationship of two women together differs or has commonalities with this, although anecdotal knowledge says that homosexual women tend to be more interested in developing relationships with each other than in engaging in casual sex.

The sex force is a great way of communing with the center of the personality.

Works Cited

Auerbach, Felix "Ektropismus, oder die Physikalische Theorie des Lebens.", Verlag von Wilhelm Engelmann, Leipzig, 1910, Google books

Baker, Elsworth "Man in the Trap", American College of Orgonomy Press, Princeton, 2000

Burroughs , William S. , Daniel Odier, "The Job", Penguin Publishing, New York, 1989.

Burroughs, William S., Brion Gysin"Third Mind", Viking Press, New York, 1978

Butler, E.W. "Magic: It's Ritual, Power, and Purpose" and "The Magician: His Training and Work", combined into one work in "Magic and the Magician", published by Aquarian Press, 1991

Carroll, Peter "Liber Lux" in "Liber Null and Psychonaut", Weiser, York Beach, 1987

"Liber Nox" in "Liber Null and Psychonaut", Weiser, York Beach, 1987

Chumbley, Andrew Azoetia, Xoanon, Hercules, USA, 2015

Grant, Kenneth "Images & Oracles of Austin Osman Spare", Fulgur Ltd, London, 2003

Gray, William G. "Magic Ritual Methods", Weiser, York Beach, 1980

Hill, Napoleon "Think and Grow Rich", Ballantine Books, New York, 1987

Hyatt, Christopher S. "Secrets of Western Tantra", New Falcon Publications, Reno, 2009

"The Tree of Lies", New Falcon Publications, reissued as "To Lie is Human, Not Getting Caught is Divine", Original Falcon publications, Tempe, 2009

"Undoing yourself with energized meditation", New Falcon Publications, Tempe, 1997

Kelley, Charles R., "Life Force...the Creative Process in Man and Nature", Trafford, Victoria BC, 2005

Mace, Stephen "Shaping Formless Fire", New Falcon Publications, Tempe, 2005

"Stealing the Fire from Heaven", Dagon Productions & Heathen World Productions, Phoenix, 2006

Massey, Gerald "Ancient Egypt, the Light of the World", vol. 1, T. Fisher Unwin, London, 1907, Google Books

Powers, Melvin "Self-Hypnosis: Its Theory, Technique and Application", Wilshire Book Company, Hollywood, 1973

Regardie, Israel "The Art of True Healing", New World Library, San Rafael, 1991
"New Wings for Daedalus: Wilhelm Reich, his Theory and Techniques", Original Falcon Publications, 2018
"Wilhelm Reich: His Theory and Techniques", New Falcon Publications, 2022
"Healing Energy, Prayer and Relaxation", New Falcon Publications, 2009

Reich, Wilhelm "Ether, God, and Devil & Cosmic Superimposition". Farrar, Straus and Giroux, New York, 1973

Spare, Austin Osman "The Focus of Life" published in 1922, available online in many formats, as well as in "Now for Reality!", published by Mandrake Press,1990.

Spare, Austin Osman, Kenneth Grant, Steffi Grant "Zos Speaks! Encounters with Austin Osman Spare", Fulgur, London, 1998

Swann, Ingo "Psychic Sexuality", Swann-Ryder Productions, USA, 2017

Frater U.'. D.'., "High Magic: Theory and Practice", Llewellyn, Woodbury,2005

Villars, Abbé Nicolas-Pierre-Henri de Montfaucon de, "Comte de Gabalis", Brothers edition, 1914, Patterson NJ, google books

Webb, Don "Uncle Setnakt's Essential Guide to the Left Hand Path", Runa-Raven Press, USA, 1999

Willis, Jack "Reichian Therapy for Home Use", e-edition at https://reichiantherapy.info/, hard copy
"Reichian Therapy: A Practical Guide for Home Use", New Falcon Publications,Los Angeles, 2013

Chapter 14
The Toadstone

The Toad Rite itself is a link between Christianity and witchcraft. The rite involves first taking a toad and killing it, then putting the corpse on a pile of ants who strip the body bare, and lastly throwing the skeleton into a stream. The Toad Bone will scream and run against the current of the water, and the practitioner of the rite has to go into the river and claim it. Once they have it, the bone will act as a talisman or vessel for magic power.

The toad here is an externalized symbol of the practitioner, and the point with the rite is to experience the same sort of dissolution that the toad undergoes. The external seizing of the toad bone is paralleled by the seizing of the parallel of the toad bone within the body, which is the pearl described in the New Testament. The bone itself is the pelvis of the toad, which is what allows it to leap from the world of the negative, symbolized by water, to that of the positive, symbolized by land, and back again. More directly, though, the bone itself never changes, whether it's in the water or on the land, and so is a symbol of the indestructible angelic soul of the practitioner. The place where the stone is located in the human practitioner is parallel to where it's located in the toad, this being behind the perineum, which is between the sexual organ and the anus.

The first thing to know about the Toad Bone rite is that you should take extreme care before deciding to carry it out. This is because it will only work if you have an angelic soul. If you undertake the Toad Bone rite and you don't possess this soul, you'll die. The toad stone that you find within you, which is the whole point of the rite, is the angelic soul. The angelic soul is the soul that people who are incarnate fallen angels possess. It's also the Luz or almond seed mentioned in Jewish mysticism. This is in addition to the Synderesis and the poential bodhicitta of the head, which everyone possesses. It is the pearl that's referred to in the gnostic "Hymn of the Pearl", as well as by Saint Paul, as the spiritual seed, though in his writings everyone was thought to possess it. The Toad Stone is also the Holy Grail, identified as the stone in the brow of Lucifer that fell to earth, this being a cipher for the angelic soul that fell from heaven in the rebellion, which needs to be found, purified and exalted for salvation. The externals of the rite are intended to allow a person to find the angelic soul within themselves, so that they can seize it and develop it. The actual bone of the toad, that swims against the water, is less important than finding the toad stone within.

Truth and the Lie.

What exactly, though, is the experience of seizing the stone? For me, I identify the angelic soul that the Toad Stone corresponds to with the base of the self. Our head corresponds to the part of the self that individuals usually relate to, and identify with, while the base of the self is a part of the self so low that it almost looks like an external part. When I say "look" I mean through the process of introspection, self examination. To seize the stone, you need to become aware of this other, base, part of the self, and not let go of it. You should be able to "see" the stone through the inner vision, that is to say you should be able to "see" with the second sight into the part of your body where the stone lives and perceive it. This awareness of this part of the self, which is localized within the body in the perineum between the sexual organs and the anus, needs to be reaffirmed again and again, with the mind returning to it, in order for the stone to be kept. It helps to have a phrase that you can associate with looking at the stone internally and becoming aware of it. This phrase is necessarily arbitrary, but should be kept secret, and silently repeated in the process of returning your awareness to the stone inside of your body. Through seizing the base of the self through seizing the stone, the snake, whose head is represented by your head, bites its tail, and completes the circle. The individual becomes an Ouroboros, a ring, that's no longer tethered to the muck, though this freedom takes time and work to realize.

Each time you return your awareness to the stone within your body, you increase the energy in your body. This is because when you return your awareness to the stone, the stone raises energy. This energy is taken from the ambient energy of the One, the Dragon Lord, from which the stone was formed as a concretization. Through returning your awareness to the stone multiple times, much energy can be raised, that can then be used in spell work.

The reaffirmation of the stone, which can and should be done many times a day, every day, is necessary because of the nature of the stone when it is found. The stone, though an angelic soul, when it is found and seized is corrupt and immersed in evil. It is the soul of a fallen angel. This soul has to be purified, the stone has to be purified and developed, in order to affect the personal redemption of the individual. This is also one reason why the stone is identified with the perineum, between the sexual organs and the anus, the lowest part of the body. The stone has to be tutored and purified. It is taken out of the muck and has to be kept from falling back into it. The stone itself, though, contains the Truth within it, in an obscured form, and this Truth has to be reaffirmed, time and time again, which leads to the purification of the stone and the purification of the rest of the body, the entity, of which the stone is the angelic soul.

The angelic soul of the Toadstone is intimately related to how it is that some people can perform magick effectively, and often, and to how some can't. The angelic soul is the soul of a demigod, and the incarnate witches that have the angelic soul, the fallen angels, are in pagan terms demigods who possess the power of creation and regulation over the world. They are not immersed completely in material reality but transcend it, and so can act from the perspective of that which is above material reality on material reality itself. The fallen angels are demigods who revolted against the gods of the Divine Mind and followed the Evil One down to the material world and became trapped.

Seizing the Toadstone, and keeping the Toadstone, developing it, which you have to do, will eventually give you the power to send forth the lightning from the Stone. This lightning reduces whatever it touches to the Truth of it, destroying the Lie that might have been behind it. This is one of the reasons why it was said that no door can hold back a toad man, and that everything is open for one. The limitations that are put on others in the external world by the Lie, whose patron is the Evil One, can be broken through the sending forth of the lightning from the Stone. This can be actualized through the secret phrase that you have established for reaffirming the stone and its existence. The lightning is not the same as a curse, in that it can't really be used to hurt someone, it can only reduce them to the Truth. Care must be taken, in that sometimes a good person is dependent on a Lie for keeping their personality together, and so eliminating that Lie can have catastrophic consequences. The powers of the Lie, the powers of the Shadow, turn against a person when they seize their Toadstone, and the constant reaffirmation of the Stone through your secret phrase counters these Shadow forces, as does attacking these Shadow forces with the lightning when they take action against you.

The difference between Lie and Truth here is the same as within both Zoroastrianism, Manichaeanism, and Buddhism. The true gods, those of the Divine Mind, the Sabbat, live within the Truth. The false gods, those who serve the Evil One, live by the Lie. The Lie is non-reality, illusion, samsara. By eliminating the Lie and the metaphysical reality of it through the lightning, the power of the Lie, of illusion, on a metaphysical level is weakened. This can lead to a spectacular collapse of metaphysical structures whose power is based on falsehood. The Evil One resents people taking their stone, their angelic soul, back into their own hands, because this leads to their liberation from his domain.

The reascent to the Divine Mind of one who has developed the Toad Stone is the reascent of Truth to Truth, with the gods of the Divine Mind being the true gods, as opposed to the false gods of the Lie who attempt to impose their rule on the material world.

What you do once you've been able to generate the Word with the Toadstone is to use it to invoke the First Sun, the Sabbat of the Ages, and so to contact the place where the angelic soul comes from Theurgically. Doing this, with a spirit of repentance for rebelling against the First Sun, reconciles the individual to the source, to the Pleroma or fullness from which he or she has come. This is the way to go from becoming a potential demon back to being an angel.

The triumph over the Evil One with regards to the Toad Stone is consummated in the defeat of the personal Shadow, which can be interpreted in the Jungian sense. The personal Shadow is the devil, evil, aspect of the personal self, and by dominating it and controlling it, it no longer is able to control you, or to act in concert with the Evil One. You can't eliminate the Shadow because it's a part of you, but you can dominate and control it.

Three Centers

The three centers come from Christian tradition. The centers are derived from Greek medical ideas, which divided the faculties of the soul, or of the individual mind/body, into the Nous, the Thymia, and the Epithymia. The Epithymia is the faculty in control of vegetative functions, hunger, and sexuality, while the Thymia is the faculty in control of the passions and higher emotions, and the Nous is the mind. These three faculties were extensively commented on by Orthodox mystics such as Maximus the Confessor, who integrated the taming and perfection of all of these into his works, which are available in English. A western Christian presentation of these is most clearly set out in the Saint Bonaventure's "De Triplici Via", or the Triple Way.

These three are the ultimate source of Austin Osman Spare's "Desire, Will and Belief". Desire corresponds to the Epithymia, Will corresponds to the Thymia, and Belief to the Nous. These three are also thought to reside primarily in three different places. The Epithymia resides primarily in the sex center, the Thymia in the Heart, and the Nous in the Head. Each of these three centers has an esoteric counterpart consisting of a stone like fragment of divinity.

Additionally, the Heart center conceals a fourth component: a version of the Microcosm, a picture of the First Sun as manifested in the body. In this, the Will is the outer correspondent to the Heart center, while the Microcosm is the hidden chamber of the heart, which can only be accessed indirectly through meditative techniques. The Microcosm is where the true self dwells, with this being a copy of Baphomet as he dwells in the Sabbat, the Microcosm being a replica of the Sabbat, the Millions of Forms of Being. Within all of this, the place of the lower center is modified from the Greek tradition. Instead of just corresponding to the sex center, it's located in the same place as the Mulahadra Chakra, that is to say between the anus and the genitals.

The esoteric counterparts of the three centers also come from Christian tradition. The Stone itself, the Toadstone which is located in the lower center, is a concept that is described in the Gospel of John as the grain of wheat that must be broken in order to bear fruit. Here, in this, Jesus is saying that for people to be redeemed, they will have to go through on a lesser level what he is going to go through on a greater level. The breaking of the grain is a parallel to the crucifixion, and the whole alchemical plan is parallel to the crucifixion, harrowing of hell, and resurrection. The Stone, as a seed, was adopted by Gnosticism, and became the angelic soul. It also became the Gnostic "Pearl", which was the subject of the "Hymn of the Pearl", also known as the "Hymn of the Robe of Glory", which describes the journey of the individual to recover the stone and bring it back to heaven. The "Hymn of the Pearl", in this, is also an alchemical allegory. This story was not confined to Gnosticism but was incorporated into Syriac Christianity in general. It was initially included in an apocryphal biblical writing about Saint Thomas, the founder of Syriac Christianity. References to the pearl can be found in the writings of Ephraim the Syrian, among others, with the motif being so widespread that a collection of Syriac Christian writings was given the title "The Wisdom of the Pearlers". It should be noted that Syriac Christianity is Aramaic speaking Christianity, and that the Syriac church, particularly the "Church of the East" or the Nestorian church, preserves lore that, potentially, goes back to the founding of Christianity itself. Notably, in this tradition, the completion of the seizing of the pearl and the work associated with it leads to the generation of the "Robe of Glory", a kind of second body, light body, or double which can ascend into the First Mind after death.

The Synderesis, or unfallen spark of divinity, is the jewel or stone that lives in the Heart center. It is a concept taken from Rabbinic tradition of the 5th century and incorporated into Christianity by Saint Jerome. In his "Commentary on Ezekiel", Jerome comments that despite his crime, Cain still retained a fragment of purity in his soul which could not be destroyed, which he derived from this Rabbinic tradition. From this mention, the concept entered into Latin Christianity. It was, unfortunately, largely discarded by extreme Protestants on the grounds that Jerome's reading of Genesis was not supported by the text itself. Some more mystical Lutherans and Anglicans retained the idea, though, as did the Quakers. It persisted in Catholic mysticism, although there, too, it has declined. The Synderesis was thought to be the origin of the Conscience, and was the object of "Listening to your Heart". It was also a means by which other communications with God, and with divinity, could be engaged in. Particularly, it was thought to be the Christ nature within, through which communion with Jesus could be possible. Here, this communion with Jesus can be equated with a communion with the god of the First Sun.

The Intellectual stone, was an inheritance from pagan philosophy, from Platonic philosophy in particular, though the conceptualization of it as a "Stone" is not usually found there. Here, the word "Intellect" has a special meaning, going beyond that of Reason. The Intellect is the mental organ that is the vehicle for Noesis, or direct apprehension of divinity. This idea was incorporated into Christian mystical practice. Though formally it was far above the imagination in its power, it was associated with the inner vision, as it was the vehicle through which visionary experience entered into the individual. Today, we apply the term "Imagination" more broadly, but in the Middle Ages it specifically meant the ability of people to consciously create images in their minds. "Imagination" in this context was associated with things that were false, while the visions that came from the Intellect were considered to be true, because they came from outside of the individual instead of from inside of them. It more closely resembles the "Second Sight" than "Phantasy", another name for the Imagination.

The faculty of the Intellect, or the immediate vision that the Intellect reveals, is equivalent to the Bodhicitta or Buddha Mind of Buddhism. The Intellect does not just act as a receiver for higher visions, but also, in self-contemplation, provides a true picture of the nature of the mind as a whole. The Bodhicitta, to be more accurate, is something that the organ or faculty of the Intellect generates through self contemplation. The faculty or organ of the Intellect itself, is the faculty of the Diamond Consciousness, which cannot be destroyed, and if it's used in meditation, in self contemplation of the faculties, it can cause Bodhicitta to be cultivated. What this means is that the Intellectual "Stone" is actually an organ of higher consciousness that cannot be destroyed, and so is stone like. Bodhicitta is not instant Enlightenment, but something which can be generated and accumulated, which puts you further on the path to liberation the more of it you generate. The Diamond consciousness, the Intellect, is also a criterion for Truth, in that if in meditation you bring something to the Intellect, it will fall apart if it contains falsehood, but will persist if it contains Truth.

The Intellectual stone is used extensively in the process of Inner alchemy, to picture the Stone in the process of reaffirming it through the Will. However, this picturing is thought, ideally, to not be a pure product of the Imagination, but to instead be a manifestation of the Inner Vision or Second Sight, where you're actually seeing the Stone on an esoteric level, instead of just creating a picture of it.

Within the three centers, the heart center, the middle center is the core of the true self. The head center is the seat of the false self of normal, everyday, consciousness. The lower center is two things: the seat of the animal consciousness, on the one hand, but the root of all consciousness through the angelic seed on the other.

Alchemical Extensions

The linkage between these concepts and alchemy was, in my opinion, at least codified at the end of the 13th century, or the beginning of the 14th, around the year 1300, by thinkers like Arnauld of Villanova and John of Rupescissa, also known as Jean de Roquetaillade. Both of these, notably, were associated with the Franciscan order, of which Saint Bonaventure had been the Minster General, or head. Raymond Llull was also a lay member of the Franciscan order, something which people have unfortunately paid little attention to. There have been several books looking at the connections between the Franciscans and alchemy.

This is the framework on which the Paracelsan "Tria Prima" or three principles of Sulphur, Salt, and Mercury were superimposed, with the actions by the different centers of the person interpreted as the interactions between Sulphur, Salt, and Mercury. This schema, with the three parts, is immensely useful, and became the framework for almost all inner alchemy in the west. However, it should be noted that before Paracelsus the primary materials were Sulphur and Mercury, with Salt being Paracelsus' unique contribution.

With regards to particular correspondences between Salt, Sulphur and Mercury and the three centers, I've seen almost every single variation of the Tria Prima corresponded to them. Sometimes, the lower center is Mercury, sometimes it's Salt, sometimes, it's Sulphur. The essential things to remember are the three centers themselves and the fact that combining the lower center and the head center creates the element of the heart center. This creation of the element of the heart center, in fact, opens the door to the fourth part, to the secret chamber of the Heart.

The current work of internal alchemy, after the Toad Stone has been seized and reaffirmed, is to open the door to this secret center, in order to speak the Word from there, to make invocations to the First Sun in the objective realm from the First Sun in the subjective or bodily realm. The secret chamber of the heart is the place of the Azoth within the body, which is behind the three principles of Sulphur, Salt, and Mercury.

The first place that I've seen the secret chamber of the heart mentioned is in the medieval mystic Richard of Saint Victor's work "The Mystic Ark", also known as "Benjamin Major". Richard was a mystic from the 12th century. Here, when he directs the individual to "Know thyself", he portrays the heart as containing a replica of the Divine Mind, where anything that's present in the external world can be found. I believe that this attribution of the heart to the contents of the macrocosm is a modification of an earlier position taken by Christian philosophers, which saw the Mind itself as being parallel to the Divine Mind. Like the Divine Mind, the human mind, with the human imagination, can create and picture anything in the world. It can visualize anything it wants, even things that are not real.

However, the ability of the human mind to do this is dependent on its possession of Ideals, which it uses in reasoning. These Ideals, in this line of thought, are present in what today we'd call a subconscious way, and are accessed by the mind in the process of thinking. In the middle ages, this was expressed by the term "Memory", with the Ideals being located there without the mind being consciously aware of it, yet drawing on them as needed. The Ideals themselves, in our subconscious, correspond more accurately to the Divine Mind and its contents than to our conscious mind itself. I believe that Richard and other mystics located the Heart as the location where these subconscious Ideals resided within the human mind/body, so that, in reality, it's the Heart and its secret chamber that the mind draws on when using Ideals in the process of thought. The Heart, then, would be the root of the mind in this secret capacity,.

Within the works of Andrew Chumbley, the heart is referred to as the "Great Watcher Within", and references to the macrocosm that's part of it, the secret chamber, can be found in different areas of the Azoetia, such as the the "Eight Fold Kiss".

Meditation and the Toad Stone.

There are several degrees of meditative practices that I've developed that are part of the Toad Stone work. These meditative practices start with the head stone, move to the head jewel, and culminate with the Toadstone, with the ultimate practice using all three at once.

The initial meditation with the Head stone, what's referred to as the diamond, is derived from the Insight Meditation, Vipassana practice outlined in the book "Seeking the Heart of Wisdom" by Joseph Goldstein and Jack Kornfield. This practice is drawn from Burmese forest monk Theravada tradition.

You start out by doing basic Insight Meditation. This meditation involves closing your eyes and observing the thoughts and feelings that come into your inner awareness.

You should first focus on your breath, breathing in and out from your nose, letting whatever other thoughts and feelings from your body that appear to you just appear and then disappear. However, this is very difficult to do, and the mind will be distracted from the focus on the breath by the thoughts and feelings. If you find yourself distracted by the thoughts and feelings, notice the thought or feeling, let it go, and then get back to focusing on the breath.

The next stage involves taking a step back and, while breathing, not focusing on the breath but on the inner awareness itself. Focus on your mental presence within yourself that you perceive when you close your eyes. Thoughts and feelings will still arise which will distract you from focusing on this presence, and when they do, behave just as in the first stage: notice them, then let them go, and return to focusing on the inner awareness. As part of this, shut down your tongue, which means do not consciously think words, but just observe your inner awareness. Do not engage with the thoughts and feelings that arise by thinking words in response to them. If you find that you've done this, notice the words, then let them go, and return to a focus on your inner awareness. The work on this level, outside of the formal meditations, involves cultivating good thoughts as well. This is a purification of "Belief", in the series of Desire, Will, Belief, with these corresponding to the Toad Stone, the Head jewel, and the Head stone.

The head stone, in this, the Diamond, is the part of you that Bodhicitta, or Buddha Mind, can be generated from. The more that you use the awareness of your inner awareness to cut through false thoughts, the more that an awareness of Bodhicitta is cultivated. The awareness of Bodhicitta is the kind of awareness that persists when the false thoughts have been slayed. This awareness of true thoughts is built up very gradually over time, through many sessions of meditation. This awareness is sometimes called a "Diamond Awareness" because what's been found to be true, in this, is indestructible, like a Diamond, though this should not cause a person to become arrogant and self assured. Instead, the ego, through all of this, must be put on hold, as selfishness is a source of false thoughts.

After having done this for a period of time, the next part can start, which brings in the qualities of the Head jewel, the diamond, into play. This inner awareness that you're focusing on is the Head jewel, and, as such, it possesses the capability of separating truth from lies. It can cut them lies in half, destroying them. When you're focusing on your inner awareness in this meditation, consider that any thought or feeling that has substantial reality will not disappear if you do not pay attention to it, but instead keep on focusing on your inner awareness. Any thought or feeling that disappears when you're doing this does not have substantial reality, and is not true in an absolute sense. Through having an awareness of this, you can learn to separate out obviously false thoughts that appear to you from thoughts that have a more substantial reality.

The thoughts that I'm referring to are unconscious thoughts that appear to the mind involuntarily. Some of these thoughts that appear to us from what psychology calls the unconscious are random and have no validity, no truth to them, while some of them are intuitions that do bear truth. These more substantial intuitions are worth paying attention to and working with. What, though, is the source of these more substantial intuitions or thoughts from the unconscious?

The immediate source of these true intuitions is the Head jewel. When you focus on your awareness and let the false thoughts destroy themselves, you will see truer thoughts arise to your consciousness from the Head jewel. Once you become aware of this, you can begin the next phase of the meditation.

This next phase is Listening to the Heart. What you do is to first direct your consciousness to be aware of itself, but then, once your consciousness if fixed on your inner awareness, you direct your inner eye to your heart, so that your consciousness is now aware of the movements of your heart and of your head jewel. You sit, and you observe. The stillness and awareness that you've cultivated with the head jewel is preserved, and this observation of the heart builds on it, so that, though the consciousness is focussed on the heart, the head stays in a still state.

Once a person has gotten proficient in listening to the heart, they'll realize that the heart, too, can be influenced by the will in obscure, but very real, ways. The will, in its root, can cause the heart to put forward thoughts and feelings to the conscious awareness through the channel of the unconscious mind. Because of this, the Heart, too, needs to be stilled from the intervention of the individual. This involves focusing on the Head jewel itself, and training the will not to intervene and to substitute its own movements for those that emanate from the jewel. Here, the process is similar to that described in the head jewel: if, when focusing on listening to the Heart, you detect that you've willed something, pay attention to that will, notice it, let it go, and then refocus your consciousness on the head jewel and on listening to it.

The Head jewel is the Synderesis, which is the source of the Conscience. Listening to the heart, outside of the formal meditation, is listening to your conscience, and obeying the voice of the conscience. The conscience represents information from the Sabbat, as well as good will in and of itself. The Head jewel distinguishes between a good will and a bad will, with the bad will provoking the Conscience to raise a signal of alarm to the mind. Listening to the heart, outside of the formal exercise, involves cultivating a good will, a will that's oriented towards doing good things, which won't provoke objections from the Conscience.

This will ultimately lead to the final stage. The Head jewel is a transmitter of impulses from the external Sabbat, from the Divine Mind, a version of which lives in the heart in a hidden way. However, these impulses are not being continuously received. The Head jewel itself is derived from the Toad Stone, which creates both the Head jewel and the Head jewel, and when the Head jewel is not receiving messages and just existing, the final stage can be engaged with. This involves having the conscious will around the heart be stilled to the point where you can detect the impulses from the Toad Stone that are transmitted to the Heart stone, and then to the Mind through the channel of the unconscious. Doing this connects you to the root of reality, and it lets the lightning that is generated by the Toad Stone flow up through the Head jewel to the Head jewel, altering it and the conscious mind in certain ways.

To do this, you essentially have to listen to the Toad Stone in a way that's similar to listening to the Heart stone, only in this you have to preserve stillness in your attitude to the Heart stone, in the same way that you preserved stillness in your observation of the awareness of your head when you shifted your consciousness to listening to the Heart. Essentially, to do this you cultivate the still awareness of your inner consciousness in your head, then move your consciousness to your heart and observe it, then still your will so that your heart can be stably observed, then when that stillness is obtained, shift your awareness one more time to the Toadstone and listen to it.

This is the inner way of reaching the Toadstone from the consciousness down. The Toadstone and its power can also be exalted through directing the energy of the Toadstone first to the Head jewel to purify it, then afterwards by directing it to the head jewel to purify it.

The Church of the East

I believe that the ultimate source of the internal alchemy described here is the Saint Thomas Christians, also known as the Church of the East and the Assyrian Church of the East and the Nestorians, possibly with some Manichean influence. This system would have been taught to the Templars, who then passed it onto the Masons, as well as the witches.

There have been consistent stories that the Templars contacted a primitive Christian group and learned from them. This group has been identified with the Johannites, by which people mean the Mandeans, but I consider this to be unlikely. The Mandeans are located in southern Iraq, a place where the Templars never were. The Church of the East, on the other hand, had a presence in Syria where the Templars were.

The Church of the East is, in fact, a continuation of the earliest post-Nicene traditions of the Church. They formulated themselves after the suppression of gnosticism, but they were also the first split in the post-Nicene church. The reason they became a separate denomination was that they accepted a heretical notion by Nestorius which was Adoptionism. This stated that Jesus was born a normal human, but that at some point the Son descended down into him and essentially commandeered his body and mind, and took over. In turn, this lead them to deny the special status of the Virgin Mary, which caused them a great deal of trouble. There have been attempts lately to try to deny the Nestorian influence on the Church of the East, but these are easily refuted by medieval works such as the Armenian "Book of Marganitha", which explicitly talks about it. In typical fashion, they say that Nestorius' views were accepted as being what Christianity originally believed, and so were not heretical at all. The Nestorians were condemned at the council of Ephesus, and from then on became their own denomination.

Facing persecution in the western Middle East of the Roman Empire, they sought refuge in the Persian lands of the Sassanid Empire, and became the official Christian church of it. This lead to an amazing expansion of their influence across central Asia, as well as into India, where the Saint Thomas Christians still exist in Kerala state. In Asia, the Nestorians managed to reach all the way to China, and to Mongolia. During the Mongol Empire one of the Khans produced a Christian bishop from Mongolia to demonstrate that despite being pagan, they too had Christians there, and the bishop was from the Church of the East. The "Pearlers", with the Hymn of the Pearl, had a great amount of influence.

I believe that there was also a crypto-Manichean influence in some Nestorian thought as well. I believe that the influence of Manicheism can be found in works such as the "Book of Steps" also known as the "Liber Graduus", an extensive Syriac text with gnostic overtones that, in my opinion, go far beyond what was normal for the Christianity of its time. The Manicheans also incorporated the "Hymn of the Pearl" into their belief system.

The Hymn itself talks about the necessity of the person going down into "Egypt", which is code for both the interior polluted world and the external corrupt world, and finding the Pearl, the Stone, seizing it and then using it to regenerate the body of light. The body of light, in this, takes the place of the outer body of corruption, which has been cast aside in the finding of the stone. These bodies are etheric bodies, and constitute the "New Man" of the Pauline letters.

Corbin, Shi'ite Gnosis and the Stone.

Henry Corbin also treats extensively of the Pearl in his essay "The Configuration of the Temple of the Ka'bah", contained in the collection "The Temple and Contemplation", in section 2 of part III. For his exegesis, Corbin is relying on a work by Sa'id Qomi, a 17th century Shi'ite scholar. Here, the stone becomes the black stone of Mecca, in the Ka'bah, and the person who journeys on the spiritual pilgrimage to their interior self seizes the stone of the Ka'bah that exists within them. This stone, which is black, becomes white, becomes the pearl on their seizing of it. The stone is within the interior temple, which is a copy of the Ka'bah, and is the "key to the Temple". Importantly, the black stone of Mecca is located in a corner of the Ka'bah, not the center, and so is a foundation stone, which is a familiar theme within Freemasonry.

The stone is said also to be an angel, and to be an angel which Adam swallowed in Paradise, and that his descendants carried with them. This recalls, to a point, Saint Jerome's idea of the Synderesis, though he does not give an account of how this piece of divinity came to be in Adam and Cain. There is a link here between the pearl and stories of Adam being granted something after the Fall which was meant to help him spiritually, whether that would be a book of knowledge, like the book of Raziel, or something else. Sometimes this is indicated by the consumption of a seed by Adam given by God that, after Adam's death, gives birth to a tree which supplies the wood for the cross that Jesus was slayed on. Significantly, Corbin also indicates that the Pearl is sometimes portrayed as a red hyacinth, a red gemstone, as opposed to a flower, and this suggests that there was a vacillation between the pearl as the lower center and the pearl as something parallel to the Synderesis in the heart center. The Synderesis is often pictured as a ruby or a red gemstone.

Corbin writes that the Pearl is concealed in the center of man, and, as an angel, is also equivalent to the Imam within, the source of spiritual guidance. However, the Pearl, when thrown down to earth, becomes the black stone, set in a corrupt place, the fallen human body, and has to be found and seized in order to become white again.

Here, though, Adam received the Pearl in Paradise itself, and the swallowing of the stone was a pact with the angel, who was to give good guidance to Adam. Corbin recounts how this pact was renewed every year by Adam with the angel in front of God. Thrown out of Paradise, Adam goes on a pilgrimage to the primal Mecca, which is the pilgrimage into one's interior being.

Corbin summarizes all of this as recounting Adam falling from the higher spiritual realms into the realm of matter, retaining the angelic stone. He then has to find the angelic stone, liberate it, then use it as the key to build the interior temple in order to regenerate himself. After the temple is regenerated, the individual, presumably, goes on to the further work of divine ascent, to return to the place from where he first fell. The Temple, in this, stands for the perfected character of man, and is located in the Heart. It's empowered by the force that stems from the Pearl, which is the Imamate or voice of Ali and his descendants as spiritual guides.

Corbin comments on how both the earthly Temple, the Ka'bah, and the Temple in the individual are copies of a Heavenly Temple around which the "Fourteen Infallibles", Muhammad, his daughter Fatima, and the Twelve Imams, constantly walk around, along with the highest angels. These fourteen are often also linked to various cosmological ideas, as we have seen.

Within all of this symbolism, a process of internal alchemy could take place, and it's tempting to see Corbin's recounting of this story as related to his own participation in the Rectified Scottish Rite, a Templar Masonic order.

The Stone and the Grail.

The grail is the Toadstone, and this was associated with the angelic soul. The source of the Masonic inner alchemy is in the Templar tradition, who got it from the Eastern Christians. Hints are described in Parzival.

Though the manuscript itself attributes these concepts to a person named "Flegitanis", who derived them from Islamic sources in Muslim Spain, I believe that this is an example of misdirection, with the actual source being the Nestorians in the Middle East, in combination with the Nusayri and the Cathars. The part in Parzival chapter 9 where Lucifer is introduced is followed by an alchemical description of the stone, which, in turn, is said to be guarded by Templars. This alchemical material includes images familiar to later alchemy. Here, at the very beginning of the tradition as it manifests in print, you have Lucifer, alchemy and Templars, although Lucifer is not being covertly honored here. Lucifer, here, would be a translation of the Nusayri Azazil, and would be distinct from the traditional witchcraft notion of Lucifer. Furthermore, the alchemical tradition talks about a Phoenix being burned to ashes by the stone and being reborn from it, which corresponds to the Toad Stone tradition. The Grail, in this, gives eternal life, which I understand as salvation and freedom for the repentant evil angels, who are now free from reincarnation and able to ascend back to the Divine Mind and live there. A Dove is described as flying down from heaven on Good Friday and leaving a Eucharist on the stone, which refers to Jesus' redemption of the evil angels through his sacrifice. Those who are called to the grail go on the grail quest, which is the quest of personal redemption linked to inner alchemy and outer acts. Seizing the stone brings great hardship on a person, in that it provokes all the powers of the Evil One to try to stop the individual from completing the act of redemption associated with the process. Conquering these forces, and succeeding in the process, is the grail quest.

The grail mountain of Montsalvache represents Paradise, the Heavenly City, the Divine Mind, the First Sun, the Heavenly Temple, which we identify with the Sabbat of the ages. Those who succeed in lifting the grail from the depths back to the heights, to the top of the mountain, lift the stone of the angels back to its source. The grail in the depths is exalted unto the heights through the completion of both the alchemical work and the quest, as well as personal repentance. The grail knights on the mountain, the keepers of the grail, are those who have succeeded with the process and the quest, and who are now associated with Paradise, both in this world and in the hereafter.

The association between Paradise and the Grail castle is made by Henri Corbin in his "The Temple and Contemplation". There, in looking at "Titurel", written as a prelude to "Parzival", Corbin looks at the jeweled grail castle on the top of Mount Salvache, and relates it to Islamic ideas about accessing the Hurqalya and the Jaribut. Here, the Grail castle is the image of the Heavenly Temple, but is not the Temple itself. Instead, Corbin describes a process where the scintilla, the Synderesis, which in this can be read as the Toadstone or the Pearl, becomes the root from which the Heavenly City is regenerated in the heart of the individual. This Heavenly City or Temple, the Grail Castle, is constructed through taming the passions after the Pearl itself has been claimed and acknowledged. After the Heavenly City has been built within the Heart, the Holy of Holies within the Heavenly City, corresponding to the Grail itself in Corbin's schema, can be accessed, which leads to communion with the Divine and mystical union through contemplative practices. This established three distinct degrees to the work, which are echoed in Masonry. As said previously, the construction of the Heavenly

Temple within is an inherently Masonic practice in a literal sense, in that building a castle in the west involves cutting and setting stones. These three degrees also contain the whole of the Toad Stone work: the first stage is seizing the stone, the second is working to purify the stone, and to purify ones self in the process through building the holy temple, while the last stage is to use the stone to effect divine union with the pleroma from which we came.

Interestingly, in describing the knight's attempt to find a cure for Amfortas, the wounded king, they describe a series of striking images. First, they describe going to the rivers of Paradise to find an herb that can heal the king. Next, they describe the golden bough, which is the branch given to Aeneas in Virgil's Aeneid. The golden bough allows him to navigate the underworld, and this was subsequently understood as an initiation. Next, they present the image of the Pelican who opens its chest to feed its young, an idea that's also associated with the Rose-Croix. After this it describes a gem taken from a unicorn's head, before talking about an herb that grows from a dragon that they harvested, and tried to heal the king with. This is related to the constellation Draco and offsetting the power of the planets and the moon through the herb. I should say that a constant alternative to the Toad Stone has been the stone in the head of a serpent, as well as a dragon. I look at these images as all being related to the Grail itself and to the process of inner alchemy which surrounds it.

Chastity, associated with Cathar belief, is requisite for achieving the Grail, and the wounded king's sin was said to be unchastity.

There's also an interesting reference to Cain and Abel in the 9th book, where, after the fall of Lucifer, and the creation of Adam, Cain is said to have destroyed the harmony of the earth by his sin. This sin on the earth is then healed by Jesus, with the blood of Abel being answered by the blood of Jesus.

The presence of neutral angels in Parzival is also significant. This is a concept that was later related to Fairy Folk in Scotland. The meaning of the neutral angels, said not to have been the worst of the fallen angels, refers to the souls of fallen angels who are still capable of repenting and ascending back to heaven. This is in distinction to the truly evil angels, who don't want to repent whatsoever, and who serve as the demons under the service of Satan. It's the neutral angels who can incarnate in human form.

Masonic Internal Alchemy

My personal belief is that a variation of this system of internal alchemy was taught in the degree of Knight of Saint Andrew, which currently forms the 29th degree of the Ancient & Accepted Scottish Rite. This degree was part of the original series of degrees associated with the Rose-Croix that was developed by the Chevalier Ramsay, and was part of the Chapter of Clermont series of degrees. This degree introduces Salt, Sulphur, and Mercury. Albert Pike's commentary on it in "Morals & Dogma", which is paradoxically located within the "Knight of the Sun" degree, and not within the "Knight of Saint Andrew Degree", comes very close to openly discussing the internal alchemical work. The active use of these to make the Masters' Word is the secret significance of the three dots associated with the master's degree in Freemasonry, even though, as I shall show in volume 2 of this work, all of this is really developed in esoteric interpretations of the Royal Arch, not in the normal master's degree itself.

The three are connected also to an esoteric interpretation of Royal Arch Masonry, which relates to the Toad Stone work as well. In Royal Arch Masonry, the individual symbolically descends into the depth of a crypt, to the Ninth Arch, and finds the Delta, the name of God that Enoch has deposited there. This is represented as the Lost Word. In reality, in this interpretation, the Delta corresponds to the Toad Stone and to the lower center of the body that corresponds to Mercury. Mercury is one of the things that the Toad Stone, as the philosophical stone, can generate. Seizing the Toad Stone is seizing the stone within. The Stone is not the Lost Word, the Masons word, but can, with the cooperation of the other centers, generate it.

The True Mason's word is generated by moving the Mercury generated by the Toadstone to the other two centers, the Head center and the heart Center. This means bringing the Mercury first to the head stone, the Bodhicitta, and then bringing the combination of the two forces down to the Heart stone, the Synderesis. When the

Mercury generated by the Toad Stone is brought into relation with these, the secret chamber of the heart is opened and the possibility of generating the true Mason's word is generated. This is not a word in and of itself, but the capacity of speaking the creative word that can create reality.

The ultimate way to do this is to first stimulate the Toad Stone, then to direct the lightning or Mercury of the Toad Stone to the head stone, then transfer the lightning from the head stone to the heart stone. The word can then be used for theurgical purposes, or for practical purposes. However, this is the last phase of the work, and the individual will have to go through intermediate stages where the linear sequence of Toadstone, heart stone, head stone is used before being able to perfect it in its final form. Before that, the individual has go through many preparatory stages of work. This involves both finding these stone individually and the moving the energy, the Mercury, from the Toad stone to these stones, to empower and purify them. The Mercury, which is the universal Solvent, can be directed like a weapon, and aimed. The person who uses it enough will be able to aim the Mercury at the head stone, and then also at the heart stone.

The lightning, as Mercury the Universal Solvent, reduces things to Truth. Its solvent properties are to destroy the Lie, to destroy illusion, and resolve things back to Being, to real existence. This is the same as the Alkahest. The universal solvent, in this, can be used to reduce you to your truth, which means purifying you of the darkness and lies which are part of your body. The character of the lightning as the Universal Solvent is the outward characteristic of the lightning, while the aspect of it as the Word is the inner aspect, which can only be accessed through this sort of meditation and energy work. This direction of energy, and the places and stones, is similar in certain ways to J.B. Kerning's interpretation of Masonic symbolism, which translates some of these centers into letters, and visualizes them in the body. Kerning's writings on this have recently been translated and published.

The sex force is not identical to the lightning, the energy, generated by the Toad Stone, although it's similar. This is where people who otherwise have some interesting ideas, go wrong. The Mason's Word is not the sexual energy that is generated by the phallus. The Toad Stone lies in the perineum, between the genitals and the anus. Similarly, the sex force itself is not specifically identified with the man, and with the phallic energy. The sex force is shared by both men and women, who are not only just as involved with generation as men, but can arguably be much more firmly associated with generation than men can, being the people who actually hold, develop, and give birth to life. However, the energy generated by the Toadstone can be channeled into the sex act, and expelled during orgasm, thereby empowering it.

The words that can correspond to the three centers, in relation to the Toad Stone, taken from the "Perfect Master" degree of the Royal Arch, are "Jah-Bul-On" for the Toad Stone/Sex Center, "Yod-He-Vau-He" for the Head Center, and "Elhannin" for the Heart Center. These also correspond to the jewels of the Pearl for the Toad Stone, the Diamond for the Head Center, and the Ruby for the Heart Center.

Extension into Traditional Witchcraft

The application to Cain and Abel in this can be applied on a personal level, with Abel representing the virgin innocence of the initiate, Cain being the force of self sacrifice or self-slaying by the initiate, although perhaps undertaken with some help, and Seth represents the perfected initiate who arises from the ordeal produced by the self-slaying resembling the perfected face of the Father, the Demiurge, Baphomet. Abel represents the Moon, Cain the star, and Seth the Sun in this. Here, applying the symbolism of the Toad Rite, we can say that the initiate slays his Abelite innocence through Cainite action, then descends into himself to claim the Stone, which is the sole indestructible thing within him, and then having claimed the Stone he rises up once again as the Sethite perfected initiate.

There's another aspect to this, however, which brings a greater symbolism into this. Cain killed Abel, and then, in exile, established the first city. In this, Cain's killing of Abel can be considered a sacrifice of innocence which, with Abel's blood, sanctified the foundation stone of the world, allowing for the Temple to manifest. This would prefigure the coming of Christ, and his similar, and more thorough, redemption of the world. Here, Abel also represents the state of human beings in ignorance to the true nature of the Evil One, who presents himself as the good god. Abel's sacrifice was pleasing to the Evil One, while Cain's was not, and the killing of Abel is similar to the eating of the fruit of the Tree of Knowledge in the reverse tradition: it shatters the innocent illusion which the Evil One had constructed around the fallen angels, and instead introduces a hard reality. In this, Cain's action, which disrupted early post-Edenic life, also disrupted the plans of the Evil One to keep society in a state of ignorance and slavery. The adept who similarly sacrifices their own innocence in the Toad Stone rite also waters their own foundation stone with their blood, then seizes it, and, in harshness but in reality, fights to regenerate themself going from the basis of the Toadstone upwards. In Lenormant's telling, the foundation stone is made from the head of Abel itself. Here, the skull or head is the persistent part of the individual which remains after death, just as the Toadstone is the bone which remains after the skeleton of the Toad has been thrown into the water.

Toads also, are symbols of resurrection, and are also associated with changes in the moon. The Toad Bone is the transition point or limit between the manifest and the unmanifest. When seized and raised it is like the central point of the three on the vertical axis. The Toad in the water corresponded to the Black or Waning Moon and to the unmanifest, the Toad out of the water corresponds to the White or Waxing Moon and to the manifest state of being, the Toad on the limit corresponds to the Full or Red moon, and is the power which can direct one or the other force. It can send things to the demanifest, or it can manifest them. This corresponds to the different uses of the lightning generated from the Toadstone. On the one hand, the outer lightning generates the Alkahest, which reduces everything to its Truth, which is an act of demanifestation. On the other, the lightning used as Word can create, can manifest things through itself.

The energies associated with the three centers of the vertical axis are also referred to by Robert Fitzgerald, in his essay "The Hidden Stone", contained in the collection "The Luminous Stone", as the
"Flaming Torch",
"Lightning Bolt" and
"Serpent's Fire", making up the Trident of Cain.

These correspond to the Head, the Heart, and the Toadstone/Sex, and it's significant that, in this, the "Lightning Bolt" of the Heart is considered to be between the head and the sex, thereby indicating that it's production is through combination of the two. [check on order]

These three make up the basis of the "Autochthonic I" described by Chumbley. The three centers can be seen both as three jewels, three stones, and as three drops, which can correspond to the three drops of "Awen" given by the Welsh goddess Ceridwen to the sage Taliesen. The stone, the seed, is also the Serpent's Egg of the Druids.

Attentive readers will have noticed a continuum between the Celtic beliefs associated with the Mabinogion and the ideas in Parzival. This isn't a trivial association. The Welsh tales were transmitted to the French through the intermediary of the Breton bards in the Middle Ages. The Bretons were Celtic Britons who decided to leave Britain after the Saxon invasions. Marie de France took down many bardic stories and translated them into her version of French, including stories about King Arthur, and from there the motifs took on a life of their own. These stories became the foundation of the Grail stories during the Crusades, and eventually influenced the German troubadour Wolfram von Eschenbach.

Works Cited

Barnstone and Meyer "Hymn of the Robe of Glory", in "the Gnostic Bible", Shambhala, Boston, 2009

Saint Bonaventure's "De Triplici Via", or the Triple Way, in "Mystical Opuscula", José de Vinck, trans. Saint Anthony Guild Press, Paterson NJ, 1960

Colless Brian E. ed. trans., "The Wisdom of the Pearlers, an Anthology of Syriac Christian Mysticism" Cistercian Publications, Kalamazoo, 2008,

Corbin, Henry"The Configuration of the Temple of the Ka'bah", "The Temple and Contemplation", KPI, London, 1986

Eschenbach, Wolfram von Parzival,, trans. A.T. Hatto Penguin, London 2004

Fitzgerald, Robert "The Hidden Stone", "The Luminous Stone", Three Hands Press,Richmond Vista, 2016.

Goldstein,Joseph, Jack Kornfield, "Seeking the Heart of Wisdom, the Path of Insight Meditation", Shambhala Press, Boston, 2001

Saint Jerome, Thomas P. Scheck trans. "Commentary on Ezekiel", Newman Press, Westminster MD, 2017

Kitchen, Robert A. and Maartien F. G. Parmentier, "The Book of Steps, The Syriac Liber Graduum", Cistercian Publications, Kalamazoo, 2004

Lenormant, François "Beginnings of History" Charles Scribner's Sons, New York, 1893, Google books

Matthews, John ed. trans. and Gareth Knight,"Titurel", in "Temples of the Grail, The Search for the World's greatest Relic", Llewellyn, Woodbury MN, 2019

Maximus the Confessor, George C. Berthold trans. "Selected Writings", Paulist Press, New York, 1985.

Mar O'Dishoo, Mar Eshai Shimun XXIII trans. "Book of Marganitha", Xlibris, 2007.

Pike, Albert "Knight of the East and West" degree in "Morals & Dogma", Kessinger Publications, nd. also Google Books

Richard of Saint Victor "The Mystic Ark", also known as "Benjamin Major", "Richard of Saint Victor", Paulist Press, New York 1979

Chapter 15
Grimoire

Now, for greater understanding of this section, I recommend that the reader do three things. First, get a notebook. Second, when the different symmetries, fourfold, eightfold, and others, are described, go to your notebook and draw them. For fourfold symmetries, draw a cross and label the different directions as indicated. For the threefold symmetries, draw a vertical line, with the beginning, middle, and end of the line corresponding to the three. For the fivefold symmetries, draw a cross like before, but at the top, the north point, place one entity before it and one entity after. For the eightfold symmetries, draw a cross and then cross quarters and label them appropriately.

Finally, take your diagrams and contemplate how each of the terms flow into the other, or change into the other. These diagrams illustrate, for the most part, cyclical change, clockwise change, and so they can be read as transforming into each other in a clockwise manner. The threefold symmetries are somewhat different, in that the bottom and the top term combine to make the middle term. After contemplating particular symmetries, compare those which have the same number of terms to each other: compare the four-fold ones to other four-fold symmetries, for instance.

Next, go back through the book, particularly to the Gerald Massey chapter, but also to previous chapters, and make diagrams of the fourfold symmetries in your notebook, and then compare these symmetries to those in this chapter and contemplate them.

Doing this will give you a much greater understanding and appreciation of what's being described.

Part 1, Cosmology and the Gods

There are two main models of the universe and of work that are presented here. The first is the ritual of Ingress, the second the model associated with the work of Congress. The actual Congress ritual will not be given. The majority of what's contained in this grimoire refers to the Ingress rite.

The ritual and model associated with the Ingress rite is based on two fundamental places and their relationship to each other: the Sabbat and the Earth. In this, the Sabbat is the source of the life energy for the earth, which comes down to it in a way parallel to that of the Sun giving life to the earth, with the life energy actually going from the Sabbat through the visible Sun to the earth. In this, there's a two way movement: of energy from the Sabbat to the Earth, and the return of the energy from the Earth back to the Sabbat. The Sabbat is considered to be the source of life while the earth without the energy of the Sabbat is considered to be lifeless. The relationship of the circle cast by the magician to the Sabbat here is the same as the relation of the Sabbat to the Earth.

Baphomet, as the the prime god of the First Sun, can be identified with Apollo in this, and the energy that flows from Baphomet to the earth can be identified with the life energy of the First Sun flowing down to earth from Apollo. Within the context of Ingress, the energy that flows from Baphomet/Apollo to the Earth is non-dual, that is, neither male or female. Because of this, even though it's possible to say that this energy flows from the phallus of Baphomet to the earth, it would be equally true to say that it flows from the vagina of Baphomet to the earth, in that it is not sperm, but undifferentiated life energy. This undifferentiated life energy is also the Schamijam.

These are the two polarities, and the Earth herself is a goddess of sorts, though a conflicted one. As has been related, the earth in this variety of traditional witchcraft is not thought to exist in purity. Instead, the earth is a product of both the creation of the good god, Baphomet, and the corruption of the Evil One. What's evil in the earth, corruption in the earth, belongs to the Evil One, while the pure life of the earth belongs to the good god. The Earth, as it exists, is, then, a goddess, and the pure form of the earth, outside of the corruption of the Evil One, should be honored. The earth itself has been redeemed through the gnostic incarnation and sacrifice of Lucifer, the parallel of Jesus, the image of Baphomet, on the earth, but the work of repair and redemption of the earth, the battle between the Evil One and life, purity, is still ongoing. The process of bringing the Sabbat down to the Earth through ritual helps to heal the earth, and to defeat the power of the Evil One.

The cosmology associated with the Congress rite is more complicated. Here, besides the general places of the Sabbat and the Earth, you have the Astrological realm and the Underworld. In this model, the Sabbat is still the source of life on earth, but the Earth is not devoid of energy. The Sabbat provides energy to the earth through the Astrological world, and this meets the energy that comes up from the Underworld of Earth itself. This earth energy flows from the Stone at the center of the earth, up through the underworld to the surface. These two energies combine to create the life on the surface of the Earth. Though the cosmology of the Congress rite gives a more thorough picture of the cosmos, the essence of what's happening is not clear without knowledge of the Ingress model of the cosmos. Here, male and female are present, and the Astral energy that flows down to the earth is male while the energy which flows from the earth upwards is female. Here, we have the divided Schamijam, which, using the alchemical imagery of Welling, sees the Astral energy and the Earth energy conjoining to make up the alchemical Salt of the reunited Schamijam on the surface of the Earth.

The Ingress model has two modalities: clockwise and counter-clockwise, the first leading to manifestation, the second leading to demanifestation. This demanifestation, in the context of Ingress, means sending something back up to the Sabbat, while manifestation means calling something down from the Sabbat and having it manifest on earth.

As this relates to the structure of the Azoetia, the vertical axis is composed of the first, second and eleventh cells, while the horizontal axis is composed of the fourth, sixth, eighth and tenth cells. These correspond to the directions of Center, Upper, and Lower, and then of East, South, West and North. The cross quarters, which are used in the congress cosmology, correspond to the third, fifth, seventh and ninth cells, these being Northeast, Southeast, Southwest and Northwest, respectively.

The Ingress Cosmology and Ritual

The Three and the Four:
The fourfold circle is fundamentally solar, while the threefold vertical axis is fundamentally lunar, within the circle.

The Three

Both the three and the four manifest differently in the completely transcendent reality than they do in the reality of the circle, and of earth.

The Three in the Sabbat

One way to think of the incorporation of the Toadstone within the Sabbat is to picture the One, who is the Dragon Lord, as the ever present darkness of the Neoplatonic One, which then concretizes a piece of his energy as a white stone. This white stone can also be thought of as the serpent or dragon's egg. This white stone, then, sends out a shoot from it which culminates in a Lotus flower, which, when opening, reveals the Sabbat of the Ages within it. The flower is also a flame, the First Sun, and the smoke from the flame congregates as the Demiurge, who takes up residence in the center of the Flower. This establishes the basis of the three: the Stone from which all originates, the Sabbat itself, the Divine Mind, which is generated from the Stone, and the Active Intelligence, the Demiurge, which is generated from the Sabbat.

The Toadstone stands for the Goddess, for the flowing out of Life, while the Active Intelligence for the God, and the flowing back of Death, with Baphomet being the product of the combination between the two.

After this initial upwards movement, there's a corresponding downwards movement. The Demiurge then subjugates the different parts of the fire of the Sabbat, of the Divine Mind, into horses or gods that serve him, these being the letters of the Azoetic alphabet, and the "conclaves" of the Sabbat of the Ages. The different characteristics of these conclaves, forces, can then be called upon and the intelligences that make them up can be consulted and learned from. The Demiurge then combines these cells with himself, and in this combination, he becomes Baphomet/Zo-I-As. Finally, Baphomet sits on the rock or stone from which the energy of the Sabbat was emanated in the first place, which signifies coordinating the conclaves or letters to the source from which they came, completing the cycle. This image completes and unites the three into one.

The initial threee also correspond to the Neo-Platonic concepts of Being, Life, and Intellect, as well as the Neo-Platonic levels of the Intelligible, Intelligible-Intellectual, and Intellectual worlds. This correspondence comes from Proclus, and involves Greco-Roman pagan concepts, which have been distantly transferred to the Craft, in changed form. While Proclus' philosophy is very complicated, I can give a simplified version which situates the triad of Being, Life, Intellect within the craft, and within the three.

For the purpose of argument, we're going to discuss Being, Life, and Intellect within the context of "Ideals" within the Divine Mind. Additionally, we're going to equate different types of "Being", with Ideals. In Proclus' philosophy, there's an enormous amount of discussion about how Ideals are formed from successively simpler elements, such as pieces of Being itself, which we're not going to deal with.

"Being", in the upper triad of Proclus' Divine Mind is not just existence, but is instead a point that the One contracts into, which contains within it all of the different potentials for the Ideals of reality. It's the seed that contains all of them. Being gives birth to "Life", which is a profusion of all of these different types of Being, or Ideals, what could be called millions of forms of Being, going forth in an undifferentiated form. Finally, "Intellect", comes into existence, which has the power of division, to divide things and organize them. This is the upflow of energy from the Stone, from Being, through Life, up to its extension as Intellect. Next comes the backflow of energy, from Intellect back down to Being.

For our purposes, "Intellect" does something very particular in the next stage: descending back down to Life, it takes all of the undifferentiated Ideals of the Divine Mind and organizes them into distinct categories. These distinct categories make up the Living

Being, the model with which the Demiurge uses to create the world. This differentiation takes the raw profusion of Ideals and creates a more usable organization of them. As described in both Plato and Proclus, the Living Being is the product of organizing the Ideals of the Divine Mind into four distinct categories, which correspond to the four elements, with a central coordinating intelligence uniting them into a single entity. Importantly, "Intellect" in Proclus in its division of the undifferentiated mass, and so fulfills the role of Intellect in the craft as being destructive. It is linked to death, albeit through destruction which is trained to a good purpose, to the fundamental organization of reality. The power of the Intellect unites itself with the Living Being, also known as the Tetramorph because of its fourfold character. Finally, the power of the Living Being and the Demiurge in combination is bound back to Being, to the Stone, the source of all types of Being. This anchors the four of the Living Being back to the essences from which it came, constraining them to them and, in a sense, grounding the Ideals within it. This completes the back flow of energy to the source, and completes the figure of Baphomet, which is a synthesis of all three centers. The energy flows upwards from Being, to Life, to Intellect, and back down from Intellect, to Life, to Being.

The upwards movement is oriented towards unfoldment and manifestation, while the downwards movement is linked to restriction and binding. The last part of the downward movement, of the Living Being back to Being is a kind of Binding. This, in general, involves a movement from a higher level of energy to a lower level of energy. The process of shaping the First Sun into the Tetramorph can also be interpreted as being a Hieros Gamos, a sacred marriage between the Active Intellect as God and the First Sun as a type of Goddess. In this, there's also resonance with the idea of the Sword or Knife penetrating the Cauldron as representing the sacred marriage as well, with the Active Intellect being the knife and the goddess of the First Sun being the Cauldron. The Tetramorph, in this, is the product of the sacred marriage. Baphomet, in this, is the product of the combination of the Demiurge, and the Tetramorph together, which combination in the last phase is bound down to the stone of Being from which all life originates.

The relationship between the Divine Mind and the active intelligence within it can also be pictured in terms of Welsh mythology. Daniel Schulke, in his essay " The Blasphemy of Things Unseen" in "Hands of Apostasy" presents an interesting correspondence to all of this. He talks about the relationship between Cerridwen and her son Affagdu or Morfan, with the latter being the Black Man. Here, the Sabbat, the Divine Mind, can be pictured as the contents of the cauldron of Ceridwen, as being the all the essences of the Awen. It is also the womb of Ceridwen from which her son proceeds. Within my understanding of the Sabbatic tradition, Ceridwen is looked at as the entirety of the vertical dimension, with her Cauldron and her Son forming subdivisions within it. The active intelligence which is formed at the center of the Divine Mind would in this be her son Morfan, also known as Affagdu.

Extending the Cauldron analogy, we can recast our story of the Lotus to be the following: There's a primal fire which heats the Cauldron, the Cauldron itself, and that which proceeds from the Cauldron as steam or smoke. The primal fire is the power emanating from the Stone, the Cauldron is the Divine Mind, which contains the Awen and all of the Ideals within it, and the steam or smoke which emanates from the Cauldron is Affagdu or Morphan. This is the upwards movement. In the corresponding downwards movement, Morfan, the black god, misshapen, becomes the beautiful sun god, through recombining himself with the contents of the Cauldron. This is equivalent to the making of Baphomet. All of this would be contained within the body of Ceridwen herself.

From what I've been able to gather, in the Sabbatic tradition Ceridwen is considered to be all of the three combined, seen in part as Gerald Massey's great goddess, the Magna Mater or genetrix of the world. This is also linked by Massey to the Dragon, though it's sometimes unclear if Ceridwen here is the dragon, or if she's the daughter of the dragon. I feel that seeing her as the daughter of the dragon lord, of the One, is a better way of conceptualizing things. She's also the black sow, or pig seen as a version of the great goddess. The Azoetia refers to her as, among other names, as Iuno or Juno and Ash-Ta-Ur-Te, the latter coming from Massey's Egyptian name for her "Ta-Urte", which is a form of the Egyptian "Taweret". Juno is the mother of the gods, the Roman equivalent of Hera, who can be taken as being the great mother of all forms.

She is thought to contain the Sabbat of the Ages within her in the form of the Cauldron of Ceridwen. This is understood as either the womb or the heart of the goddess. Her child, Affagdu or Morfan, is contained within this cauldron as well, as a black god who later becomes a sun god. This god is dual, first black and then golden, with the golden aspect being equated by Massey to the neo-druidic sun god Hu Gadarn or Hu the mighty. I believe, in this, that the black portion of her son most closely corresponds to the waning phase of the moon.

The three within can esoterically be linked to Cain, Abel, and Seth in the following way: the goddess of the Stone refers to Abel, the demiurge refers to Cain, and Seth is the product of Cain, the Demiurge, working on and carving the Divine Mind into the four elements of the Living Being. The virgin innocence of the Sabbat in its phase of "Life", before being sacrificed and shaped, is also of the nature of Abel. When Cain shapes the virgin nature of the divine mind, he sacrifices Abel, and the product which results, the full picture of Baphomet, is Seth. As Seth, Baphomet resembles the face of the Father, the manifest form the Dragon Lord, the One. This is slightly different from how these things work within the human body in the process of internal alchemy.

Very importantly, the level of Cain is one of the entities which Chumbley describes as the "Opposer", which is a translation of the Hebrew "Satan" into English, which needs some explanation. This ultimately derives from figures referred to as the Devil in the craft. The discourse around the "Opposer" appears to be Chumbley's attempt to find a deeper meaning connecting the mask of Lucifer to the underlying reality of what he represents in the craft. This leads to two different interpretations, the first linking the etymology of Satan as "Opposer", an alternate interpretation of "Accuser", to the Demiurgic process of creation through cutting, and secondly linking the figure of Death to the "Opposer" through the process of breaking.

However, though the effort here is strong, I feel that Chumbley's use of the term allows for literalistic interpretations that cause the mask to be confused with what is masked, and that therefore lead to

Satanism and to Satanic interpretations of things which are not Satanic in any way. This has manifested itself copiously in the writings of people who have literally interpreted the Opposer as Satan and then integrated it, in a very flawed way, into a greater Satanic belief system.

The Devil in traditional witchcraft is not Satan, but, in my opinion, is a mask that comes from the Cathar reversal interpretation of the Bible that witchcraft comes from. Here, it's more profitable to link Cain with Lucifer than with Satan. Lucifer, in this, is the true god, who resembles the Neo-platonic Christian interpretation of Jesus. Satan is the true form of the false god who represented himself as the true god to the people of the Old Testament, and who is the false god that many Christians today worship. In this, we are not "Devil Worshippers".

Here, also, Nigel Pennick's alternative interpretation of "Devil" as linked to the Indo-European "Deva", or bright one, is instructive as well. Though Cain in the three is dark, the combined figure of Baphomet, which we will go through below, is very bright, as an embodiment of the First Sun. This figure of light is a fitting object for the label of the bright one. He also corresponds to Apollo as well, as the god of the First Sun, and in this, the brightness of Apollo can be linked to the brightness of Lucifer. Through this, he can emanate life energy from himself to the Earth. The energy of the First Sun, that which contains all the ideals within it, is the same as the Schamijam referenced earlier, and the emanation of life energy from Baphomet/Apollo is an emanation of the Schamijam to earth.

Here, as well, Baphomet is a semi-pagan reinterpretation and adaptation of the Neo-Platonic Jesus.

However, as we have seen previously, the figure of Jesus himself in the original Christianity may well have been much more pagan than is commonly acknowledged, and while Baphomet as the Sabbatic Goat is clearly very different, it's much less clear if Abraxas was truly as different from Jesus in the original Christianity as is sometimes claimed.

Also, Eliphas Levi's own description of Baphomet as being the scapegoat that was released as an offering into the wilderness is instructive, in that, far from being a representation of the demon Azazel, the scapegoat is traditionally associated with Jesus. Not only that, but in Judaism the goat is an offering to the demon, not the demon itself. As a former priest, Levi would surely have been aware of the link of Jesus with the goat given as a sin offering on Yom Kippur, the Day of Atonement, the day in Judaism where one's sins are forgiven. In this, the goat would be the antithesis of Azazel, and Jesus would be the ultimate sin offering. He would be the offering that defeated, and overthrew, both Azazel (in the Judaic interpretation) and Satan.

Within this, the combined figure of Baphomet can also be interpreted as Tubal-Cain, the Demiurgic god of the Forge, which is the First Sun. In fact, in the account of the Timaeus, where the Platonic Demiurge is described, Plato portrays this figure as a blacksmith who forges together the different components of the cosmos as if they were different types of metal.

The Three in the Circle, and on the Earth

Here, the drama that we've outlined above is masked by the three phases of the moon. This is the outer veil for the inner reality. The energies of these three phases of the moon can be manipulated to open up the door to the fourth path of the moon, the dark or completely new moon, which leads to the transcendent reality of the Sabbat itself.

The three refer to the creation of the Sabbat itself as manifested in the body of the initiate. It stands for the vertical axis. This axis consists of: the Stone, the Moon-stone, which was first created by the One, which generates the Divine Mind, the Sabbat itself, which is the Eternal Sun containing the Millions of Forms of Being, which generates, as "Smoke", the concretization of itself in the form of the Active Intelligence, the Demiurge, which can correspond to a generic Star.

The Toad Stone in the initiate corresponds to the Moon Stone generated from the One, the Dragon Lord. The Synderesis to the Heart, corresponds to the Divine Mind, which is also the Cauldron of Ceridwen. The Head, the Bodhicitta, the Diamond stone, corresponds to the Demiurge, the Opposer in its first form. These can also correspond to the white, red, and black moons, as well as to the waxing, full, and waning moons.

Characteristics of the Three:

The three correspond to the center of the circle. The three as they manifest in the vertical column of the individual, as used in ritual, are the following:

Lower Center—Diana and the White Moon, the Waxing Moon

Heart Center— Venus and the Red Moon, the Full Moon

Head Center—Selene, the Horned Goddess, and the Black Moon, the Waning Moon

The lower center and Toadstone corresponds to Diana and the White Moon, as well as to the Depths, and to Sleep, unconsciousness, to the alchemical Mercury, and to Desire, as well as to Virgin innocence and the Virgin woman. Desire present but unrealized. The altar stone, as well as the shod Stang. Abel. The Rock from which Mithras and the Bull are born. The Serpent's Fire. The Toadstone in this can be paralleled to the Pearl. The pure Lunar force. The Moon in the vertical column.

Diana, Virgin goddess of the waxing moon, goddess of beginnings, corresponds to the Stone, to the fragment of Being that everything comes from. Corresponds to the underworld, the depths. Mercury, standing here for the first matter. Also Desire, and Virgin desire, linked to sleep and unconsciousness as naivete, and innocence. Tenth Cell of the Azoetia

The heart center and Synderesis corresponds to Lady or Dame Venus and the Red Moon, the Full Moon, which is a combination of Black and White. It's also parallel to the surface of the earth. The Heart center contains a version of the Sabbat itself hidden within it. It corresponds to the Red goddess, and the red woman, the fertile woman. It corresponds to the Will, and to the inner alchemical Sulphur. Also, corresponds to Dreaming in its outer aspect and to the path of Trance in its inner aspect. Will in its outer aspect, the microcosmic Sabbat in its inner aspect. Also, the First Sun, the bale file or smaller fire on the altar, the cauldron of Cerridwen, the cauldron used as a container on the altar. Container of the Awen.

The middle part of the Stang. Abel. The Mithraic Bull. The Lightning Bolt. The Synderesis can be paralleled to the Ruby. The First Sun, and the Sun in the vertical column

Venus, the sexually mature goddess, "Mother", but more accurately the Red Woman, the Red Goddess, in other traditions known as Babalon, the very sexual woman, who also conceives and gives birth. Not a "Mother" in the homey sense. She corresponds to the Sabbat in its undifferentiated form, which comes from the Stone. She's the embodiment of Life, in all of its forms, which proceeds from the seed of Being. Red, the Red Moon, in this, corresponds also to the Full Moon, between the moons of waxing and waning Corresponds outwardly to Will, and inwardly to the Sabbatic energies of the First Sun themselves. Sulphur, standing here for the Azoth, the fundamental force and power of the First Sun. The expansion of the First Matter into its full life. The Zeroeth Cell of the Azoetia. The center point of the vertical axis.

The head center and Bodhicitta corresponds to the Horned Goddess, Selene, and the Black Moon, the Waning Moon, and to the Heights, and to the Waking state. Corresponds to the alchemical principle of Salt, as well as to the principle of Belief. Also corresponds to Reason. The Crone goddess. The horns of the Stang. Cain. Morfan or Affagdu, son of Ceridwen, in Welsh mythology, the Black Man. The Active Intelligence and Demiurge within the Sabbat. Mithras as the Bull slayer. The Flaming Torch. Corresponds to the Diamond consciousness, which is the concealed Bodhicitta within the mind. The Star within the vertical column.

The Horned Goddess, Selene, who is also a Black Goddess, goddess of the New Moon, is horned because she wears the horns of the crescent moon on her head. The moon in its sliver state is pictured being fixed sideways on her head, which makes it appear as two horns. She corresponds to Cain, the Demiurge, and to the power of the Intellect. She is the crone goddess, of whom Chumbley describes as the goddess so old yet the goddess so young. The senior goddess of the three. Corresponds to Belief, in relation to Intellect, the Mind, and Reason. Goddess of Wisdom. There's confusion, perhaps intentionally introduced, in the Azoetia between this goddess and the goddess of the West, but they're two distinct figures.

Salt, the desiccation or byproduct of the fire of the First Sun, the opposite of Sulphur, dead, with the idea that Reason itself kills as well. However, the force of death, and of Reason, in its form of "Ratio" or division, is necessary for analysis and also for producing things from the First Sun and from the Azoth themselves, for manifesting things in reality. First Cell of the Azoetia

Selene as moon goddess has a more direct parallel with Cain, though, in that there are various "Man in the Moon" symbols which feature the horns of the moon which can be linked to Cain. This is through the idea that Cain was exiled to the moon. In this, the horns of the Stang, which are parallel to the level of Selene, are representative of the dividing power of Cain and of the waning crescent of the Moon.

The three also correspond to the White, Red, and Black Moons, with the Red being the moon in between the White and the Black Moon. The Red moon is literally half white and half black, thereby connoting a unity between male and female. These are the White virgin goddess of the foundation stone, the Red goddess of sex, generation, and motherhood corresponding to the Sabbat itself, and the Black goddess, the Crone goddess, beyond motherhood, standing for the Opposer. As translated out into the actual cycles of the Moon, the White Moon can be considered the waxing moon, which starts from the day after the New Moon, while the Red Moon can be equated with the Full Moon, and the Black Moon with the Waning Moon.

With these lunar correspondences in mind, we can present once more the story of the three in another fashion:

The stone, concreted from the One, the dragon lord, is the source of Life. It is Zoa and the source of manifestation. It corresponds to the Waxing moon. It gives forth its life, which culminates in the fullness of the Sabbat, the First Sun, which corresponds to the Full Moon. The fire of the Sabbat, the fire of the First Sun, then generates smoke, which turns into death, Azoa, which culminates in the Waning moon. The point of Death that's generated is also the point of consciousness within and beyond the First Sun. This is the upward movement.

It's followed by a downward movement where the Active Intelligence, Death, applies itself to the stuff of the Sabbat, and carves it into the four sectors of the Tetramorph, corresponding to the four elements. This creates the model of the world, and, in fact, in applying itself to the Sabbat in this way, Death is transformed into something more positive. The creative aspect of Death, in forming the model of the world out of the profusion of life in the Sabbat, is the light part of Death. After this, the model of the four elements of the Tetramorph, is bound back to the stone of Life from which everything first emanated. In this process, the expansive power of Life goes against its nature to bind and to contract, making this act the dark part of Life. Once in place, you have the complete figure of Baphomet: the Active Intelligence, or Death, fused to the Tetramorph, who in turn is fused to the rock of Life. The complete figure, then, includes all of the four elements, as well as life and death, which can also be seen as male and female. The whole figure of Baphomet interacts with the world outside of the transcendent realm through the creative word, which goes from this realm into that of earth.

The Four:

The entirety of the four is contained in the middle number of the vertical column of the three. As in the schema of the three, the structure of the four differs according to whether it's considered as it exists within transcendental reality, or whether it exists within the circle, and on the earth. The Circle is an application of the primal pattern of the Tetramorph, of the generation and arrangement of the four elements, united around a common center, to the earth. Here, in Ingress, it represents the inflow of energies from the Sabbat to the earth, and the outflow or return of energies from the earth to the Sabbat.

The Four in the Sabbat

Another way of describing all of this is to start with the First Sun, the first Fire, the Divine Mind, the Sabbat of the ages and look at why exactly fire was chosen to describe it. Fire, such as a campfire, if you look at it can be seen to contain a myriad of shapes within it, which is a good way of describing the Millions of Forms of Being in the Ideal realm, in the Divine Mind. Fire in this can be extended to the Sun as the example of a fire writ large, with the Sun then being seen to contain these millions of forms of Being, or Ideals, within it. The Sabbat of the Ages, the First Sun, is also made up of the Azoth, which is the material the First Sun is made of, which contains the Ideals within it, which, in turn, is the same as the Schamijam.

The inner nature of the active intellect within the First Sun is Death, and the relation of Death to the nature of creation is outlined by Chumbley in the section of the Azoetia dedicated to explaining the nature of the Arthame, the dagger. There, Chumbley outlines that the God, within the First Sun, grabbed a handful of the stuff which would become matter, and shaped it with the knife, sculpting the human form out of it, before breathing in the fire which is the life of the Sabbat into it. This process can be expanded to an account of the creation of the model for the entire world. A sculptor, or carver, in this works by removing material, and in this the action of Death is related to creation. But, the nature of Baphomet, the Demiurge is more complicated than just Death.

The cells of the outward directions, the elements, as part of the divine mind, are subdivisions containing the various aspects of the divine mind in a progression of manifestation. These subdivisions correspond to number, but they're also gods, places, and conglomerations of essences, which contain wisdom and knowledge within them. They correspond to the different schemas of subgods around the throne of the main god, who is represented by the Center. They are agglomerations of Ideals. Proclus, following Plato, thought that the Ideals of the world existed in a pure, perfected, form, in the Living Being, the Tetramorph, who exists within the divine mind. The Living Being is the Paradigm, or model on which the world is based.

Going into more detail about this process, though we're in the transcendental realm, there still are directions. Starting from the center, Fire is created first, in the South. Fire represents the most active, energetic, Ideals, which are contained within the Divine Mind. Then, going back in the opposite direction, Earth is created, in the North. Earth represents the completely passive Ideals within the Divine Mind. Next, the Ideals which are between active and passive, but which are more active than passive, are collected together in the East, these corresponding to Air. Finally, the Ideals which are between active and passive, but which are more passive than active are collected in the West, and these correspond to Water.

Fire—South
Earth— North
Air— East,
Water— West

Baphomet, Tubal-Cain, within the Sabbat

The Tetramorph is related to the idea of Baphomet in that the Living Being can be said to combine the creatures of the four elements into one in his/her body. The tetramorph is the Chimera in this. In the description of Baphomet by Eliphas Levi, that of the Sabbatic goat, the duality of devil and angel, man and woman, united in one is emphasized, however, in other representations, such as those associated with traditional witchcraft, Baphomet can be pictured as being made up of the composite parts of the animals of the different elements, in addition to male and female, light and dark, etc. In this, Baphomet is pictured as a composite being made out of animals that correspond to the four elements. In these portrayals, it incorporates the features of a fish, a bird, a land animal, and a man, with the man standing for fire. The figure of the sphinx, as understood in 19th century occultism, also combined many of these animals, with it often being featured with wings, and this figure could also be understood as combining the four elements within itself.

Additionally, within recent mythology, meaning of the post-Renaissance world, including that associated with esotericism in France, the Egyptian Sphinx was analyzed in a way that attributed its different parts to different animals of the four elements. This picture of the sphinx included wings, prominently, and is equated with Baphomet by Chumbley in the Azoetia, with expressions such as "Sphinx to all that lives" meaning that the deity incorporates the different animals of the elements within him/her. The Manticore is another similar being. Many of Chumbley's portrayals of the sphinx in the Azoetia actually use the imagery of the Manticore, which can be distinguished from the Sphinx itself by having a viper for a tail.

This portrayal of Baphomet is also adapted into Christian tradition by equating him with the Tetramorph or Cherub of Jewish tradition. Here, the idea of a being composed of a lion, an ox, an eagle, and a man, are used as a substitute for the elemental animals. I believe that the original where this came from was Neoplatonic, and was from Greek pagan religion, not esoteric Judaism.

In this, through the combination of the elements with each other and with himself, Baphomet would also be Androgynous in several ways. It would also be Hermaphroditic, or double Hermaphroditic, in the sense that the four that are bound, correspond to two male and to two female elements each. Fire and Earth are first united with each other, then Air and Water, and then the two combined forces are combined with each other to make a fourfold unity. As each of the two combined forces are combinations of male and female in themselves, we could call the joining of the two the formation of the double Hermaphrodite or Androgyne. This double Hermaphrodite, united in turn to the Demiurge, is also referred to as Zo-I-As in Chumbley's Azoetia.

Baphomet, in this, combines all of the Ideals within himself, and is simultaneously the world creator, who creates the world with these Ideals. He can also be identified with Apollo as the god of the First Sun, who spreads fertility to the world from the First Sun. Here, the First Sun is also the Azoth as well as the Schamijam.

Baphomet is also identified with Tubal-Cain in traditional witchcraft, with the identification being based on the Demiurgic function of Baphomet. Tubal-Cain was a worker in metals who is of the line of Cain, and this working of metals is generalized into the powers of a creator deity in general. Tubal-Cain, in this, is also associated with the Forge, used to make the implements, which is equated with the First Sun.

Additionally, we can incorporate the two arms of Levi's Baphomet, which feature the terms "Solve" and Coagula" into the figure by equating them with Decrease and Increase. Decrease here, associated with the poewr of Water, is a transition between the manifest and the demanifest, as Solve is, while Increase, associated with the power of Air, can be associated with Coagula as the transition from the demanifest to the manifest. Within the body itself, the genitals of Baphomet can be equated with Manifestation, while the head of the goat, and the divided horns, can be equated with Demanifestation or destruction, and death. This incorporates the four elements into the diagram in another way. The heart, or core, of Baphomet, is the meeting place of all of these four.

The Tetramorph, in addition to all of this, is the primal plan of the world, in the sense of representing the four quarters of the world within itself, the four directions, the four elements, the four tendencies, united by a center. As the Living Being, it's literally the model on which the world is created based on, with this including its foursquare character.

The Four as Translated into the Earth, and into the Circle

The Frame of the World

This is how the structure of the Living Being, the Tetramorph, manifests itself on the Earth and in the Circle. The structure, and the creation of the structure of the world, is different from the functioning of the world. The same is true for the circle itself. Here, we go over the formation of this structure before presenting how it works in practice, when the structure is activated. Now, in this, we have the elements joined to manifestation and demanifestation,

Before looking at the actual casting of the circle, it's helpful to look at how this works in the Earth in general. With regards to manifestation and demanifestation on Earth, it's important to define terms, because the word "manifest" can be taken in several ways, particularly in ways that don't represent what's going on. One of the common definitions of manifestation is that things that are the most concrete are the most manifest. In other words, things which are most solid and earthly are the most manifest. Another definition, using "manifest" as a verb, is that the results of a spell are manifestations, and that, in this, to manifest something means to make it completely real and concrete, often in an earthly way. The terms, instead, should be read in relation to the life force of plants, animals, and other living entities. This life force is the same as the Azoth, the quintessence, which is the stuff that the First Sun is made out of. Similarly, the term "Demanifest" is linked to the withdrawal of life force, and so to death.

The most "Manifest" in this, is the plant or animal that's at the peak of their life force and flourishing. Because of this, a corpse of an animal, though more earthly, would not be more "Manifest", and instead would be more "Demanifest". This includes fruit and vegetables, things which are harvested. Their flourishing is when they're still connected to the plant that generates them. In that state, they are most "Manifest", because their life is in its most complete state. When the plant is harvested, their life force is diminished, in that they're no longer connected to the plant which has generated them. In this, the harvested fruit has gone into a more "Demanifest" state. Here, the final destruction of the fruit or grain, liberating the seed, can be taken as representing the end point of Demanifestation, and as being the completion of the death of the being.

The elements can also be thought of as forms of manifestation and demanifestation, the going forth and the withdrawal of the life force, which are also known as life and death, Zoa and Azoa. They are also called by Chumbley Excreation and Increation. Here, we have the fundamental components of the Platonic vision translated into Witchcraft terms. To each of the four elements, we now add the attributes of manifestation and demanifestation, as well as those of increase and decrease.

As we start from the center, the production of the element of Fire is the first movement outwards, of manifestation, of life. Fire, the Sabbat in general, the Divine Mind, goes out to the South. This is followed by the production of the element of the Earth, which is the first movement inwards, of demanifestation and death, which goes to the North. This is followed by the production of the element of

Air, which is a lesser type of movement outwards, called increase, which is the transition between the demanifest and the manifest states, which goes to the East. Finally, there is the production of the element of Water, which is the lesser type of movement inwards, from manifestation to demanifestation, which is decrease, which goes to the West. Air is the medium for fire, Water is the medium for Earth. Air is a mixture of the nature of Fire and Earth, with Fire predominating, while Water is a mixture of Fire and Earth, with Earth predominating. Each of these, in turn, is a fragment of Baphomet, who stands at the center, with Baphomet combining all of these into One.

In this, the four fundamental powers, Manifestation, Demanifestation, Increase, and Decrease, are formed and are associated with each of the four elements, Fire, Earth, Air, and Water. Manifestation and Demanifestation are also Life and Death, Zoa and Azoa, whereas Increase and Decrease are modifications and combinations of these two factors.

> Fire— Manifestation, Life, South
> Earth—Demanifestation, Death, North
> Air—Increase–change from Demanifest to Manifest, East,
> Water—Decrease–change from Manifest to Demanifest, West.

The link between the powers of the three and the four, for the purpose of the Ingress ritual, is the following: The powers of Manifestation, of Life, of Excreation, of the energy going forward, are an echo of the life of the Divine Mind itself, of Abel, or the Goddess. The powers of Demanifestation, of Death, of Increation, of the energy going back to the Sabbat, are an echo of Cain, of the Active Intelligence. For the purpose of the Ingress ritual, the Stone, which generates both of these, is not incorporated into the working. It is incorporated into the Congress working.

The production of Fire is the pure power of Manifestation, and is the same as excreation, the manifestation of Life. This force is the same as the Sabbat in the three, and is associated with the energy of the Goddess, and so the point of the South is consequently female.

Earth, the pure power of Demanifestation is the same as increation, which is the same as Death, the removal of life, which is the same as the God of the Three, Cain, and so the point of the North is male.

Air, in the East, is a combination of Fire and Earth, and is transitional, being the transition between Earth in the North and Fire in the South. It's a combination of the two in which Fire predominates, but it proceeds from the point of Earth. Being the transition point from Earth in the North to Fire in the South, it retains its male character in its power of Increase. Water in the West, a combination of Fire and Earth with Earth predominating, is the transition point between Fire in the South and Earth in the North. Being the transition point from Fire in the South to Earth in the North, it retains its female character in the power of Decrease.

Fire—Manifestation, Life, South, Female
Earth— Demanifestation, Death, North, Male
Air—Increase–change from Demanifest to Manifest, East, Male
Water— Decrease–change from Manifest to Demanifest, West. Female

The Functioning of the World

The transcendental realm exists completely with reference to itself, but the circle does not. Instead, the translation of the four into the circle, and into the process of circle casting, involves the Sabbat, the transcendental realm, in its relationship to the circle. This relationship is similar to that between the Sun and the Earth. The connection between the two, the elements as they manifest within the circle, is the flow of life from the Sabbat, from the First Sun, to the Earth, and the withdrawal of life from the Earth back to the Sabbat, the First Sun. The Sabbat is the source of the energy which manifests in the circle, and its also the place where the energy of the circle departs back to. In this, there are actually two circles that are involved, one standing for the transcendental realm, the other for the earthly realm, although in this case only one circle is marked out and defined in the physical world. In other types of workings, a representation of both circles can be used. The Sun of the Sabbat, in sending down energy into the Earth and into the circle, actualizes the framework that's been established, and sets it into motion.

The circle itself represents a microcosm of the world, the world in miniature, with its times and seasons, its directions and its center. In this, the circle resembles the wheel of the year, and the life that's metaphorically stated to come into the Earth from the Sabbat through the North at the Winter Solstice comes into the circle through its north point, which is also the point of exit of the energy from the circle to the Sabbat. The gate of the north leads through the empty realm of the One, the unmanifest realm, or demanifested realm, the ground of all being, to the Sabbat, which exists within it as a golden sphere. Here, as well, the energy of the Sabbat as the Eternal Sun comes down through the physical sun, which travels throughout the wheel of the year, dispensing its life energy throughout the seasons.

Here, the four movements of Manifestation, Demanifestation, Increase, and Decrease, can be linked to the different seasons, as well as to the different directions. Demanifestation corresponds to Winter, Increase corresponds to Spring, Manifestation corresponds to Summer, and Decrease corresponds to Fall. In this, the Earth represents a receptacle for the energy of the First Sun, mediated through the physical Sun. For the purpose of the Ingress ritual, the Sun is considered to be the source of all life, with the Earth not contributing its own energy. Energy, in this, goes from the First Sun to the Earth, and then it is withdrawn from the Earth, going back to the First Sun.

In the winter, the Earth is dead, deprived of the warmth and life energy of the Sun. At the Solstice, the point of Death or demanifestation, the life energy starts to come back, to come through. The positive life energy overcomes the power of Death in the Spring, in the East, the station signifying Increase, and from there it further increases, reaching its pinnacle in the Summer. The Summer stands for the power of the Manifestation of Life at its fullest. After this, the life energy starts to be withdrawn once more, with the power of Decrease rising. It overcomes the power of life at the Autumnal equinox, the point of the West, and then continues into demanifestation until the energy reaches its lowest point at the Winter Solstice, the point of the North.

In this, in the circle version of the Sabbat, "Demanifestation" is particularly connected to Death. This can be seen in the parallel of the clockwise circle with the harvest season. Here, what is most "Manifest" is not the completed work. Instead, the flourishing of the plant at midsummer is a preface to its being harvested at the equinox. The harvesting of the plant at the Equinox does not add to the "Manifestation" of the plant, but diminishes it, cutting it off from life and instead binding it to the Earth, introducing death into it. Going further, the fruit or grain which is cut and harvested in the West, in order to reproduce, has to be destroyed so that the seed can go forth from it, and land in the ground. This final death is represented by the North, by demanifestation or Death in its purest form. In this, the first half of the circle, from the Winter Solstice to Midsummer, is ruled by Life, while the second half of the circle, from Midsummer to the Winter Solstice, is ruled by Death. Here, the movement of the fruit back to the seed, through harvesting and then destruction, is parallel to the movement of the energy from the earth back to the Sabbat, while the movement of energy from the seed, through growth, to flourishing is parallel to the movement of energy from the Sabbat down to earth. Both come through the gate of Death in the North.

> North, corresponding to Earth, is the pure form of the God, associated with Death, Demanifestation.
>
> South, corresponding to Fire, is the pure form of the Goddess, associated with Life, Manifestation.
>
> East, corresponding to Air, is a mixture of the God and the Goddess, Death proceeding to life, and is Increase and Male.
>
> West, corresponding to Water, is a mixture of the Goddess and the God, is Life proceeding to Death, and is Decrease and Female.
>
> Each of these elements and powers of the directions can be pictured as gods.

Considerations of the circle.

Here, though, we have a key difference between the Tetramorph or elemental arrangement as it exists within the Sabbat and the arrangement as it exists within the circle. Within the circle, the point of Earth in the North is not just a purely passive entity. Instead, it serves a dual purpose as both Earth and the gate to the energies of the Sabbat. In the Divine Mind, the point of Fire is the source of all power, but here, after the circle is formed, the North, the place of Earth, becomes the gate where the divine fire comes down from the Sabbat, from the First Sun, into the Circle. The energy that comes through the gate of the Earth in the North is said to manifest in the point of Fire in the South. This is the life energy of Baphomet/Apollo as well as the creative word of the same, these being identical, with these also being the same as the Schamijam. For the purpose of the Ingress ritual, the Earth itself, before the energy is brought down into it, is thought to be dead, and to be a pure receptacle of the power from the forge of Tubal-Cain

Within practice, as we shall see, there's another variation, this time in the function of the West. The West is the place of Decrease, and in this it's the place of binding, particularly the place of binding spells and entities to earth. There are two possibilities here in practical work: the spirit that's been called forth can either be dismissed and go back to where it's come from, without doing any work for the person, or it can be charged and bound to do specific work on earth. If the latter happens, then the spirit is bound in the west, to the earth and to material things, with this binding likewise being a reduction or decrease from its pure form. Here, the binding can be paralleled to the harvesting of the plant.

Importantly, in the Ingress or invocation ritual, there's only one energy that's being dealt with—the energy of the Sabbat. This energy is non-dual, the Creative Word. The energy generated from the vertical axis of the individual through the inner alchemy of the Word is non-dual, and is the same energy as that of the Sabbat, it is both the life energy and the Schamijam. The energy of the horizontal plane can either be non-dual or dual, depending on the type of rite. The Ingress rite of evocation uses non-dual energy, calling it in and sending it back.

As for the Evil One, he doesn't figure into the wheel of the year, and, instead, is a force outside of the circle which figures as a general antagonist to the work. In opposition to the astrotheists, the Evil One is most emphatically not the north figure of the circle, and is not to be reduced to the passive force of death, or demanifestation. Instead, he exists outside of both of the currents, that leading from the Sabbat to the earth, and from the earth to the Sabbat, and instead features as a general obstructive principle of both. The natural decline of the earth in the winter is not a result of the Evil One. Instead, his work appears in unnatural misfortunes that exist outside of this natural functioning.

The Gods of the Circle and their Correspondences.

There are four sources for these god names: First, the Azoetia, second, Paul Huson's "Mastering Witchcraft", third, Neo-Druidic writings mentioned in the "Pickingill Papers", and finally, the writings and traditions of Robert Cochrane, 1734 and Clan of Tubal Cain.

East: Hu Gadarn, Goe-Magog, Hercules, Lugh, Invocation, Increase, Air, Male, Wand, Lucifer, Phallus, Dawn. Constellation Orion, Gerald Massey's Horus, Third cell of the Azoetia, Watchtower of Air

South: Bride, Habundia, Freya, Rahab Massey's Isis. Manifestation, the work of the rite, Fire, Female, Cup, Hand, Noon, Sirius, the Light Twin. Fifth Cell of the Azoetia, Watchtower of Fire

West: Ariadne, Arianrhod, Goddess of the Silver Wheel, Hekate, Rahab. Binding and Loosing, Decrease, Water, Female, Pentacle, Hesperus, Mouth, Dusk, Constellation Great Bear, Gerald Massey's Nephthys, Seventh Cell of the Azoetia, Watchtower of Water

North: Mahazael, Herne the Hunter, Odin. Demanifestation, breaking, Earth, Male, Knife, Eye, Midnight, Polaris, the Dark Twin. Ninth Cell of the Azoetia. Massey's Set, Watchtower of Earth.

Mahaziel in the north, which Paul Huson labeled Herne the Hunter, would be a manifestation of Morfan in material reality, while Bride, Habundia, in the South would be a manifestation of the Life of Ceridwen, of the Divine Mind, within manifest reality.

Increase and decrease, on the horizons, are also Lucifer and Hesperus, Venus as the morning and evening star, with Lucifer being the light bringer of the dawn in the East, and Hesperus being the bringer of night in the West, corresponding to Arianrhod, Hekate, Ononshu. This is one of the reasons that the god of the East is sometimes referred to as Lucifer-Tubelo in traditional craft. East literally corresponds to Dawn while West corresponds to Dusk.

The Four Gods of the Circle.

These four are externalizations of the one at the center of the circle, of Baphomet.

Hu Gadarn, Goe-Magog, Hercules, Lugh, Tubal-Cain, Massey: Horus

Orion, in this, also corresponds to Gog-Magog, one of the Watchers who was supposed to have inhabited Great Britain before the coming of other humans, whose story is recounted in "The Magitians Discovered" volume 3, and also Semyaza, a Watcher who, repentant, was suspended in the sky permanently instead of sent to hell. As Goemagog, he's celebrated in the City of London in an annual parade. When Chumbley refers to Iuj-Majuj, this is Gog-Magog, with I, J, standing for G. Juj-Majuj is the Islamic reading of Gog-Magog, which appears in the Book of Revelations as a giant in the north. Apeth-Iuj, then, would be Apeth-Gog. T.C. Lethbridge wrote an interesting book called "Gog-Magog" where he collected many legends, which he related to an earthworks made in chalk in the English countryside. This, the Cerne Abbas giant, is represented naked with a large club and a huge erect phallus. This figure can also be corresponded to Hercules, who similarly carried a large club, and was a symbol of masculine power. Here, too, Goe-Magog as Hercules can be corresponded to the constellation Orion. Though it's an outside possibility, Chumbley's use of Greek names and words in the

Azoetia makes it possible that the "Apeth" in "Apeth-Iuj" is really Arete-Juj, "Arete" that is to say "Virtue" in Greek, with a number of different shades of meaning attached to it, such as glory and fame, as well as goodness.

In all of this, Gog-Magog, represents the god in his Life aspect, which captures quite a lot of the principles of Baphomet within him. Remember, the four gods are aspects of Baphomet, the central androgyne, that have been broken up and split into the four directions. In fact, the clearest parts of the Azoetia about Baphomet, which are contained in the fourth cell, deal with the different stars of Orion. Lugh as well, with a connection to Lucifer as Light Bringer, the Venus of the dawn, of increase, the victory of light over darkness. Here, Lugh is the god of the rising sun.

A parallel figure is the Irish Lugh, and the Welsh character of the Mabinogion known as Lleu Llaw Gyffes, with this being connected to Lucifer as the lightbringer in later practice, though this is not linguistically correct. Arianrhod, who we shall meet, is an antagonist of Lleu Llaw Gyffes in his youth, with Lleu overcoming her power with the help of the sorcerer Gwydion, before coming into his own as a powerful warrior and magician. In this, no association should be made between this Gwydion and the god of the north. The figure of Lleu, as well as Hercules and Orion, points to the martial, sacred king or warrior aspect of this figure, with a parallel to the anachronistic figure of King Arthur.

The figure of Hu Gadarn is ahistorical, but is the product of the Neo-Druidic revival of the 19th century, and subsequent traditions based on it. It originally comes from one of the historical fabrications of Iolo Morganwg as a god of the sun, and so subsequently as one connected to agriculture and to growth. From there, Faber included it in his "Origins of Pagan Idolatry".

Tubal Cain is used in various craft traditions to mean Baphomet himself, the Demiurge, the world creator, and to signify the power of the East. This is because the eastern power is the more creative aspect of the Demiurge, the power of increase, as opposed to the power of destruction. By shaping the world, Death becomes Tubal-Cain, the shaper of the world.

He is also the Tetramorph aspect of positive masculinity. As such, the breakthrough of the light that he's associated with also contains the millions of forms of being of the Sabbat within it. In the Azoetia and other Sabbatic writings, he's associated with the different animals that make up the Tetramorph and Baphomet. He's also labeled the Red Man there, a term that may be derived from Gerald Massey's work.

Bride, Habundia, Freya, Rahab, Massey: Isis

Bride, Hadbundia, this is the goddess of the South and of Manifestation. She corresponds to the pure going forth of life from the Sabbat into the earth, and reflects the corresponding growth of life that's generated from that. She corresponds to the cup, which is filled with life, and in her male aspect is the Green Man as an embodiment of life. In the male aspect, this force can be related to the Green Man as a going forth of life itself into the world. This can be linked to the earth, though strictly speaking it doesn't need to be. The Celtic Bride, in various Neo-Druidic thought, has a similar role, and is associated with the hearth fire of life, in this being similar to the Roman Vesta. The vestal hearth fire is the manifestation of the life force on earth, within the household.

Habundia is a goddess of love and fertility who is described in Paul Huson's "Mastering Witchcraft", whose ultimate origin is in the medieval poem "The Romance of the Rose". There, she appears as Dame Habundia, who is described as leading souls out of their bodies three times a week to the Sabbat. This is a version of the story of Diana or Herodias, but the name "Habundia" is an Old French variant of Abundance, and therefore connotes the aspect of fertility and plenty as well. This is important because it suggests that she's not a psychopomp in the form of death, but is instead linked with life and fertility in her nocturnal journeys. The passages that she appears in, in "The Romance of the Rose" are contained within a greater treatment of dreams, with the author considering the leaving of souls to be with Dame Habundia as an example of dreams as opposed to reality. Bride could also be interpreted as the southern goddess, Bride or Bridget, who is the force of fertility coming down from the Sabbat to earth. Corresponds to Sirius as the star symbolizing manifestation.

Freya here is the Norse name of a pan-Germanic goddess of fertility whose name is the origin of the modern German word "Frau", "Lady", through "Frouwa".

Rahab appears in the Dragon Book but not the Azoetia. There, she's "Maheleth-Rahab", which is better spelled as Mahalath-Rahab. These are two different people, Mahalath and Rahab. Rahab was a prostitute in Jericho who did virtuous actions. In the run up to the conquest of the Holy Land by the Hebrews, Joshua sent spies to Jericho to report on the city. She appears in the "Book of Joshua" book 2, verses 2-22. Rahab ran an inn, and the spies stayed there. While they were staying there, the authorities of Jericho, searching for the spies, came and asked her where they were. She hid them, and told the authorities that they'd already left. After this, she says to the spies that the victory of the Hebrew god over Canaan is certain, and that's why she hid them. In return, she asks them to spare her when they take Jericho, which they agree to. Here, the relevant part is that she's a prostitute, and so becomes a goddess of fertility and the manifestation of life.

Mahalath, besides being a wife of Esau, is one of the "mothers of demons", who mated with a demon in the desert and gave birth to semi-demonic offspring. Both of these figures also appear, along with other female names used in the Dragon Book, in the Zohar, where they're transformed into evil demon goddesses. The Zohar tradition is the likely source.

Massey associates Isis with the star Sirius, and from there with fertility through the rising of Sirius with the sun in the summer months corresponding to the flooding of the Nile. The rising of Orion in the East, in a sense, leads or points to the rising of Sirius in the South, when the powers of Increase reach their fullest form in the manifestation of life.

Arianrhod, Hekate, Ononshu, Massey: Nephthys

When referring to astral lore, Arianrhod/Hekate, the power of Decrease, is linked to the Big dipper, with Life, while Hu Gadarn, the power of Increase, is linked to the constellation of Orion. Arianrhod is the power in the West, while Hu Gadarn is the power in the East. Now, the Big Dipper is in the North, and the constellation of Orion is in the South. The power of Decrease leads to demanifestation, and to egress out of the circle, which happens through the northern portal, while the power of Increase, of invocation, leads to the manifestation of Life and Ingress of forces into the circle at the southern point. The constellations represent the two pillars, of Increase and Decrease, but in a way that's removed from the literal correspondence of them to East and West.

The Big Dipper is also identified with "Caer Arianrhod", which is a place of testing and initiatory trials. In this, "Caer Arianrhod" is not the Sabbat itself, but a place to go through in order to get to the Sabbat, which is beyond the stars. The Sabbat itself can be pictured as Ceridwen's "Caer Sidi", he Castle of the Four Winds if Celtic imagery is to be used, because this implies that it's the place of the Cauldron, which is another name for the Sabbat, the Divine Mind, the Eternal Sun. The constellation of Corona Borealis can also be linked with Caer Arianrhod, with similar caveats.

Ariahnrod, the goddess who leads the path of testing that leads to the Sabbat, is identified with Ariadne as the goddess who leads the thread to the center of the maze, the center of the labyrinth, which is the Sabbat itself. Here, the foursquare city lies at the center of the Labyrinth. Alternately, the journey to the center of the Labyrinth is a journey to the center of the self, where the Minotaur of the lower self is slain, this being similar to the seizing of the Toadstone. The Minotaur is half animal, half human, with the animal being his upper half. This is the default, disordered, nature of man. By slaying him, the initiate rises as a Centaur, with the man on top, and the animal on the bottom. This is similar to the position of a rider on his horse, with the horse obeying him. The Castle of Arianrhod is in the North, the place testing, and going there leads to the Sabbat itself. The Celtic Arianrhod is also associated with testing, in that in the Mabinogion she curses her son, Lleu, three times, with her brother intervening each time to counteract the curse. More info about the labyrinth in relation to this can be found in the section on Gerald Massey.Arianrhod is the goddess of the West.

Arianrhod in the "Hanes Taliesin" is linked to the underworld, and to imprisoning people there. Her epithet "Of the Silver Wheel", connects her to Fate and to the spinning of fates, in the same way in which Hekate is linked to them.

The power of Decrease is linked both to the power of binding and loosing. Decrease can be seen as loosing bounds, and what's been loosed can be bound again, and vice versa. Instead of taking what's been invoked and sending it back, you can bind what's been invoked to the material plane, so that it will continue to exist there in a spirit form, doing its work.

Here, we have the other aspect of Hekate/Arianrhod—she can bind spirit to matter, or spirit to the material plane. Within Greek pagan theology, Hekate was in charge of the World Soul, among other things, and the Daemons that were under her control played a role in binding souls down to new bodies. Similarly, here, Hekate/Arianrhod as goddess of the west can bind and complete the work which has been done, fixing it and making it real.

In this, she's also a spinner of fate, which also intersects with the golden thread of Ariadne, a thread spun from a spinning wheel. This is similarly related to the three fates in Greco-Roman thought, who, with thread, measure the life of a person, and cut the thread to signify the length of the life.

Death, Mahaziel, Odin, Herne the Hunter, Gwynn Ap Nudd, Massey: Gwydion, Set Anubis Thoth

Death, if he's represented within the circle is at the north. There, he serves as a guard towards that which is beyond the circle, to the Sabbat itself. Using Chumbley's notion of the "Opposer", Death, in this, is both guardian of the Sabbat and the person who summons the individual to the Sabbat. Opposition can mean many things, such as guarding the Sabbat with a sword and opposing access, protecting it. In this, Death as opposer resembles Saint Michael the Archangel, as well as the Cherub with the flaming sword protecting the Garden of Eden, Paradise. Mithra, the Zoroastrian deity who became a Roman god, agrees with this notion of the Opposer as well.

Death, in this, is also directly derived from the Biblical angel of death, Azrael. The angel of death appears several times in the Bible, but most directly in Exodus. There, God, in liberating the Hebrew people from slavery in Egypt, sends the angel of death down to claim the first born sons of everyone in the country. The Hebrews are instructed to place a mark on their doors so that the angel of death will pass over them, and not take their children. This passing over gives its name to the yearly commemoration of the liberation of the Hebrews in Judaism. The story would also be familiar to Christian audiences, and this story most likely combined with already existing pagan ideas about death and beings associated with it. Notably, the angel of death is not an evil being. It is not satanic, but instead serves God, and so has a more ambiguous status, despite the character of its function.

Death, as Opposer, has another meaning as well, which is as the guide that accompanies the dead to the other realm. Death, as an embodied figure, both does the actual removal of the soul, and guides that soul to where it needs to go. The other realm, in this, includes both the Sabbat and other, lesser, places that the dead can go. The Sabbat, known as the "Rest of the Saints" in medieval Christianity, is the place where the honored dead live, where those who have either lead an exemplary life or have succeeded in mystical practices of divine union during life find themselves. Because of this, Death, the embodied Grim Reaper like entity, the Opposer pictured as Charon, is the one who takes you across the river, and so is the proper person to guide you and take you to the Sabbat. Death in this is identified by Paul Huson with Mercury, the conductor, psychopomp, and guide. Huson also identifies him with Herne the Hunter, who is both a psychopomp and a guardian spirit. Death in this, is a guide and an emmisary of the Sabbat, and can serve as a general spiritual guide to teach you about the Craft, and lead you to the Sabbat and its understanding.

Herne the Hunter is documented in Shakespeare's "The Merry Wives of Windsor", where it's said of him that he's a ghost of a game keeper who haunts Windsor forest, who wears horns on his head, and who curses cattle. Variant versions of the "Merry Wives" show his name as "Horne", which has several added significances. In Shakespeare's english, it's possible that the "e" would be pronounced, making the name "Horny" and "Horny the Hunter". This would associate him with "Old Horny" as a name for the devil, as well as with death as a ghost and guardian spirit. This read also makes sense in the context of the play. There, the character Falstaff, who is pursuing a married woman, is instructed to meet her at Herne's oak wearing the horns of Herne the Hunter.

Shakespeare is making a double entendre in this, in that not only is Falstaff literally "horny" for someone, but wearing the horns is an expression for being a cuckold, someone whose wife has cheated on them. Falstaff, in this, who's trying to cuckold another man, is made to wear the horns himself, which is a sign of humiliation, and is further humiliated by a group of people once he gets to the tree.

Odin is another concept of the Opposer, which links him with the leader of the Wild Hunt. The Wild Hunt was a procession of the dead, and the dead, in this case, can either go to the underworld, or to the Sabbat of the ages. Therefore, the germanic Odin can also lead the way to the Sabbat, and can take his place in the north of the circle. Also, in Welsh tradition, he's associated with Gwyneth Ap Nudd as the leader of the Wild Hunt. Here, the Wild Hunt itself is composed of the Cwn Annwn, or "Hounds of Hell".

As a psychopomp, the Opposer, Death, can go backwards and forwards to the Sabbat from the Earth, and serves as the bearer of the energy of the Sabbat to the Earth. In this, he serves as a gateway for the energies of the Sabbat, which enter the circle in the North and go to the South. In this form, he's most closely associated in recent literature with Mahaziel.

Mahaziel, transliterated as Machasael elsewhere. is the angel who in legend had sex with Ham's wife, conceiving Sihon, a giant, and who therefore brought the Luciferian spark of fire back into the human bloodline. Mahaziel, in this, is literally the being who brought the fire of the Sabbat into the human realm, and through this can bring the fire of the Sabbat into the elemental realm in the context of the circle. Therefore, Mahaziel, serves as a gate which you can literally go through to either reach the Sabbat or to call energy from the Sabbat down to earth.

Mahaziel is the vehicle and bearer of the Creative Word, but is not the Word itself. The Creative Word, in this, appears to be a combination of the ideas of the Holy Spirit and of the Christian Word as Jesus, which have been collapsed into one entity and depersonalized. It is the Word of Baphomet. Mahaziel is a psychopomp, transporting both people and energy, and is a gateway in that sense. In addition to this, as the bearer of the Creative Word to the circle, and as the gateway to the circle, Mahaziel is the bearer of the life energy generated from Baphomet/Apollo, which is identical with the creative word, with Baphomet/Apollo being syncretized with Jesus in this. The Creative Word of which he is the bearer is also the Schamijam. He also corresponds to the Pole Star, standing in the symbolic and spiritual north as the gateway to the Sabbat.

Here, in the figure of Mahaziel, you have a more authentic notion of Death as the Devil of the Sabbat. Again, here, I believe that Death was chosen as a reverse mask. Jesus is life, and so if the Bible lied about who exactly is who, perhaps Death is the true savior. The role that Mahaziel plays is like that of Jesus, facilitating the Word, and, in this, he can also be identified with Lucifer as a light bringer, as he who brings the creative word from the Sabbat to earth. In this, the Devil of the circle, the leader of the circle, stands in a role similar to that of Jesus in the rites, just as a priest does while conducting the Mass, in this case serving as Lucifer, the conductor of light, the psychopomp who brings the light from the Sabbat to earth as well as souls from earth to the Sabbat. This is the inner meaning behind the Devil as the leader of the circle.

This story of Mahaziel goes back to a 4th century Christian writer Sulpicius Severus, and was resurrected during the Renaissance, appearing, in, among other places, the writings of one Thomas Bång or Bangius. A Danish Orientalist, Bång wrote "Coelum Orientis et Prisci Mundi", which was published in 1657. The purpose of this work was to refute ideas about an Adamic or Antediluvian language. However, in the process of doing so, Bång compiled and translated almost any source he could get his hands on concerning the Watchers, including both Severus and large sections of the Ethiopic version of

Enoch itself. Through this, he inadvertently made this knowledge available to a learned audience who may have had other motives for pursuing it.

He is the Caduceator, the figure of Mercury, carrying the Caduceus, who the leader of the mysteries in Greece imitated and embodied in sacred processions. As bearer of the Caduceus or rod, he can be thought to direct power to the circle, and, in the syncretism with Mercury or Hermes as psychopomp, can direct both souls to the Sabbat and energy from the Sabbat to the earth.

As the two way gate, though he's identified with demanifestation, he also brings the seed of life at the winter solstice in the North which will break through in the spring in the East.

He also corresponds to the Pole Star. In this, the Pole Star is the gate to the Sabbat, and its this star to which the constellation of the Great Bear in the West points.

These are the seven gods, with Baphomet being the eighth god, who exists at the intersection of the vertical and horizontal axes at the center of the circle.

The Four as Found in Paul Huson's work

The four gods, plus the Sabbat and the Earth, that have been described are parallel to those described in Paul Huson's "Mastering Witchcraft".

> The god of the north, the leader of the Wild Hunt, Odin, Opposer, is Herne the Hunter, linked to Mercury by Huson and described in the chapter on divination.
>
> The god of the East, Hu Gadarn, is described by Huson as Cernunnos, which is a term that's used to describe two different gods. The Cernunos that's described in the chapter on "Vengeance and Attack", the martial Cernunnos, is the god of the East. The god of the East also has erotic aspects to him in Huson's account, which is the other god form, that is properly related to the center as Baphomet.
>
> The goddess of the South is Habondia, talked about in Huson's chapter on Love Magic.

The goddess of the West, Arianrhod/Hekate, is linked by Huson to the Saturnian character of the earth goddess Hertha, and to the dark power of Habondia, known as Noctiluca. She is described in vivid detail in the chapter on "Vengeance and Attack", where her death like aspect is emphasized.

However, besides these four there are two other gods described: Cernnunos as the Horned God of the Eternal Sun, the Sabbat, who is Baphomet, and described as pure eros by Huson, and Hertha, the goddess of the Earth. Hertha is derived from Tacitus' "Germania". In the rites that Huson describes for coven work, the fire of the First Sun, that of the Sabbat of the Ages, is drawn down into the earth through the ritual of the lighting of the Bale Fire, with a person who stands for Cernunnos lighting the candle and starting the fire with the coven's cooperation.

Additionally, these four can be related to Huson's four sides of the "Witch's Pyramid". These would be Imagination in the East, Will in the South, Faith in the West, and Silence in the North.

Part 2, Elaborations

Tools of the Circle:

The attributions of the tools here may surprise people. Fundamentally, however, they're not elemental tools in the conventional understanding of the term so much as tools connected to the particular god form and phase of manifestation and demanifestation in the cycle of the year. The correspondences are derived from the particular way the elements are derived, with the fundamental duality being fire and earth, with air and water being means between these that facilitate the change and transformation from one to the other. These attributions also differ from those given in the Azoetia.

Weapons of the Four

North—Opposer, Athame, Death.
East—Hu Gadarn, Wand, Invocation.

South—Goddess of Life, Grail or cup holding the wine of the Sabbat, Bride Habundia.

West—Arionrhod, Hekate, Pantacle, Binding. Alternately, knotted cord

Center of the Four, Baphomet and the Vertical Axis,

Weapons of the Three, of the Vertical Axis:

Lower — Altar stone
Middle — Fire on the altar, cauldron, skull, rose
Upper —Stang

The Athame corresponds to the God, to the North, and to the Eye, while the Cup corresponds to the Goddess, to the South and to the Hand. The cup contains the wine of the Sabbat, which is a representation of the First Sun, in the form of Spirit, which corresponds to Essence. The cup holds the Essence, the Azoth, which the Divine Mind is made out of. The Eye and the Hand conjoined, the Athame and the Cup, make the Pen and its Ink. The Pen is a version of a knife, and the ink it uses is the blood of the Sabbat, and the writing of the Pen, in sigils and symbols, is a re-presentation of the Forms that the Sabbat contains in a pictorial way, with the Ink used to represent them being the Essence of the Sabbat itself.

The union of the knife and the grail, in this, is the shaping of the all potential that the Sabbat of the Ages contains into a concrete, manifest, reality. It's also a representation of the Hieros Gamos that creates the Tetramorph, these being the same thing. The body itself is also a vessel for the Azoth, and is like the Cup and the Hand on another scale.

The wand is for raising general magical energies and directing them. Its power and form is like that of the Phallus.

The Pantacle is a diagram of the macrocosm, of the planetary and elemental energies, inscribed on a disc, which might be wood, stone, metal. It can be painted, but should be carved into it. The inscribing of the image of the macrocosm on the disc is a type of binding, symbolically binding the pattern of the universe itself, of the First Sun, into matter. This can also be represented by a knotted cord. In this, the knots in the cord stand for the stations of the horizontal and vertical axes, so, depending on on what you're doing, this would either be five fold and three or ninefold and three. The extra knot there is to indicate that the place you're starting in is also the place you're ending in, which will be discussed below in relation to the phallus, eye, hand, mouth.

A cord can also be used to indicate the circle as a whole, forming the outer boundary of this. In both cases, the cord represents a literal binding.

With regards to the use of a cord as a boundary of the circle, the cord becomes a binding force similar to the binding of the material of the First Sun into the four directions done by the Demiurge. Here, that same kind of binding unites the power of the Sabbat to earth. In this, the cord no longer corresponds to the West, but has a much broader significance. Here, the duality of Tetramorph, or bound power of the Sabbat, is balanced by the Demiurgic force of the Knife or Athame. In this, the Athame is, likewise, not simply the North, but is considered to be the action of the magician at the center in general in casting the circle, and binding the four quarters in a way which lines up with the cord.

Center, Altar, Cube or double cube, indicative of the Moonstone from which the Sabbat comes, the Foundation stone. Cauldron, or Fire, a Bale Fire in the center of the circle, on top a buried stone, symbol of First Sun, the Sabbat. A brass vessel with hot coals inside can serve as a fire on top of a cubical altar. If you're actually using the Cauldron to cook something, as opposed to another use, the stone should be buried under the ground on top of which you place the fuel for the fire that cooks the cauldron. Stang, at the center, with the forked branches indicative of the Demiurge on the vertical axis, next to and above the cauldron or Fire. The forked stang indicates division, as well as creation. The Stang itself, with the bottom "Shod" or encased in metal, can stand for all three of the centers on the vertical axis: the "Shod" part standing for the stone, the middle part standing for the Sabbat, and the divided part standing for the Active intelligence or Demiurge. All three of the pieces of the vertical axis combined create Baphomet seated upon the stone.

Interestingly, there is a parallel with the Stang in the "Coven of Atho" tradition of Charles Cardell. In this, they use the "Trident Position", where the priest assumes the position of the arms outstretched and then bent in at 90 degrees, so that the two arms are raised up with the head in between. These three make the Trident. This was used to project power. The Trident, here, is said to be the weapon of Atlas, the king of Atlantis, which, taken out of cipher, means Baphomet as the king of the Sabbat, in his manifest form. Atho himself is related by Melissa Seims to "Athor", a corrupted Egyptian name used in Hargrave Jennings' "Rosicrucians, their Rites and Mysteries", to refer to the king of queen force of the concentrated energy of the world of the gods, in other words, to refer to Baphomet once more as the king of the First Sun. There may be a connection here with what's asserted in the Pickingill letters, which is that some of Hargrave Jennings' ideas either a) originated from witches or b) influenced witches, which will be discussed more in volume 2 of this work. Atho, here, would be the same figure as Atlas. Importantly, though, in the Coven of Atho material, Atho is male, not hermaphroditic. Additionally, though, the "Head of Atho" played a very prominent role in their work. This was a horned head that had all of the core symbols of the group painted or inscribed on it. This head brings to mind the heads of Baphomet that the Templars were thought to venerate.

Instead of a cauldron, a skull can be used, and this on top of the stone can represent Baphomet as well. For instance, the Azoetia contains two rituals that are centered around a skull, which should be placed on top of the cubical stone of the altar, in the center of the circle. In this, the skull itself is the container for the First Sun, the Sabbat of the Ages. It's identical to the cauldron in this. It's identified with Baphomet because there are accounts of the Templars using oracular heads as centers of worship. Baphomet, as the Tetramorph, would technically be at the center of the skull, rather than the whole skull itself. Here, too, the figure of the skull and cross bones can be explained as the cup of the Sabbat on top of a representation of the four directions. The Skull on top of the double cubical altar is the same as the Rose on the double cubical stone in Freemasonry. A rose can be used, on top of the altar, with the rose being a feminine representation of the First Sun, which, in its many petals, represents both the ideals in the First Sun and is also suggestive of the female organs of generation.

The cubical stone in this is the Baetyla, the biblical standing stone that is the focus of some of the worship in the Bible, and within the craft stands for the foundation stone generated from the One, the great Dragon Lord, from which the Sabbat itself, the Eternal Sun, is generated. The Baetyla, in turn, the Double Cubical altar, with the skull on top of it, can also be identified with the Xoanon, the stone carving of a protector spirit which was present in many Greek cities. The Xoanon was thought to have fallen to earth, and here, the stone can be thought of as the angelic soul, or the Toadstone, inherent in those with witch blood, which, fallen from heaven through the angelic rebellion, can be lifted up by the person who possesses it to the keystone of heaven once more.

The Athame is the fundamental tool of the circle casting, and the purely mental form of Ingress can be performed using it alone, or even without any tools. In this, the individual would just use their will and their hands and arms to do the various gestures.

Zodiac Arrangements and Time.

Doing my own research, I've come to the conclusion that the Zodiac was originally oriented around ancient Draconic and other mystery religions, but that this has not only been lost but obscured. The obscuration comes from not pegging the start of the year to a star, as they do in Indian Sidereal astrology. The original Zodiac, in my opinion, was exactly the same in the order of the signs as the current Zodiac, but its rising sign for the Vernal equinox was different. We have Aries, but I believe that when the Zodiac was first established, it was Taurus, the Bull, which was the ruler of the Vernal Equinox. With this in place, Scorpio would be the ruler of the Autumnal Equinox. The Scorpion, in this, is an alternate symbol of the Snake or Dragon. Here, in the Age of Taurus, you have the mysteries of the Bull and the Dragon, which are the ruler of the

Eternal Sun itself and the One, the great Dragon Lord. The Bull, in this, is the power of increase, while the Snake or Dragon is the power of decrease in more general terms.

Following through this shifting of the circle, you find that the Winter Solstice in the North, you have Capricorn and Aquarius, male and female Saturn, standing guard at the point of demanifestation.

At the South point of the circle, corresponding to the summer Solstice, you have Leo and Cancer, the manifest powers of the Sun and Moon. To me, it makes quite a lot of sense that the Solstice's were originally supposed to be, on the one hand, between the power of the Sun and Moon, and, on the other between the two signs of Saturn, rather than how they're arranged currently, where the Summer Solstice is between Gemini and Cancer, and the Winter Solstice is between Sagittarius and Capricorn.

However, these two later arrangements have their own symbolism, including within the craft, in that the gate of Gemini is significant as a portal back to the Sabbat, and is linked to the rising of Orion.

Speaking in general about the Solsticial points, the classical world recognized the North point as the gate of Horn, where souls can go back outside of the circle to the spirit world, with the South point signifying the Ivory gate of life, the gate of souls coming down into manifest reality. This schema was broadened by later writers to mean that the gate of Ivory was the point of life energy coming down into the world in its fullest form, while the gate of Horn was the point of life energy most fully going back up from the world to the Sabbat.

With regards to this alternate Zodiac arrangement, it would also imply that, in the original Zodiac, Taurus was identified with the 1st house, Gemini was identified with the 2nd House, and so on.

There are many things that could be observed about this arrangement, but let's just note that both of the Equinoxes are governed by signs relating to Mars and Venus: The Vernal equinox here is the transition between Aries and Taurus, with Venus following Mars, while the Autumnal equinox is the transition between Libra and Scorpio, with Mars following Venus. One is associated with increase, the other decrease, and here Venus can be associated generally with increase and Mars with decrease.

The time when the procession of the Equinox would have been on the Age of Taurus corresponds with the rise of the megalithic civilizations of Europe, as well as with monuments associated with previous Draconic civilizations elsewhere in the world.

With regards to time of days, there's what could be called the natural arrangement of night and day, which everything else is derived from. On one of the equinoxes, on the equator, night and day being completely equal, we have the following: Sunrise is at 6 AM, Midday is at 12:00PM, Sunset is at 6:00 PM, and Midnight is at 12:00PM. Similarly, for the cross quarter times, in this natural arrangement, they would be 9:00 AM, 3:00 PM, 9:00PM, and 3:00 AM. For all other times, and all other places, the actual times of day for these varies. Exact timing is not required, and often not practical, but, for those interested in extra precision, to do a ritual at true midnight, you should look up your local sunrise and sunset times and do the ritual at the exact middle between them, which will be true midnight.

Similarly, if you are doing things on the cross quarter days, it's important to realize that astrologically they're precisely one and a half signs, or 45 degrees (30 + 15) after the closest solstice or equinox.

Also, it's helpful to know that the Moon roughly runs through three signs of the Zodiac each week.

Celebrations

Though the cross quarters have been given much importance, I believe that the celebrations at the cardinal points of the compass are important as well. With this, the north, and the northern Solstice, is the celebration of the time of death, which has the point of life within it. This is the void that has within it the Pole Star, which is the point of light in the darkness from which life will come back down to earth from the Sabbat. The Spring Equinox is the celebration of increase, of life bursting out from the ground into life. The Summer Solstice is the peak of life and manifestation. The Fall Equinox is the beginning of the time of decrease and death, and is the harvest, the harvest of life itself, as the final quarter of the year starts. The celebrations of the different points of the year can provide a fixed goal for the coming together of the covine of the Quadriga in sexual unity.

Planets and the Compass

Though the directions of the compass are not fundamentally planetary, there have been some attempts to correspond the directions with the planets. The most major one is that given in the "Sworn Book of Honorius". This diagram is reproduced in "Magitians Discovered, vol. 2".

North is Saturn, ♄
Northeast is vacant, or fixed stars
East is the Sun ☉
Southeast is Jupiter, ♃
South is Mars, ♂
Southwest is Venus ♀
West is the Moon ☽
Northwest is Mercury ☿

While this doesn't come from a traditional witch source, I feel that if you switch the Sun and Mars, it can be a functional description of the compass.

North is Saturn ♄
Northeast is vacant, or fixed stars
East is the Mars ♂
Southeast is Jupiter ♃
South is Sun ☉
Southwest is Venus ♀
West is the Moon ☽
Northwest is Mercury ☿

Another arrangement, this time using the three and the four, is to see the axis of the three as consisting of this:

Lower— Moon ☽

Middle — Sun ☉
Upper— Saturn ♄

The axis of the four, then, would correspond to

North—Mercury ☿
East—Mars ♂
South—Jupiter ♃
West—Venus ♀

Though this is speculation, and I have no proof that these are the real correspondences that he uses, it may be profitable to investigate whether this particular planetary arrangement is compatible with the Cantrefs described by David Conway, with the Cantrefs of these directions potentially serving as substitutes for the Sephiroth. The planetary correspondences of the Sephiroth are particularly important in his work "Magic: an Occult Primer".

The Heavenly City and the Circle.

A common way of casting the circle in traditional witchcraft is by castle, which means opening a castle in the East, South, West, and North. Though in some traditions, like that of 1734, these are attributed to castles from Welsh and Celtic mythology, I believe that the practice precedes the revival of Welsh mythology. Instead, I believe that the opening from Castle ultimately derives from a practice where the Heavenly Jerusalem of the Book of Revelations is used as a model for the circle, and brought down to earth. As we've discussed, the Heavenly City is another cipher for the Sabbat of the Ages, the Divine Mind, the Eternal Sun. Here, the four directions are the four quadrants of the city, and by casting each of them, you're bringing that quadrant of the city down to earth. This is the ultimate source of the "Opening by Watchtower" in the Gardnerian tradition. The idea of "Watchtowers" prompts the question of where are they and what do they watch? A castle can have four watchtowers, one for each direction, which protect the space within. The four watchtowers correspond to the four elements of the Tetramorph, the Living Being, while the fifth in the center corresponds to the Active Intelligence, the Demiurge.

This concept of the foursquare Heavenly City is, I believe, the source of John Dee's work with the four elemental tablets and the four watchtowers. I believe that his grand tablet, with the "Tablet of Union" at the center, is a representation of the Heavenly Jerusalem, and that he took this idea from the popular ideas about the Heavenly City that were circulating during his time. Work with each of the quadrants, with their Seniors and other figures, would then be work with that part of the Sabbat or the Heavenly Jerusalem.

Putting it in the context of traditional witchcraft, the four sectors of the city correspond to the four directions, and to the four winds, with each of the quadrants of the city having three gates each, making a total of twelve, also corresponding to the signs of the Zodiac. This plan is also the origin of the "Paradise Garden", which is based on similar divisions. The middle of the garden, the "Devil's plot" or no man's land, in this, is the center of the Heavenly City, which is where Jesus, or Baphomet in this case, dwells and oversees the rest. The circle, when casting it in this way, becomes a mandala. This pattern of the circle as the Heavenly Jerusalem is particularly associated with East Anglian traditions of witchcraft, and is also the organizing principle behind Daniel Schulke's work "Viridarium Umbris".

This version of the Heavenly Temple can also be combined with the idea of the cosmic axis, this being represented by the Three. The depths can be represented by the Stone, the middle part by the First Sun itself, and the Heights by the Active Intelligence, by Cain. Here, the generation, of the Tetramorph by the active intelligence is simultaneously the generation of the horizontal axis, the generation of the Temple or City itself.

The process of casting the circle, starting with the three and then extending to the four, thereby recapitulates this process of creation once again.

What we're doing when we cast the circle, in the way described, is creating a Yantra or Mandala in real life, a Temple with deities within it emanating from a central point, with the construction of the vertical axis taking place before the emanation of the Temple from it.

Alternate Reading of the Four

There's another way to analyze the procession of the four as well. This one derives the four points of the circle from the upwards and downwards motion of creation in the vertical axis. The south derives from the Stone, and corresponds to the Goddess, and to life. The north corresponds to Cain, and corresponds to Death. The East corresponds to Tubal-Cain, and represents Cain shaping the energy of the Sabbat with his knife. The West corresponds to the Goddess Hekate, and represents the binding of the completed Tetramorph back to the stone of creation from which all emanated.

Going into more detail, here, we're looking at the North-South axis and the East-West axis. The North-South axis is parallel to the upwards motion up the vertical column. It expresses manifestation, is linked to Life and to the Goddess of the stone, while the East-West Axis is linked to the downwards motionm expresses demanifestation and Death, and is linked to the God of the head, Cain, the Demiurge.

This attribution is based on the following readings of the vertical axis: it expresses the three parts of the sigil, which are the beginning, which stands for manifestation, the center, which is a combination of manifestation and demanifestation, and the end, which stands for demanifestation. Here, the lower center, that of the Stone, stands for manifestation, while the top center, that of the head, stands for demanifestation, with the Heart center being a combination of the two. The motion of the Vertical axis is from the bottom up, from the Stone upwards, in a process of manifestation.

However, it's also possible to invert the sigil. In the inverted reading of the sigil, manifestation would be at the head, a combination of manifestation and demanifestation would be at the heart, and demanifestation would be at the bottom. The direction here goes from the Head downwards, and is a process of demanifestation rather than manifestation.

The upright sigil of the vertical axis is feminine, while the inverted axis is masculine. In the feminine sigil, the lower center, corresponding to desire and to manifestation, corresponds to the womb, which generates, while the head is relatively impoverished. In the male, inverted, manifestation of the sigil, the head is empowered, while the lower center, corresponding to the sex, is impoverished.

Within the four, the North-South axis is the feminine sigil, while the East-West axis is the masculine, inverted, sigil. Since it's inverted, the Head of the sigil, so to speak, which is Hu Gadarn, Tubal-Cain, is associated with manifestation, while the bottom of the sigil, associated with Arianrhod/Hekate/Onoshu, is associated with demanifestation. The East-West axis is equated with the horizon, the rising and setting of the sun, while the North-South axis is equated with the Midnight and Noonday manifestations of the Sun.

The intersection of these two types of sigils, in the common center, is the place of the union of male and female, and of manifestation and demanifestation in two separate forms: Manifestation/Demanifestation and Demanifestation/Manifestation. These two forms have four terms as a whole, which correspond to the four directions of the circle. Putting all four of these together both formulates the double Hermaphrodite, Baphomet, and unites the male sigil with the female sigil to generate completeness in the Congress ritual. Baphomet as the Double Hermaphrodite is as follows: the top and bottom halves of the Baphomet figure are the North-South axis, while the upwards and downwards pointing fingers and hands are the East-West axis. Both of these individual axes are made up of male and female, positive and negative components, so the unity of all four is that of a Double Hermaphrodite which is unified with itself to create one entity.

Second Alternate Reading of the Four

Another way of reading the four is this: relating the circle as a whole to the downwards movement on the vertical axis as whole. Here, the upwards movement on the transcendental vertical axis does not correspond to the points of the circle at all.

First, power travels up the vertical axis, from the stone to the Sabbat, to the the active intelligence. Second, power travels down the vertical axis, and, in this, the travel down the vertical axis is also the travel clockwise around the circle. Here, from the point of Cain or the active Intelligence in the North, the point of death, the power travels down to the Sabbat itself, penetrating it, being Tubal Cain in the East. Next, the power of the Tetramorph itself is created, this being the actual work of the Demiurge, in the South. Following this, the power of the Tetramorph is bound to the Stone in the West, and then what is bound to the Stone is killed in the north. The conclusion of this is that what is killed in the north manifests in the center.

This could also be illustrated by the following: Cain, Death, in the North pierces the Sabbat in the East, then the working of the magic happens in the South, before its bound to the power to the Earth in the West. Following this, what has been made is cut from its source, and sacrificed in the North, which leads to it completely manifesting in the world.

The Hand and the Eye, Mouth and Phallus.

These are referred to by Chumbley as the "Witches' Tetragrammaton", and I would like to remind the reader that the Tetragrammaton is the fourfold name of God, which indicates that when these four are combined in the right way, the essence of God, signified by the name, is invoked. Within this context, that god is Baphomet.

The Hand and the Eye Taken in Isolation, as Two Aspects of Reality.

The Eye symbolizes the perception and inner vision of the various essences that make up the Sabbat and the Spirit world in their pure form, as well as personal, pure, creative activity. It simultaneously represents Death and killing, as we shall see. The inner vision of the Eye corresponds to the seed of energy which comes down from the Sabbat in the North at the Solstice. The Hand is the representation of these various essences within the material world, as well as the container that can hold these essences. This container can either be the Earth or the human microcosm.

The Eye, in being linked to Death, is linked to the projections of the Eye as well, to the Evil Eye, which traditionally is linked to jealousy and envy projected through the eyes, but is, in a more general sense, linked to the Eye of someone who possesses the spark of magic. In this, the Eye, in line with Greco-Roman and Medieval ideas of sight, constantly generates light from itself that exits itself in the form of rays that go out and influence the world around it, then bounce back to it. In people with the spark of magic, this outgoing of rays from the Eyes can work magic on that on which they're trained, and can work to either harm or help. The rays of the eye can cut like a knife, and therefore shape things, or they can support that which they connect to. Moreover, the rays projected by the Eyes are completely spiritual, and so are a unmanifested way of affecting change in the world, in opposition to the manifest way of making change in the world that's accomplished through the literal works of the Hand, the personal Hand, as well as the body as a whole which uses the personal Hands.

The Eye, then, can correspond to personal visualization, or perception of the higher essences, and it can correspond to the projection of the rays from the eyes, which can hurt and cut. In this cutting aspect, or death aspect, it also corresponds to the act of orgasm, the destruction and liberation of energy. Like a knife, like the Athame, it can destroy, or it can create, through carving. Through this, it's linked with Demanifestation. It also is symbolized by Mahaziel, Odin, Herne the Hunter. The Eye is associated with death, Azoa, and the Opposer.

The Hand as a whole can symbolize man or the microcosm and the actions of man as a whole, where what is perceived by the Eye can be represented in other ways, through physical actions, through creating things. In this, the Hand, and the body, physically create and manifest that which the Eye perceives, and so are linked in a fundamental way with the process of manifestation. Through this, the Hand symbolizes that which is the most manifest. The Hand also manifests as the body of the initiate, and in this is the Microcosm. The body of the initiate, and specialized organs such as the heart, contain a replica of the Sabbat itself and the millions of forms of Being within it. The Hand, the Body, in this, can call down the energies from the external Sabbat that correspond to that which is present within itself micro-cosmically. It can also, in this, receive those energies, as a vessel, in this corresponding to a grail. As a vessel, it concentrates the power of life into one location. There, the hand is the receptacle of the power in its manifestation, and can also take the power that's been transmitted to it and manifest it in physical form through subsequent actions. The hand also can stand for the five senses, which are five different ways of approaching truth, as we shall see.

An example of this can be seen in the union of the Eye and the Hand through the use of the Pen by the Hand. The Hand can symbolize the holding of the pen, and in this, the pen can write out what the Eye sees or perceives, thereby making the abstract essence physical. The Pen in this is a sword, taken in another form, and so is an athame, with the union of the Pen and the Hand being a combination of the Hand and the Eye. The union of the Hand and Eye in this can take those energies which have been received into the hand and manifest them in physical reality through concrete actions, through drawing or through writing. Therefore, the Hand is associated with Life, Zoa, Bride, Habundia, the goddess, Manifestation, creation.

Here, too, you can see that the duality of male/female exists between the Eye and the Hand, in that the projective power of the Eye is male, while the receptive power of the Hand is female. Beyond this, though, taking these two symbols in isolation from the others, the Hand as the body is also the portal in women through which new life is created and manifests in the world. The power of the Eye is analogous to the Phallus, which is projective, while the receptive power of the Hand is female, and analogous to the Vagina, which is also receptive.

The Hand, Eye, Phallus, and Mouth Taken Together, Ritual and Practice, Sexual Practices.

These four taken together correspond to the four points of the circle, and their significance is intertwined with these points, as well as with the stages of magical practice. As stated in the previous chapter, on Gerald Massey, this is not the only way of looking at the four.

The way that these four work together in ritual can most clearly be seen in the masturbatory sigillic rite. This can be seen as the prototype of the ritual within the circle, with the different phases of this rite being adapted to the more formalized work engaged in there. Several things that might seem confusing, such as why the

Mouth corresponds to binding while the Phallus corresponds to Invocation, make more sense when the original context of the sigil rite is taken into account. The masturbatory sigillic rite does not need the casting of a circle.

In terms of sigil magic, what you have is a course of work where the actual making of the Sigil and the planning of the work, the planning and establishing of the desire to be realized, corresponds to the Eye. Then, through the masturbatory action of the Phallus, the energy is initially raised. Then, through the work of the Hand, a process of picturing the sigil combined with complete Desire, then letting it go and letting the Eye of the mind wander, then picturing it again, is done as the key work of the rite. Next, at the moment of orgasm, the full intent of the sigil and the sigil itself is brought to mind and projected onto the energy of that orgasm, this being the binding of the Mouth. Finally, the orgasm itself, as a break in consciousness and a going forth of energy, happens. This destructive power of orgasm corresponds to the Eye once more, and is complemented by the destruction of the physical media associated with the sigil, and in this both the orgasm and the physical breaking correspond to the power of the Eye.

Now, with that in mind, it's possible to look at the four within more general ritual work.

The Eye corresponds to the North, Earth
The Phallus to the East, Air
The Hand to the South, Fire
The Mouth to the West, Water

These four encipher the process of invocation and spell craft.

Eye—Planning,
Phallus—Beginning, Invocation
Hand—Middle, Working,
Mouth—End, Binding
Eye—Completion, Breaking.

This is the preparation of the work, the invocation of the powers of the work, the Work itself, the binding of the work, and then the end or casting of the Rite itself.

First, the Eye refers to Visualization of the pure essences, and planning based on them, the Phallus refers to invocation, while the Hand refers to the work of the Rite, and then the Mouth refers to binding, and the Eye, again, refers to breaking. Planning, Preparation, working, binding, casting. The breaking, here, is also a sacrifice to the gods of the Sabbat, the First Sun, to the sexual genii that are part of it, which can take many forms. The sexual genii are succubi and incubi, who receive the sacrifice as part of their feeding. This feeding, and the genii, are motivated by love, which is the same as the love energy of the Sabbath, part of its essential nature. Their essential nature is that of love itself.

The Phallus does not represent the most physical. Instead, it's between the purely mental and the physical, like the Mouth. The Phallus is in between the Hand and the Eye. This is because it contains within itself the stuff of generation, which is inherently living and spiritual, but it is not the full manifestation of these powers in reality. This power is literally expressed through sexual gametes as well as the reproductive energy that comes with them, which can be expressed and shaped in work and projected at the moment of orgasm. The sexual energy can be shaped into spells. The sexual energy of the Phallus is the raw "stuff" that's formed in the subsequent processes of the rites.

The Phallus is connected with invocation of the energies of the rite. Abstracting from the sigillic application of this stage, the invocation can metaphorically be dancing to raise power, singing to raise power, verbal invocations to raise power, combinations of all three, and other techniques as well.

The power of the Hand, in relation to the four, is the power of the South, which is the point of the key work of the rite. That which has been raised in the process of invocation is now worked with. Some people advocate for suppressing all intent of the sigil while doing the work, leaving its presentation until the end. Others go for the opposite, and advocate focusing on the intent throughout the work. Chumbley advocated a combination of these two, bringing the intent to the surface strongly during the masturbatory work, then letting it go and settle down, in a cyclical form. This is supposed to echo repeated phases of manifestation and demanifestation, with the binding at the point of orgasm being a joining of the true essence of the spell to the orgasmic sexual energy, done through an empowered projection of the sigil and intent.

The power of the Mouth is binding the spell after work is done, based on the exclamation during orgasm. The Mouth binds through the power of speech, this being a passive power in relation to that of the Phallus. The mouth literally consumes, as well, and so destroys, as well as enchants. It can stimulate, but it cannot fecundate like the Phallus. It can also quite literally "earth" or ground something, through the process of eating food, leading to nourishment for the body. Here, the consumptive power of the Mouth exists in contrast to the generative power of the Phallus. The binding at this stage can be expressed as a physical binding of a vessel that contains the invoked power as well.

Both visualization and breaking correspond to the Eye. The Eye, in relation to the four, and to rituals performed with the four, can stand both for the initial planning of the ritual as well as for the destruction and banishing that takes place at the end of the ritual. In this, the planning and the construction of the various things necessary for the ritual, such as sigils, correspond to the capacity of visualization associated with the Eye. In this, the Eye is, in a way, both the first and the last with regards to the ritual, it is the Alpha and Omega, in the North.

Death is connected with the Eye, with orgasm being connected both with completion and with death, and so facilitating the realization of what has been ordained.

However, the most important part is the final act: the destruction of what has been manifested. This brings the wheel back to the start, to the north. It liberates the Essence behind the image, and allows the essence to manifest. The destruction of the sigil casts the sigil. It is also the sacrifice given to the gods of the Sabbat, to the sexual genii of the First Sun, as is the sigil directed in orgasm. This sacrifice, extended to general ritual work, is the sacrifice of the completed work of the ritual to the sexual genii of the Sabbat, which the process of ritual work has built up as an aetheric or energetic construct. This construct, in breaking the circle and ending the rite, is sacrificed to the gods, in order for them to manifest the work contained in it.

Here, the sexual genii are the parts of the Sabbat which correspond to the essence, or quintessence of the rite itself. The breaking, the sacrifice, liberates this essential meaning of the rite, its Azoth, and this liberated Azoth resonates, and vibrates, with the corresponding Azoth of the First Sun. This calls down the sexual genii, who embody this aspect of the First Sun's Azoth, to come down and to claim their offering. After they take it up, they oversee the manifestation of it in reality. They feed on this energy as Succubi and Incubi, and their motivation is fundamentally that of love. The essence, the Azoth, which the Sabbath is made out of, has the essential nature of love. In cases where what's being done is not a sigil, but a rite where a spirit is called down, the spirit itself is sent out to do its work, but the sacrifice still happens, and the sexual genii still claim the energy of the rite. They act to guide the whole of the process.

In specifically sacrificing, or breaking, the sigil or rite to the sexual genii, they may appear, or they may not. Their appearance may be purely spiritual and psychological, or it might be more subtle.

After the destruction of the sigil, the working should similarly be put out of your mind, creating another "Break".

The final moment of orgasm is like death, the final break, the final banishing, the experience of the North and the Opposer. It ends the substantive part of the auto-sexual sigil ritual, with the literal cleanup and disposal of material being a secondary type of banishing.

Orgasm, in this, is similar to sleep. This is because even though the physical breaking of circles in banishing, as well as the destruction and disposal of perishable items used in the working, are necessary, the end of consciousness in sleep after the ritual is what ultimately casts the rite. The consciousness that a person retains, the image of the rite, the energy of the rite, are all linked together, and the going to sleep of a person at the end of the day, after the ritual has ended, provides a concrete break in consciousness that, in its way, casts what has been accomplished magically during the day into the cosmos. It provides the same sort of "Break" in normal consciousness that orgasm does.

Dreaming in general is a path that, taking place in a "Break" can act as a portal to the Sabbat. The path of Dreaming at night is echoed by the potential visions and travel which can happen in the wake of the "Break" of orgasm in a ritual. Just as sleep, not just in the wake of a ritual but in general, can lead upwards to the Sabbat, so too can the dreams that happen after orgasm lead a person upwards to the Sabbat.

This idea of sleep as a "break" can be applied to dreams in general, as a time when human beings can take advantage of the "break" in consciousness to go upwards to the Sabbat of the Ages. Here, the gate of sleep is similar to that of the gate of the north, and to the point of orgasm. In dreams, a person's soul can venture into the unmanifest and upwards to the Sabbat, to receive instruction, though the conclaves of the Sabbat may not appear as people may expect.

These four stages can also be linked with Paul Huson's four side of the "Witch's Pyramid".

> Invocation in the East is linked with the power of Imagining what it is you want very intensely.
> Will, in the south, is linked with the main work.
> Faith, in the West, in linked with Binding, and
> Silence, in the North, is linked with Breaking and final casting.

Interestingly, in the Coven of Atho material, a pyramid is also mentioned, linked to the four directions and to the four Kerubic animals. In this material, the four sides of the Pyramid are put together to form the Sphinx, the synthesis of the four Kerubic animals, which is a symbol for Baphomet.

A modified version of Wilhelm Reich's four stage model can also be corresponded here to the working model for general rituals. Here, "Orgasm" stands for the main working. It's possible to encapsulate the sexual working within the whole working stage itself. In this, what would happen is that Invocation would be casting the circle, followed by the sexual work as a whole, in all of its stages, followed by a separate formal binding of the whole work, followed by the breaking, final casting, and clean up of both the ritual as a whole and the physical ritual components:

The Eye, Planning, Tension
The Phallus, Invocation, Charging,
The Hand, Working, Orgasm
The Mouth, Binding, Discharge
The Eye, Breaking, Relaxation.

The Four, more generally, can be related to rites as follows:

The Eye corresponds to the going forth of life in the North
The Phallus to Increase in the East,
The Hand to Manifestation in the South,
The Mouth to Decrease in the West.
The Eye corresponds to the Demanifestation in the North,

Practical Considerations in Sigil Work.

In this sigil working, the three can be integrated into the four in the following way: "Thee Temple Ov Psychick Youth"'s "Sigil ov Thee 3 Liquids" makes use of the three within it. This rite involves taking the saliva, hair, and blood from the individual and anointing the sigil with it before beginning the work. The saliva corresponds to the head center, the hair to the lower or bodily center, the blood to the heart center. The sigil thus anointed can then be worked with, with the seminal or vaginal fluid applied to it post-orgasm, before the destruction of the sigil takes place. As with any practice involving drawing blood from ones self, please be careful not to unduly hurt yourself while engaging in this practice. Hair can be snipped with scissors.

The writing of the Sigil itself, to be used in the rite, can be empowered through this symbolism as well. Here, it would be the final drawing of the sigil which is empowered, rather than the process of arriving at the sigil from a statement of desire. Here, one would be aware of the Hand as the vessel of the Eye, with the pen or other writing implement used to scribe the sigil being the Athame or knife on another level. You would correspond the intent of the sigil to the Will, which is scribed through a combination of Belief and Desire, with Belief corresponding to the Eye and Desire corresponding to the Hand.

The Hand as a Map of the Four, the Five.

The Hand is linked to man as the manifestation of the Five, with five fingers being linked to four limbs and the head, which manifests life in human form. The hand, like the Eye, is also a prime transmitter of magical energy.

In that the process of spinning the wheel of the four starts from the Eye and ends in the Eye, it can be said to have five points, which can correspond to the five fingers of the hand. The correspondences are the Thumb to the initial planning stage of the Eye in the North, the Index finger to the East, the Middle finger to the South, the Ring finger to the West, and the Little Finger to the North once more.

Chumbley, in the Azoetia, gives the following correspondences: Thumb to tactile sense, Index finger to Smell, Middle Finger to Hearing, Ring finger to Taste, and little finger to Sight. I disagree with this, in that I think that the Thumb much more fully reflects the Visual sense, while the Little finger more correctly represents the tactile sense.

This tracks very well with the circle, first, in that the Thumb, and the sense of Sight, corresponds to the planning of the rite and the manufacture of any visual material needed for the rite's work, while the sense of smell, as commented on by Chumbley, is a force which evokes memories, or powers, through incense and perfume. The sense of Hearing, corresponding to the core work of the Rite and to the South, is called the ultimate sense, and is linked to the direct work between the summoner and the summoned. The senes of Taste, the West, the Ring finger, incorporates matter into the body, and so binds what is consumed into the earth. The Tactile sense, in the North, once more, corresponding to the Little Finger, is what underlies everything, and which is revealed in the power of breaking the circle and casting the spell. Through this, the five points of the ritual and circle follow in from Thumb to Little Finger.

We can summarize this as follows:

Thumb—Vision, planning, North
Index Finger —Smell, invocation, East
Middle Finger —Hearing, main work, South

Ring Finger —Taste, binding, West
Little Finger —Touch, breaking, North

These also refer to different aspects of the physical ritual. Here, the palm of the hand is the sixth point, which corresponds to the particular characteristic of the spirit which is being invoked. This is the hidden six in the five, which is the point or intent of the ritual. This corresponds to the center of the pentagram, which is the same as the center of the fourfold circle.

As said in the section on the hand itself, the five senses can be used in a purely internal way to summon communion with a spirit, through picturing the sight, taste, smell, sound, and touch of a particular sigil.

Importantly, in this set of correspondences, the middle three fingers correspond to East, South, and West, with the Middle Finger corresponding to South. Thumb and Little Finger, used together, represent the Alpha and Omega of the North and of the Eye.

In this, the upright pentagram can be taken as the hand, with the middle finger corresponding to the upper most point, and to the power of spirit in manifestation, and the other fingers following, with the lower two points corresponding to the thumb and little finger. This symbolism can be applied to the human body as well.

This symbolism can also lead to the hand being considered as a pentagram. The pentagram interrelates all of the five with each other. In this, the pentagram which is "Averse", with the two points upwards, does not relate to evil. Instead, the two points upwards relate to the "End" and the "Beginning". Between these two points, after the End, is the quintessence, which makes up a six in this way of looking at things. The quintessence can either go out, upwards, or it can be drawn inwards, from beyond the circle, in which case it empowers the space at the center of the pentagram. The quintessence, here, can come in many different forms, in planetary, deific, and more abstract forms and Ideals.

I'm partially taking the idea of the invoking pentagram being the usually called "Averse" one from a column by Madeline Montalban on the tarot, titled "Star of Peace, Lighting the Way to Happiness", published in Prediction magazine in 1957, as well as Tony Willis' commentary on it. The column, along with many other of

Montalban's columns on the Tarot, is available free for non-commercial use on the "Auntie Tarot" website, http://www.auntietarot.wordpress.com. There, invoking is signified by the averse pentagram and banishing by the upright pentagram, with it being possible to use the two together to banish something while bringing in something new to take its place. These two pentagrams can also refer to the left and right hands of Baphomet, with one hand taking influence from the sky and the other transferring an influence down to earth. Charles Cardell's "Coven of Atho" used a pentagram position, where the person did just this, taking influence from the sky with one hand, processing it through the body, and then giving the excess to the earth through the downturned right hand.

This five-fold symbolism, which goes around the circle with the north repeated twice, can also be found in the Clan of Tubal Cain material as well as the Coven of Atho material. As described in the letters in "The Taper that Lights the Way", Shani Oates' collection of Robert Cochrane material, the five of the Clan of Tubal Cain are Life, Love, Maternity or Maturity, Wisdom, and Death. These can five can be linked to the in the way I've described, linked to the: Life can be linked to the Tetragrammaton in the following way.

> North as the initial going forth of Life;
> East as Love can be linked to the Phallus and Vagina through linking Invocation with an initial love making, which will manifest in the
> South through Maternity. There, Maternity corresponds to the Hand in being Manifestation in its pure form. The Virgin Maiden, in the East, has been made love to, and has given birth in the South, and, in the
> West, has become the wizened crone of Maturity. In the
> North, the Crone, the dark goddess of the West, goes forth to death.
> This also recapitulates the working year: the seed is sown in the spring,the East, comes to fruition in the summer, the South, is harvested in the fall, the West, and the land is vacant and dead in the Winter, the North. This way of operating also combines lunar symbolism: for the Clan of Tubal Cain, the East is the

waxing moon, the south is the Full Moon, the West is the waning moon, and the north is the Dark Moon, which is the complete New Moon.

The Coven of Atho material, given by Melissa Seims, lists the five as Birth, Survival, Reproduction, Death, and Return. These are linked with five circles: Fertility, Brotherhood, Vitality, Travel, and Return.

Within this, Birth and Fertility can be linked to general Life.

Survival and Brotherhood can be linked with Invocation through the sense of coming together for strength, and so with Love.

Reproduction and Vitality can be linked with Manifestation, and Maternity.

Though Death is listed as the fourth attribute, the corresponding circle is that of Travel, which signified the witch going forth into the other realm through scrying and other means. This can be linked to the goddess of Decrease in the West and to the travel of the individual to the Sabbat, as well as Maturity.

Return, in both of these, is the attribute which more properly relates to Death, in that it's related to the now dead spirits of individuals who, in this state, return either through psychic communication or through reincarnation. Return, in the North once more, the place of Death, completes the cycle, and its link with rebirth leads once more into Fertility and Life.

Like the rest, the following are my own embellishments on the material that Seims provides, and may or may not be accurate to the tradition. These five can also be linked to the circle in the following way:

North is the place of Baphomet, or the Head of Atho, as well as the link to the Water City or the Sabbat, on top of being the place of both Return(from Death) and Birth.

East, place of joining together for Survival and Brotherhood, is also the place of Initiation and the Joining of Fertility. This may be linked with male dominant sex in the sense of planting a seed, which can be equated with sex from behind, commonly known as "doggy style".

South is the place of Vitality, the force of Love, the power of the Trident as a projector of force, female dominated or more equal sex, woman superior, on top of the man, as well as women serving as oracles.

West is the place of both Astral travel and vision, the power of the imagination, "Death" in a more temporary sense.

Seims provides much more material about the five in the Coven of Atho in her book, going far beyond this brief description, and interested readers should consult it for further details and correspondences.

The Eight Paths.

This is a valuable teaching found in the Gardnerian tradition that I believe derives from traditional witchcraft. The Eight Paths are eight modes of approaching the divine, which can be corresponded to the eight directions as well.

The First Path is intention and visualization

The Second Path is trance states and astral travel

The Third Path consists of talismans, charms, and rituals that are sometimes referred to as "Low Magic"

The Fourth Path consists of drugs of various sorts, mind altering substances, from wine and alcohol through marijuana to psychedelics.

The Fifth Path consists of dances used in a ritualistic sense.

The Sixth Path consists of binding, in the sense of kink and BDSM, which means both tying and restraining with cords as well as using tight cords to change and cut off blood circulation. Included in this is breath work, which means either auto or mutual erotic asphyxiation. This, obviously is a dangerous one.

The Seventh Path consists of flogging, whipping, and scourging.

The Eighth Path consists of the "Great Rite", which is invoking the gods through sex magic. I would add drawing down the Moon and drawing down the Sun to this, even though it might appear that these rituals would be associated with the second path and the trance state.

Each of these are treated in detail by the Gardnerian priestess Lady Sable Aradia in her book "The Witch's Eight Paths of Power", which is recommended.

As for the correspondences between these eight and the spokes of the wheel, I'm not certain that this pattern is really in the correct order, and that it actually corresponds correctly to the eight spokes of the compass.

Another ordering of them, which relates them to the eight quarters of the circle is the following:

> North: Trance states and astral travel, the Second Path
>
> Northeast: Drugs of various sorts, mind altering substances, from wine and alcohol through marijuana to psychedelics, the Fourth Path.
>
> East: Dances used in a ritualistic sense, the Fifth Path.
>
> Southeast: Talismans, charms, and rituals that are sometimes referred to as "Low Magic", the Third Path
>
> South: The "Great Rite", which is invoking the gods through sex magic, but also drawing down the Moon and drawing down the Sun, the Eighth Path.
>
> Southwest: Flogging, whipping, and scourging, the Seventh Path.

West: Binding, in the sense of kink and BDSM, which means both tying and restraining with cords as well as using tight cords to change and cut off blood circulation, the Sixth Path,

North West: Intention and Visualization, Meditation, the First Path

These paths are not meant to all be used together in rituals. In fact, doing so would be very dangerous.

Particularly, using BDSM work after taking intoxicants, even those as mundane as wine, is dangerous. To really participate in rituals such as binding and flogging in a safe way, both parties need to be in a sound state of mind, and different states of intoxication, including experiencing full hallucinations, are easy ways for people to hurt both other people and themselves. It is not adequate for one person to be in a sound state of mind while the other is not, because whoever is not will not be able to adequately communicate their inner state to whoever they're collaborating with. This can lead to serious physical injury, as well as psychological harm. Personal and interpersonal safety are paramount during ritual, as well as in non-ritualistic kink activity. Also, binding to the point of seriously altering blood flow is very dangerous, and should be overseen by someone with experience in these matters. Less serious binding, though, is less dangerous, and can have similar effects.

This latter arrangement of the paths strikes me as being authentic. Particularly, look at the four cardinal directions and the rites attached to them:

North, Astral Travel,
East, Dancing,
South, the Great Rite,
West, literal Binding.

These can be corresponded very directly to the four aspects of the wheel, which is turned to complete the rite.

East, Dancing corresponds to invocation,
South, the Great Rite in the South to the main work of the rite, which can be either practical or religious,
West, Binding in the West to literal binding of the work of the rite to the world, and
Norht, Astral travel to the ending and breaking of the rite, which in certain cases can lead to astral experiences, but which also releases the working into the astral realm.

More importantly, though, the North, corresponding with astral travel, is an obvious direction of exit from the circle, the path from the circle to the Sabbat itself, as well as the pathway of energy from the Sabbat to the circle.

Within this, the South can correspond not only to the Great Rite, but to the drawing down of the Moon, and of the Sun, in the capacity of receiving the spirit which has been invoked in the rite of Ingress. The Great Rite itself corresponds to what happens in Congress, while a reception of a spirit, or a god or goddess, in this corresponds to what happens in Ingress.

Alternately, a statue or other physical form can function as the receptacle for the incoming spirit. In this, the physical binding would be perhaps a binding with cords of the statue, as opposed to a binding of people.

Similarly, corresponding the Sabbatic tetragrammaton to this, we find that

East, Dancing, corresponds to the Phallus,
South, the Great Rite, corresponds to the Hand,
West, physical Binding, corresponds to the Mouth,
North, Astral Travel, corresponds to the Eye.

Significantly, the Coven of Atho material also has an eightfold path, but this is somewhat different. In the section on the fivefold symbolism, I've given readers enough hints so that they can consult Seims' book and find the proper orientation of the compass, and readers are invited to do their own research, comparing these paths to Gardner's.

I do have my own idea of how the Coven of Atho compass can be reconciled with this arrangement of Gardner's compass. This is completely my own work, and so I have no proof that this is something their coven would have known or approved of.

Here, we have the following:

North, Baphomet, the Head of Atho, corresponding to astral travel and other trance working.

Northeast: the Cup, containing wine, drugs and other intoxicants as a path to trance. Element of Water

East: Fertility in the sense of Brotherhood, Initiation, male and female joining together, planting a seed, here linked to Dancing in Gardner's compass as something that joins male and female together but is not inherently sexual. Also corresponds to coming together for survival and "Brotherhood", though it involves both sexes.

Southeast: the incense platter, corresponding to Earth. In this, the incense can be taken to signify actions taken by the participants, with this standing in turn for low magic and charms. The Cardells make the association between Earth and Action in their booklet on the symbolism of the "Wishan Wands", where every wand stands for a point in the compass.

South: given as a fertility rite that explicitly includes sex in the Atho material, corresponds to the Great Rite in Gardner's compass.

Southeast: the horn in the Atho material, corresponding to the element of Air and to sitting out and listening to the spirits of nature. Can correspond to flogging in the Gardner material through the correspondence of Air with the life energy, which flogging stimulates.

West: the hand of glory, associated with teaching the tradition. This can be paralleled with binding in the sense of binding the tradition, or the energy of the Sabbat, to earth through teachings. The teachings are embodied in symbols, and it's the binding of mystical concepts to symbols

Northwest: the Eye, corresponding to visualization in both Atho and Gardner material, and to Fire in the sense of the Fire of imagination in Cardell's elemental correspondences.

Invocation

Ingress is basically an evocation, evoking energies and powers, and gods, from the First Sun, from the Divine Mind, the Sabbat of the Ages, down into the circle. However, you can also invoke these energies into you as well. This division follows the current definitions of evocation as something external and invocation as something internal.

The process of invocation has been touched on in the chapter on Gerald Massey. The process of doing this is to picture the letter in your mind, then will yourself to "hear" the sound of the letter, to "smell" the letter, to "taste" the letter, and then to "touch" the letter. After doing this, bring all of these together into one, so that you simultaneously perceive the letter with all five of your senses. This opens up a door to the pure energies of the letter, which come forth from it in what Chumbley refers to as "Telaesthesis". This is a term that Spare originally used for the coming together of all emotions in "The Zoetic Grimoire". This process of opening the door to energies through this five-fold picturing can be done with any sigil.

Sexual Permutations, the Quadriga.

The name Quadriga comes from the four horses of the chariot that was used to carry Apollo, the sun god, across the heavens. Apollo here is equivalent with Baphomet, and by engaging in this transgressive and unificatory sexual action, the four horses reconstitute Baphomet at the center, in completeness and unity. This can also be interpreted as binding all of the people involved into unity as the body of Christ, with the sexual rites being the focus of the Agape or love feast. The power of the Quadriga to come together in unity can also be yoked to the materialization of a particular god, or goal.

The making into one of the four, according to the four different parts of Eye, Hand, Phallus, and Mouth, can be interpreted in a purely sexual way: Here, the Eye stands not just for the physical Eye, but for the secret Eye of the Anus, which is stimulated by others, while the Mouth stimulates the sexual organs of the other people, the Hand similarly stimulates the sexual organs, and the Phallus or Vagina is stimulated. Through a combination of homosexual and heterosexual coupling, with mouth to phallus or vagina, hand to phallus or vagina, phallus to vagina, and all to the secret eye of the anus, all of the four can be brought into one. Interestingly, with these attributions, the anus as Eye would be in the north, the place of the transmission of the energy to the circle.

This fusion of homosexual and heterosexual acts implies a Quadriga, a four person group, made up of two men and two women, each of whom engages in heterosexual and homosexual sex with the others. Engaged in with male and female, partner and non-partner, all the possible permutations of sexual behavior are fulfilled, making a total union of the four in all possible ways. The four of Baphomet, the four stations of the circle, are made into one. Traditionally, a Quadriga is made up of two couples, and in this act civil laws, those of marriage and against homosexual behavior, are broken, at the same time a new unity is forged.

In non-western countries where things like the Quadriga are practiced, the two couples, who are married to each other, make a pact for a group marriage and often live in the same house or compound. The children of the two couples are considered brother and sister, and are forbidden from intermarrying for seven generations. Considering that practice of the Quadriga for long periods of time can bring up questions about the parentage of children, this is a reasonable idea.

However, in this, do not ignore the capacity of the normal eye as a vessel of the projection of magical power. Additionally, the use of the eye in its capacity as a projective power of energy has relevance to the magical aspect of sex work, as does the capacity of the hand not only as a manipulator, but as a similar transmitter of magical power. In this, the Eye in its projective capacity as the actual seeing eye also corresponds to the first stage of preparation, while the hidden eye or anus corresponds to the Eye in its destructive capacity.

On another level, the progression of Eye, Hand, Mouth, Phallus can also correspond to the progression of a sexual relationship: first, mutual seeing, then contact through hands, then kissing through the mouth, then sex through the phallus. This can also function as an introductory pattern for sex work in general.

The Non-Sexual Working Quadriga.

In this work of the first circle, one individual can face north, the direction of vacancy, and invoke the powers of the Sabbat into himself and into the circle. However, this role can be split into four. In this case, a man takes the place of the East, a woman of the West, a woman takes a position to the South, and a man in the North. However, these roles are flexible and people of either sex can take them up as needed. The man in the North is the leader of the Circle, and, occupying the place of Mahaziel, serves as the gateway for the powers outside of the circle, from the Sabbat of the Ages to come through, as well as the director of all the other members.

The role of East is to facilitate the invocation. The goal of invocation is to bring something from the unmanifest, the north, into the manifest, which is the South. The East corresponds to the rising sun and to the powers of increase. This naturally forms a bridge between the unmanifest and the manifest.

In one version of the work, the role of the person of the South is to serve as the medium or Oracle, who the invoked energies go into and speak through. The work of the rite, communication with spirit either for charging it with practical work or just asking it questions, is mediated through the Oracle. This is not the only way to proceed. Alternately, a statue or other physical form can be the focus for the reception of the spirit, or the spirit can be called forth in an abstract form. The Oracle works to annunciate the message and communication to the other people in the circle. The spirit invoked into the Oracle can be one of the gods of the circle, and, as well, the union of the spirit with the Oracle is the union of spirit with matter, causing it to manifest within the world.

The role of the West is to facilitate either the binding of the rite to earth, or the charging of the spirit, this being the commanding of the spirit to do what you've first told it to do in the main working. The Charging, giving it a charge or a task, is a forceful reiteration of what has already been agreed to. This binds the spirit to do what has been agreed to. The person in the West corresponds to the setting Sun, the intermediary between the manifest state and the demanifest state.

The leader in the North does the final dismissal and breaks the circle. The banishing, or dismissal, of the spirit, and the breaking of the circle, serve as a bridge between the manifest and the unmanifest.

When there's just one person in the circle, they can perform all of these roles, including having the mystic vision and communing with the Spirit.

Part 3, the Ritual

Working Considerations, Circle Casting with the Three and Four, Frame Ritual.

The basic fourfold working practice, consisting of Invocation, Work, Binding, and Completion or Breaking is described in the section on the Hand, Eye, Phallus, and Mouth, which should be consulted prior to this work.

East corresponds to the beginning invocations of the Rite, South corresponds to the main work of the Rite, west corresponds to the Binding of the Rite, and the return to the North represents the ending of the Rite, the return to the place of the unmanifest.

What can be called the neutral arrangement of the four is what has been described, North demanifestation, South manifestation, East the power of increase, West the power of decrease, but when you work magic for particular purposes you either work clockwise or counter-clockwise.

This way of working goes clockwise around the circle. The clockwise motion creates manifestation, while the counter-clockwise motion banishes. Counter-clockwise motion returns things to their source in the ground of being. It can be used for offensive magic in this capacity. Counter-clockwise is also the way of working for the Egress ritual, which involves a return to the ground of being on the part of an individual, prior to them coming forth once again to the Sabbat.

Clockwise is for the Ingress rite, and for manifestation, while counter-clockwise is for Egress and demanifestation. The Egress rites are extremely dangerous and advanced works, and so won't be dealt with here.

Spinning the wheel in the counter-clockwise direction takes a person from manifestation to demanifestation,

Within the Ingress Rite, working clockwise, you can work in two ways: first, you can work to either accomplish something which involves charging a spirit to do something in reality, or you can just talk to a spirit and dismiss it.

If you want to accomplish something in reality, you have to use the capacity of Arianrhod/Hekate in the West to bind it to reality. If you're just talking with a spirit, the function of the West is to loose the spirit from its bonds, which is a preface to dismissing it in the final act of banishing.

Viewing this, there are two different paths that can be taken: what has flowed in from the unmanifest into manifest reality can flow back out, or it can be bound and take on a more permanent form. Drawing on Buddhist thought, you can call the pure inflow and outflow of energy from the unmanifest to the manifest and back again the way that things proceed if there's no attachment. However, sometimes you want attachment to happen, such as when you cast a spell. Attachment is also responsible for the process of incarnation and for the more permanent manifestation of objects in reality. In that case, instead of the West releasing that which has been given manifestation, it instead binds what has manifested in the circle more permanently to existence within material reality. The power of Demanifestation or Decrease, in this, is the power of Loosing, and that which is loosed can be Bound as well. If that which has been called on is bound, it will manifest in reality according to the binding. If it has not been bound, it will instead just return to the unmanifest.

Instead of taking what's been invoked and sending it back, by working clockwise you can bind what's been invoked to the material plane, so that when the ritual is complete and everything has been struck it will continue to exist there in a spirit form, doing its work. Here, Hekate/Arianrhod as goddess of the west can bind and complete the work which has been done when the person has adopted the guise of Bride/Habundia, fixing it and making it real. Likewise, Hu Gadarn has another aspect, which in the counter-clockwise work, can be used for destructive purposes, as well, he can tear down what has been invoked.

The final step in the work is the banishing and ending of the rite itself, after its consummation in binding. There should be a final signal and act that dismisses the entity summoned, or that in another way signals the end of the rite. This completes the circle, returning the position to the North.

The rite itself can, in a sense, be seen as the construction of the ideal object that embodies the intent of the working, and the completion of the rite, it's closing, and the destruction of the circle and of all products associated with it, can be seen as parallel to the final destruction of a sigil that lets the essence within it manifest in the outside world.

Cross Quarters

The cross quarters aren't used in the Ingress ritual, but they do have a particular significance. They act as "Breaks" or spaces of demanifestation, which break the form and the function of the previous cardinal point and allow for the manifestation of the form, and the performance of the function, of the next cardinal point. Practically, this means letting the god or goddess of the quarter depart from you, and then letting the next god or goddess into you as you go through the different working processes of the circle. Chumbley, in this refers to the cross quarters as the "non-integral" spaces, with the "integral" spaces being the four cardinal directions. They're non-integral in that they resemble the demanifest realm of the One, the same space that's traversed in the journey from the circle to the Sabbat and back again. However, though this is the case, it's very important to note that in the Congress ritual and its cosmology the cross quarters have a very different definition, one which, though in a sense related to this definition, is not that of the demanifest realm.

Physical Working

What's presented below is a purely mental working of the rite, by which is meant no physical ritual beyond just gesturing with a consecrated instrument. This can be adapted and combined with a physical interpretation. For the physical interpretation, consult the "Eight Paths" section. The way the two can be combined is to proceed with spinning the wheel in a physical way until you get to the South, and then, at the point of work, start with verbal invocations, then proceed to the core work, then announce the verbal binding. After this, complete a physical binding, then proceed to the North and both dismiss the spirit and physically end the rite.

In this, the process of physical invocation should be to generally draw down the energy of the Sabbat, with the particular invocation which follows specifying just what fraction of spirit you want to call down.

The Spirit itself, a fraction of the Sabbat of the Ages, the Divine Mind, the Eternal Sun, comes into the circle from the station of the North. This, the spiritual North, faces Midnight's Dawn, the demanifest realm, within which is the Sabbat of the Ages as a globe of fire.

Casting the Circle

To work magic in a circle, the three centers of the Body are activated and brought into relationship with the four directions of the circle. The four directions, in this, are the "Aetheric I". What that means is that, fundamentally, they're not things in themselves but are instead creations by the magician, creations which he or she has associated with the various directions. Because of this association, the aura of the practitioner in its various orientations to the body takes on characteristics of each direction. They're present within the "Aetheric I" of the magician. A person looking North looks towards demanifestation, which is the direction of absence or vacancy, through which they can see the higher realms that transcend the material. Looking North, their right hand has the characteristics of East, of increase, which includes invocation, while their left hand has the characteristic of West, and of decrease, or dismissal and banishing. The material world corresponds to their back. However, in the actual process of casting the circle, you face south first for the first of the four invocations, then turn around and face North for the rest of the invocations.

The conjunction of the three and the four is very important, and the symbolism is life inserting itself into death. Here, the three, the vertical axis, represents the Goddess, Life, along with the Sabbat itself taken into its component parts. The horizontal axis represents the Earth, which, without the power of Life flowing from the Eternal Sun of the Sabbat, is barren and lifeless, is dead. By extending the power of Life, the vertical axis, outwards to the four directions as outlined, you bring life to the otherwise lifeless matter around you.

Of course, this matter isn't completely lifeless, in that the Sabbat, and the earthly Sun which is a representative of it, empowers the world both seasonally and daily. However, this empowerment is not total, in that the world is fallen, with the Evil One having polluted and corrupted it.

In the following ritual, the conjuration of the three is done within the circle, followed by the conjuration of the four. In other traditions, the conjuration of the three takes place outside of the circle, and then then energy is brought from the place of conjuration outside of the circle into the circle in order to cast the four.

One of the things that casting the circle does is to restore the energies in the local area to the primal pattern on which everything is based, represented by the pattern of the Tetramorph in the Sabbat. Because of this, the casting of the circle itself has beneficial effects in the world. Nigel Pennick talks quite a lot about this aspect of circle casting in "Secrets of East Anglian Magic", where the construction of the nine-fold plot, which is the East Anglian version of the circle, is related intimately to the local energies of the earth. The nine-fold plot, in turn, is a representation of the Sabbat, which in our case includes the pattern of the Tetramorph, as a Temple or Building that has been brought down to earth. Within ritual, bringing energy down from the Sabbat to Earth, in the form of invocation of entities from the First Sun, also has a positive benefit not just for the individuals involved but for the local area. Both of these have the effect of countering the damage that the Evil One has done to the Earth, damage that was partially made at the time the earth was formed through the Evil One serving as a co-creator of the world. These rites, in themselves, irrespective of the practical purpose to which they may be put, help with the victory of good over evil and with the perfection and reparation of the world, bringing that piece of the world in communion with Paradise, the Sabbat itself. This general benefit is also present if you do rituals indoors or even within an apartment in a city, though this effect is somewhat lessened. Similarly, the individual who casts the circle also reestablishes the primordial pattern or order on the earth, and acts like a sacred king in this way too, recapitulating Pennick's "Tyrmagent", or Tyr the mighty, as a Demiurgic figure like Baphomet.

This ritual is for an individual, but it can be adapted for multiple people.

A Ritual Format Incorporating both the Three and the four

The place of the three, of the vertical axis, is the center of the circle.

Standing in the center, facing south, you first call up the three through focusing on them.

First focus on the Toadstone and invoking the power of the white moon and its goddess in your sexual center, invoking the power of Diana, the power of the Pearl, the power of Desire, and the holy name of Jah-Bul-On. If you have actually done the Toadstone ritual and have seized the stone, you should use your word or phrase of affirmation several times to establish a connection with the stone before beginning the invocation.

Then focus on the Head stone and invoke the power of the black moon, and its goddess, the horned goddess Selene in your head, the power of Belief, as well as the power of the Diamond, the Boddhicitta, and the holy name Yod-He-Vah-He.

Then focus on the Synderesis, the Ruby, the Heart stone, invoke the power of the red goddess and of the red moon, Venus, or Venus Genetrix, as well as the power of the Synderesis, of the Ruby, of Will, and of the holy name Elhannin.

While doing this you should picture the corresponding jewel within you and address the invocations to it. You should also both visualize the particular goddess at each point, and picture the goddess merging with you in your mind and working with you while you focus on that particular point.

The reason for this particular pattern of calling up the three has already been given in the section on the stone. By combining the lower center with the higher, we formulate the key that opens the gate to the Heart in between them. The Heart contains the Sabbat as it manifests in the microcosmic realm, which is the source of the Creative Word which, after opening the gate of the Heart, the operator can then speak. The Word, here, is the same as the life energy generated by Baphomet/Apollo. In this, you yourself have become like Baphomet/Apollo, and can give forth the creative word. It is also the Schamijam, which is directed by the operator to a particular purpose.

The words that can correspond to the three centers, in relation to the Toad Stone, are taken from the "Perfect Master" degree of the Royal Arch. "Jah-Bul-On" for the Toad Stone/Sex Center, "Yod-He-Vau-He" for the Head Center, and "Elhannin" for the Heart Center. These also correspond to the jewels of the Pearl for the Toad Stone, the Diamond for the Head Center, and the Ruby for the Heart Center.

The three centers can be seen both as three jewels, three stones, and as three drops, which can correspond to the three drops of "Awen" given by the Welsh goddess Ceridwen to the sage Taliesen.

The three of these, aligned through the body, form the figure of the letter "I", which contains all potentiality within it. The line, with the point, line, and another point, corresponds to the point of the Toadstone, the line of the Heart and the end point of the Head. "I" in this, is the primal sigil, the first sigil, corresponding to the start, the middle, and the end. The line itself expresses the magic of the sigil, which corresponds to fraction of the Sabbat which is embodied within it. The line itself is a gateway to the Sabbat, and in this corresponds both to the Heart and to the potential of the Word, which expresses a fraction of the Sabbat itself. This process is the formulation of the Word.

This completes the three. The transition from the Three to the Four is symbolically associated with the Northeast, which is the only cross-quarter used in the Ingress ritual. The Northeast is the bridge between the Autochthonic "I" and the Atmospheric "I". Speaking the word bridges the gap between the two, and is symbolically associated with the Northeast, though in this circle casting you're physically facing South.

After you've activated the Word of the Heart, speak forth and breath forth the energy of the Azoth from your heart to the South of the circle and state that with this action you have manifested Bride, Habundia, the power of manifestation, at the southern point of the circle.

Next, take that energy and thrust it backwards behind you out of the circle, to the North, across Midnight's Dawn to the Sabbat of the Ages, and declare that you have manifested, Mahaziel, Odin, Herne the Hunter, the power of demanifestation.

Next, with your right arm, go to the North, go through the gate of Mahaziel, and take the energy from beyond the circle, from the Sabbat that sits in Midnight's Dawn, and bring it back into the circle, through the gate of Mahaziel, putting it in the South, declaring that you manifest Go-Magot, Hu Gadarn, Hercules, and the power of increase on your right.

Finally, take the energy in the South and with your left hand bring it back to the North and send it out through the gate of Mahaziel, through Midnight's Dawn to the Sabbat, declaring that you make manifest the power of Arianrhod, Hecate, Ononshu on your left. This practice invokes all four of the gods of the directions from the inside, and establishes them in the four points of the circle.

With regards to sending the energy to the Sabbat and drawing energy from the Sabbat, it's done through going through Midnight's Dawn in to the demanifest realm, and through the demanifest realm to the Sabbat itself. The demanifest realm, Midnight's Dawn, is the body of the One, of the Dragon Lord, as the ground of all Being, within which the Sabbat of the Ages sits.

It's a separate dimension, whose door can be opened. Paradoxically, it's the "Thirteenth Knell" of the clock. For details on how to find it and open it, consult the essay "The Blasphemy of Things Unseen" by Daniel Schulke, in the collection "Hands of Apostasy", where he provides encrypted directions for this and for much else.

However, if you can't do this, it's adequate to just picture the Sabbat as a ball of fire outside of the circle, and to symbolically reach your hand out to the ball of fire in giving energy to the Sabbat and picture yourself taking energy from the ball of fire in bringing the energy back in. In doing this, don't actually put your hand outside of the circle, but rather picture the circle as being a sphere, half of which extends above the circle, half of which extends below it. Bring your hand outside of the part of the sphere that extends above you, but which on the horizontal axis is not beyond the boundary of the circle. From there, picture your hand going to the Sabbat of the ages, which is conceived as a ball of fire, either putting energy into it or drawing energy from it. This will not be as effective as actually opening the door to Midnight's Dawn, but it will do something. I should note that this partially going beyond the circle only works for solitary rites. For collective rites, a door specifically linked to Midnight's Dawn should be drawn and opened.

Similar considerations can be for the Toadstone and the manipulation of the different internal energies within the body. If you have not seized the Toadstone, you can still manipulate these energies to a lesser degree. As with everything, it will be less powerful, and your "Word" will not be as authentically creative and powerful as it would otherwise be, but it will still have an effect. The process of seizing the stone, the experience of keeping the stone, and the practice of internal alchemical purification associated with the stone is the ultimate base of power, and lacking these things will correspondingly limit your power.

I should say that this practice of sending energy to the Sabbat and taking energy from it makes the Sabbat itself into a second circle, and then intertwines the first circle with the second. The two circles together resemble the Dual Ouroboros featured in the Dragon Book of Essex, and, in fact, my belief is that the second circle in the Dual Ouroboros, and the work that goes on there, is a physical representation or enactment of things experienced in the spirit when Chumbley or others actually went to the Sabbat of the ages. In this, you can picture the two serpents of manifestation and demanifestation linked to each other in a way that describes a figure eight, with the two circles of the Sabbat and the earthly circle being the two circles contained within the figure eight. Within the Coven of Atho system, the two circles, which here refer to the earth and to the Sabbat, were thought to refer to the earth and the otherworld, with the snakes that describe the figure eight referring to the process of rebirth, where people go from the earth to the otherworld, and from the otherworld to the earth. Now to return to the process.

Ingress Rite Frame

Next, if you're invoking a force, you can split the operation into four parts: the invocation of the force, which corresponds to Hu Gadarn and the East, the main work, which corresponds to Bride, Abundia in the south, the binding of the work, which corresponds to Arianrhod,Hecate in the West, and the ending of the work, which corresponds to Mahaziel in the North. This spins the wheel in the clockwise direction.

In this, start with the East and state, "At the East, Hu Gadarn and powers of increase, at the South, Bride,Habundia and the powers of manifestation, at the West, Arianrhod,Hekate,Ononshu and powers of decrease, at the North, Mahaziel, Odin, Herne the Hunter, and the powers of demanifestation". It's important to declare this in a clockwise direction, in the series that follows from that, instead of in the series that these were originally evoked. This cements the purpose of the rite as Ingress, working clockwise.

If you're doing this alone, you should invite the spirits of each of these into you in turn, so that it's they who, with you, perform the respective roles. Start with Hu Gadarn, take the persona of Hu Gadarn back into yourself and perform the invocation. Then switch to Bride, and perform the work of the rite, then switch to Arianrhod,Hekate, Ononshu and bind what you've worked into reality. Finally, switch to Mahaziel and dismiss the spirit, declare that the work of the rite is complete.

When the rite is complete, thank and dismiss each force, starting with the four gods, in a reverse order. First thank North, then West, then South, then East. After this, thank the three gods in reverse order, starting with Venus in the Heart, then Selene the Horned Goddess in the head, and then Diana the virgin moon in the Toadstone/Sex. After this, you need to physically leave the circle. If you're using candles or other media such as fire or incense, extinguish these, and then leave the circle. Next, come back to the circle. This completes the breaking of the circle. Be sure to completely dispose of any moveable material that you've used, incense, candles, etc. after this to complete the casting of the rite.

Traditionally, a feast of some kind follows this, where people both eat and drink. This serves to further earth the current. If you're alone, this can be a modest meal instead of a feast.

Ultimately, the rite will be cast when the participants wake up the next day after sleeping for the night. Sleep here serves as a further break, on par with both breaking the circle, disposing of the portable material, and orgasm. Though it's possible that there might be significant dreams after this, personal experience has shown that this is often not the case. If there aren't, don't be concerned. The important part is the break in consciousness that sleep provides.

Using Consecration of All Things, Secrets of Helios

This is an example of how to apply the four parts of the mental part of the rite of Ingress in practice.

This discussion of the framework has so far not gone into invocations themselves, or how to use them. A great way to apply the framework, and the Word of inner alchemy, to Theurgy is to use the spell from the Greek Magical Papyri titled "The Consecration of All Things". This spell, which has been issued in a retranslated and annotated edition by Hadean Press under the title "The Secrets of Helios", invokes the Eternal Sun itself for personal benefits. This version is edited by Alison Chicosky and translated by Cory Childs. This spell corresponds exactly to a description of an Egyptian theurgic spell given by Iamblichus in "On the Mysteries", and so has very good provenance.

There are many good things to say about this spell. First of all, its structure contains the series of invocation, work, and binding that corresponds to the circle. After the initial start of the spell, there follows a section of invoking the secret names of Helios, then there follows the work of the spell, and finally the spell ends with a binding, where what's been asked is confirmed. The initial part of the spell is an invocation too, but it's different in quality from the more pure invocation of the names in the second part.

The working part of the spell states the god form and names of twelve subdivisions of the Eternal Sun, corresponding to animal forms, and then asks for a boon or benefit from each of them. Contrary to the annotations of the current edition, I believe that the boons that are asked for correspond to the qualities of the animals themselves. This series of twelve covers the entirety of the circle of the Sun, though the symbolism, being from Egypt in the first centuries AD, is quite different from current use. You can use the spell both in its given form and as a frame rite that can be adapted to many other uses.

The way to integrate it into the framework of the circle and its casting is to have it follow the traditional set up of invocation given in the Azoetia: after the circle has been cast fully, you would first consider your stone, the lower center, or the ground as a fragment of Being, and be in silence, then consider your heart and say "I" very loud, as the coming forth of Life and all its possibilities, then consider your head and say your name "vel Eternal Sun", or similar. In this, picture yourself speaking the Word forth from yourself. This is a way of invoking the three once, more, and it makes use of the framework of energies that have already been set up by casting the three in the casting of the circle. The sequence of concentrated silence, then "I", then the declaration, echoes the sequence of Being-Life-Intellect described by Proclus.

Then, you would follow this with first saying that you banish Satan, then stating that you hail the Eternal Sun, following this with as many other names for it as you can possibly find. Also, hail the Active Intelligence, Zo-I-As, Baphomet, Living Being, Tetramorph, and Demiurge, that lives within the Eternal Sun. Also use as many names for this as you can find. Particularly with this spell, make sure that Zeus is one of the names of the Demiurge, and that Serapis is one of the names given to the Eternal Sun as a whole. The very last line of the "Consecration", done at the end of the Binding, is "One Zeus is Serapis", and using these names in the Litany makes this line more effective.

After this, state that you're invoking the Sabbat of the Ages, the Eternal Sun, or the Divine Mind in its form of Helios with the following, at which point you start the "Consecration of All Things".

Be sure to follow the "Consecration" with a dismissal of the spirit and a declaration of the end of the rite of your own making, as this is not included within the spell.

Every successful operation which draws down the Essence from the Divine Mind down into the Circle, which draws the gods down into the circle, is a victory of the good gods, and of the Truth, over the Evil One. Therefore, the invocation of the Sabbat benefits the world in general, as well as the people who participate in it in particular. It's a gnostic ritual of restoration and overcoming.

The Different Levels of Reality.

This does not derive from traditional witchcraft, but overlaps with it. It may be of interest to people.

Here, we're going to discuss the different planes of reality using the term "Dimension" and "Higher Dimension". The fundamental planes of reality here are the physical, the etheric, the astral, the mental, and the spiritual. The spiritual dimension is the Sabbat of the Ages, the Divine Mind. The etheric plane is really an extension of everyday reality into a fourth dimension that's usually unseen with the eyes. It can be perceived by an illumined eye. Every object, including human beings, has this fourth dimensional extension. This etheric dimension, or etheric plane, is somewhat bound by time and space, just as the physical world is.

The astral plane, strictly speaking is the unseen extension of the world in the elemental realm, which exists below the realm of the planetary energies. The difference between the astral proper and the etheric is that the astral energy and the astral realm is not directly connected to any particular organ or being. The astral energy exists independently of any material body, yet the human mind can call it up, accumulate it, imprint it, and send it out into the universe. There is a connection between the etheric energies within the individual and the astral energies, in that the human mind can take the etheric energetic extensions, liberate the energy, turn it into an abstract astral energy, and then manipulate it and send it out.

The astral plane is a modified double of the earth which, though under the influence of both time and space, is not directly bound to the material world. Instead, it floats relatively freely above the world.

It receives influences from the planetary mental realm above it, which shape it, and transmits those to the earth. Within this scope, it's malleable to a good degree, with abstract beings within it which similarly have freedom of action. Within the schema of dimensions, the astral is a kind of intermediary between our conventional three dimensional world and the fifth dimensional world of the mental plane. It's still somewhat bound by time and space, but not totally. Space, particularly, is malleable, which is what makes things such as "astral traveling", possible, which is really the projection of consciousness to particular places.

People unconsciously create things on the astral level with their thoughts, with collective thoughts creating more definite forms. These forms unconsciously effect others. In fact, the personal unconscious mind is continually influenced by astral forces, many times without the knowledge of the conscious mind. Belief systems and constructs take on a life of their own, in this, but, equally, these astral constructs can be manipulated, destroyed, and changed, through magical action and engagement. These belief systems, too, can be used as symbols of a higher reality, on the mental or spiritual level, and in being so used can serve as vessels for the energy of those higher realities. The astral forms, in turn, are affected by the time and tides of planetary forces as well, with these limiting, extending, and shaping them. In this, the astral forms don't have unchecked dominion over people, because of this limiting force of the planets on the negative constructions which can form on the astral. These planetary influences also should be taken into account in attempts to manipulate astral constructs created by group thought. Advertising and other types of intentional manipulation of the minds of individuals on a mass scale also help to create group astral thought forms that influence people, for ill or for good. The astral forms, in this, can be shaped not just by the nobler thoughts and desires of humanity, but by ones that are less noble, and ones that bring people to a lower level of existence rather than towards a higher one. Nonetheless, higher forces can intercede and break through these astral forms. The accumulation of astral detritus derived from lower impulses is one of the reasons why people have said that the astral plane is ruled by the Evil One. This is only partially true. However, it does present a mass of influences that the beginner will have to rise through in order to get to a more liberated state where the transcendent influences can be more clearly felt. Forces that deny the transcendent do live on this level, and do not want individuals to rise above them, but this is not the whole of the astral level itself, which contains more pleasant beings and energies as well.

The mental plane, on the other hand, is a fifth space dimension, which is not bound by space, but is bound by time. There is an idea in physics that says that higher dimensions may, in fact, be "compactified", that is, rolled up into very small spaces, so small that we might not notice them otherwise. In the mental plane, everything is much closer together, which means that it's possible to influence things at a distance. Two objects might appear to be very far apart in the three dimensional world, but on the fifth dimensional plane they may be very close. Therefore, it's possible to influence them on the fifth dimensional world and thereby give the appearance of action at a distance, even though that is not actually happening. Compactification of this higher dimension might be the cause of this. If the whole dimension is wrapped up into a microscopic tube, everything would be much closer together.

The mental plane is the plane where astrology manifests itself, where the planetary energies influence people's reality. I believe the source of this is quantum entanglement, in that all the planets, and all of the matter of the earth, were at one time part of a previous physical sun that existed in our solar system. While in this sun, everything was entangled on a quantum level. That entanglement persisted once that sun went nova, exploding and creating the cloud of matter that both our own sun and the planets formed from. I believe that the level of quantum entanglement, which also accounts for seeming action at a distance, happens across this fifth dimension. The planets, being very large objects, still influence people on earth through this fifth dimension, which is not bound by spatial distance but is still bound by time. Because of this, astrological cycles in time influence people, though the planets themselves are millions of miles away from us, and don't exert any influence in a conventional way.

The mental plane is called that because, among other reasons, it's accessed through the inner sight of the mind exclusively. Though the astral plane can be accessed in this way as well, it's possible to see the astral aspects of reality without using the mind's eye. The mental plane in this appears as a very black place with different points of consciousness and influence here and there. It's also the place where telepathic communication takes place. People who know each other, who are familiar with each other's minds, stay in contact with each other through the mental plane, even if they're not aware of it.

The spiritual plane, or sixth dimension, is the Sabbat itself, the Divine Mind, the Pure Land. This is unbound by either time or space.

One of the best presentations of all of this, which includes descriptions of the Sabbat as he experienced this dimension, is contained in the book "Resurrecting the Mysterious" by Ingo Swann. This individual was one of the pioneers of remote viewing, but had a very spiritual background, inspired by Theosophy and other currents. However, his work is focused on actually doing and experiencing these things, and is not primarily ideological. The work is composed of two parts: one called "Resurrecting the Mysterious" and one called "Beyond the God's Devices". The second part is the one that gets to the core of it, with the first part being introductory. Swann refers to the Sabbat dimension as the "Emerald Realm", which is very on point, considering the many testimonies to its appearance from Islamic sources and others who talk about its greenness. This book gives much advice on how to develop psychic vision on all the levels outlined here, and is recommended, especially for beginners, along with Swann's "Psychic Sexuality".

Works Cited

Aradia, Lady Sable "The Witch's Eight Paths of Power, a complete course in magick and witchcraft", Weiser, York Beach, 2014

Chumbley, Andrew Azoetia, Xoanon, Hercules, USA, 2015

Chicosky, Alison ed, Cory Childs trans."The Secrets of Helios", Hadean Press, London, 2022

Cochrane, Robert, Shani Oates ed. "The Taper that Lights the Way", Mandrake of Oxford, Oxford, 2016

Huson, Paul "Mastering Witchcraft",Berkeley Publishing Group, New York, 1980

Jennings, Hargrave "Rosicrucians, their Rites and Mysteries" John C. Nimmo, London, 1887, Oxford University, Oxford, 1838, Google Books.

Lethbridge, T.C. "Gogmagog", Routledge, Kegan & Paul, London 1957

Levi, Eliphas, trans. AE Waite, "Transcendental Magic", William Rider & Sons, London, 1923, google books

Liddell,E.W. "Pickingill Papers", Michael Howard ed., Capall-Bann, Chieveley, 1994

Montalban, Madeline "Star of Peace, Lighting the Way to Happiness", Prediction magazine in 1957, as well as Tony Willis' commentary on it, refer to 1957 Prediction Annual,

Mun, Jean de, F.S. Ellis trans. "The Romance of the Rose, vol. III",J.M. Dent, London, 1900. Google Books

Pennick, Nigel "Secrets of East Anglian Magic" Capall-Bann, Milverton, 2004

Schulke, Daniel " The Blasphemy of Things Unseen" in "Hands of Apostasy", Michael Howard and Daniel Schulke eds., 2014, Three Hands Press

Schulke, Daniel "Viridarium Umbris". Xoanon Ltd. 2005

Scott, Reginald, John Madziarczyk ed. "Magitians Discovered, vol. 2". Topaz House Publications, Seattle, 2016

Seims, Mellisa "Here be Magic", Thoth Publications, Loughborough, 2022

Shakespeare, William"The Merry Wives of Windsor", many editions available

Swann, Ingo "Psychic Sexuality", Swann-Ryder Productions, USA, 2017

Swann, Ingo "Resurrecting the Mysterious, Ingo Swann's 'Great Lost Work'", Swann-Ryder Productions, USA, 2020

Appendix

Other Witchcraft: Aradia.

Research by Robert Mathieson, reproduced in his critical edition of Leland's Aradia, has shown that the document that was given to him as the "Gospel of the Witches" really only consisted of chapters I, II and IV. This is significant because it's chapter III, "How Diana Made the Stars and the Rain" which contains the overwhelming majority of the theology in Aradia. This is supposed by Mathieson to have been written by Leland himself.

With chapter III taken out, and chapters I, II, and IV looked at in isolation, a different picture of the document presents itself. Though Diana, Cain, and Lucifer are mentioned, the status of "Aradia" herself, the daughter of Diana and Lucifer, is ambiguous. The first chapter recounts that her mother Diana teaches her that she should curse the Church and revolt against the rich, but in chapter II, where the blessings of the food are made, the invocation to Aradia talks about Aradia being a bad person and urges her to repent, saying that her mother had already repented, and wants Aradia to be a good person. This interpretation is strongly encouraged by the new translation of the verses from Italian by Mario and Dina Pazzaglini, included in the book. Additionally, the conjurations in chapter II are not unambiguous songs of praise. The conjurations to both Cain, Diana, and Aradia, involve threats and potential condemnations if the spirit does not obey them. To me, this suggests that to Maddalena these were black magical practices, which a person should engage with in a way similar to that of working with demons from a Christian perspective. What could be going on here?

My feeling is that, in reality, the first chapter of the "Witches Gospel" was presented to Leland by his informant Maddalena not as something positive, but as something negative, as a story of bad witches, and of their leader, who did bad things, with Leland turning the condemnation into something positive. Through Leland presenting this document as something positive, something that Maddalena endorsed, he manufactured something that was not real. What people have been basing their rites on is a combination of Leland's own philosophical speculation on the nature of Diana and Lucifer, joined with a tale of badly behaving witches that is inverted and presented as something good, that should be emulated.

However, what about Leland's non-historical invention? If you look at it, there are resemblances to the primal vision of the Sabbat that I've been describing. Diana, in this, gives birth to Lucifer. I understand Diana in this to be the primal seed, the foundation stone, the Toadstone of the world of the gods, that gives birth to the lotus or rose flower. The rose flower or lotus is the Sabbat itself, with Lucifer, the active intelligence of the Divine Mind, being generated from its center, as the king of the Sabbat. This is somewhat different from Leland's version, which considers Diana to be associated with darkness, and Lucifer to be associated with light, and that says that the darkness in Diana wanted to bring the light of Lucifer within her. Nonetheless, the juxtaposition of the two is still present.

I think it's possible that Leland derived the theology that he puts into Aradia from Hesiod's account of the gods, which starts with Chaos and its children Erebos, twilight, and Night, Nyx, who then generates Brightness or Aethyr, who then go on to generate the rest of reality.

Witchcraft and Fanny Hill

John Cleland was the author of the erotic novel "Fanny Hill", or "Memoirs of a Woman of Pleasure", published in 1749. Cleland was also a reconstructionist Druid who wrote a very interesting essay called "Essay on the Real Secret of the Free Masons", which he included in his book on Druidry, "The Way to Things by Words and to Things by Words". What, then did this secret consist of?

Before going into that, Cleland was also associated with a club in Scotland called "The Beggar's Benison", which has been examined in "Hell-Fire Clubs" by Evelyn Lord. The "Beggar's Benison" was a bawdy club that featured group masturbation, the (chaste) viewing and examination of naked women, and featured an initiation rite where all the members would touch the penis of the initiate with their penis before the member masturbated to completion onto a plate. "Fanny Hill" in an unpublished form, was read at the meetings, which also featured reading of other erotic fiction. Interestingly, with regards to the "Beggar's Benison", Evelyn Lord says that the nucleus of it in East Neuk in Scotland was formed from merchants who traded with Norway, Sweden, and the Baltic.

Cleland's secret had multiple layers. The first was that Freemasonry was a continuation of Druid rites that had continued in the form of secret societies. Secondly, these rites had also been associated with witchcraft, which had been unfairly stigmatized and mischaracterized by the public. With regards to this, Cleland spends time defending the idea of the witches' Sabbat as a Druid institution, and, in the main part of the book about Druids, spends two whole pages talking about the supposed etymological origin of the word "Sabbat". In this, he links it with, among other things, two Celtic words that mean "Man of the Word", which he explicitly says refers to Cunning-Men and Wizards, with these terms being his exactly.

From there, he relates Druidry to the Cathars, the Albigensians, though he insists that their doctrines have been misunderstood and that they were not, in fact, dualists. He laments the destruction of the Cathars, and says that they were persecuted for continuing the Druid mysteries under another form.

Interestingly, and very significantly, Cleland also links the Druids to the Persian Magi. Again, for some reason he's adamant that the Persian Magi were not dualists, and condemns the Manicheans in relation to them. I believe that in talking about the Magi, Cleland is making a covert reference to the Templars, and to the Templar tradition, thereby associating the Druids with both the Cathars and the Templars, as well as witches, and associating both of them with Masonry.

This brings us to Masons, which to him are inheritors of both the Cathar tradition and Druidry. The core secret of Freemasonry, Cleland indicates is Phallic Druidic principles. Particularly, Cleland associates Hiram Abiff of Masonry with the Phallic power of generation, and with the May Pole, both of which he says were at the core of Druid beliefs. This, combined with other statements in his book about Druids, indicates that he thought that the Mason's Word was associated with the sexual generative principle, something that Theodore Reuss of the OTO would also endorse about a hundred and fifty years later.

His book about Druidry, where the essay is reprinted, bears examination. It's organized as a word list of names and terms which Cleland claims were originally Druidic in origin, with Cleland supplying the restored meaning. These are interspersed with Cleland's own commentary. The definition of the term "Sabbath" runs for several pages.

The format of the book, is, in fact, very similar to that of Christopher Irvine's "Historiae Scotiae Nomenclatura Latino-Vernacula", talked about in "Magitians Discovered" vol. 1, and the similarities don't stop there.

Like Irvine, Cleland introduces a historical theory of the Druids that draws from the Swedish Gothicist tradition, with Cleland directly naming late Gothicist Olaus Rudbeck and his "Atlantica" in the work. In fact, Cleland adapts Rudbeck's ideas to Great Britain, saying that Hyperborea and Atlantis were actually Great Britain and that the keepers of the pristine knowledge were the Druids. This is integrated into a theory of some of the pagan gods being embodiments of men who claimed to be gods that is reminiscent of the historical ideas of Annius of Viterbo, gone over in "Magitians Discovered", volume 1. In fact, Cleland develops a whole historical theory about the development and degeneration of Druidism in relation to the beliefs of Scandinavia and elsewhere, with the Druids, particularly those in Scotland, being thought to have preserved the pure tradition.

Many things that Irvine, in his work, leaves implicit are made explicit by John Cleland: for instance, that Witches were really Druids and were unfairly persecuted. They had a source of pristine wisdom.

Though Cleland defends the witches' Sabbath as being relatively harmless, the fact that at its core he believed that Druidism had to do with phallic worship of sexual energy, with the Maypole being the Druidic equivalent of the Cross, suggests that this might not have been the case.

Cleland, in talking about this in his word list, devotes quite a lot of space to defining Circles, which surrounded the Maypole in Mayday dances, as well as magic circles, and wands, with the wand being implicitly a penis in this. Within his wordlist there are also many strange additions that seem to serve no obvious purpose, such as "Aceldama". This word is the term for the field of blood, the "Blood Acre", the place where Judas Iscariot hung himself after betraying Christ. As such, it appears in contemporary traditional witchcraft traditions as a name for the Circle, though the explanation for it is sometimes associated with the death of Abel by Cain rather than the death of Judas.

All of this suggests, to me, that whatever Christopher Irvine was a part of, and cryptically communicated to the world through his "Historiae Scotiae", continued for at least a hundred years, and manifested in part through this work by Cleland.

All of this can be observed, and verified, very easily by searching one of our contemporary oracles, Google Books, for the title "The Way to Things by Words" and Cleland.

From "The Way to Things by Words"

Sabbath. This word has two significations, the one in the Hebrew, the other in the Celtic; the near affinity in which of one to the other, is but a reason the more for drawing the line of separation, especially as it accounts for the prevalence of a vulgar error, in the days of ignorance and superstition.

In the Hebrew, according to Josephus and Eusebius, the word Sabbath-day signifies a day of rest. The Dutch translate it so, literally De Rustdag. About this derivation then there is no difficulty.

But in the Celtic, the same word, Sabbath, signifies a Teacher's or Doctor's instruction. The true word is Sab-aith, from Sab, a knowing-man, or, to use the antient term, a cunning-man, or Magus, in the sense of Sage, or wise person, and Aith, Preachment, Doctrine, or with more emphasis, the word. It is strictly synonymous to the Welsh Celfydd, skilled in the Faith, and to the old word Kel or Caldey. It is to be observed, that Sab, in the sense of knowing or wise, is the radical of Sapiens, and of Sofos in the Greek, of Savio in the Italian, of Saber in the Spanish, & c. It was also, like the word Good, employed to express the Deity; thence Sabasius, or the Being excellent on Wisdom. The Sabines took their name from this pretension. In the Gauls and in Britain, it signified precisely a Druidical teacher; Sabus,or Zabus, was an Hyperborean word, and equivalent to Galeota, or Caleotæ, the Druids of Sicily mentioned by Cicero.

The word Aith, besides its signification of Oath, had also that of the Word (of God, or of Wisdom, elliptically understood.) It is the radical of the theological term Faith, and of the Icelandic Edda, which ought to be pronounced like the dd in the Welsh, or the Greek Theta, which is, in fact,the form of a double D , the one D upon the other.

Sabbaith then, in this combination, signifies clearly the Word, or doctrine of the Cunning-man,or Wizzard, neither of which last expressions were originally understood in a bad sense; till the time that the Druidical worship being proscribed, and supplanted by the Roman paganism, and by Christianity, the private assemblies of the remaining adherents to the Religion of the Grove (which being, according to primeval institutions, essentially, not only at midnight, but, independently of the circumstance of persecution, held in caverns, or in the most secret places) were stigmatised with the appellation of nocturnal meetings of witches to worship the Devil. The French gave, or rather preserved, to this resort, the old name of Sabbat; thence aller au Sabbat, with which they associate the idea of a thousand ridiculous horrors, beneath confutation. It is also remarkable, that certain points of Instruction, or Theses, agitated in the College at Paris, were called Sabbatines, more properly from Sabbat, in the pre-mentioned sense, than from their being on a Saturday; as in the first place,that was not the Christian Sabbath-day; and in the next, those exercises were not confined to that day, but indifferently held on any.

The word Sabbath also affords me an occasion of hazarding what at first view may appear a very rash conjecture it is this, that not only the Chaldeans, but the Sabaens,which I take to be synonymous terms, or nearly so, are designations not of those countries,whose names they bear,but of profession, non ex gentis, sed ex artis vocabulo,

[...] To say the truth, there was, in the first foundation of the meetings of the Free-masons, some very untoward circumstances, which were very innocently and independently inherent to the very essence of their cause. In the first place: the assemblies were originally in the dead of night, an hour not at all chosen for the sake of guilty concealment, but because it happened to be specifically the time consecrated not only to the solemnities of the Druidical religion, but to any extra ordinary mirth, festivity, or revels (reveils). When the assembly was for a religious purpose of hearing instruction, it was called Sabaith, whence the French expression, "allerau Sabat," (asinp.44.) But as these meetings must have been sovereignly obnoxious to the Christians of those days, they not only persecuted but decried them, in the heat of pious zeal, accusing them of much such abominations as had been very falsely imputed to themselves, by the heathens, before the liberty of their public worship had done justice to the innocence and purity of their private.

From "Essay on the Real Secret of the Free Masons"

But the word Manichæans gives, in its decomposition, clearly the sense, of the religionists of the Grove, which I do not here particularise, that I may not be imagined to lay any stress on any thing so precarious as etymology, though the least receivable an one I could offer, could hardly be more absurd than the strange, incoherent romance of the Persian Manes, who has, at a great expence of imagination, been made the founder of a doctrine, which had existed for ages before his supposed birth, and was long preserved in various parts of the world, in Asia, Africa, and Europe; but in France especially, under the name of Manicheism, which was nothing more than the remains of the Religion of the May, of Druidism, in short. But if the doctrine of the Druids may be judged by that of the Magi of Persia, there never was a more groundless accusation than that of their making any power co-ordinate with that of God, whose supremacy was the capital tenet of their religion. It is, however, but too true, that with this primary, this sublime, this divine truth, there came to be errors mixed; which, as it is the nature of errors, begot other still greater ones.

The Druids then invented, or adopted, most probably in favor of the multitude, the secondary doctrine of Spirits or Imps (whence the mythological words numen and nympha) with which their fertile imagination peopled every part of the creation, sun, moon, stars, planets, air, earth, water, fire, mountains, vallies, groves, rivers, and even ships. They animated every thing. To these spirits they not only assigned their respective departments and functions in the natural world; but, pursuing the idea, they created allegorical personages, under the mystic adumbration of which they conveyed truths, moral, natural, and religious: thence their Jupiter, the Spirit of paternal Goodness; Pallas, the Spirit of Wisdom and of Arts; Mars, the Spirit of War; Ceres, the Spirit of Agriculture; Juno, the Spirit of conjugal Union; Venus, the Spirit of genial Love; Bacchus (L'Iber, L'Yvre) the Spirit of Drinking; Osiris, the Spirit of Government; Isis, the Spirit of Nature, &c. Names of fancy, which, being assumed by real human personages, came afterwards to be literally understood: and these imaginary abstracts passed (as abstracts often do to this day in argument) for essential substances.

Thence arose another mythology, in which the Egyptian, the Greek, and the Roman Gods manifestly sprung out of the corruption of Druidism, or rather of the worst part of Druidism.

These spirits were also divided into classes; but principally into the celestial and infernal, to whom were assigned their nature and mansion, according to the prevalent idea, among the antient Celts, of heaven and of earth. Heaven they considered as the origin of all good, natural and moral. Earth of all evil. Every thing pure, every virtue, every blessing, in every sense, they believed descended from on high, from the celestial regions. Everything gross, polluted, painful, wicked, they imputed to terrestrial influence. Dreams they accounted earthly vapors. Man, whom they esteemed a production out of the earth, they judged to retain too much of the gross earthy nature to assign any part of him a place in Heaven; but, as the immortality of the soul was one of their principal tenets, their imagination provided for him, not only a place of punishment and of purification but of rewards, in the bosom of the earth, from whence he sprung. Thence the Elyzium, adopted by the Heathens of Greece and Rome, in which the souls of the brave and virtuous were to remain provisionally till this time of their recall into the animation of some human creature; for there is not the least ground to charge the Druids with the tenet of the transmigration into animals of any other species. The Odyssey, and the sixth book of Virgil, contain, with no variations but those of a poetical licence, the Druidical mythology on the state of the dead.

This is in brief their doctrine of good and evil spirits, subordinate to one supreme God: a doctrine in which there was more of folly than of guilt; but the misinterpretation of which, combined with so many prejudices against them, antient and modern, seconded withall by the jealous zeal of the religion in power, could not but reduce the unhappy remnant of the Druidical votaries to the last extremities of ruin and despair. In France, they never appeared in any considerable body after the destruction of the Albigenses, by the Cruzade begun against them under Simon de Montfort. In Britain, after the reduction of the Picts, such as held out against the new religion, would naturally form assemblies, for the safety of the members of which, the utmost privacy was required, for reasons of fire and faggot. This probably produced the oath of inviolable secrecy, in nearly the form it is now administered to the initiates of Freemasonry. Hitherto I have not made use of any argument drawn from words or proper names to establish the conjecture of this existence of a Druidical remnant, of which the difficulty would be to believe, that, after the destruction of the main body of Druidism, it did not exist, especially in Britain, the head-seat of it for ages. Proceeding then on the strongest presumptive consequences from established facts, from things, in short to words, the name of Free-mason offers a corroboration, of which I readily submit the degree of justness to the judgment of the reader. The adherents to Druidism had various names, Guydeliens, Paulicians, Manicheans, Leogrians, Ougbers, May's-ons, besides others. [...]

Celtic Commentary.

The Giants

The pagan gods were sometimes portrayed as giants surviving from Ante-Diluvian times in medieval epics. This was beside the Euhemerization of gods, where they were turned into positive heroes. Here, the explanation for their powers was that they were the children of fallen angels and men. This can be seen in the second branch of the Mabinogion, where Ceridwen and her husband are portrayed as giants. Cerwiden, the Giantess, makes the Awen which blesses Taliesin with powers that are associated with the Holy Spirit, and her Cauldron is arguably turned into the Holy Grail in later works.

However, this has to be measured against the pagan traditions from which they come from. Particularly, the Norse pagan tradition already had giants within it, who were recognized as evil beings, and, in this, the explanations of giants as being the product of fallen angels was adopted not to explain the main gods themselves, such as Odin, but these other beings. This can be seen in Beowulf, where Grendel is portrayed as being of the race of Cain. Not only that, but the author of Beowulf makes this general statement about the "race of Cain"

"On the race of Cain the Eternal Lord brought death as vengeance, when he slew Abel. Nor did he find joy in the feud, but God for the crime drove him far thence. Thus it was that evil things came to their birth, giants and elves and monsters of the deep, likewise those giants who for a long while were striving with God Himself. And well He requited them. " (Beowulf, Part 1, section 1)

Also, Saxo Grammitcus appropriates Christian ideas of the Watchers to describe giants in his "Gesta Danorum", which is excerpted in "Magititans Discovered, vol. 3". Though the link between Giants and Christian tradition is present in both Welsh and Germanic traditions, Giants in the Norse and Germanic traditions also partake of a set of theological ideas that do not appear in Welsh mythology.

In the Welsh tradition, though, besides Ceridwen being the creator of the holy Awen, we can see the ambiguity of giants in the tale of "How Culhwch won Olwen" in the Mabinogion. Here, Olwen is the daughter of the "Chief Giant" Ysbaddaden. Olwen is presented as being a very beautiful, and normal sized, woman, and not evil at all, and though Ysbaddaden does not want Culhwch to marry her, he has reasons for this besides malice, and does not appear to be particularly evil.

Being a giant here is a disfavored thing, but not something that puts one into the category of an evil being. For instance, in the second branch of the Mabinogion, the giants are portrayed as harassing people and causing problems, leading to them being expelled from their land, in an echo of the idea of the giants of the Ante-Diluvian times being degenerate, although later in the story they're said to have settled in Wales and to have been good people.

Geoffrey of Monmouth's portrayal of giants in his "History of the Kings of Britain", lines up with this as well.

This work, particularly its passages on giants, is excerpted in volume 3 of "The Magitians Discovered". Geoffrey sees Brutus, a character from the Aeneid who is originally from Troy, as the founder of Britain. Though Brutus is, of course, a pagan, I think an argument can be made that Brutus is portrayed by Geoffrey of Monmouth as a "virtuous pagan", whose descendants duly adopt Christianity, in opposition to the "Bad pagans", represented by the giants in Cornwall and elsewhere. The polytheism of Brutus is looked on as a bad but unavoidable thing, which was soon overthrown when Christianity came to Britain, as opposed to the beliefs associated with the giants, who are looked on as irredeemably bad. These giants were the people that Brutus supposedly encountered when he and the rest of the team from Troy landed in Britain. Here, they may represent the bad pagan gods themselves.

Here, as well, the bloodline of the giants and Ante-Diluvians is the bloodline of the gods. Geoffrey's original work talks about the giant Goe-Magot that Brutus from Troy found in Cornwall and defeated. A part that was added to Geoffrey's work gives a bigger perspective: Goe-Magot, and other giants in Britain are thought to have been children of exiled evil women from Greece who had sex with evil spirits and practiced witchcraft, living in a matriarchal society. Here, an exact parallel to the story of the Watchers before the Flood is transferred into Britain.

This addition to Geoffrey's work was not the first example of this transference. In the "Getica" of Jordanes, a history of the Goths written in the 6th century, the Huns are portrayed as being the product of Gothic witches having sex with evil spirits.

Geoffrey's history was later used to justify the idea that he was actually talking about Ante-Diluvian times in Britain, with Britain being a blessed isle that was a type of Atlantis. Descent from giants in Britain, then, becomes descent from the Watchers. Goemagoe, then, appears as a brother to the giants mentioned in the Mabinogion, such as Ceridwen.

The Cauldron

The Cauldron itself is an interesting symbol. It contains the Awen, and is also mentioned both in the second branch of the Mabinogion and in the Preiddu Annwn. In the Mabinogion, it's origin is out of a lake, brought by two giants who are presumably Ceridwen and her husband, who appear out of nowhere. In this tale, it grants a partial resurrection to warriors who are dipped into it, partial because they lack the power of speech. This is perhaps a nod to Christian doctrine, in that in Christianity the only true resurrection which would be possible would be that which happened at the end of time. All other resurrections that happened before this would have to be partial or flawed in some way, as this resurrection is. Plus, the Cauldron is of course a pagan object. This would be overcome by transforming it into the Holy Grail, where it would be the blood of Christ that would renew the individual, and give them an eternal life which was understood to be a metaphor for Christian redemption.

In the Preiddu Annwn, or the "Spoils of Annwn", about Arthur and his warriors conquering various fortresses, the cauldron is listed as one of the things plundered. It's associated with nine virgins, who help brew its contents, and with poetic inspiration. The fortress or castle in which it's found is the castle of drunkenness, according to Higley's translation, thereby connecting it once again with intoxication and inspiration. Also in the Preiddu Annwn, a sword is raised to the cauldron, and this is echoed in Robert Cochrane's rituals where daggers are put into the cauldron before being put into the ground.

Additionally, in the Preiddu Annwn, and indirectly in the second branch of the Mabinogion, the cauldron is something that's quested after, which in a way makes it a prototype of the Holy Grail, said to grant immortality and other powers. Arthur is the leader of the warriors in the Preiddu Annwn, and of course Arthur is famous for later stories that are centered on the grail quest. Later, in the third branch of the Mabinogion, another container, a golden cup, shows up. Here, it's related to a supernatural castle that appears in an afflicted land, and whoever touches it is paralyzed and stuck to it, which may be a prototype of the caution against greed in trying to seize the grail.

The Cauldron is also associated in the first branch of the Mabinogion with resurrection, particularly with the resurrection of dead warriors. However, the resurrection is incomplete, as the resurrected warriors cannot speak. That the Cauldon contains the Divine Mind, and that the Awen is the substance of the Divine Mind, is suggested throughout the Taliesin literature by the sheer number of things which being granted three drops of the Awen is said to grant to Taliesin. The Sabbat, in this, is the same as the Divine Mind within the Cauldron. Here, the Cauldron can also be linked to the Grail, with the quest for the grail being the quest for communion with the Sabbat. When the grail, the energy of the Sabbat, is found and consumed, it transports the individual to Paradise and bestows the pagan form of the Beatific Vision. Related to this are the three drops of Awen as the three drops of internal alchemy.

Hanes Taliesin

Taliesin's chase and the coal blacksmith. The transformations of Taliesin in his flight from Ceridwen is echoed by later folk songs such as the "Coal Blacksmith". A key difference, though, is that in the "Coal Blacksmith" or "Twa Magicians" songs, it's a man chasing a woman, while in Taliesin it's a woman chasing a man. The process of the transformation chase has the one who is fleeing realizing all of the four elements or potentials within a person, through transformations into animals of all of these four elements.

Perhaps the fact that Taliesin was given inspiration from the Awen indicates that he was the First Sorcerer of witchcraft lore? This granting of the gift of sorcery through Awen is what could be called a primary way of getting power, that is, a way of getting power that directly flows from the source, instead of it either being taught or passed on.

Taliesin, in his poems, says that he speaks with the Druids words, and so this is arguably a real synthesis of Celtic paganism with Christianity. The Awen, however, comes from a pagan cauldron prepared by a giantess, with five sacred herbs. In the Preiddu Annwn, there are seven virgins who kindle the fire of the cauldron with their breath.

The Book of Raziel is also mentioned in the last poem contained in the "Hanes Taliesin". The Book is a supposed text given to Adam after his expulsion from Paradise that contained the "Prisca Theologia", or old, original, theology, or knowledge, which was passed down orally from Adam to his descendants. Some stories identify the Book of Raziel as being given to Adam by Raziel as part of God's mercy to Adam after his transgression. Taliesin is said to have received his knowledge from similar books. The book itself was also identified as containing magical knowledge and words of power, and so several grimoires were manufactured in the middle ages that claimed to be the Book of Raziel. Here, the things that it legendarily contains is similar to the different types of knowledge that Taliesin is supposedly granted, about the mysteries of the world. The poem also connects this knowledge to that received by Moses in the river Jordan, which allowed him to construct the mystical rods that he used in his contest with the Pharaoh. This emphasis on books contradicts the entirety of the story of Ceridwen and the Awen which has been narrated previously. Perhaps this change was an attempt to shift the focus of the work away from a pagan context to a Christian one.

Is Taliesin possessed by the Holy Spirit? The variety of things that he says that he was present for would seem to imply it. This suggests a Christo-pagan synthesis. The Holy Spirit in Catholicism gives seven gifts, which are Wisdom, Understanding, Council, Fortitude, Knowledge, Faith, and Fear of the Lord. Though each of these are broken down into more specific powers, nonetheless, Wisdom, Understanding, Council, which means good advice from a supernatural source, and Knowledge, can certainly overlap with the pagan powers that the Awen is said to provide. Also, one version of Taliesin's poems says that he comes from the world of the Cherubim, while another says that he comes from the place of the summer stars. In this, it's likely the spirit which is speaking through Taliesin that's talking, describing where it comes from, and that the heaven of the Cherubim, is being equated with a more pagan idea of Paradise. Most of the things that Taliesin in his first poem says he was present for are events from the Bible. Within Christian mysticism, the Holy Spirit is the force that lifts a person up to the Beatific Vision, which is variously, at different levels, a vision of Paradise, of Heaven, and of God himself. In this, the Holy Spirit gives vision of a higher world, in the same way that the Awen gives Taliesin insight into "All Futurity" plus the sacred mysteries of the universe, including the heavens and god himself.

The Tower of Babel is mentioned in Hanes Taliesin as one of the places where he was, the translation being that he was with a foreman on the Tower of Babel, but, even though the Tower, and Nimrod are mentioned in traditional witchcraft traditions, this is an example of the Holy Spirit connection. By being present with a foreman, he's saying that he was there when the tongues were confused, which implies that he was the one who confused the tongues. This lines up with Taliesin identifying himself with the Holy Spirit, in that it was this entity who as a servant of God confused the tongues at the Tower of Babel. Taliesin refers to the British as the remnants of Troy, thereby building on the theory found in Geoffrey of Monmouth's "History of the Kings of Britain".

Arianrhod and Lleu

I have adapted the use of Arianrhod from the Pickingill letters where she appears as a goddess of the West, concerned with Fate and binding. Here, in our usage, Arianrhod and Lleu form the East-West axis of the circle, with Lleu being a Welsh equivalent to the Irish

Lugh, the bright warrior, who can be syncretized with Lucifer, the light bringer as the actual warrior bringing light as the rising sun in the Eastern part of the circle.

The actual myth of Arianrhod and Lleu takes place in the fourth branch of the Mabinogion. There, the story of Arianrhod is somewhat disjointed. This is because it appears her story is a continuation of that of the character Goewin, though they're not labeled the same person. Assuming that they are the same person, the story goes like this: during another adventure, Goewin, a kinswoman of the king Math son of Manonwy, was sexually assaulted by the magician Gwydion and his brother Gilvaethwy. In punishment, they're turned into a series of pairs of animals by Math, and made to have sex with each other and to bear children as animals as a kind of humiliation. After going through this three times, being turned into deer, pigs, and wolves, they're restored to human form, and their children are also turned into humans in the process. Next, Math asks them who he should marry, and the answer is Arianrhod. He requires her to test her virginity, by stepping over a magic rod, and when she does this she drops, or gives birth, to two babies, one of which she raises, one of which is hidden away by Gwydion. This is a shameful thing for her, since she presented herself as a virgin. The second child is Lleu.

Now, the subtext indicates that these are the children that are the product of the sexual assault on Goewin, who is now Arianrhod, and that Gwydion, in this, is one of the children's father. Gwydion acts as the child's protector. The child Lleu grows at a supernatural rate and is extremely strong. He also proves to be the best at anything he pursues. But when he's presented to Arianrhod and told that he is hers, she curses him, denying him a name. This is the first of three curses against Lleu by Arianrhod. It's hard to see why she would have such enmity to her son unless he was the product of the sexual assault. Gwydion helps Lleu to overcome all of the curses, using magic. Gwydion's helping of Lleu also makes much sense if he's his father. The cursings can be equated with bindings by Arianrhod. Though it's not Lleu himself who counters Arianrhod's magic, nonetheless, he can be equated with a divine king who overcomes darkness through struggle, with him and Arianrhod being interpreted as the divine twins that stand for the positive and negative sides of the circle. These can be equated with Set and Horus, or, drawing on the later symbolism, Nephthys and Horus, with Nephthys being the wife of Set.

Works Cited

Cleland, John, "The way to things by words", L. Davis and C. Reymers, London, 1766, Google books

Cleland, John, "On the Real secret of the freemasons" in "The Way to things by Words", google books

Guest, Lady Charlotte, "Hanes Taliesin" in "The Mabinogion", Bernard Quaritch, London, 1877, sacred-texts.com

Gantz, Jeffrey Mabinogion, Penguin, London 1976

Higley, Sarah "Preiddu Annwn", online edition, Camelot project, University of Rochester USA, https://d.lib.rochester.edu/camelot/text/preiddeu-annwn

Kirtlan, Ernest J.B. trans "The Story of Beowulf", Charles H. Kelly, London, 1913

Leland, Charles, Robert Mathieson, Mario Pazaglini & Diana Pazaglini trans. "Aradia, or the Gospel of the Witches, A New Translation", Phoenix Publishing, Blaine WA, 1998

Lord, Evelyn, "The Hell-Fire Clubs", Yale University Press, New Haven, 2008

Madziarczyk, John, "The Magitians Discovered" vol 1, Topaz House Publications, Seattle, 2016

Madziarczyk, John, ed. "Magitians Discovered" volume 3, Topaz, Seattle, 2016

Works Cited

Many of the very old books that are listed here are in the public domain and easily available online. For ease of finding, I've listed the online sources where I found them. Some of these sources, such as Google Books, are self explanatory. Others are more obscure. Where IAPSOP is listed, this refers to the "International Association for the Preservation of Spiritualist and Occult Periodicals", which is located at http://www.iapsop.com. The Hathi Trust also makes available texts for non-commercial use, and is located at http://www.hathitrust.org. Finally, EEBO-Text Creation Partnership 2 refers to the Early English Books Online Text Creation Partnership, which transcribes books from the 16-17th centuries into text files and releases them into the public domain. It can be found at https://textcreationpartnership.org/tcp-texts/eebo-tcp-early-english-books-online/.

Aelred of Rievaulx "Mirror of Charity", Elizabeth Conner trans.,Charles Dumont ed., Cistercian Publications, Kalamazoo, 1990

Agostini, Domenico and Samuel Thrope trans, "Bundahishn". Oxford University Press, Oxford, 2020

Anklesaria, Behramgore Tehmuras, trans. "Greater Bundahishn" 1956, made available by Joseph Peterson at the "Avesta.org" http://www.avesta.org/mp/grb.htm.

Aradia, Lady Sable "The Witch's Eight Paths of Power, a complete course in magick and witchcraft", Weiser, York Beach, 2014

Asatryan, Mushegh, "An Early Shi'ite Cosmology, Kitab al-haft wa-'l-Azilla and its Milieu", published in Brill's "Studia Islamica 110" in 2015. Available on the author's Academia.edu page

Auerbach, Felix "Ektropismus, oder die Physikalische Theorie des Lebens.", Verlag von Wilhelm Engelmann, Leipzig, 1910, Google books

Badakhchani, S. J., "Spiritual Resurrection in Shi'i Islam", I.B. Tauris, London 2017

Baker, Elsworth "Man in the Trap", American College of Orgonomy Press, Princeton, 2000.

Bar-Asher, Meir M., Aryeh Kofsky "The Nusayri-Alawi Religion", Brill, Leiden, 2002

Barnstone and Meyer "Gnostic Bible", Shambhala, Boston, 2009
    "Hymn of the Robe of Glory", in "the Gnostic Bible", Shambhala, Boston, 2009
    "Umm al-Kitab", translated in "Gnostic Bible", Shambhala, Boston, 2009

Birge, John Kingsley "The Bektashi Order of Dervishes" Hartford Seminary Press, Hartford, 1937

Saint Bonaventure "Collations on the Hexaemeron", Franciscan Institute Publications, St. Bonaventure NY, 2018
    "De Triplici Via", or the Triple Way, in "Mystical Opuscula", José de Vinck, trans. Saint Anthony Guild Press, Paterson NJ, 1960

Bonwick, James "Egyptian Belief and Modern Thought", C. Kegan Paul & co., London, 1878, Google Books

Borchart, Samuel "Phaleg", or "Geographica Sacra, Phaleg et Canaan", Leiden, 1692, google books

Brisson, Barnabe "De formulis et solennibus populi Romani verbis", 1754, Google Books

Budge, E.A. Wallis "The Book of the Dead, The Papyrus of Ani in the British Museum", British Museum, London, 1895, Google Books, Sacred-Texts.com

Bunsen, Christian Karl Josias Freiherr von "Egypt's Place in Universal History", vol. 5, by, published in 1867. Google books,

Burroughs, William S., Daniel Odier, "The Job", Penguin Publishing, New York, 1989.

Burroughs, William S. and Brion Gysin "Third Mind", Viking Press, New York, 1978

Butler, E.W. "Magic: It's Ritual, Power, and Purpose" and "The Magician: His Training and Work", combined into one work in "Magic and the Magician", published by Aquarian Press, 1991

Works Cited

Callataÿ, Godefroid de trans. Bruno Halflants trans., On Magic I: An Arabic Critical Edition and English Translation of EPISTLE 52a (Epistles of the Brethren of Purity), Oxford University Press, 2012

Carroll, Peter "Liber Lux" in "Liber Null and Psychonaut", Weiser, York Beach, 1987
"Liber Nox" in "Liber Null and Psychonaut", Weiser, York Beach, 1987

Charles, R.H. "A Critical and Exegetical Commentary on the Revelation of Saint John" vol. 2, Charles Scribner's sons, 1920, Google Books

Chicosky, Alison ed, Cory Childs trans."The Secrets of Helios", Hadean Press, London, 2022

Chumbley, Andrew Azoetia, Xoanon, Hercules, USA, 2015
Dragon Book of Essex", Xoanon, Hercules, 2014

Cleland, John, "The way to things by words", L. Davis and C. Reymers, London, 1766, Google books
"On the Real secret of the freemasons" in "The Way to things by Words", google books

Cochrane, Robert, Shani Oates ed. "The Taper that Lights the Way", Mandrake of Oxford, Oxford, 2016
"Basic Structure of the Craft", Cochrane , "Taper that Lights the Way", Shani Oates, Mandrake of Oxford, 2016
Cochrane,Robert to Joe Wilson "#3 Transcript", "The Taper that Lights the Way", Shani Oates, Mandrake of Oxford
"A Midsummer Ritual", "The Taper that Lights the Way", Shani Oates ed., Mandrake of Oxford, 2016
Cochrane, Robert,Shani Oates ed. "Bowers to Joe Wilson #5", "The Taper that Lights the Way", Mandrake of Oxford, Oxford 2016

Colless Brian E. ed. trans., "The Wisdom of the Pearlers, an Anthology of Syriac Christian Mysticism" Cistercian Publications, Kalamazoo, 2008,

Conway, David, "Magic: An Occult Primer", The Witches' Almanac, Newport RI, 2016
"Magic without Mirrors", Createspace Independent Publishing, 2011

"Secret Wisdom, the Occult Universe Explored", The Aquarian Press, Wellingborough, 1987

Corbin, Henry "The Temple and Contemplation", KPI, London, 1986

The Configuration of the Temple of the Ka'bah", "The Temple and Contemplation", KPI, London, 1986

"The Imago Templi in Confrontation with Secular Norms", in "The Temple and Contemplation", KPI, London, 1986

Nancy Pearson trans. "Spiritual Body and Celestial Earth", Princeton University Press, Princeton, 1977

Cummings, William L. "The Spurious Rites of Memphis and Mizraim", written in the mid 1930s but republished by the Scottish Rite Research Society journal "Heredom" in 2001, with updates.

Daftary, Farhad "The Isma'ilis, Their History and Doctrines", Cambridge University Press, Cambridge, 1999

Davies, Edward "The Mythology and Rites of the British Druids", J. Booth, London, 1809, Google books

Deledda, Grazia "Ashes", John Lane, London, 1908, Google Books

Delumeau, Jean "The History of Paradise, the Garden of Eden in Myth and Tradition", Continuum International Publishing, New York, 1992

Dupuis, Charles François "The Origin of All Religious Worship" the "Abridgement", New Orleans, 1872, Google Books

Encyclopedia Iranica, "Cosmogony and Cosmology vi. In Ismailism" https://www.iranicaonline.org/articles/cosmogony-vi.

"Manicheans, general survey" https://www.iranicaonline.org/articles/manicheism-1-general-survey

Ephrem the Syrian "Hymns on Paradise" , Sebastian Brock ed. trans, Saint Vladimir's Seminary Press, Crestwood New York, 1990

Eschenbach, Wolfram von Parzival,, trans. A.T. Hatto Penguin, London 2004

Evans-Wentz, W.Y.,"Fairy Faith in Celtic Countries", Citadel Press, New York, 1994

Faber, George Stanley "Dissertation on the Mysteries of the Cabiri"vol. 1 and 2. Oxford University Press, Oxford, 1803, google books

"The Origin of Pagan Idolatry", vol. 1, 2 and 3, F and C Rivingtons, London, 1817, google books

Fitzgerald, Robert "The Hidden Stone", "The Luminous Stone", Three Hands Press, Richmond Vista, 2016.

Friedman, Yaron "The Nusayri-Alawites, An Introduction to the Religion, History, and Identity of the Leading Minority in Syria", Brill, Leiden, 2010

Gantz, Jeffrey Mabinogion, Penguin, London 1976

Gardner, Gerald "Witchcraft Today", Citadel Press, New York, 2004

Goddard, David "The Sacred Magic of the Angels", Weiser, York Beach, 1996

Godwin, Joscelyn "Atlantis and the Cycles of Time", Inner Traditions, Rochester VT, 2011

Goldstein, Joseph, Jack Kornfield, "Seeking the Heart of Wisdom, the Path of Insight Meditation", Shambhala Press, Boston, 2001

Grant, Kenneth "Images & Oracles of Austin Osman Spare", Fulgur Ltd, London, 2003

Gray, William G. "Magic Ritual Methods", Weiser, York Beach, 1980

Guest, Lady Charlotte, "Hanes Taliesin" in "The Mabinogion", Bernard Quaritch, London, 1877, sacred-texts.com

Gurdjieff, George "Meetings with remarkable men", many editions

Hämeen-Anttila, Jaako "The Last Pagans of Iraq", Brill, Leiden, 2006

Hammer-Purgstall, Joseph "Mysterium Baphometis Revelatum", Vienna, 1818, Google Books

Harrison, Michael "The Roots of Witchcraft", Tandem, London, 1975

Herbert, Algernon "An Essay on the Neo-Druidic Heresy in England", Henry G. Bohn, London, 1838, Google Books.
"Nimrod", vols. 1-3, Richard Priestly, London, 1828, Google Books,
"Nimrod", vols. 4, Richard Priestly, London, 1829, Google Books,

Higgins, Godfrey "The Celtic Druids" Cosimo Inc., New York, 2007

Higley, Sarah "Preiddu Annwn", online edition, Camelot project, University of Rochester USA, https://d.lib.rochester.edu/camelot/text/preiddeu-annwn

Hill, Napoleon "Think and Grow Rich", Ballantine Books, New York, 1987

Howard, Michael "Children of Cain", Three Hands Press, Richmond Vista, 2011

"Pillars of Tubal-Cain" and Nigel Jackson, Capall-Bann, Milverton 2003

"Book of Fallen Angels", Capall-Bann , Milverton, 2004

"Teachings of the Light" from "The Luminous Stone", Three Hands Press, 2016, Richmond Vista, USA

Howard Michael ed. Daniel Schulke ed. "The Luminous Stone", Three Hands Press, 2016, Richmond Vista, USA

Hoyos, Arturo de ed. "Collectanea, vol. 20", parts one and two, issued by the Masonic Grand College of Rites in the United States in 2008

Hughes, Pennethorne "Witchcraft", Penguin Books, London 1965

Hunzai, Nasir, "The Wise Quran and the World of Humanity" Danishgah-I Khanah-I Hikmat, Pakistan, 2003

"The Institute for Spiritual Wisdom and Luminous Science" at www.monoreality.org

Huson, Paul "Mastering Witchcraft",Berkeley Publishing Group, New York, 1980

"The Devil's Picture Book", iUniverse, 2003

Hyatt, Christopher S. "Secrets of Western Tantra", New Falcon Publications, Reno, 2009

"The Tree of Lies", New Falcon Publications, reissued as "To Lie is Human, Not Getting Caught is Divine", Original Falcon publications, Tempe, 2009

"Undoing yourself with energized meditation", New Falcon Publications, Tempe, 1997

Jennings, Hargrave "Rosicrucians, their Rites and Mysteries" John C. Nimmo, London, 1887, Oxford University, Oxford, 1838, Google Books.

Saint Jerome, Thomas P. Scheck trans. "Commentary on Ezekiel", Newman Press, Westminster MD, 2017

Kelley, Charles, "Life Force...the Creative Process in Man and Nature", Trafford, Victoria BC, 2005

Kerning, J.B., Ian Gladwin trans. "Letters on the Royal Art", Pansophic Press, 2022

Khan, Razib, http://www.razibkhan.com
"Razib Khan: Anatolia over 10,000 years", https://www.razibkhan.com/p/anatolia-over-10000-years
"Ararat's long shadow: Asia Minor's major impact on humanity", https://www.razibkhan.com/p/ararats-long-shadow-asia-minors-major
"Hittite Words, Byzantine Walls: what the West as we know it owes Anatolia's empires"
https://www.razibkhan.com/p/hittite-words-byzantine-walls-what

Kirtlan, Ernest J.B. trans "The Story of Beowulf", Charles H. Kelly, London, 1913

Kitchen, Robert A. and Maartien F. G. Parmentier, "The Book of Steps, The Syriac Liber Graduum", Cistercian Publications, Kalamazoo, 2004

Layard, John "Stone men of Malekula", Chatto and Windus, London, 1942

Laurence, Richard, "The Book of Enoch the Prophet", Oxford University Press, Oxford, 1838

Leland, Charles, Robert Mathieson, Mario Pazaglini & Diana Pazaglini trans. "Aradia, or the Gospel of the Witches, A New Translation", Phoenix Publishing, Blaine WA, 1998

Lenormant, François "Beginnings of History" Charles Scribner's Sons, New York, 1893, Google books

Lenormant, François and Charles"Histoire et mémoires de l'Institut royal de France", volume 25, published in 1861, and titled "Mémoire sur les Réprésentations qui avaient lieu dans les Mystères D'Éleusis", Google Books

Lepsius, R., "Das Todtenbuch der Ägypter", Georg Wigand, Leipzig, 1842, Google Books

Lethbridge, T.C. "Gogmagog", Routledge, Kegan & Paul, London 1957

Levi, Eliphas, trans. AE Waite, "Transcendental Magic", William Rider & Sons, London, 1923, google books

Liddell, E.W. "Pickingill Papers", Michael Howard ed., Capall-Bann, Chieveley, 1994

Lord, Evelyn, "The Hell-Fire Clubs", Yale University Press, New Haven, 2008

Lynch, Richard "The Travels of Noe" EEBO-Text Creation Partnership 2

Mace, Stephen "Shaping Formless Fire", New Falcon Publications, Tempe, 2005
   "Stealing the Fire from Heaven", Dagon Productions & Heathen World Productions, Phoenix, 2006

Madziarczyk, John, "The Magitians Discovered" vol 1, Topaz House Publications, Seattle, 2016
   Madziarczyk, John, ed. "Magitians Discovered" volume 3, Topaz, Seattle, 2016

Maple, Eric "The Dark World of Witches", A.S. Barnes & Company Inc., New York, 1964

Marconis de Negre, E.J. "The Sanctuary of Memphis or Hermes", Kessinger Publications, Kila MT., nd.

Massey, Gerald "A Book of the Beginnings" vol 1. and 2, Williams and Norgate, London, 1881, Google books,
   "Ancient Egypt, the Light of the World", vol. 1 and 2., T. Fisher Unwin, London, 1907, Google Books
   "My Lyrical Life, Poems Old and New", First Series. Watts and Co., London,1896, google books
   "The Natural Genesis", vol.1 and 2.,Williams and Norgate, London, 1883 , google books,

Matthews, John ed. trans. and Gareth Knight,"Titurel", in "Temples of the Grail, The Search for the World's greatest Relic", Llewellyn, Woodbury MN, 2019

Maximus the Confessor, George C. Berthold trans. "Selected Writings", Paulist Press, New York, 1985.

McDannell, Colleen, Bernhard Lang."Heaven, a History" Yale University Press, New Haven, 1988

McGinn, Bernard trans."Treatise on the Spirit and the Soul", in "Three Treatises on Man, A Cistercian Anthropology", Cistercian Publications, Kalamazoo, 1977

Mebes, G.O. "Tarot Majors", Shin Publications, England, 2020

Michell, John "At the Center of the World, Polar Symbolism", Thames and Hudson ltd. London, 1994
   "The Dimensions of Paradise", Inner Traditions, Rochester VT, 2008

"New View Over Atlantis", Hampton Roads publishing, Charlottesville, 2013

"The View Over Atlantis", Ballantine Books, New York, 1977

Monod, Paul Kléber, "Solomon's Secret Arts", Yale University Press, New Haven, 2013

Montalban, Madeline "Star of Peace, Lighting the Way to Happiness", Prediction magazine in 1957, as well as Tony Willis' commentary on it, taken from the 1957 Prediction Annual, https://auntietarot.wordpress.com/2012/11/06/the-star-pentagram-magic/

"Horned god and the Devil card of the tarot", Prediction Mag., February 1967 https://auntietarot.wordpress.com/2014/02/19/angel-or-devil/

"The Rayed God", published in Prediction mag. in April of 1962, https://auntietarot.wordpress.com/2013/07/02/the-mystic-tarot-the-devil/,

"Love Must be Earned", from Prediction Mag. November1959 https://auntietarot.wordpress.com/2013/01/17/the-5-of-rods/

"Daughter of the Mighty", about the "Empress" card of the Tarot, published in Prediction Mag. in March of 1961, https://auntietarot.wordpress.com/2013/06/06/the-mystic-tarot-the-empress/,

"Four Watching Kings", Prediction Mag. August 1965, https://auntietarot.wordpress.com/2013/11/23/the-magical-tarot-the-kings/,

"The Watcher Within Ourselves", Prediction June 1963, "https://auntietarot.wordpress.com/2013/08/27/the-mystical-tarot-the-wheel/"

Moore, William D. "Darius Wilson, Confidence Schemes, and American Fraternalism 1869–1926", published in 2013 in the "Journal for Research into Freemasonry and Fraternalism", available from author's Academia.edu page.

Moosa, Matti "Extremist Shiites, the Ghulat Sects", Syracuse University Press, Syracuse, 1988

Mouni Sadhu "The Tarot: A Contemporary Course of the Quintessence of Hermetic Occultism", Wilshire Book company, North Hollywood, 1971

Mun, Jean de, F.S. Ellis trans. "The Romance of the Rose, vol. III",J.M. Dent, London, 1900. Google Books

Mar O'Dishoo, Mar Eshai Shimun XXIII trans. "Book of Marganitha", Xlibris, 2007.

Odeberg, Hugo trans. "3 Enoch or the Hebrew Book of Enoch", Cambridge University Press, Cambridge, 1928, google books

Oliver, George, "The History of Initiation in Three Courses of Lectures", Washbourn, London, 1829, google books,

Oliver, George, "The Theocratic Philosophy of Freemasonry in Three Lectures", R. Spencer, London, 1856, google books.

Pelley, William Dudley "Starguests", Soulcraft Press, Noblesville IN, 1950, IAPSOP

Pennick, Nigel "Earth Harmony", Capall-Bann, Chieveley, 1997
Secrets of East Anglian Magic" Capall-Bann, Milverton, 2004
"Secret Games of the Gods", Weiser, York Beach, ME, 1990

Phillips, Julia and Amy Hale video presentation "Madeline Montalban: Magus of the Morning Star", "The Last Tuesday Society", https://www.thelasttuesdaysociety.org/event/madeline-montalban-magus-of-the-morning-star-by-julia-phillips/
"Madeline Montalban: Magus of the Morning Star" in "Essays on Women in Western Esotericism", ed. Amy Hale, Palgrave Macmillan, 2023

Pictet, Adolphe "Du Culte des Cabiris chez les Anciens Irlandais", J.J. Paschoud, Geneva, 1824, google books

Pike, Albert "Morals & Dogma", Kessinger Publications, nd. also Google Books
"Knight of the East and West" degree in "Morals & Dogma", Kessinger Publications, nd. also Google Books

Powers, Melvin "Self-Hypnosis: Its Theory, Technique and Application", Wilshire Book Company, Hollywood, 1973

Prest, John, "The Garden of Eden, The Botanic Garden and the Re-Creation of Paradise" Yale University Press, New Haven CT., 1981

Pseudo-Macarius, "Fifty Spiritual Homilies and the Great Letter", Paulist Press, New York, 1992

Ramsay, Chevalier Andrew Michael "Travels of Cyrus",2 vols.. Woodward, London, 1727, google books

Randall-Stevens, H.C. "The Book of Truth, or the Voice of Osiris", Rider & co. London, 1927, Hathi Trust
"The wisdom of the soul", Aquarian Press, London, 1956
Regardie, Israel "The Art of True Healing", New World Library, San Rafael, 1991
"Healing Energy, Prayer and Relaxation", New Falcon Publications, 2009
"New Wings for Daedalus: Wilhelm Reich, his Theory and Techniques", Original Falcon Publications, 2018
"Wilhelm Reich: His Theory and Techniques", New Falcon Publications, 2022
Reich, Wilhelm "Ether, God, and Devil & Cosmic Superimposition". Farrar, Straus and Giroux, New York, 1973
Richard of Saint Victor "The Mystic Ark", also known as "Benjamin Major", "Richard of Saint Victor", Paulist Press, New York 1979
"Benjamin Minor", also called "The Twelve Patriarchs", in "Richard of Saint Victor", Paulist Press, New York 1979
Rhodes, H.T.F. "Satanic Mass", Citadel Press, Seacaucus, 1974
Rose, Jenny "Zoroastrianism: an Introduction" I.B. Tauris, London 2012
Ross, Peter, "Standard History of Freemasonry for the State of New York", "Book XIII--The Rite of Memphis", 1899, Google books
Russell, Jeffrey Burton "Witchcraft in the Middle Ages", Cornell University Press, Ithaca, 1984
Sanders, Maxine "Fire Child", Mandrake of Oxford, Oxford 2007
Schelling, F.W.J., "Über die Gottheiten von Samothrake", "On the Divinities of Samothrace", Frank Scalambrino trans, Magister Ludi press, Castalia, 2019
Schulke, Daniel " The Blasphemy of Things Unseen" in "Hands of Apostasy", Michael Howard and Daniel Schulke eds., 2014, Three Hands Press
"Viridarium Umbris". Xoanon Ltd. 2005
Scot, Reginald, John Madziarczyk ed. "Magitians Discovered, vol. 2". Topaz House Publications, Seattle, 2016
Seims, Mellisa "Here be Magic", Thoth Publications, Loughborough, 2022
Shakespeare, William"The Merry Wives of Windsor", many editions available

Skjærvø, Prods Oktor "The Spirit of Zoroastrianism", Yale University Press, New Haven, 2011

Spare, Austin Osman "The Focus of Life" published in 1922, available online in many formats, as well as in "Now for Reality!", published by Mandrake Press,1990.

Spare, Austin Osman, Kenneth Grant, Steffi Grant "Zos Speaks! Encounters with Austin Osman Spare", Fulgur, London, 1998

Stoyanov, Yuri "The Other God", Yale University Press, New Haven, 2000

Swann, Ingo "Resurrecting the Mysterious, Ingo Swann's 'Great Lost Work'", Swann-Ryder Productions, USA, 2020

"Psychic Sexuality", Swann-Ryder Productions, USA, 2017

Thomson, Matthew McBain, "Tabloid History: Rites and Orders Other than the Scottish Rite in America." in "The Universal Freemason", vol. XI num 2, August 1918, IAPSOP

Trench, Brinsley le Poer "Men Among Mankind", Venture Bookshop, Evanston, 1963

"Sky People" Tandem, London 1971

Frater U.'. D.'., "High Magic: Theory and Practice", Llewellyn, Woodbury, 2005

Villars, Abbé Nicolas-Pierre-Henri de Montfaucon de, "Comte de Gabalis", Brothers edition, 1914, Patterson NJ, google books

Vogh, James alias of John Sladek, "The Thirteenth Zodiac: the sign of Arachne", Granada Publishing, London, 1979

Volney, Constantin François de Chassebœuf,"The Ruins of Empires", Rossange Freres Booksellers, Paris, 1820, Google Books

Waite, A.E. "The Secret Tradition in Freemasonry, Volume II", appendix, Rebman Limited, 1911, google books

Wakefield, Walter, Austin P. Evans "Heresies of the High Middle Ages", Columbia University Press, New York, 1991

Walker, Benjamin "Man and the Beasts Within", Stein and Day, New York 1977

"Gnosticism, it's History and Influence", the Aquarian Press, Wellingborough UK, 1983

Walker, D.P. "Spiritual and Demonic Magic from Ficino to Campanella", Pennsylvania State University Press, University Park PA, 2000

Bishop Warburton "Divine Legation of Moses", tenth edition, Vol. 1, Book II, pg. 254, , for Hekas, Hekas Este Babeloi, Thomas Tegg, London, 1846, google books

Webb, Don "Uncle Setnakt's Essential Guide to the Left Hand Path", Runa-Raven Press, USA, 1999

Williamson, George Hunt "Other Tongues, Other Flesh", Neville Spearman, London, 1965

"The Road in the Sky",Neville Spearman, London, 1973

Willis, Jack "Reichian Therapy for Home Use", e-edition at https://reichiantherapy.info/, hard copy

"Reichian Therapy: A Practical Guide for Home Use", New Falcon Publications,Los Angeles, 2013

Wilson, Peter Lamborn "Sacred Drift", City Lights Publishers, San Francisco, 1993

Wright, Dudley "Druidism, the Ancient Faith in Britain", Ed. J. Burrow, London, 1924, Google Books

Yarker, John "Arcane Schools" Cosimo Inc., New York, 2007

Zacharias,Gerhard, Christine Trollope trans. "The Satanic Cult" by George Allen & Unwin, London, 1980

www.ingramcontent.com/pod-product-compliance
Lightning Source LLC
Chambersburg PA
CBHW071939220426
43662CB00009B/919